Civil Tongues *&* Polite Letters

Civil Tongues

Published for the
Institute of Early American
History and Culture,
Williamsburg, Virginia,
by the
University of North Carolina Press,
Chapel Hill and London

& Polite Letters

IN BRITISH AMERICA

David S. Shields

The
Institute of
Early American
History and
Culture is
sponsored jointly
by the College
of William and
Mary and
the Colonial
Williamsburg
Foundation.

Library of Congress Cataloging-in-Publication Data
Shields, David S.
Civil tongues and polite letters in British America / David S. Shields.
p. cm.
Includes bibliographical references and index.
ISBN 0-8078-2351-1 (cloth : alk. paper) —
ISBN 0-8078-4656-2 (pbk.: alk. paper)
1. Etiquette — United States — History.   2. Social interaction —
United States — History.   3. Associations, institutions, etc. —
United States — History.   4. Literature and society — United States —
History.   5. English language — Discourse analysis.   6. United
States — Social life and customs — To 1775.   I. Title.
E162.S555   1997
306'.0973 — dc21   96-37377
CIP

This volume received indirect support from an unrestricted book
publication grant awarded to the Institute by the L. J. Skaggs and
Mary C. Skaggs Foundation of Oakland, California.

01 00 99 98 97   5 4 3 2 1

FOR LUCINDA

ACKNOWLEDGMENTS

This book is the product of my tenure as the Citadel Development Foundation Faculty Research Fellow. For its continuing and enlightened support of faculty research at a time of financial retrenchment in academia, the Foundation deserves praise.

A subsection of Chapter 7, "The Religious Sublime," is an adaptation of "The Religious Sublime and New England Poets of the 1720s," *Early American Literature*, XIX (1984–1985), 231–248. I thank the editor and the University of North Carolina Press for permission to reprint portions of the article.

The opening portion of Chapter 6 is an alteration of a Note, "Anglo-American Clubs: Their Wit, Their Heterodoxy, Their Sedition," *William and Mary Quarterly*, 3d Ser., LI (1994), 293–304, and it appears here by permission of the editor, Michael McGiffert.

The poems of Henry Brooke reproduced in Chapter 3 were drawn from the Commonplace Book, Peters Collection, Historical Society of Pennsylvania, Philadelphia, and appear by its kind permission. Thanks are due to curator Linda Stanley.

Joseph Norris's poem "On E. Magawley Pres[um]ing to Write," found in the Joseph Norris Commonplace Book, appears courtesy of the Trustees of the Huntington Library, San Marino, California.

The poetic quotations from Elizabeth Graeme Fergusson's "Poemata Juvenilia" found in Chapter 4 appear courtesy of the Library Company of Philadelphia. I also owe a personal debt to curator James Green for his aid in tracking down a number of facts.

Joseph Green's letters to Captain Pollard (Smith-Carter MSS) quoted in Chapter 7 appear courtesy of their owner, the Massachusetts Historical Society, Boston.

The correspondence of Dr. Thomas Dale of Charleston to Thomas Birch used extensively in Chapter 8 appears by permission of the Trustees of the British Library, London. They have also granted permission for my use of Captain Thomas Walduck's 1710 letter from Barbados to James Petiver, Sloane MS 3202.

The American Antiquarian Society, Worcester, Massachusetts, has allowed me to quote from its notebook collection of the "Poetry" of Deborah Pratt Ruff. Thomas Knowles, the manuscript curator, kindly assisted in answering several biographical questions concerning Ruff.

I wish to thank the archival and library staffs at the Folger Shakespeare

Library, Washington, D.C.; the British Library; the Southern Historical Society Collection, Perkins Library, Duke University, Durham, North Carolina; the Virginia Historical Society, Richmond, Virginia; the New-York Historical Society; the New York Public Library; the Houghton Library, Harvard University, Cambridge, Massachusetts; the Scottish Record Office, Edinburgh; the Huntington Library; the South Carolina Historical Society, Charleston; the South Caroliniana Library, University of South Carolina, Columbia; the American Antiquarian Society; the Connecticut Historical Society, Hartford; the Alderman Library, University of Virginia, Charlottesville.

Conversations with a number of scholars have determined the direction of this study; indeed, certain people have operated as my imaginary audiences for chapters: Chapter 1: Bernard Herman; Chapter 2: Dena Goodman and Lawrence Klein; Chapter 3: Mitchell Snay, James Green, and Dennis Barone; Chapter 4: Carla Mulford, Pattie Cowell, and Susan Stabile; Chapter 5: Judith Cobau; Chapter 6: Wilson Somerville, Robert Micklus, and J. A. Leo Lemay; Chapter 7: Jeffrey Walker, David D. Hall, and Leon Jackson; Chapter 8: Daniel Williams and David Moltke-Hansen; Chapter 9: Michael Warner and Fredrika J. Teute. Although the specific obligations I have to particular scholars are indicated in my notes, by a curious happenstance four persons are not directly cited whose work greatly determined my general understanding of the cultural situation of early America: Jack P. Greene, for his elaborations of the political dimensions of the process of anglicization in the colonies; William Speck, for his explorations of the literary-commercial ambience of the empire; Rhys Isaac, for his work on the transformation of domestic space by the increasingly public use of dwellings; and Robert Ferguson, for insights into the aesthetics of state proclamation.

Philip Gura, David D. Hall, Robert Ferguson, and Lawrence Klein have critiqued my manuscript, offering substantive improvements in both style and structure. Gil Kelly at the Institute has with great good humor refined the prose and tightened the annotation.

I owe special gratitude to my editor, Fredrika J. Teute. Her interest in the institutionalized practices of civility was so intense, and her thoughts on the subject so complementary (albeit centered a century later), that what began as a searching and lively conversation quickly evolved into collaboration. Our joint studies of the republican court and the women's domain of the public sphere in the early Republic should be considered the intersection of this book and her researches into the social life of the governing classes in the 1830s in Washington, D.C. Thank you, Fredrika.

CONTENTS

ILLUSTRATIONS

Introduction: Of Civil Discourse and Private Society

In 1709 Anthony Ashley Cooper, the third earl of Shaftesbury, coined the term "private society" to describe the range of voluntary associations he saw coming into being in Europe.[1] These bodies were private in the sense that they came into being and operated outside the superintendence of the state. Many, if not most, lacked charters or official warrants for association. Nevertheless, they were truly societies; they made for themselves covenants, articles of agreement, laws binding members into community. They met in the name of common interest, pleasure, feeling, or appetite. By 1709 several sorts of private association existed: salons, coffeehouse coteries, clubs, tea tables, and projecting societies. All formed beyond the periphery of the royal courts. To varying degrees these private bodies cultivated manners that stood at odds with the codified etiquette of the courts. Liberties of conversation and conduct made private society seem for Shaftesbury a social space in which opinion might be formed, manners refined, and arts encouraged. In private society persons took part in — and were transformed by — the great project of civility.

Shaftesbury recognized private society as a distinctive feature of the political and cultural life of his day in part because he could not avoid doing so; the proliferation of coffeehouses, clubs, salons, and tea tables made the consolidation of this social zone hard to ignore. These institutions spread wherever Europeans congregated or settled. Their increasingly distinctive styles of conduct and conversation traveled with them. They, as much as

1. Anthony Ashley Cooper, third earl of Shaftesbury, *Sensus Communis: An Essay on the Freedom of Wit and Humour . . .* (London, 1709).

any government, seemed requisites of civil order, for in them persons entered into a sense of communal identity and found a happiness in society. This civil acculturation was particularly important in two sites of social disruption where populations loosed from customary ties of neighborhood, congregation, and family coalesced: in urbanizing towns and cities and in the new settlements.

This is a study of the role of private society in invoking civility in British America. It explores from a transatlantic perspective American cultural provinciality. Modern inquiries into the institutional character of British American provinciality have concentrated on religious denominations, military organizations, chartered corporations, and agencies of state. This study examines several forms of private society. By private society, I mean pretty much what Shaftesbury meant when he coined the term — groups formed outside the jurisdiction of the state so that people might share pleasures, promote projects, and fashion new ways of interacting. I will anatomize several forms of private society, marking the distinguishing features of tavern companies, coffeehouse fellowships, tea-table gatherings, salons, dancing assemblies, routs, card parties, gentlemen's clubs, and college fraternities. I will also chronicle their florescence in the American colonies.

My purpose, however, is not to tell how fraternity and sorority became popular or to chronicle America's growing dependence on voluntary association to achieve happiness in society. These oft-told tales need no retelling. Instead, I trace the development of distinctive and culturally powerful modes of communication in each arena of private society. I ask why these different modes developed concurrently and in tension with one another. I have presumed that new ways of communicating pleasure gave rise to novel ways of associating: that is, that aesthetics instructed politics in private society. I contend that each form of private society that flourished in British America depended upon a distinctive manner of discourse for its effective operation. So necessary were these discursive manners to the conduct of these societies that we can speak of coffeehouses, clubs, salons, and tea tables as "discursive institutions" — social entities bound to linguistic formations.

The cultural power of private society has been freshly appreciated by historians. Jürgen Habermas prompted this change in attitude. *The Structural Transformation of the Public Sphere: An Inquiry into a Category of Bourgeois Society* argued that the coffeehouses, clubs, salons, and private associations were central to the constitution of the authentic "public sphere" in Western states. Habermas and Reinhart Koselleck understood "the public" to have been a complex structure, deriving in part from "the private" and in part from the depersonalized authority of the state.[2] Habermas understood that the articulation of an authentic "public opinion" required a public independent of state control and capable of criticizing state power. How did a critical public come into being? Its independence derived ultimately from the permissions accorded the private conscience during the Reformation. The power of independent judgment became public through the mediation of various "communities of conscience" — conventicles, coffeehouse discussion groups, reform associations, and political clubs. Thus private societies were instrumental in the formation of the public sphere, and their modes of discourse necessary to the creation of public opinion. They made up the constituent territories of the "republic of letters."

Habermas's history of the public sphere has begun to influence the historiography of early America.[3] Much of the scholarship confesses a sympathy with Habermas's ambition to learn how discursive institutions effectively form and communicate a public opinion critical of ruling powers. Habermas envisions a politics dependent upon communicative reason. In his view, the evacuation of God from the political language of the West transmuted the judgments of Christian conscience into the judgment of human reason, a reason not validated by divine law, but tested in the arenas of human conversation and exchange. There is a problem here, as the widespread criticism of this turn of Habermas's thought indicates. However admirable Habermas's political ambition to inject the echo of conscience into public debate may be (and who would deny the attractiveness of a theory that challenges the modernist myth of alienation and the postmodernist myth of mutual incomprehensibility by offering a vision of a common language enabling communal judgments?), "reason" presents insuperable difficulties as an explanation for what was and is at work in communications that founded communities. Although reason was repeatedly invoked in Anglo-American political criticism as an authoritative ideal, these polemic uses of "reason" had a peculiar way of rationalizing one's passions — one's love of liberty, life, or property. The disingenuous identification of reason with one's political affections suggests that "feel-

2. Reinhart Koselleck, *Critique and Crisis: Enlightenment and the Pathogenesis of Modern Society* (Cambridge, Mass., 1988); Jürgen Habermas, *The Structural Transformation of the Public Sphere: An Inquiry into a Category of Bourgeois Society*, trans. Thomas Burger (Cambridge, Mass., 1989).

3. David Waldstreicher, review of Craig Calhoun, ed., *Habermas and the Public Sphere, William and Mary Quarterly*, 3d Ser., LII (1995), 175–177.

ing" rather than "reason" more accurately names what was at work in communication.

I do not dispute Habermas's claims that "communities of conscience" made up a range of private society and that these contributed critically to the formation of public spirit and public opinion. Rather, I would argue that these communities — conventicles, reform societies, charitable groups, associations for the promotion of practical knowledge, political parties — constituted that domain of private society that Daniel Defoe called "projecting" societies, associations that prosecuted programs promoting the welfare of persons besides their memberships.[4] Private society encompassed more than projecting communities. Sodalities that exclusively cultivated their own welfare also existed. Many of these groups confessed wit, affection, or appetite as the grounds of community, not conscience. Some of these groups were secret, others exclusive, others casual about membership. All experimented with means other than law or self-interest for binding society in a practical order. My particular concern is to bring to light the discursive practices that served as verbal glue for these communities of appetite and feeling.

Findings in the intellectual history of sociability help. Lawrence Klein, Susan M. Purviance, and John Dwyer have constructed a genealogy of sentimentalist theories of society from Shaftesbury to Adam Smith. Particularly pertinent is Klein's *Shaftesbury and the Culture of Politeness: Moral Discourse and Cultural Politics in Early Eighteenth-Century England.*[5] Shaftesbury astutely grasped the connections between power, morality, desire, and wit in the association of people. He saw private society as both an experimental haven of play superintended by wit and an arena of political morality where honesty was possible because friendship gave persons the liberty to critique everything. He, more than any other commentator of the age,

---

4. D[aniel] Defoe, *An Essay upon Projects* (London, 1697). Much of the book encouraged the formation of these sorts of reformative associations.

5. Lawrence E. Klein, *Shaftesbury and the Culture of Politeness: Moral Discourse and Cultural Politics in Early Eighteenth-Century England* (Cambridge, 1994); John Dwyer, "Enlightened Spectators and Classical Moralists: Sympathetic Relations in Eighteenth-Century Scotland," in Dwyer and Richard B. Sher, eds., *Sociability and Society in Eighteenth-Century Scotland* (Edinburgh, 1993), 96–118. See also Dwyer, *Virtuous Discourse: Sensibility and Community in Late Eighteenth-Century Scotland* (Edinburgh, 1987); Susan M. Purviance, "Intersubjectivity and Sociable Relations in the Philosophy of Francis Hutcheson," in Dwyer and Sher, eds., *Sociability and Society in Eighteenth-Century Scotland*, 23–38.

saw the role that feeling played in informing the "public spirit" and recognized the power of wit to promote fellow feeling.

Shaftesbury's cultural analysis envisioned both the exoteric and esoteric developments of private society. His discussions of public spirit and political morality grounded later Scottish elaborations of the theory of social projects. In particular, he anticipated Francis Hutcheson's empiricist moral epistemology, which identified "perception of virtue and vice as the product of a moral sense: a disposition to respond to the motivations of others by way of feeling."[6] It is through Hutcheson's sentimentalist politics that we can understand communities of conscience in terms of a moral sense grounded in shared feeling, rather than as a Habermasian communicative reason. From it we can see why the discourses of projecting associations were so bound to the rhetorical task of sensitizing the hearts of an insensate audience. Hutcheson's picture of sociability as a frame for communal moral action is the theoretical dimension of private society most familiar to American historiography, explaining the post-Revolutionary zest for voluntary association. Yet even in the most morally earnest of projecting societies, there were playful elements in their communication unexplained by Hutchesonian moral epistemology: the feasting of fire insurance societies, the theatricality of the Democratic-Republican clubs, the toasting rituals of militia companies, and the Freemasons' mystagogy.

Play was important to private society, projecting or no. Shaftesbury's remarks in *Sensus Communis: An Essay on the Freedom of Wit and Humour* suggest why. Wit, he argued, grounded one's sense of common cause with one's fellows. In shared laughter tacit values come into the open, permitting strangers to become fellows.[7] Viability of the public spirit depended upon giving manners sufficient scope to allow wit and humor. Shaftesbury's insistence upon discursive permissions reacted against the tendency for politeness to calcify into "correctness," particularly in court society.

6. Purviance, "Intersubjectivity and Sociable Relations in the Philosophy of Francis Hutcheson," in Dwyer and Sher, eds., *Sociability and Society in Eighteenth-Century Scotland*, 23. Purviance here is commenting upon Hutcheson's *System of Moral Philosophy* (1755).

7. Shaftesbury, *Sensus Communis: An Essay on the Freedom of Wit and Humour* . . . , in Shaftesbury, *Characteristics of Men, Manners, Opinions, Times, Etc.*, ed. John M. Robertson, 2 vols. (London, 1900), I, 49–53. For a meditation of the present applicability of Shaftesbury's theory of the social utility of humor, see Joel Weinsheimer, "Shaftesbury in Our Time: The Politics of Wit and Humour," *Eighteenth Century Theory and Interpretation*, XXXVI (1995), 178–188.

Shaftesbury's signal insight was that this license in discursive manners could not operate in society at large, or in the court, but could in institutions such as clubs that preserved an element of privacy and enjoyed the mutual tolerance endowed by friendship.

To underscore Shaftesbury's point about the ability of certain communications to institute communities of interest and fellow feeling, I will use his term, "sensus communis," when discussing how speeches and texts create and sustain various forms of private society. Sensus communis should not be understood as "common sense," either in its guise as conventional wisdom or a generally apprehended experience. It is, rather, a form of communal identity brought into being by speech acts or writing.

At this point the intersection of this study with the concerns of the history of political thought becomes visible. Since J. G. A. Pocock resurrected manners as a political category by arguing that the enrichment of manners was the commercial imperium's payoff to a citizenry with little direct access to power, the politics of politeness has been an issue. With Lawrence Klein and Dena Goodman, I hold that the cultural struggles between politeness and Grub Street incivility, resort heterosociability and libertinism, and salon conversation and print polemic must be situated in a context of institutional contestation (thus the libertine extravagances of the Tory tavern oppose the polite conversation of the Whig coffeehouse).[8] One cannot say much of value about civilizing until one recognizes the variety of discursive manners and their institutional features. There was no uniform civility during the seventeenth and eighteenth centuries, but a variety of behavioral and conversational practices that claimed the name. For this reason, I am not greatly concerned with expounding *the* theory of politeness or tracing *the* development of the code of manners as revealed in sequences of conduct books. What mattered most then and matters most here was the evolution of discursive practices in the variety of provincial institutions over the eighteenth century. (This is more a cultural history than an intellectual history.) Yet theories of sociability, politeness, and gentility cannot be ignored, for an important function of conversation in private societies was to advertise the glories of participating in the com-

8. J. G. A. Pocock, "Virtues, Rights, and Manners: A Model for Historians of Political Thought," in Pocock, *Virtue, Commerce, and History: Essays on Political Thought and History, Chiefly in the Eighteenth Century* (Cambridge, 1985), 49–50; Dena Goodman, *The Republic of Letters: A Cultural History of the French Enlightenment* (Ithaca, N.Y., 1994). Goodman makes this argument in connection with the French salons, the subject of her study.

pany. Clubs were perpetually confessing how delightful and improving it was to belong to a club. Theories of sociability, politeness, and gentility do illuminate how British America's clubs, tea tables, and salons cultivated a mystique about themselves.

My use of discursive practice as a key to understanding the evolution of cultural institutions should be viewed as a latter-day adaptation of Norbert Elias's historical sociology, *The History of Manners*, volume I of *The Civilizing Process*. When I undertook this study, I feared that reliance upon Elias's scholarship might be regarded by historians as a methodological archaism. I had no idea that civility would become a hot trope of political rhetoric in the United States during the 1990s. I did not anticipate that intense theoretical and historical consideration would be given to how a disparate population works toward mutuality by making use of manners, polite discursive formulas, rituals, play, and entertainment. Now scholarly interest in civility approaches the intense concern that political scientists have always evinced in civil society. The issue has been taken up in a number of ways by historians. Some (Carol F. Karlsen exemplifies the approach) employ Elias's portrait of civilizing to frame the often dire consequences of Europeans' cultural project of overcoming the "savagery" of native Americans. This sort of history explores what might be called the external dialectic of civility — the encounter between various native cultures and various European projects of settlement driven by the imperative of remaking the natives in their image. Others treat what might be termed the internal dialectic of civility within Anglo-American culture. Richard L. Bushman, for instance, offers an analogue of civilizing in his portrait of the spread of gentility among the middling orders during the late eighteenth century.[9] He shows how instruction in the material and behavioral forms of gentility informed the creation of middle-class identity in nineteenth-century America. I, like Bushman, am interested in how manners, fashions, and modes of conversation influenced the horizontal integration of American society. Yet the period that most concerns me, the colonial era (roughly 1690 through the 1760s), predates the formation of an American middle class. It was a time during which society was organized by a general distinc-

9. Norbert Elias, *The Civilizing Process*, I, *The History of Manners*, trans. Edmund Jephcott (New York, 1982); Carol F. Karlsen, "The 'Savagizing' Process and the Practice of Race in Western New York, 1770–1850," conference paper, "Possible Pasts: Critical Encounters in Early America," Philadelphia, June 4, 1994; Richard L. Bushman, *The Refinement of America: Persons, Houses, Cities* (New York, 1992).

tion between the leisured quality and the working commonality. Within these two layers existed hierarchies of rank, profession, and calling. Status was further complicated by ethnicity, religious affiliation, sex, and locality. Civility — and civil discourse particularly — enabled persons to bridge distinctions.[10] It enabled congenial communication between persons of different ranks and permitted one to make common cause with them. Within ranks, it enabled persons to put aside the perpetual struggle for precedence and so establish fraternal or sororal familiarity.

Gordon Wood's *Radicalism of the American Revolution* has argued that the meaning of the Revolution resides in the transformation of a colonial society profoundly hierarchical in structure — a society organized vertically — into a democratic society, integrated horizontally.[11] According to Wood, the Revolution gave substance to egalitarian republican political ideals driving the transformation of society. Studying the development of the forms of private society in British America reveals that the integrating of society horizontally was already begun well before the Revolution. We see how certain discursive institutions permitted a coalescence of interest between ranks — how, for instance, the coffeehouse became the space where gentlemen communed with merchants because news became their common idiom (Chapter 2); or how the town madams of urban tea-table society of the 1710s and 1720s used fashion as a means of building a general feminine interest that encompassed country wives and city girls (Chapter 4). Some civil institutions — those championing free conversations, such as clubs and salons particularly — used their privacy as a hedge to rearrange society on other than customary grounds. Yet a question of scale arises. A club might pretend that it was a state (as did the Schuylkill Fishing Company, in Chapter 6) and that liberty and consent governed the res publica; in reality, the familiarity of the membership suggested that the old politics of personal relations was at work in a new form. Wood argues that the innovation of the American Revolution was the way in which its

10. Indeed, the status-bridging function of civil discourse made it anathema to the more exclusionary sorts of elite persons. Consider the complaint of Lady Bab Lardoon in John Burgoyne's play *The Maid of the Oaks:* "Oh, my dear, you have chose a horrid word to express the intercourse of the bon ton; *civility* may be very proper in a mercer, when one is choosing a silk, but *familiarity* is the life of good company." John Burgoyne, *The Dramatic and Poetical Works of the Late Lieut. Gen. J. Burgoyne* (1806; rpt. Delmar, N.Y., 1977), 64.

11. Gordon S. Wood, *The Radicalism of the American Revolution* (New York, 1992), 11–42.

political ideology supplanted personal politics with the impersonal imperatives of democracy in the United States. Yet the Republic was far from being a democratic logocracy. Rather, the United States seems intent during the 1780s and 1790s with personalizing every ideal in its political and cultural lexicon, forming voluntary associations in the name of benevolence, learning, utility, liberty, and virtue. Moreover, citizens distressed by the post-Revolutionary disregard of rank or person found solace in civility, with its personability, sociability, formality, and exclusivity. A whole range of antirepublican values was preserved in private society and would flourish quite handsomely into and through the nineteenth century. To the extent that civility condoned pleasure, and the pursuit of pleasure evaded virtue and utility, it enabled a sense of communal enrichment freed from republican discipline.

Although I discuss the fate of civility and civil discourse in the early Republic in my final chapter, it is proper to suggest here at the outset how the changed circumstance of society amplified the importance of polite manners and a civil tongue after the American Revolution. Like the 1990s, the 1790s were obsessed with civility — in terms of cultural adequacy compared to Europe, in reaction to the rancorousness of politics, in contrast to the rudeness of native peoples, and in terms of the relations of the sexes in public places. The issues and the language were not then and have not now been exhausted.

To summarize: this history recalls what various groups of persons did in the name of civility to rearrange their conversation and behavior in British America. I concentrate on private societies and discursive institutions driving certain social and intellectual transformations because they most clearly show that something more was entailed than consent or dissent or custom in creating the public world. The richer and more mutable category of manners stands at the center of politics when private society comes into view. This is an institutional history of manners, a historical sociology of mannerly discourses, and a meditation on the aesthetic dimension of provincial society.

I have written this history in a language that I hope different sorts of readers will find inviting. It approximates civil discourse — talk that is not the esoteric speech of my academic tribe. I hope I can speak to informed common readers, historians, political scientists, students of communication, sociologists, and those troubled folks who have civility much on their mind these days. There is, however, one audience to which I speak with particular pointedness, people interested in early American literature. A reason why I have composed a history of the communication of private society in British America is to provide an avenue for understanding why British American belles lettres became largely meaningless for posterity.[12]

What did British American literature mean? This is not the question, What does it mean? — the hermeneutic question that anyone might answer by reflecting on one's sense of the writings. Rather, this is the more troubling problem: What did it *once* mean? What was it that was once so important that it moved hundreds of persons to write thousands of works from the 1690s through the 1770s, yet quickly seemed so unimportant that it seemed unworthy of comment by the first literary historians of the United States and by literary historians subsequently? What was the spirit, motive, message that perished?

Why is belles lettres the most profoundly dead of all the literatures produced in British America? Other sorts of colonial writings survive: "Yankee Doodle" and other provincial folk songs are still sung; certain eighteenth-century hymns have never ceased playing a part in Protestant worship; proverbs and moral sayings (Franklin's particularly) still contribute to the fund of common wisdom; early natural histories have rarely been out of print; political speeches and tracts, particularly those advocating libertarian or republican ideals, have been canonized as part of the curriculum in American civics; neo-Calvinist presses reissue many Puritan sermons and nearly every colonial writing on practical piety for the edification of conservative denominations. Yet British American belles lettres survives only in the few pages allotted in college literature anthologies to excerpts from William Byrd's *Histories of the Dividing Line*, Ebenezer Cook's "Sot-Weed Factor," Sarah Kemble Knight's journal, and maybe Richard Lewis's "Journey from Patapsco to Annapolis." None of these writings is a masterwork in the technical sense of being a writing whose provocations commanded immediate notice and whose problems proved so durable as to compel the uninterrupted attention of posterity. Only Lewis's poem mattered in the eighteenth-century republic of letters, and its fame did not survive the rise of romanticism. Scholars exhumed and revived these pieces,

12. William C. Spengemann, in *A New World of Words: Redefining Early American Literature* (New Haven, Conn., 1994), 1–50, has given a masterful account of how early American literature has been assigned a proleptic, attenuated status in the narrative of the rise of American letters as a function of evolving political concerns in the academy. But my explanation is intended to be more radical: to account historically for those qualities of British American literature that defy subsequent attempts to memorialize it.

justifying their places in the canon of American letters as exemplary works. What they exemplified remains an open question; our understanding of British American literature in general, and belles lettres in particular, is so tentative that it should be called speculation, rather than knowledge.

We do know, however, that British American literature lost whatever vitality it once possessed — that it died. Consequently, some hard tasks fall to us: to explain how the desires it embodied became passé, to determine how its pleasure became less piquant, to discover how the belles lettres began to seem no longer beautiful.

The history of modern aesthetic practice, replete with retromovements and neorevivals, suggests that desire is sufficiently recursive to permit old forms of pleasure to revive and old beauty reappear. Hegel argued that the return of what was lost is the characteristic path of Western aesthetics, and in confirmation of Hegel's dictum we have seen John Barth in *The Sot-Weed Factor* refurbish with postmodern dress Ebenezer Cook's burlesque of commerce and colonization. Yet the beauties of British American literature remain, for the most part, intractably alien.

The extent of this estrangement was made clear in 1990 when the Institute of Early American History and Culture published Dr. Alexander Hamilton's *History of the Ancient and Honorable Tuesday Club*. If any work of British American letters could have engaged the postmodern imagination, this extravagantly crafted parody of world history, the republic of letters, and masculine society should have. Alas, it did not. We who own copies of the three hardback volumes form a readership on the scale of those who snapped up Thoreau's *Walden* on first issue. *Very* select.[13]

The failure of Hamilton's work to find an audience beyond the cognoscenti prompted me to rethink literary historiography. Until 1991 I understood the loss of British American literature in conventionally political terms. Subscribing to Terry Eagleton's view that the history of aesthetics should be understood as a struggle for political hegemony, I regarded the disappearance of British American belles lettres as signaling the eclipse of the mystique of British mercantile colonialism by patriot republicanism. The beauties of colonial belles lettres were so implicated in imperial occasions they could not survive the crack-up of the empire. This is at best a limited truth, most telling for the poetry upon affairs of state that I exam-

13. Dr. Alexander Hamilton, *The History of the Ancient and Honorable Tuesday Club*, ed. Robert Micklus, 3 vols. (Chapel Hill, N.C., 1990).

ined in *Oracles of Empire*.[14] It failed to explain the aesthetic problem of *The History of the Ancient and Honorable Tuesday Club*. Hamilton's work did not perform as a hegemonic discourse should; it did not critique the power of the state or the conduct of society in light of its own utopian politics of sympathy; nor was its parody so stable that it operated as burlesque. It resembled a game that evolved in the course of practice some truly peculiar rules, yet managed to attract a cult of enthusiasts who played along for the sake of its absurdity. So I wondered whether the *Tuesday Club*'s politics was a by-product of aesthetic play. My perspective flipped: no longer did politics possess explanatory force, revealing the occult motives of aesthetics; rather, the play of desire explained the formation of politics and societies. I found myself validating the primacy of aesthetics in eighteenth-century philosophy against the prevailing orthodoxy in cultural studies that politics is the nexus of meaning. I began reading British American literature as a register in which political innovation was revealed to be a function of new modes of communicating desires and pleasures. My attention shifted from explicitly political expressions to those that were implicitly political, seizing upon the one powerful discourse that came into being during the seventeenth century as a medium for sharing pleasure — belles lettres.

In 1991 Sacvan Bercovitch asked me to write a summary of British American literature for the first volume of *The Cambridge History of American Literature*. I agreed, with the proviso that I treat a much more concentrated matter, belles lettres. The essay, published in 1994, told how an elite provincial culture flourished by devising new ways of communicating politeness, mannerliness, gentility, and elegance — modes of pleasurable social engagement. Involvement with the history of the book and encounters with the work of David D. Hall and Michael Warner disposed me to represent an array of urban literary scenes to show how conversation, manuscript, and printed text cooperated and competed.[15] The story: belles

14. Terry Eagleton, *The Ideology of the Aesthetic* (Cambridge, Mass., 1990); David S. Shields, *Oracles of Empire: Poetry, Politics, and Commerce in British America, 1690–1750* (Chicago, 1990).

15. David S. Shields, "British-American Belles Lettres," in Sacvan Bercovitch, ed., *The Cambridge History of American Literature*, I, *1500–1820* (New York, 1994), 307–343; Michael Warner, *The Letters of the Republic: Publication and the Public Sphere in Eighteenth-Century America* (Cambridge, Mass., 1990); David D. Hall and John B. Hench, eds., *Needs and Opportunities in the History of the Book: America, 1639–1876* (Worcester, Mass., 1987); Hall, *Worlds of Wonder, Days of Judgment: Popular Religious Belief in Early New England* (New York, 1989).

lettres borrowed qualities of courtly address from the bon ton of London and Paris, capturing them in manuscript writings that mimicked conversational modes. These exclusive communications were themselves imitated by the periodical press to construct subscriberships in the image of genteel society. This tale undergirded a portrait of British American belles lettres that emphasized its unfamiliarity by an extensive presentation of new material. Its novelty implied a critique: to the extent that previous literary history of the American colonies restricted attention to products of the press, it missed belles lettres, for the bulk of belletristic production circulated in manuscript or scripted oral performance.

Composing the *Cambridge History* survey proved useful in forming a general sense of British American belles lettres. The essay failed, however, to appreciate the historical justice of the banishment of belles lettres from the affections of posterity. Instead, it claimed places for the writings of Archibald Home, Elizabeth Graeme Fergusson, James Kirkpatrick, and Dr. Alexander Hamilton in the canon of American literature, arguing their vitality, reflexivity, political prescience (choose your virtue).[16] But these writings did not insist that a posterity attend to their message; they did not demand to be monumentalized. The historical sketch should have recognized the consequences of the use of belles lettres as scripts for occasions of shared pleasure: that these writings were profoundly occasional; that they were frequently instrumental, being consumed or absorbed in the act of keeping conversation amusing and alive; that their longevity as writings depended upon their effectiveness in reactivating social pleasures or in giving body to rituals of sociability. Most belletristic writings were designed *not* to seek eternal regard. A historical significance of belles lettres was the disavowal of durable learning and undying truth in favor of a passing, shared amusement. Even the seemingly monumental *History of the Tuesday Club*, with its two-thousand-page rumination upon club / world / social / political / literary affairs, mocked the aspiration for literary immortality, ridiculing the vanity of history.

Which brings us to the problem of this study: Can literary history be written without a chronology of classics, without fixing upon master texts, and without depending upon a rhetoric of revisionism or a vision of a new canon? This study presumes that it can. A number of scholars have fash-

16. Shields, "British-American Belles Lettres," in Bercovitch, ed., *CHAL*, I, 307–343.

ioned innovative literary histories that promise to overcome the objection of social and cultural historians that accounts based on masterpieces suffer from the unrepresentativeness of their superlative expression. Franco Moretti's *Signs Taken for Wonders*, an experiment in the sociology of literary forms, blazed paths in the direction of a history of popular discourses organized not so much by genre as by their figurations of society.[17] This study will go in a similar direction—away from history constructed as interpretations of a series of classics toward a narrative reconstituting a dynamic of discourses imbedded in substantial bodies of texts.[18]

I want to dramatize the variety of belletristic discourses, showing how they organized around different ways of achieving social pleasure; furthermore, I want to show how each discursive mode fixed on a particular site of conversation: the tavern, the coffeehouse, the tea table, the salon, the club, the college. A history of British American literary culture must recover the constellation of institutional styles that emerged and must reconstruct the dynamics of communication. What grabs attention in such a history is, not the progress of refinement or democratization of civility, but the flowering of a precise array of discursive manners, each manner entailing its own politics, relation to the public realm, image of society, and aesthetics. By recovering the tensions between politeness and Grub Street incivility (Chapter 2), tavern jest and wit (Chapter 3), coffeehouse news and truth (Chapter 3), tea-table gossip and news, tea chat and salon sense (Chapter 4), ritual play at balls and card parties and free conversation in salons and clubs (Chapter 5), club raillery and state proclamation (Chapter 6), the college's Christian belles lettres and evangelical piety (Chapter 7), we overcome hidebound dichotomies between religious and secular, elite and popular, and public and private, replacing them with a complex of discriminations that suggests the richness and variety of discursive manners.

Individuals could and did perform in more than one of these institutions concurrently, mastering several discursive modes while seeking amusement, social advancement, and a secure place in the provincial world. Chapter 8 recounts the career of a master of civil discourse, Dr. Thomas Dale, tracing his trajectory upward through Charleston's social domains.

---

17. Franco Moretti, *Signs Taken for Wonders: Essays in the Sociology of Literary Form*, trans. Susan Fischer et al. (New York, 1988). It is among Cultural Studies scholars that Moretti's work has had some influence; traditional literary scholars have passed it by.

18. Or: this study will lead away from a Gadamerian hermeneutics of the classics toward Habermasian anatomy of discourses. Hans-Georg Gadamer, *Truth and Method*, trans. Garrett Barden and John Cumming (New York, 1985), 176–191.

In one year, 1732–1733, he went from being a debt-plagued social outcast from London to a fixture at the very highest levels of society, married into one of the exalted families and tapped for public employments by the colonial executive.

Mastering sociable discourses had instrumental value, permitting one to perform effectively in private society; yet it could also be an end in itself, providing pleasure and enabling the self-cultivation that was the hallmark of civility. Being polite was pleasurable. Performing one's role correctly and well in one of British America's cultural arenas was gratifying. Mastering the discursive manners of sociable institutions secured one's happiness. The students of happiness as a political ideal have tended to view the matter in one of two ways: as satisfaction of the individual citizen or as a national *sensus communis*, contingent upon the fulfillment or nonfulfillment of a consensual American Dream. Yet this study will argue that there existed other accesses to happiness in the communication and play of bodies that lay intermediate between the private person and the state. Consequently, any history of the discursive institutions of civil society in British America must entail a social aesthetics sensitive to the varieties of shared pleasure.

The question of social aesthetics is important for political history, cultural history, and literary history, and it is the ground where these fields might have their most useful conversation. Studying pleasure as a ground of society moves the question of public happiness beyond the restrictions of Habermas's communicative reason or Hutcheson's communities of moral sense. The pursuit of pleasure was not (could not be?) constrained by normalcy, morality, and moderation. In those times and places when happiness became identified with pleasure and divorced from reason or moral sense, then private society could experiment with the limits of expression. Over the course of the eighteenth century, the coffeehouse, tavern, tea table, salon, club, and college advanced the liberty of expression beyond personal expressions of jest, ridicule, parody, gossip, scandal, giving voice to a *sensus communis* articulating extravagant social appetites and passions (as well as moderate feelings of friendship and public spirit). The interest of these discursive institutions was their experimental liberties. In them desire, interest, power, and law became issues of playful interrogation — and targets of total raillery.

Throughout the century, the speculative liberty of these discursive institutions subjected them to attack from champions of evangelical piety and from sentimental moralists demanding authenticity of heart from humanity. During the latter half of the century, certain republican ideologues attacked the sociable institutions on other grounds. Having defined public virtue as a private morality of self-sacrifice, discipline, and maturity, Radical Republicans challenged all communities predicated on pleasing the self—those pursuing recreation, amusement, good-fellowship, shared consumption, or shared pleasure. Republicanism attacked the value of a social aesthetics, asserting the dominion of morality in public affairs. A person's seeking pleasure in company was conflated with self-interest under the heading of "luxury."

The culture clash of the 1780s and 1790s revealed the extent to which belles lettres was subsumed under the category of manners in republican thought and in genteel practice. The history of belles lettres became incidental to the history of manners. The contest over manners erupted because the discursive institutions nurtured by provincial belles lettres had survived the Revolution and projected their competing visions of gentility in the new Republic. Chapter 9 speculates on the effect of the republican critique and the spread of print on the discourse of the coffeehouse, tavern, and salon and marks the path toward the creation of a synthetic national practice of polite manners in the sociability of the republican court.

What did British American belles lettres mean? The question might be answered if restated, What did British American belles lettres do? It invoked an array of discursive institutions enabling societies to form. It contributed to the life of these groups by celebrating the common appetites, defining and encouraging the pleasures, furthering play, and promoting the free conversation that bound persons in community. And it idealized the values of friendliness, liberty, gentility, mannerliness, wit, and politeness that served as philosophical warrants for the conduct of these private societies in the ideological contests that agitated Anglo-American culture. There were historical consequences: the range of discursive manners contributed by these private societies to the American public accounted in large measure for the richness of expression found in public discourse at the end of the eighteenth century. The persistent vitality of the club, the salon, and the college as cultural institutions well into the nineteenth century owed much to discursive practices descended from those first enacted in British American belles lettres.

What should a history of British American belles lettres do, besides recount the work of polite letters in creating and sustaining the various discursive institutions? It should communicate something of the peculiar power that various modes of polite conversation and writing exerted within their proper habitats. So we shall visit Enoch Story's tavern in Philadelphia in the 1700s to witness a wit's attempts to counteract male crudity. We shall watch the women of the Boston tea tables in the 1720s project their influence through the city's public spaces and into the countryside by means of fashion and talk. We shall see a young salonniere in Philadelphia of the 1750s learn that the perils of mixed company require that she cultivate wit as well as sense and sensibility. We shall attend balls in Williamsburg and the West Indies to ponder the role of the arts in contests for precedence in provincial society. We shall play a game of crambo with college undergraduates and sit on the sidelines of a poetry contest between two beaux in Barbados. We shall wonder why various fishing clubs in Philadelphia pretended that they were sovereign states. We shall review the trial of the secretary of the Homony Club of Annapolis for leaving unattended the minute books. We shall follow a cagey Harvard student as he fashions a literary reputation for himself by manipulating the public prints until he provokes a classmate to become his literary nemesis and gets his comeuppance in the pages of London's most fashionable magazine. We shall chart the rise of an impecunious English physician to the highest level of South Carolina society within a year of his settlement because of his mastery of several styles of sociable self-presentation.

I have chosen to treat a variety of urban scenes rather than to explore the institutional world of one city intensively. The discursive cultures of three cities — Charleston, Philadelphia, and Boston — are described in some detail to indicate the institutional dynamics of cities. I want to suggest the pervasiveness of these developments in British America. Wherever urbanization occurred, conversation and literary communication coalesced around the same institutions. Local politics, local religion, and local society influenced the specific conditions of this institutionalization (the Pennsylvania Council legislated strictures on the public diversions in taverns, for instance), yet the institutions invariably cosmopolitanized public affairs and public discussions in each locality. This pattern defined the discursive dimensions of American provinciality. Coffeehouses, colleges, tea tables, salons, and clubs were not indigenous to British America. All owed their births to the European metropolises. Their Old World nativity would become, in the course of time, a basis for criticism by republican nationalists. The republicans' inability to create or imagine native institutions in which to refigure manners and reconceive social happiness became a cause of anxiety, driving them to ever more extreme espousals of antiurban agrarianism. Cities, however, could not be wished away. They flourished rather than failed, and the forms of associations that had characterized European and colonial urban life remained in power in the new Republic.

British American belles lettres might have been consumed in the making of discursive institutions, but, so long as those institutions remained intact, new works designed for inspiring social pleasures were called for. Printers and booksellers saw that they could provide for a price what had been provided before by persons in salons and clubs for free. The print market burgeoned as it supplied texts that, read aloud, became a foundation for company keeping. The transatlantic market for print kept this institutional arrangement in place until at least the 1830s.

How British America's discursive institutions related to the press and how the booksellers and publishers of periodicals constructed a print replica of the urban world and its institutions will be only subsidiary concerns in this study.[19] Chapter 7, however, will present enough material about the spread of print to enable everyone to grasp a paradox: the virtual sociability of the framing club of a periodical (in which each subscriber was a "corresponding member") did not supplant the arenas of conversational sociability; rather, it popularized clubbing, company keeping, and personal communication by enhancing the mystique of private society. One phenomenon that *shall* be treated extensively is the self-conscious avoidance of print by participants in certain of these institutions. This avoidance of print became at times a condition of communication. The cultivation of exclusivity, intimacy, and an aura of personal connection became part of the mystique of clubs and salons. Once this is realized, we can see that the avoidance of print by the partisans of gentility, male or female, was often a matter of preference, not of exclusion. The manuscript was the favorite vehicle of communication in several arenas of sociability until late in the eighteenth century. For salonnieres the greater cultural effectiveness of manuscript writing, particularly letters, was an article of faith until the 1830s. My point: the question of the relation of sex to print must be recast entirely in light of knowledge how discursive institutions communicated in early America.

At this juncture, the relationship between this study and other projects in the history of the book, early American literary history, and cultural studies becomes apparent: it explores for the history of the book the arenas

19. The first volume of David D. Hall and Hugh Amory, eds., *The History of the Book in America* (New York, forthcoming), takes up this matter, providing a summary assessment of the cultural effects of print culture in British America and the early Republic.

of manuscript publication, where an economy of gift rather than a market determines the circulation of most texts; it also illuminates certain cultural conditions that limit the employment of print for communication.[20]

My project assists the revision of feminist historiography by aiding current attempts to conceptualize women's institutions of communication in order to define the discursive conditions of their presence in the republic of letters. It recovers for British America the sort of exchanges documented for France by Dena Goodman in her landmark study of salon culture, *The Republic of Letters*. It supplies a provincial context for the salon culture of the early Republic under reconstruction by Carla Mulford, Susan Stabile, Daphne O'Brien, and Fredrika Teute. It provides matter for their interrogation of the domesticity thesis that currently superintends most inquiry into the condition of early national women. It also provides colonial antecedents for the intellectual history of elite women of the United States pioneered by Mary Kelley and Elizabeth Fox-Genovese.[21]

20. This book is less concerned with the production than the performance of writings, so differs from the work of Harold Love in *Scribal Publication in Seventeenth-Century England* (Oxford, 1993). Because of this study's preoccupation with discursive institutions, it differs from Richard D. Brown's useful *Knowledge Is Power: The Diffusion of Information in Early America, 1700–1865* (New York, 1989).

21. Carla Mulford, Introduction, in Mulford, ed., *Only for the Eye of a Friend: The Poems of Annis Boudinot Stockton* (Charlottesville, Va., 1995); Susan Stabile, "American Women Writers of the Middle Colonies, 1770–1820" (Ph.D. diss., University of Delaware, 1996); Stabile, " 'I Wou'd Wish Our Present Leaders Might Have a Three-fold Dose, at the Dawn and Close of Every Day': Philadelphia Women Political Satirists as Moral Physicians," paper presented to the Philadelphia Center for Early American Studies, Winterthur Museum, May 5, 1995; Catherine La Courreye Blecki and Karin A. Wulf, *Milcah Martha Moore's Book* . . . (University Park, Pa., 1997); Daphne Hamm O'Brien, "From Plantation to Parnassus: Poets and Poetry in Williamsburg, Virginia, 1750–1800" (Ph.D. diss., University of North Carolina at Chapel Hill, 1993); O'Brien, "The First Congress, Polite Society, and Courtship in New York City: The Case of Margaret Lowther [Page]," paper presented at the Sixteenth Annual Meeting of the Society for Historians of the Early American Republic, Boston, July 15, 1994; Fredrika J. Teute, "Roman Matron on the Banks of Tiber Creek: Margaret Bayard Smith and the Politicization of Spheres in the Nation's Capital," in Donald R. Kennon and Barbara Wolanin, eds., *"A Republic for the Ages": The United States Capitol and the Political Culture of the Early Republic* (Charlottesville, Va., forthcoming); Teute, " 'A Wild, Desolate Place': Life on the Margins in Early Washington," in Howard F. Gillette, Jr., ed., *Southern City, National Ambition: The Growth of Early Washington, D.C., 1800–1860* (Washington, D.C., 1995), 47–66; Teute, "Reading Men and Women in Late-Eighteenth-Century New York," paper presented at the Twenty-fifth Anniver-

Like the work of Mary Kelley, this study takes up the matter of the reception of writings, yet it differs from most reception history (aside from work in theater and mass media) in understanding the event of reception communally, occurring within institutional constraints, and registered in the permutations of spoken or written conversations. The recoveries performed by this history are not of individual texts so much as of the conversations that lent point to writings. This programmatic inclination *not* to treat the text as a self-substantiating aesthetic object reveals the seriousness of this study's commitment to history. An attentiveness to aesthetics does not mean one must buy into the New Critical mystique in the literary work of art as autonomous object.

By viewing literary texts as contributing to performance in conversation, this study recognizes the primacy granted to oral communication in early American culture. It assists in the investigation of the culture of performance, offering a view of expression in arenas other than the forensic venues examined by Jay Fliegelman in *Declaring Independence: Jefferson, Natural Language, and the Culture of Performance.*[22]

In the end, this study presumes that by immersing ourselves in the languages of the tavern, the coffeehouse, the tea table, the salon, the club, and the college, by attuning our ears to the differences in talk, we can learn to identify each discursive institution's contribution to the power of public discourse to fashion new forms of group identity. With this end in mind, let us enter into the provincial world of letters, for an introduction to the promise of civility of belles lettres. Let us visit Philadelphia, the greatest of North America's cities, shortly after the close of the Revolution.

---

sary Meeting of the American Society for Eighteenth-Century Studies, Charleston, S.C., Mar. 12, 1994; Mary Kelley, *Private Woman, Public Stage: Literary Domesticity in Nineteenth-Century America* (New York, 1984); Elizabeth Fox-Genovese, *Within the Plantation Household: Black and White Women of the Old South* (Chapel Hill, N.C., 1988).

22. Jay Fliegelman, *Declaring Independence: Jefferson, Natural Language, and the Culture of Performance* (Stanford, Calif., 1993).

Civil Tongues & Polite Letters

Prologue

The following account of the French fete in Philadelphia in honor of the birth of Louis-Joseph, dauphin of France, given on Monday evening, July 15, 1782, is excerpted from a letter of Dr. Benjamin Rush to a lady.

PHILADELPHIA, 16 July, 1782.

DEAR MADAM:—For some weeks past our city has been amused with the expectation of a most splendid entertainment to be given by the minister of France, to celebrate the birthday of the Dauphin of France. Great preparations, it was said, were made for that purpose. Hundreds crowded daily to see a large frame building which he had erected for a dancing room on one side of his house. This building, which was sixty feet in front and forty feet deep, was supported by large painted pillars, and was open all round. The ceiling was decorated with several pieces of neat paintings emblematical of the design of the entertainment. The garden contiguous to this shed was cut into beautiful walks, and divided with cedar and pine branches into artificial groves. The whole, both the building and walks, were accommodated with seats. Besides these preparations, we were told that the minister had borrowed thirty cooks from the French army, to assist in providing an entertainment suited to the size and dignity of the company. Eleven hundred tickets were distributed, most of them two or three weeks before the evening of the entertainment.

Forty were sent to the governor of each state, to be distributed by them to the principal officers and gentlemen of their respective governments, and, I believe, the same number to General Washington, to be distributed to the principal officers of the army. For ten days before the entertainment, nothing else was talked of in our city. The shops were crowded with customers. Hair dressers were retained; tailors, milliners and mantua-makers were to be seen, covered with sweat and out of breath, in every street. Monday, July 15th, was the long expected evening.

The morning of this day was ushered in by a corps of hair dressers, occupying the place of the city watchmen. Many ladies were obliged to have their heads dressed between four and six o'clock in the morning, so great was the demand and so numerous the engagements this day of the gentlemen of the comb. At half past seven o'clock was the time fixed in the tickets for the meeting of the company. The approach of the hour was proclaimed by the rattling of all the carriages in the city. The doors and windows of the streets which led to the minister's were lined with people, and near the minister's house was a collection of all the curious and idle men, women and children in the city, who were not invited to the entertainment, amounting, probably, to ten thousand people. . . . The minister was not unmindful of this crowd of spectators. He had previously pulled down a board fence and put up a neat palisado fence before the dancing room and walks, on purpose to gratify them with a sight of the company and the entertainment. He intended further to have distributed two pipes of Madeira wine and $600 in small change among them; but he was dissuaded from this act of generosity by some gentlemen of the city, who were afraid that it might prove the occasion of a riot or some troublesome proceedings. The money devoted to this purpose was charitably distributed among the prisoners in the jails, and patients in the hospital in the city. About eight o'clock our family, consisting of Mrs. Rush, our cousin Susan Hall, our sister Sukey [Stockton] and myself, with our good neighbours Mrs. and Mr. Henry, entered the apartment provided for this splendid entertainment. We were received through a wide gate by the minister and conducted by one of his family to the dancing room. The scene now almost exceeds description. The numerous lights distributed through the garden, the splendor of the room we were approaching, the size of the company which was now collected and which consisted of about 700 persons: the brilliancy and variety of their dresses, and the band of music which had just begun to play, formed a scene which resembled enchantment. Sukey Stockton said "her mind was carried beyond and out of itself." We entered the room together, and here we saw the world in miniature. All the ranks, parties and professions in the city, and all the officers of government were fully represented in this assembly. Here were ladies and gentlemen of the most ancient as well as modern families. Here were lawyers, doctors and ministers of the gospel. Here were the learned faculty of the college, and among them many who knew not whether Cicero plead in Latin or in Greek; or whether Horace was a Roman or a Scotchman. Here were painters and musicians, poets and philosophers, and men who were never moved by beauty or harmony, or by rhyme or reason. Here were merchants and gentlemen of independent fortunes, as well as many respectable and opulent tradesmen. Here were Whigs and men who formerly bore the character of Tories. Here were the president and members of congress, governors of states and generals of armies, ministers of finance and war, and foreign affairs; judges of superior and inferior court, with all their respective suites and assistants, secretaries and clerks. In a word, the assembly was truly republican. The company was mixed, it is true, but the mixture formed the harmony of the evening. Everybody seemed pleased. Pride and ill-nature for a while forgot their pretentions and offices, and the whole assembly behaved to each other as if they had been members of the same family. It was impossible to partake of the joy of the evening without being struck with the occasion of it. It was to celebrate the birth of the Dauphin of France.

How great the revolution in the mind of an American! to rejoice in the birth of an heir to the crown of France, a country against which he had imbibed prejudices as ancient as the wars between France and England. How strange! for a protestant to rejoice in the birth of a prince, whose religion he had been always taught to consider as unfriendly to humanity. And above all how new the phenomenon for republicans to rejoice in the birth of a prince, who must one day be the support of monarchy and slavery. Human nature in this instance seems to be turned inside outwards. The picture is still agreeable, inasmuch as it shows us in the clearest point of view that there are no prejudices so strong, no opinions so sacred, and no contradictions so palpable, that will not yield to the love of liberty.

The appearance and characters, as well as the employment of the company naturally suggested the idea of Elysium given by the ancient poets. Here were to be seen heroes and patriots in close conversation with each other. Washington and Dickinson held several dialogues together. Here were to be seen men conversing with each other who had appeared in all the different stages of the American war. Dickinson and Morris frequently reclined together against the same pillar. Here were to be seen statesmen and warriors, from the opposite ends of the continent, talking of the history of the war in their respective states. Rutledge and Walton from the south, here conversed with Lincoln and Duane from the east and north. Here and there, too, appeared a solitary character walking among the artificial bowers in the garden. The celebrated author of "Common Sense" retired frequently from the company to analyze his thoughts and to enjoy the repast of his own original ideas. Here were to be seen men who had opposed each other in the councils and parties of their country, forgetting all former resentments and exchanging civilities with each other. Mifflin and Reed accosted each other with all the kindness of ancient friends. Here were to be seen men of various countries and languages, such as Americans and Frenchmen, Englishmen and Scotchmen, Germans and Irishmen, conversing with each other like children of one father. And lastly, here were to be seen the extremes of the civilized and savage life. An Indian chief in his savage habits, and the count Rochambeau in his splendid and expensive uniform, talked with each other as if they had been the subjects of the same government, generals in the same army, and partakers of the same blessings of civilized life.

About half an hour after eight o'clock the signal was given for the dance to begin. Each lady was provided with a partner before she came. The heat of the evening deterred above one half of the company from dancing. Two sets however, appeared upon the floor during the remaining part of the evening.

On one side of the room were provided two private apartments, where a number of servants attended to help the company to all kinds of cool and agreeable drinks, with sweet cakes, fruit and the like.

Between these apartments and under the orchestra, there was a private room where several Quaker ladies, whose dress would not permit them to join the assembly, were indulged with a sight of the company through a gauze curtain.

This little attention to the curiosity of the ladies marks in the strongest manner the minister's desire to oblige everybody.

At nine o'clock were exhibited a number of rockets from a stage erected in a large open lot before the minister's house. They were uncommonly beautiful and gave universal satisfaction. At twelve o'clock the company was called to supper. It was laid behind the dancing room under three large tents, so connected together as to make one large canopy. Under this canopy were placed seven tables, each of which was large enough to accommodate fifty people.

The ladies who composed nearly one half the whole assembly, took their seats first, with a small number of gentlemen to assist in helping them. The supper was a cold collation; simple, frugal and elegant, and handsomely set off with a dessert consisting of cakes and all the fruits of the season. The Chevalier de la Luzerne now appeared with all the splendor of the minister and all the politeness of a gentleman. He walked along the tables and addressed himself in particular to every lady. A decent and respectful silence pervaded the whole company. Intemperance did not show its head; levity composed its countenance, and even humour itself forgot for a few moments its usual haunts; and the simple jest, no less than the loud laugh, were unheard at any of the tables. So great and universal was the decorum, and so totally suspended was every species of convivial noise, that several gentlemen remarked that the "company looked and behaved more as if they were worshipping than eating." In a word, good breeding was acknowledged, by universal consent, to be mistress of the evening, and the conduct of the votaries at supper formed the conclusion of her triumph. Notwithstanding all the agreeable circumstances that have been mentioned, many of the company complained of the want of something else to render the entertainment complete. Everybody felt pleasure but it was of too tranquil a nature. Many people felt sentiments, but they were produced by themselves, and did not arise from any of the amusements of the evening. The company expected to feel joy, and their feelings were in unison with nothing short of it. An ode on the birth of the Dauphin, sung or repeated, would have answered the expectations and corresponded with the feelings of everybody. The understanding and taste of the company would have shared with the senses in the pleasures of the evening. The enclosed ode written by Mr. William Smith, son of the Rev. Dr. Smith, was composed for the occasion, but from what cause I know not, it did not make its appearance. It has great merit, and could it have been set to music, or spoken publickly, must have formed a most delightful and rational part of the entertainment. About one o'clock the company began to disperse, our family moved with the foremost of them. Before three o'clock the whole company parted, every candle was extinguished, and midnight enjoyed her dark and solitary reign in every part of the minister's house and garden. Thus I have given you a full account of the rejoicing on the birth of the Dauphin of France.[1]

1. Benjamin Rush, "The French Fête in Philadelphia in Honor of the Dauphin's Birthday, 1892," *Pennsylvania Magazine of History and Biography*, XXI (1897), 257–262; see also L. H. Butterfield, ed., *Letters of Benjamin Rush*, I, *1761–1792*, Memoirs of the American Philosophical Society, XXX, pt. 1 (Princeton, N.J., 1951), 278–284.

I

Overture: The Promise of Civil Discourse

What shall we make of this event—the first national celebration in the wake of the Revolution? Here in a temporary dance pavilion erected by Anne-César, chevalier de La Luzerne, the French minister to the United States, it seemed the new "world" coalesced for the first time. The government of the Confederation could never do what the chevalier did with his entertainment celebrating the nativity of the dauphin: bring all the actors in the new nation into a civil harmony. In Benjamin Rush's report it seemed an occasion of achieved civility, yet one whose circumstances were quite exotic. The national family was brought together only in the name of pleasure. The good order of the company was maintained by manners, not laws. The superintendent of manners and the guarantor of pleasure was a courtier from the courtliest of Old World regimes.

The contributions of the chevalier were of several sorts. He constructed a precinct of otherworldly beauty, a fenced-off garden and painted temple amid the urban landscape, in which the miniature world could gather. He invited a sufficiently various company so that seven hundred persons might seem a world. He enacted a number of traditional rites of sociability—concert, dance, fireworks display, feast—that permitted the universal participation of the assembled company, suggesting a communal identity. He supplied spaces in which persons were free to converse with one another individually, and he personally engaged women in conversation, recognizing their place in the world.

The invitees responded to the extraordinary occasion by wholeheartedly entering into the spirit of the event. They suspended prejudice and interest in the spirit of liberty to engage in conversation with others. Like devotees putting aside worldly care when entering a sacred precinct, the guests put by their ordinary concerns when they entered the temple of social pleasure. Conflict ceased. They assumed a spirit of decorum, demonstrating, in Rush's view, a new capacity for self-government hitherto unseen in the new nation.

Despite the unanimity of decorous manners, despite the communal sensitivity to the aesthetics of the occasion, Rush and others felt that something was missing. What was lacking? A universal sense of joy surpassing social pleasantry. This, Rush suggested, could have been provided by the performance of a literary work of art, a poem to the dauphin. A performance would have concentrated the stimuli of the evening into a meaningful clarity. The sort of emotional elevation that the chevalier forfeited can be gathered from the closing lines of Annis Boudinot Stockton's poem composed for the event. The Genius of America speaks to two attendant Sylphs:

> Tritons, convey to Gallia's royal ear
> The pleasing transport on our hearts engrav'd,
> To none more dear is France's blooming heir,
> Than to the people whom his father sav'd.
> Oh! tell him, that my hardy gen'rous swains,
> Shall annually hail this natal day;
> My babes congratulate in lisping strains,
> And blooming virgins tune the chearful lay.
> For him their pious vows the skies ascend,
> And bring down blessings on his lovely queen;
> May vict'ry ever on his arms attend,
> And crown his days with peace and joy serene.[1]

Stockton imagined a Greek festival when invoking "joy serene." William Moore Smith intensified emotion by making the audience witnesses to the paternal affection of America's "great Protector," Louis XVI.

---

1. Annis Boudinot Stockton, "On the Celebration of the Birth of the Dauphin of France," in Carla Mulford, ed., *Only for the Eye of a Friend: The Poems of Annis Boudinot Stockton* (Charlottesville, Va., 1995), 142. Dated June 2, 1782, Stockton's poem was intended to be performed while "The Genius of America enters the garden of the Chevalier de la Luzerne, with two attendant Sylphs, carrying baskets of flowers in their hands" (141). Stockton was a poetical correspondent of Rush and a friend of the Reverend William Smith, whose son's poem is mentioned in Rush's letter.

This rising Empire's future Friend;
Pleas'd his own lineaments to trace,
Upon the smiling Infant's face,
See, o'er the couch, the God-like Father bend.[2]

The auditors, having won their liberty with Louis's help, could stomach the epithet "God-like" as a neoclassical formula for expressing his potency. They were helped by Smith to forget the Protestant stereotypes of French kings as Catholic tyrants, by an argument that Louis reincarnated France's great Protestant king, Henry IV. Smith further argued that the infant dauphin inherited these ancestral values and would serve as a guarantor of America's future safety from Britain's "lawless Tyrant." The symbolic distance between France and the United States was shortened by viewing the latter as a "rising Empire" rather than a republic. Republican rhetoric sounded only in abstractions — freedom, virtue, happiness. Rush understood that only in such symbolic and rhetorical manipulations could general amusement be amplified into authentic joy among the participants. What Rush missed in the celebration was that expression of genius that could move amusement to a communal sense of serene joy.

Rarely do writings from early America map so precisely as Rush's letter the place of literature in connection with the sister arts, the rites of sociability, the practice of conversation, mannerly conduct, styles of political publicity, and cultural mythology. The most telling feature of Rush's account was his indication that celebratory poetry had been prepared and submitted but had not been used. Rush's implication: the inadequacy of French courtly practice in framing a communal feeling among the new American world was its dependence on the techniques of courtly spectacle; the chevalier failed to realize that the sensus communis among Anglo-Americans almost invariably formed around spoken texts. By making the eye the ruling organ, rather than the ear, the chevalier failed to touch the citizenry's profoundest sensibilities.

We should appreciate the care with which the chevalier used the methods of courtly spectacle to organize the event as a political experience. It is by sight that the host connects the ten thousand uninvited persons with the select seven hundred. He destroyed visual barricades, erecting a see-through palisade fence, enabling the urban populace to participate passively in the event. Vision is the least intimate and engaged of the senses,

2. [William Moore Smith], "An Ode, on the Birth of the Dauphin of France . . . ," in [Smith], *Poems, on Several Occasions, Written in Pennsylvania* (Philadelphia, 1786), 75.

the one that can most attenuate participation, so it is invariably the resort of authoritarian regimes in enlisting the participation of the ruled in ceremonies of state. Having cleared the sight lines, the chevalier supplied a fanciful set upon which the new nation's actors would move. The greater the disparity of scene with the surroundings, the greater an indication of the power deployed by the master of ceremonies. The chevalier's set is predicated on a number of reversals: amid urban structures he erects an artificial grove; against the sparsely ornamented facades of permanent modern buildings, he places a temporary antique temple vivid with painted pillars. The absence of walls in the temple permitted the dancing guests to be viewed by the people in the street, so they seemingly performed for the amusement of the spectators. Yet a hierarchy of visual access governed. Those within the temple not only were closer to one another; they alone could see the painted ceiling that revealed the "design of the entertainment." The guests, not the multitude, had access to the emblems that conveyed the meaning of the celebration. Consider: if a recited poem had been the means of conveying the meaning of the celebration, it would have been heard, just as the music was heard, by the multitude, and they would have been privy to the "family feeling" and "joy" the ceremony would have inspired. Yet this was not the desire of the chevalier. He wished to inspire among the privileged seven hundred something of the aristocratic sense of the Old World court. To do so he wished to convey both a sense of privileged access to knowledge, experience, and one another and a sense of being actors in a political theater.

Certain of the attendees had a more exquisite sense of their roles than others. Thomas Paine, for instance, successfully played at being the solitary philosopher brooding in the grove of contemplation while visible to more people at one time than he would otherwise appear before during his entire life. Count Rochambeau in full dress uniform, heeding the theatrical principle of conspicuousness through contrast, sought out the figure in the company attired in clothing least resembling a uniform, an Indian chieftain, thereby forming a visual vignette of civility and nature for the spectators. Rush's litany of "here were to be seen" was an index of the attractiveness of the spectacle to the participant actors. Indeed, the scene proved so attractive that it enticed some of the foes of extravagant display, the Quakers, who from a private chamber viewed the splendor through a veil.

Even to attendees the finest of the fete's attractions was the company. To Rush the assembly was so remarkable that it seemed the Elysium of ancient poetry. It included many of the most conspicuous persons in the recently concluded struggle for Independence yet also represented all areas of political, religious, social, and cultural endeavor — as various as a "world." To late-twentieth-century readers trained to notice the "curious and idle" multitude beyond the pale, Rush's ideas of variety might seem an instance of the ordinary myopia of a member of the privileged ranks. Yet if we are to understand in detail the character of the new American civil order and the hopes that citizens of the new country entertained about society and manners, we must study the discriminations that Rush made in his illustration of the company's variety. It is a sophisticated first glimpse of the American public. The company has an aristocratic component: "the most ancient as well as modern families"; representatives of the professions: "lawyers, doctors and ministers of the gospel"; and those cultural actors who were not deemed professionals: artists and academics. There were merchants, tradesmen, and gentlemen of property — officers of the army and members of the new governing class. Half the company were women. That these elements met together and engaged in a concerted conversation was an unprecedented event in American history. It was, as Rush indicated, a signal of a type of achieved civility, a sign of the maturation of a public community.

Rush's republican world did not spring full-blown, an emanation of the Revolution. Well before the chevalier's fete, certain of the groups that composed the Assembly had entered into conversation and established havens of sociability in which exchange could occur. The party for the dauphin can be viewed as a culmination (by no means the only one) of a long process of social and cultural expansion in British America associated with the idea of civility. It presents itself as a demarcation of this study because it declared emphatically the aesthetic dimension of politics (not simply happiness, but "joy" was the highest communal passion). Furthermore, it captured the peculiar tension that existed between Old World courtly forms and republican ideals of disinterested civic communion. It also named the actors who stood center stage in the creation of an American civil society. Most important, it posited a world — a comprehensive pattern of society — that in design and detail differed from that first identification of the world as the beau monde that emerged from the courts of Europe at the beginning of the colonial era. Between the courtly world and Rush's republican world we can chart a vivid complex of developments, secured by a common metaphor.

2

Belles Lettres and the Arenas of Metropolitan Conversation

When publication of the voyages first gave literate Europeans a global sense of the world, they took to calling their society, the high society that revolved around the royal courts, "the world"—"le monde," "el mundo." Let us not mistake the nature of this presumption. It was no act of bravado, no compensation for a growing sense of insignificance before an expanding globe. Quite the contrary; the joke was the baldness of their vanity, the candor with which they made the globe theirs. When the world came to light, they used it to supply novelties—uncanny things, tastes, sights, and sounds—to give relish to their "world," making it a "beau monde." The desire of the beau monde for strange and luxurious things drove the imperial expansion of the great mercantile powers. Spain, France, Holland, and Britain extended global networks of trade and settlement to gather commodities and merchantable goods from foreign lands for the delectation of metropolitans. In exchange colonists and natives were offered civility and arts.

> COMMERCE gives Arts, as well as gain
> By Commerce wafted o'er the main,
> They barbarous climes enlighten as they run.
> Arts, the rich traffic of the soul
> May travel thus from pole to pole,
> And gild the world with Learning's brighter sun.[1]

1. Edward Young, "Imperium Pelagi: A Naval Lyric, Written in Imitation of Pindar's Spirit, Occasioned by His Majesty's Return, September 10th, 1729 and the Suc-

The metropolitans did not doubt that the world at large would engage in the transaction or aspire to become an image — a refracted, lesser image — of the beau monde. The great despair of the critics of metropolitan luxury from Montaigne to Tobias Smollet was the city nobility's confidence in the rightness of their world. The spread of the practices and institutions of civility around the globe vindicated the metropolitans' faith. Every West Indian nabob tricked up as a town beau, every provincial lady with her hair arranged à la mode testified to the potency of "the world." Fashions, manners, and conversation were the vehicles of civility. Where populations had little experience of the metropolis, writing presented the ways of court and town. In British America, imported books and periodicals portrayed the beau monde's glories so compellingly that a cadre of writers dedicated themselves to creating similar worlds in Halifax, Boston, Newport, New York, Trenton, Philadelphia, Annapolis, Wilmington, Charleston, Savannah, and Kingston.

Belles lettres enabled the transmission of a secularized, cosmopolitan, genteel culture into North America during the seventeenth and eighteenth centuries. In belles lettres (or "polite letters," as it was anglicized) an American "world" came into being — a protopublic of clubs, women's tea tables, and coffeehouses. These arenas flourished, then transformed, when print adopted the forms and symbols of belles lettres, fashioning from them the republic of letters and the "public sphere." The passage from "world" to "public sphere" was no triumphal progress. When the printed page usurped the prerogatives of urbane conversation, a pleasure was sacrificed. In pleasure's stead, the prints offered a middling readership the opportunity to participate imaginatively in a discursive analogue of genteel company.

"The world" was something greater than the European royal courts and less than "the public sphere." Norbert Elias, the sociologist of court culture, indicated how the palace replicated itself in the *hôtels* and the court of Louis XIV in the salons over the course of the seventeenth and eighteenth centuries. Between the court and "the world" there developed a crucial difference. The court became increasingly ceremonious. Behavior became ritualistic, striving to fix the dynamic hierarchy of power arrayed around the royal center. Etiquette, as Elias argued, became constraint upon royal

---

ceeding Peace: The Merchant, Ode the First, on the British Trade and Navigation," in Young, *The Complete Works: Poetry and Prose*, ed. James Nichols (1854; rpt. Hildesheim, 1968), strain II, stanza 1.

power, binding it to a sphere of contracted obligation.[2] Outside the court and palace, salons, clubs, and coteries became places where a greater latitude of expression could be exercised because of their peripherality to the center of power. The rituals of court could prove too inhibiting for the exercises of familial and self-promotion needed in the contest for social precedence.

A penumbra of social arenas developed beyond the royal palaces where greater liberty of display and conversation could be attempted. In distinction to the etiquette of the court was the stylish gentility of the "world." Illustrious courts — as of Elizabeth I, for instance — engendered courtly companies whose attractions vied with the royal company. The countess of Pembroke's coterie possessed one clear advantage over the court: the power of its patroness was sufficiently modest to distance one from the necessities and interests of state, enabling aesthetic enjoyment and reflection. The countess of Pembroke was "Urania," not the sun. One did not risk getting scorched.[3]

When courts became graceless in their ritual, the impulse to form alternative societies increased. The barbarism of the Gasgoine court of Louis XIII prompted Catherine de Vivonne, marquise de Rambouillet, to open her famous Hôtel de Rambouillet, the town house out of which the extensive constellation of French salons would grow. Even before the court exfoliated into the world, it developed an aestheticized sense of self, an alternate identity. One reads of Thomas Wyatt's "company of courtly makers," which transformed the court of Henry VIII into a pastoral academy of love. Masquerading as an Arcadia was standard recreation at royal courts until the days of Marie Antoinette. In England, the principal literary vehicle of this play identity was the masque. Noble actors and the royal family idealized their power relations in fictive characters and actions.[4]

2. Norbert Elias, *The Court Society*, trans. Edmund Jephcott (New York, 1983), 80, 117–145.

3. Gary F. Waller, *Mary Sidney, Countess of Pembroke: A Critical Study of Her Writings and Literary Milieu* (Salzburg, 1979). Much of the modern scholarship about Mary Sidney has concentrated upon the relation of Sidney's writings to the discursive forms of patriarchy rather than inquired into the structure of her relations with her circle and its symbolic representations.

4. Barbara Krajewska, *Mythes et découvertes: le salon littéraire de Madame de Rambouillet dans les lettres des contemporains*, Papers on French Seventeenth-Century Literature (Paris, 1990); Raymond Southall, *The Courtly Maker: An Essay on the Poetry of Wyatt and*

Adopting pastoral identities was essential in the courtiers' play, on stage and off. The conversation between the sexes greatly depended upon this device. (In belles lettres the practice survived in the near universal use of cognomens—idealized names such as Damon, Laura, Amynta, and Sylvio by which writers were known in the "world.") The participation of women in the play of the court marks the distinctively aristocratic character of the social relations. As Elias has shown, the court aristocracy's practice of dynastic marriage vested women with status under the patrimonial scheme, for wives and potential wives represented the families of their birth. Marriage bound families in alliances.[5] The court existed in part as a social space where marriageable persons from aristocratic families could consort and where the contest for dynastic preeminence could be performed without threat of violence (because of the presence of the crown), by matchmaking, conspicuous display of wealth, or the securing of offices. Creating new modes of refined living was a means of gaining some control over the contest of display—a way of altering the rules in one's favor. The innovations of the salons when they had established a new taste were imported back into the court.

Women began to exercise dominion over the conversation in certain of the Italian courts during the sixteenth century. It has been suggested that a cultural disposition to lady worship enabled this assumption of power.[6] Whatever the case, the way Italian noblewomen deployed their newly got power was striking. Into the conversation of the aristocracy, they invited the scholars of the new humanism. They brokered an intellectual marriage between the academies and the princely courts. A distinctive aspect of the arrangement was that the language of courtship became suffused with the ideals of Platonism. The new heterosociability required that talk of desire be sublimated into espousals of spiritual love or displaced into the realm of ideas.[7] When this new scheme of relationship was transmitted to France

---

His Contemporaries (New York, 1964); Matthew H. Wikander, *Princes to Act: Royal Audience and Royal Performance, 1578–1792* (Baltimore, 1993).

5. Elias, *The Court Society*, trans. Jephcott, 49–51.

6. This point was made by Chauncey Brewster Tinker, one of the first serious English students of the cultural history of salons, more than eighty years ago. See *The Salon and English Letters: Chapters on the Interrelations of Literature and Society in the Age of Johnson* (New York, 1915).

7. The historiography of sixteenth-century Italian salons remains undeveloped. The best glimpses of their operation may be had in recent treatments of the rather anoma-

and England, it proved congenial only to the court of Elizabeth. Where male monarchs ruled, the Italian scheme offended the economies of power inscribed in etiquette. Consequently, women wishing to superintend the conversation of the "world" set up imitation courts, salons beyond the royal company's pale.

Whether located in country estates or town houses, the salons were marked by innovations in worldly intercourse. The patroness redesigned the architectural space in which the conversation was held, adopting a new intimacy of scale more congenial for sociable exchange encouraged by a new decorative warmth. She concentrated conversation on literary and philosophical matters while subordinating amusements such as cards and eating to ancillary pastimes. She freed conversation from court protocol without sacrificing aristocratic tone. She encouraged an ethic of heterosexual friendship, platonic rather than domestic, exemplifying in her own behavior the ideal of amiability. She also fostered a cult of personality around herself, accepting the role of muse or proprietary goddess for a circle of devotees who were often clients of her patronage. Writers in the circle (most of whom were male) paid tribute to the presiding spirit, certifying her fame in the wider world. "Urania" enjoyed the devotion of Spenser and so won, according to Aubrey, a reputation as "the greatest patroness of wit and learning of any lady of her time." Samuel Daniel celebrated the dominion of Lucy Russell, countess of Bedford, over the circle at Twickenham Park in the "Vision of the Twelve Goddesses," where she was Vesta. Her circle included Ben Jonson, George Chapman, Sir John Davies, Michael Drayton, and Daniel.[8]

---

lous figure of Veronica Franco, a poet and court mistress in Venice. Alvise Zorzi, *Cortigiana veneziana: Veronica Franco e i suoi poeti, 1546–1581* (Milan, 1986); Margaret F. Rosenthal, *The Honest Courtesan: Veronica Franco, Citizen and Writer in Sixteenth-Century Venice* (Chicago, 1992).

8. Barbara K. Lewalski, "Lucy, Countess of Bedford: Images of a Jacobean Courtier and Patroness," in Kevin Sharpe and Steven N. Zwicker, eds., *Politics of Discourse: The Literature and History of Seventeenth-Century England* (Berkeley, Calif., 1987), 52–77.

The issue of female patronage in England has best been treated by David M. Bergeron, "Women as Patrons of English Renaissance Drama," in Guy Fitch Lytle and Stephen Orgel, eds., *Patronage in the Renaissance* (Princeton, N.J., 1981), 274–290; and Mary Ellen Lamb, "The Countess of Pembroke's Patronage," *English Literary Renaissance*, XXI (1982), 162–179. The essential works in the literature of the French salon are Carolyn C. Lougee, *Le Paradis des Femmes: Women, Salons, and Social Stratification in*

Participation by several court poets in the countess's salon shows that the "world" was a constellation of groups in which individuals held concurrent membership. Each coterie had its distinctive attractions. Courtiers sampled the company at several salons for variety of conversation and a multiplicity of venues in which to display one's parts. Then, too, the ability of a patroness to dispense favors and influence appointments waxed and waned.

During the seventeenth century, skill as a conversationalist in mixed company became, for gentlemen, a requirement for advancement in society and state. French court ethics at the turn of the seventeenth century shifted from valor, a masculine military virtue, to politeness ("hônnêteté"), a heterosocial virtue manifested in conversation. In France, Italy, and England, the tongue eclipsed the sword as the instrument of power. Elizabeth C. Goldsmith witnesses the apotheosis of conversation in the change in conduct books from Nicolas Pasquier's *Le gentilhomme* (1611) to Nicolas Faret's *L'honnête homme ou l'art de plaire à la cour* (1630), which provided detailed instructions on how to talk with gentlewomen. She observes, "Conversation was an artifact as much as an activity, and it was through conversation that all other cultural forms were assigned or denied their place in 'le monde.' "[9]

In "le monde," writing was understood to be a precipitate of conversation. "Writing is none other than a kind of speech which remains in being after it has been uttered, the representation, as it were, or rather the very life of our words." Writing also performed service as a script for oral delivery. Most court poetry was made for declamation. Drayton's verse, except for the translations, derived essential aspects of its meaning from its role in court conversation; Daniel's performances as laureate were all social apostrophe. Ben Jonson's writings, from the most elaborate masque to the most casual impromptu, were performances in the ceremonies of court or the sallies of the salons. Even those poets whom critics regard as having been textually oriented because of their biblicism or their reliance on

Seventeenth-Century France (Princeton, N.J., 1976); Dena Goodman, "Governing the Republic of Letters: The Politics of Culture in the French Enlightenment," *History of European Ideas*, XIII (1991), 183–199, Goodman, "Enlightenment Salons: The Convergence of Female and Philosophic Ambitions," *Eighteenth-Century Studies*, XXII (1988–1989), 329–350; Goodman, *The Republic of Letters: A Cultural History of the French Enlightenment* (Ithaca, N.Y., 1994).

9. Elizabeth C. Goldsmith, *Exclusive Conversations: The Art of Interaction in Seventeenth-Century France* (Philadelphia, 1988), 2.

metaphysical conceits operated in the world of conversation. Thus John Donne has been seen as the example par excellence of a coterie poet.[10]

One cannot, after Jacques Derrida, be glib about insisting upon the orality of communications. Beneath the repartee of the salon lay a fixed pattern, a deep text. It may be read in the symbolisms employed by the arenas of conversation to establish their authority. Each circle grounded itself in a myth of society, explaining how and why it came together. Like myths of monarchical statehood, these myths of private society attributed the activity of the community to the influence of a single person. The charisma of this person was signified by fictional divinity. The patroness of a salon was usually identified with one of the nine Muses or, less frequently, an Olympian goddess. Invariably pagan mythology, not Christian symbolism, supplied the icons of authority. This was true even when the patroness wrote and encouraged religious works. As muse, the patroness exerted an aesthetic power over devotees, compelling their senses and imaginations. All reflected the glory of the patroness in their tributes and compliments.

The point of representing salons as cults of individual muses lies in the primordium of religious society. States confessed the origin of their authority in divine commission. Only the family rivaled divine sanction in the reckoning of thinkers about the primacy of social institutions. When Ben Jonson, court poet extraordinaire, devotee of Lucy, countess of Bedford, formed his innovative annex to the world, the Apollo Club, he combined both religious-mythological and familial schemes of symbolism to warrant it.

What distinguished the Apollo Club from the host of informal tavern companies was its conscious cultivation of a social identity in terms of myth, rite, law, and sign. Like the salons, the Apollo was a charismatic company. Following the countesses of Pembroke and Bedford, Ben Jonson masked his authority in mythic divinity. He mirrored Apollo and the "sons of Ben," the sons of Apollo. The patent fiction of a court of male muses shows that Apollo operated as a "ridiculous club," mocking the creeds and ceremonies of church, state, and the learned world.

While the symbolic linkages between Jonson's club and the salons are clear, we should also note certain analogies between the Apollo and its habitation, the Devil Tavern. Taverns, being licensed by the Company of Vintners and not the City Corporation or the crown, had long enjoyed the

10. Jean R. Brink, *Michael Drayton Revisited* (Boston, 1990); Arthur F. Marotti, *John Donne, Coterie Poet* (Madison, Wis., 1986).

status of social spaces beyond the immediate jurisdiction of the state.[11] Despite the imposition of royal licensing with the Restoration, taverns remained privileged havens so long as they kept tolerable order. House rules were posted and generally enforced. The tavern had a better reputation than the alehouse, scene of unruliness. Taverns were characterized by a tension between the permissions of alcoholic revelry and the good order of regulated self-government.

A tavern catered to the quality. It differed from the alehouse by vending wine as the house beverage, supplying good victuals, being more commodious (accommodation consisted of something more than sleeping on the tables and benches), and maintaining a core clientele of local citizens. Inns dominated the carriage trade; alehouses served the tramping classes.[12] The tavern occupied an intermediate station. It provided space for a host of civic activities — auctions, plays, exhibitions, governmental meetings. The success of a city tavern depended upon its possessing some distinguishing quality: good wine, good food, good lodging, good talk, good tobacco, a notable clientele. All taverns, good or bad, were known by their signs.

During the seventeenth century, London was blazoned with signs. Each public establishment brandished its symbol painted on a board; sometimes a motto was affixed, sometimes not.[13] In the medieval period these signs had borrowed from heraldry, the culture's dominant symbolism of power. Taverns identified with great figures by bearing their coats of arms and borrowing their fame. A second body of imagery was drawn from folklore. The Devil Tavern, for instance, was the shortened name of the Devil and St. Dunstan, famed of nursery rhymes. When Jonson's club met under the portrait bust of Apollo, it used a material token of identity like that used by the tavern in which they met. The salons might have been courts of the muses, yet they did not physically indicate what they were. The clubs did,

11. The tavern patent of the London Vintners survived until 1757, withstanding several challenges. During the 1630s the Vintners were granted powers of licensing beyond the bounds of London. Peter Clark, *The English Alehouse: A Social History, 1200–1830* (London, 1983), 12.

12. For the markers in the hierarchy of inn/tavern/alehouse, see ibid., 6–14. The precision of these distinctions diminished with their importation into British America; while "inn" retained its sense of being a place of elite accommodation, "tavern" came to signify any public house that sold wine, spirits, or ale.

13. George Berry, *Taverns and Tokens of Pepys' London* (London, 1978).

perhaps because they were born in the taverns, where identity was organized around a material sign.

It is difficult to judge the contemporary fame of Jonson's club. Its greatest measurable influence dates from the 1650s, when Alexander Brome's English translation of two club documents, the "Leges Convivales" and "Apollo's Oracle," began to circulate. The texts became important to persons organizing a new sociable institution in the metropolis, the coffeehouse. In England the coffeehouse came into being during the Commonwealth, when the court languished in French exile. Like a tavern, the coffeehouse was a public establishment organized to vend beverages. The beverage was nonalcoholic, giving it a cachet among Puritans. Like the tavern, it advertised its identity by a sign. In 1665 a poet wrote:

As you along the street do trudge,
To take the pains you must not grudge,
To view the Posts or Broomsticks where
The Signs of Liquors hanged are.
And if you see the great Morat
With Shash one's head instead of hat.
Or any Sultan in his dress,
Or picture of a Sultaness,
Or John's admir'd curled pate,
Or the great Mogul in's Chair of State,
Or Constantine the Grecian
Who fourteen years was the onely man
That made Coffee for th' great Bashaw,
Although the man he never saw;
Or if you see a Coffee-cup
Fil'd from a Turkish pot, hung up
Within the clouds, and round it Pipes,
Wax candles, Stoppers, these are types
And certain signs . . .

.   .   .   .   .

That in that house they Coffee sell.[14]

14. *The Character of a Coffee-House . . . by an Eye and Ear Witness* (London, 1665), reprinted in Aytoun Ellis, *The Penny Universities: A History of the Coffee-Houses* (London, 1956), 256.

Orientalia dominated the symbolism of coffee. Introduced into England through the Levant trade, coffee had been popularized by Pasqua Rosee of Smyrna, who set up a coffeehouse in St. Michael's Alley during the 1650s. Although the original constituency was Dissenting brethren, the new institution won favor after the Restoration with several other sorts of persons: businessmen who did not want a fuddled head when negotiating, cosmopolitans intent on following the latest consumption fad, and persons who frowned on indulgence of the grape. City wits could complain that "the drench has credit got, / And he's not a gentleman that drinks it not."[15]

A peculiarity of coffeehouse society was its overwhelmingly masculine cast. In inns and taverns women might be seen if they were wives or girlfriends of a male customer or when a female company gathered for refreshment. (The Apollo Club's "Leges Convivales" welcomed women under certain conditions.) Coffeehouses were homosocial. Coffeehouses contributed to segregating the sexes in Britain, moving men and business out of private households. In the description of the company in *The Character of a Coffee-House* (1665), no woman appears.[16]

The coffeehouse can be seen as the central institution in the elaboration of a postcourtly civility in England. With the reestablishment of the court, which attempted to resume old patterns of conduct in church, state, and society, the activities of the coffeehouse appeared to challenge the Restoration. Lawrence E. Klein has noted three objections to the coffeehouse: it "allowed promiscuous association among people from different rungs of the social ladder, from the artisan to the aristocrat," it "served as an unsupervised distribution point for news, transmitted in either oral or printed form," and it "encouraged free-floating and open-ended discussion."[17] The conversation of the coffeehouse differed from that of worldly mixed company in that political disquisition, lecture, and critical excursus were permitted; that is, individuals could monopolize the talk. The second novel

15. *A Broadside against Coffee* (London, 1672), reprinted in John Timbs, *Clubs and Club Life in London, with Anecdotes of Its Famous Coffee-Houses, Hostelries, and Taverns* (London, 1873), 272.

16. Clark, *The English Alehouse*, 225; *The Character of a Coffee-House*, in Ellis, *The Penny Universities*, 255–263.

17. Lawrence E. Klein, "Coffee Clashes: The Politics of Discourse in Seventeenth- and Eighteenth-Century England," paper given at the Annual Meeting of the American Historical Association, Chicago, 1991, 7.

PLATE 1 Court of Equity; or, A Convivial City Meeting. *Painted by Robert Dighton, printed by Robert Laurie. England, 1778. Courtesy, Colonial Williamsburg Foundation*

feature of coffeehouse talk was its obsession with news. A jaundiced observer of the talk observed:

> Here Newes by subtile Tongues is spread,
> To try the listening crowd;
> But what is Truth's a secret made,
> Whilst Lyes are Talk'd aloud.
> Beau Fools in Clusters here Resort,
> And are so saucy grown,
> They'll ask my Lord,
> What News from Court?
> Who smiles, and Answers None.[18]

In truth news had more value than its detractors granted, for milord was beginning to haunt the coffeehouse now as much as the palace. Despite objections, the court made its uneasy accommodations with the institution.

The great contest of aristocratic display was relocating from the royal

18. *News from the Coffe-House* (London, 1667).

palaces to the coffeehouses, theaters, and parks of the city. The most significant of the coffeehouses in this regard was Man's in Scotland Yard. Designated the Royal Coffeehouse, its proprietor claimed to be "declar'd Cofee-Man to Charles the Second."[19] Here the beaux — the young men of fashion who were not yet fixtures in the court (because of youth, insufficient fortune, or insignificance of family) — conducted their contests of dress and manners. It became the school of masculine fashion, the recruiting depot where established courtiers came to enlist likely young men in their schemes.

If Man's was the arena of the beaux, Will's was the temple of the wits. Tom Brown, the humorist, facetiously observed: "A Wit and a Beau set up with little or no Expence. A pair of Red Stockins and a Sword-knot Sets up one, and Peeping once a Day in at Wills, and two or three Second hand Sayings, the other."[20] At Will's John Dryden presided over a miscellaneous company of persons who claimed acquaintance with the muses. Here the scripts for the polite world were written, critiqued, and tested. Here the discourse of civility was renovated from its courtly exclusivity to something more demotic and applicable to the world at large.

In the coffeehouse "the world" finally began to converse with the world.

A Conversation in the Suburbs

In 1693 two of London's premier booksellers, Richard Bentley and Jacob Tonson, jointly published a mock exposé, *The Humours, and Conversations of the Town.* Curiously, the conversation that dominated its pages did not occur in the city.

The scene: a road in the suburbs of London, late spring. Three gentlemen ride into the country: a town beau, Mr. Sociable; a schoolman, Mr. Pensive; and a hearty man of the counties, Mr. Jovial. Delighted with the scenery, Pensive and Jovial wax enthusiastic about the benefits of country living: simple manners, plain-dealing folk, leisure for thought, quiet. Sociable listens tolerantly to the recital, though disbelieving it thoroughly. For him simplicity is a pleasant name for crudity; quiet, a promise of tedium. He declares his preference for the town, doubting that country talk satisfies as much as city conversation. Pensive, hoping to convince Sociable otherwise, ventures a definition of "satisfying conversation." Such

19. Ellis, *Penny Universities,* 72–73.
20. [Tom Brown], *Laconics; or, New Maxims of State and Conversation . . .* (London, 1701), 96.

conversation has to produce "Profit and Pleasure; the *improvement*, or *diversion* of the mind; and if it deviate from this, or tend wholly to diversion, 'tis certainly faulty." Sociable demurs:

> A pretty regulation of Conversation this, if I mistake not! So that you wou'd reduce the World to that pass, that ev'ry Company shou'd be an Academy, or a *Convivium Philosophorum*; ha! ha! ha! but I am of much a contrary Opinion; I think that Conversation was ordain'd for the passing away our idle hours with pleasure: Thus far however I'll agree with you, as to grant it shou'd sometimes be consider'd as an improvement, when we endeavour for the converse of Men of Sense and Wit, which may bring us to a habit of talking wittily.[21]

With a brusque laugh Sociable dismisses learning, profit, and philosophy from conversation. In their stead, he exalts pleasure. In 1693 a London beau no longer reckons it faulty to speak "wholly to diversion" — diversion for him is the fundamental purpose of conversation. Sociable's laughter signals a rupture between the old ethic that favored durable knowledge over transient pleasure and the new urban manners that make the pursuit of pleasure, and perhaps wit, the highest good.

Something should be said about Sociable's technique as a disputant. By making a joke of scholastic analysis, Sociable is injecting the favorite device of sociable wits in promoting sense: raillery. Anthony Ashley Cooper, the third earl of Shaftesbury, in *Sensus Communis*, emphasizes the importance of raillery in furthering reason, for by "raising a laugh" conventional wisdom, superstition, and melancholy delusion could be put to flight.[22] If companions laughed at a witticism, then a new degree of common sense might emerge. What is noteworthy in this conversation is the impasse that Sociable's joke occasions. We are left with a failure to construct a common sense among countryman, collegian, and citizen.

Part of the difficulty lay in the inability on the part of Pensive and Jovial to credit Sociable's wholehearted identification with the "man of pleasure." Or perhaps it was the novelty of Sociable's vision of that figure. Since Epicurus, persons had measured their contentment by the quality of pleasing sensation they had experienced. Epicurus and his followers, however,

---

21. *The Humours, and Conversations of the Town, Expos'd in Two Dialogues: The First, of the Men; The Second, of the Women* (London, 1693), 17.

22. Anthony Ashley Cooper, third earl of Shaftesbury, *Sensus Communis: An Essay on the Freedom of Wit and Humour* . . . , in Shaftesbury, *Characteristics of Men, Manners, Opinions, Times, Etc.*, ed. John M. Robertson, 2 vols. (London, 1900), I, 49, 53.

located their utopia of pleasant sensations in a secluded garden; Mr. Sociable searched it out in the bustle of the city. Indeed, he insisted that the greatest satisfaction was to be had in those places most devoted to the service of the senses, the tavern and the townswoman's boudoir.

> JOVIAL: Then you are for no Conversation, but in a Tavern, *Sociable?*
> SOCIABLE: Yes, yes, Jovial, I am for Conversing in a Lady's Chamber too.

Explaining the attractions of public house parley, Sociable likens speaking with eating: "To avoid the cloying our selves with the same Dish, we vary our Company, and so meet with the variety of *Wit,* and always something *New,* and *Surprising.*" Novelty, variety, satiety. Sociability is an appetite that talk fills; satisfaction comes when novelty and wit sauce the vitals.[23]

Sociable's championing of pleasure in conversation challenges Pensive's scholastic idealism. The excitements of tavern talk make academic discourse seem "grave starch'd Debates." Historically, the eclipse of the English universities during the long eighteenth century began at precisely that juncture when Mr. Pensive's rhetoric lost its force against Mr. Sociable's wit.[24] Thereafter, youths migrated from campus to town to learn to speak and write. Jonathan Swift first published under his own name in 1712 to complain about this migration:

> Several young Men at the Universities, terribly possessed with the Fear of Pedantry . . . think all Politeness to consist in reading the daily Trash sent down to them from hence: This they call *knowing the World,* and *reading Men and Manners.* Thus furnished, they come up to Town; reckon all their Errors for Accomplishments, borrow the newest Set of Phrases; and if they take a Pen into their Hands, all the odd Words they have picked up in a Coffee-House, or a Gaming Ordinary, are produced as Flowers of Style. . . . To this we owe the strange Race of Wits, who tell us they write to the *Humour of the Age.*[25]

---

23. *The Humours, and Conversations of the Town,* 50, 51.
24. Perhaps as early as 1667, when *News from the Coffe-House* declared,
So great a Universitie
I think there ne'er was any
In which you may a scholar be
For spending of a Penny.
Ellis took this as the epigraph of *The Penny Universities.*
25. Jonathan Swift, *A Proposal for Correcting, Improving, and Ascertaining the English*

Swift recognized and regretted the triumph of the coffeehouse and tavern over the college. Nevertheless, he hoped to reform the education of the young nobility by supplanting the modish talk of the coffeehouse with conversations with the dead — which is to say, literary study. In *A Proposal for Correcting, Improving, and Ascertaining the English Tongue* (quoted above), Swift argued for the establishment of a national academy of letters. This temple of the true English word would enforce orthodox usage and counteract the novelties and oddities spawned by town wit.

Swift's remedy was too authoritarian (too French?) to find favor with his countrymen, but his diagnosis of the ills suffered by English letters proved influential. In *Tatler* no. 230 he gave a name to the literature "written for Entertainment, within fifty Years past," a term borrowed from across the channel: "belles lettres."[26] By distinguishing writings on the basis of their capacity to entertain, Swift drew attention to a difference that might exist between edifying works and those designed for social pleasure. He forced his fellow critics to see aesthetics as a problem.

Another influential element of his analysis was his argument that the disfigurement of belles lettres was owing to its perversion of language. It was "filled with a Succession of affected Phrases, and new conceited Words, either borrowed from the current Style of the Court, or from those, who, under the Character of Men of Wit and Pleasure, pretend to give the Law." Swift understood the corruption of literary style to have been caused by the invasion of fashionable society's speech into the precinct of writing. For Swift, literature, not conversation, was where the genius of the English language dwelled. When belles lettres sanctioned the *"Humour of the Age"* by preserving it in writing, it insulted the timeless quality of great literature. Because of the bondage of belles lettres to the modish wit of the court and coffeehouse (note their linkage in Swift's thought), it was an evanescent literature, offending the nature of writing as a perfect memory created to retain those transactions too important to be consigned to mere human memory.

Swift was Mr. Pensive with a pen. His premises, like Pensive's, stood entirely at odds with Sociable's. That lettres should be belles would have been no reason for complaint to Sociable; he did not doubt that they would be belles if they contained some of the pleasing novelties of expression

Tongue, in Swift, *A Proposal . . . Etc.*, ed. Herbert Davis [vol. IV of The Complete Prose Works] (Oxford, 1973), 12.

26. [Jonathan Swift], *Tatler*, no. 230, Sept. 28, 1710, 2.

found in the coffeehouse, the tavern, and the court. Furthermore, Sociable would not have objected if writing were used in the service of conversation: "Here we always have a numerous Club, sometimes of a dozen, seldom under ten; and they by the time one has done with his Intrigues, the next has fresh Adventures to impart, or some Poetic Essay perhaps to Communicate, and so we never want Discourse, nor ever are troubled with the same."[27] Swift wanted the timeless sameness of a canon; Sociable wanted a piece whose timeliness, novelty, and wit might give point to sociable talk. For Sociable, literature was a dead letter unless read aloud or discussed in company.

Conversation and writing converged in the most vital literary genre of the age, the play. Restoration comedy mimicked the talk of the town, polished it, and publicized new patterns of compliment and repartee. The plays mapped the fashionable terrain, locating the various sites of conversation and reproducing (sometimes recreating) the new sociolects spoken there. Sir Thomas St. Serfe gave coffeehouse raillery a stage voice in *Tarugo's Wiles* (1667), Thomas Shadwell documented the new courtship talk of the spas in *Epsom-Wells* (1673), Thomas Wright captured the parley of the women's tea table in *The Female Vertuoso's* (1693), and Susannah Centlivre mocked the duplicities of the gaming room in *The Basset-Table* (1705). Most popular were Sir George Etherege's evocations of London drawing room conversation in *The Man of Mode* (1676). We can no longer identify with any surety all the "newconceited words" and "affected phrases" being featured in these imitations of city life, but we can grasp the two general stylistic qualities common to all of these venues of metropolitan conversation: politeness and wit.

Politeness and Wit

Politeness in conversation meant an easy, mannerly, and agreeable style of expression in good English.[28] Polite discourse, therefore, encouraged sociability. Wit, on the other hand, was the apposite and novel adjusting of language to thought to form a memorable expression. A reciprocal rela-

---

27. *The Humours, and Conversations of the Town*, 52.

28. The English discourse of politeness has been anatomized by Lawrence Eliot Klein, "The Rise of 'Politeness' in England, 1660–1715" (Ph.D. diss., Johns Hopkins University, 1984). For French developments, see Peter France, "Polish, Police, Polis," in France, *Politeness and Its Discontents: Problems in French Classical Culture* (Cambridge, 1992), 53–73.

tionship existed between polite expression and wit. The novelty of wit shone against the mannerly conventionality of polite conversation. Witty sentences, when repeated, replenished the stock of polite formulas. Old wit lost the sharpness of its novelty yet retained sufficient of its ingenuity to be pleasant. Sociability thrived on pleasantries.

We should not ignore the social utility of pleasantries. To encourage sociability, one must address one's fellows in a way seemingly fresh, to provide the pleasure of novelty, yet familiar, for the stranger cannot be incorporated into the sense of community if he or she speaks or acts new to the point of strangeness. The stage operated as a bank of mannerly expression.

The critics of the stage, like Jeremy Collier and Jonathan Swift, recognized that the language of comedy was becoming a lubricant, smoothing courtship and play in the city and the spas. Manners had become a code of conventions aiding social interaction; they had ceased to be the public face of morals. A second charge laid against the stage was its encouragement of hypocrisy. When people mouthed the pleasantries learned from characters in plays, they were not speaking authentically.

Was their criticism cogent? Yes: even when Cromwell's Protectorate darkened the London stages, the citizenry's demand for models of polite conversation was such that John Cotgrave published a "Theatre of Courtship" in his *Wits Interpreter, the English Parnassus* (1655), supplying "Complements a la mode":

> [SHE]: Sir, you are welcome to this homely fare, I am sorry tis no better for you; *I* could wish it handsomer, but truly Sir, our house affords it not.
>
> [HE]: Courteous Lady, I am so much indebted to the matchlesse bounty of your house, that my thanks are such poor things that they would but shame me.[29]

Eighty years later, Swift pointed out the witlessness of such scripted courtesy in *A Complete Collection of Genteel and Ingenious Conversation, according to the Most Polite Mode and Method Now Used at Court, and in the Best Companies of England* (1738). Swift's parodic premise was that politeness in conversation was a system that could be learned by rote, and the *Collection* presumed to sum up "the whole Genius, Humour, Politeness, and Eloquence of *England.*" Simon Wagstaff, Swift's mask, observes, "There is not

29. J[ohn] C[otgrave], *Wits Interpreter, the English Parnassus...* (London, 1655), [iii], 100 (third numbering).

one single witty Phrase in this whole Collection, which hath not received the Stamp and Approbation of at least one hundred Years."[30] In Swift's version of the polite mode, wit had degenerated to formulaic repartee, and conversation to the exchange of clichés. In sum, belles lettres debased literature because it depended upon the temporary beauties of modish conversation for its pleasure; politeness debased social commerce because it subordinated genius to system and reduced wit to formula.

What Swift found pernicious in the confusion between the written and the spoken in belles lettres and polite conversation, Restoration playwrights found enlivening. The two most memorable stage wits, Etherege's Dorimant and Congreve's Mirabell, are great quoters. Dorimant's first words are recited lines, and Mirabell's wooing of Mrs. Millamant is conducted by trading favorite verses. Of even greater interest, Dorimant, Mirabell, and Millamant quote the same poet — Edmund Waller. If there was any progenitor of belles lettres in England, the lip tribute of the stage wits gave unambiguous notice who it was.

The Model of Belles Lettres

Edmund Waller's lyrics addressed to Sacharissa during the 1630s were the prototypes for English belles lettres. The distinction of these verses may not be apparent from a distant vantage. Like much Cavalier poetry, they celebrated the sovereignty of beauty, yet there was none of the platonizing of the beautiful so apparent in the court verse of Richard Lovelace and Sir John Suckling.[31] Like metaphysical poetry, Waller's lyrics employed the devices of wit — metaphor, paradox, antithesis — yet the intellectual effort that the metaphysical lyric advertised in its breadth of conceit or extravagance of simile has been abandoned. What Waller accomplished in his art may best be understood by reading the most reputable of his verses.

Go, Lovely Rose!

Go, lovely Rose!
Tell her that wastes her time and me

---

30. Jonathan Swift, *A Complete Collection of Genteel and Ingenious Conversation* . . . , in Swift, *A Proposal . . . Etc.*, ed. Herbert Davis [vol. IV of Complete Prose Works], 100–102.

31. Warren L. Chernaik, "Beauty's Sovereignty: Waller's Cavalier Lyrics," in Chernaik, *The Poetry of Limitation: A Study of Edmund Waller* (New Haven, Conn., 1968), 52–114.

That now she knows,
When I resemble her to thee,
How sweet and fair she seems to be.

Tell her that's young,
And shuns to have her graces spied,
That hadst thou sprung
In deserts, where no men abide,
Thou must have uncommended died.

Small is the worth
Of beauty from the light retired;
Bid her come forth,
Suffer herself to be desired,
And not blush so to be admired.

Then die! that she
The common fate of all things rare
May read in thee;
How small a part of time they share
That are so wondrous sweet and fair![32]

To grasp the innovation of the poem, we must note what is traditional. The motif of the rose as a message from a young man to a young woman, a text to be read communicating the youth's regard, derived from the classical epigrammatists. The circumstance of the poem, a gift from a young man in the world to a retired beauty, accompanying a request that she abandon her retirement, could be found throughout the ample corpus of neo-Roman English verses addressed to coy mistresses. Finally, the conceit of the rose as a mirror of mortality comes from an epigram by Rufinus (in *The Greek Anthology*). So what is new? First of all, the fact that Waller's lyric adverts to none of its classical precedents. There is no play of allusion or display of learning. That which is traditional in the poem has been incorporated because of the simplicity that convention lends argument. The lyric's simplicity, almost to the point of abstraction, is its most striking quality.

This discursive quality, identified by critics as "ease," became a hallmark of belles lettres and its principal point of distinction from the elaborate wit of metaphysical poetry. When Joseph Addison caricatured the typical belletrist of Queen Anne's reign, he marked both the influence of Waller and

---

32. Edmund Waller, "Go, Lovely Rose!" in *The Poems of Edmund Waller*, ed. G. Thorn Drury (1893; rpt. New York, 1968), 128.

the cultivation of poetic ease: "Ned Softly is a very pretty poet, and great admirer of easy lines. Waller is his favourite: and as that admirable writer has the best and worst verse of any among our great English poets, Ned Softly has got all the bad ones without book, which he repeats upon occasion, to show his reading, and garnish his conversation."[33] Ned Softly was not only a belletrist but a master of polite conversation as well.

Just as polite conversation had its detractors, so did belles lettres. The poetry of ease, with its learning that appeared to be no learning and its stripped-down simplicity of wit, disavowed the arcana of the schools and the self-referentiality of the court. The communicability of the poetry of ease, its wresting of the treasure of the muses from the care of the most learned and most high to enrich a more general audience, tarnished the treasure for those who believed the encounter with literature to be an occasion of apprehending rare truth rather than experiencing pleasure. From Waller's time, the poetry of ease has, despite its popularity, endured critical denigration as vers de société.

The sociability of "Go, Lovely Rose" may be detected in the sole innovation of its argument. Unlike classical lyrics that enticed the reluctant beauty to participate in the joys of the poet's private embrace, Waller's lyric entreated the beauty to realize her "worth" in social commerce. The value of beauty was realized only by means of admiration by "men" (note the plural). Only by circulating in company and by suffering "herself to be desired" did she apprehend her value in a social economy of desire. The poet's rose (the poem) served as a token of her value. Its significance was not simply confronting the woman with a sense of her own value by presenting a mirror of her beauty but also instructing her that no escape from the economy was possible. The rose presents an either-or. Either the woman participated and exercised the power of her beauty in society, or she suffered the "common fate" of creatures, despite their rarity and fairness — decay into worthlessness.

The choice between power and powerlessness, between exercising the exchange value of one's beauty and falling subject to the "common fate," denied that any benefit lay in retirement. Equanimity and wisdom, the traditional fruits of retirement, mean nothing in the poem. The sum of a woman's worth lies in her beauty, and, since beauty depends upon the eye of the beholder, only subjecting oneself to social admiration — submitting

33. [Joseph Addison], "Will's Coffee-house, April 24," *Tatler*, no. 163, Apr. 25, 1710.

to the masculine gaze — imbues the woman with value. Beauty is an engine of social pleasure, a force animating sociable commerce. Circulation, not retirement, nor settling into a fixed domestic relationship, constituted a beauty's meaningful exercise of her worth. Sociability abhorred a fixed or solitary circumstance.

Sociability

Mr. Sociable was a distinct type by the 1690s, more tolerant and facetious than his country companion, Mr. Jovial, more worldly, easy, and pleasure-loving than Mr. Pensive. Mr. Sociable retained the old rank of gentleman yet behaved with the condescending spirit and easy manners of the town. His identification with urbanity says something about the history of sociability. In England it was a mode of conduct associated with the intensive urbanization of post–Great Fire England. Sociability distinguished itself ethically from the old hospitality, politically from theories of society claiming divine sanction or perpetuity for the social order, and civically from creeds making much of one's virtue. In practical terms, it signified the eclipse of the traditional social organizations in which one was bound to one's fellow by ties of neighborhood, congregation, family, and common employment. Friendship, mutual interest, and shared appetite were the grounds of sociability.[34]

Society so grounded stood distinct from state, church, country, court, and street. Sociability promoted more intimate (and artificial) forms of association: clubs, corporations, routs, friendly circles, parties, and assemblies. Sociability flourished as cities grew and nations urbanized. As London, Paris, and Amsterdam drew enterprising citizens from the provinces to the center, they congregated in chocolate shops, coffeehouses, and public rooms and eventually coalesced into coteries. The formality of these groups may be contrasted with the fluidity of the public house world, where new faces continually appeared and disappeared. Coffeehouse societies and tavern clubs emerged espousing an ethic of friendship conceived in terms of social contract. The icon of the clubs was the handshake, which was also the mark of the completed deal.[35]

Once a man had been accepted into the fellowship of one of these city

---

34. Peter Clark, "Sociability and Urbanity: Clubs and Societies in the Eighteenth-Century City," lecture to the Victorian Studies Centre, University of Leicester, 1986.

35. Sarah Elizabeth Freeman, "The Tuesday Club Medal," *Numismatist*, LVII (1945), 1313–1322.

companies and had shown his good manners and contributed to the conversation, he might be invited into the more exclusive circle of drawing room society, the mixed-sex salons, and house parties. In these way stations of the world, the gentleman might come to the notice of someone who would sponsor his access to the inner circles of society where preferment, place, and fame might be had. Barriers of class remained to be negotiated. But one feature of life during the Restoration was the increasing permeability of degrees and ranks for persons adept in the genteel graces. If an earl could marry an actress or a minister's son win the welcome of every fashionable house in London for his way with impromptu poetry, then much might be ventured. As the world became more diffuse and less centered on the doings of the court, acceptance in arenas other than the court answered personal ambitions. Of particular interest is the adoption of the manners and discursive styles of the coffeehouse by the merchants and enterprisers who manned Europe's commercial empires.[36]

These mobile individuals conveyed the practices of the metropolis to the provinces and colonies. In coastal cities throughout British America, merchants took the lead in forming outposts of sociability that imitated London's club culture. Some of these institutions — the Freemasonic lodges and the societies devoted to the national patron saints, Saint George, Saint David, Saint Patrick, Saint Andrew — were founded on the basis of institutional charters dispensed from the British Isles. Others simply acknowledged London as the prototype of civility by aping metropolitan rites and fashions.

In Barbados during the early decades of the eighteenth century, every October 29 was marked with a Cockney Feast open to all "gentlemen of this Island, that were born within the Sound of Bow Bell." The feast was a rite of devotion to London. The meeting room was decorated with "the queens arms finely carved and guilded, on the right hand the Arms of the August City of London, next the Arms of the 12 Companies, out of wch the Lord Mayor is Chosen." Besides various pictures of the great buildings of London, the space was dominated by an allegorical painting reflecting upon sociability, representing

> Men societated together Some eating some drinking and dancing and
> playing upon Musick full of Variety of Exercise. Over head the Gods,
> looked down upon them Smileing — the Moral shews that when men

---

36. Paul Langford thoroughly explores the role of civil discourse in the conduct of business in *A Polite and Commercial People: England, 1727–83* (Oxford, 1989).

are met together through an Innocent design, Heaven above are well pleas'd as we poor mortals below.[37]

Here a work of art sanctions the social designs of the Barbadian Cockneys. Like the salon legends and the tokens and rites of the tavern clubs, the painting supplied a warrant for private society in the pleasure of the pagan gods. That the innocent designs approved by the gods were all worldly amusements — eating, drinking, dancing, and playing music — showed that the common motive shared by man and god was love of pleasure.

Mercantile sociability, like the other modes of association in the world, stood at symbolic odds with Christianity. Christian doctrine modeled its sense of society on the Trinity, out of which emanated the society of family, church, and nation (Chapter 7). The love that animated Christian associations, even those forms of association structurally analogous to secular private societies (the classes, the conventicles, the prayer meetings), was love of Christ, or the love of society itself. Society was understood to be a refraction of an innate, divinely inscribed attraction between human beings. Never in any Christian symbolization of society was pleasure deemed an end in itself; neither was love of pleasure deemed an innocent affection.

Art at the Cockney feast served as a vehicle of pleasure or as a mirror reflecting on the role of aesthetic diversions in their society. The literature of sociability generally performed these two services. In company, writing, like dancing or music, might serve as the amusement of the moment. Or it might reflect symbolically on the nature of "being societated," working like the great painting in the Barbadian hall. Whether performing either function — stimulating thoughtless sensation or promoting the more refined delights of philosophical self-understanding — sociable literature operated in camera. It spoke to the fellowship by preference, not to an anonymous populace. Sometimes it invited someone new into the fellowship. When Addison and Steele adopted a club as a mask for the *Spectator*, the friendly, conversational intimacy of belles lettres became the means by which an anonymous readership was recruited into a sense of print fellowship. The conversationality of belles lettres was conveyed in a number of ways: by parataxis in prose; in verse by cultivation of the quality of ease; in prose and verse by the resort to forms associated with conversation: dialogue, epigram, anecdote, joke, impromptu, toast, bon mot, witticism, and compliment.

37. Thomas Walduck to James Petiver, Nov. 12, 1710, Sloan MS 2302, British Library.

The scintillating conversation captured in belles lettres required more craft than many men of commerce could manage. Richard Steele allowed that false wit and jest plagued talk among the "trading part of mankind" because "the packer allows the clotheir to say what he pleases, and the broker has his countenance ready to laugh with the merchant, though the abuse is to fall on himself, because he knows that, as a go-between, he shall find his account in being in the good graces of a man of wealth."[38] The crudity of the wealthy man was indulged because self-interest inhibited companions from the criticisms and raillery that polish talk among equals. The merchants found it difficult to "be easy," to suspend self-interest. Yet within the merchant community there were those who, having tasted the refinements of the metropolis, wished to instill the taverns and coffee-houses of the world at large with urbane wit. In Philadelphia circa 1710 one such wit, to prevent the table talk of his ship captain friends from degenerating into shop talk, composed

A Rule For Conversation seriously
recommended to a certain Club

[Sloops] and Snows and Brigantines
Brigantines and Sloops and Snows.
[Su]re 'tis own'd, as fit machines
As the world of Trafique knows.

Sailors Bo'swains, Skippers, Mates
(Members that compose a Crew)
Are, for vessels, of all Rates,
Necessary hands; 'tis true.

Granting this, I dare proclaim
That, for fellowships best ends,
These shou'd be no more my Theme
Than These my chosen Bottle friends.[39]

Artful conversation required that persons treat matters other than those recommended by the necessity of affairs, one's interest, and one's self—

38. [Richard Steele], *Tatler*, no. 225, Sept. 16, 1710.
39. Henry Brooke, "A Rule for Conversation Seriously Recommended to a Certain Club," [Henry Brooke Poetry Collection], Commonplace Book, Peters Collection, Historical Society of Pennsylvania, Philadelphia.

the commonplace concerns of the world of traffic. The first of Benjamin Franklin's "Rules for Making Oneself a Disagreeable Companion" stipulated, "If possible engross the whole Discourse; and when other Matter fails, talk much of your-self, your Education, your Knowledge, your Circumstances, your Successes in Business, your Victories in Disputes, your own wise Sayings and Observations on particular Occasions, etc. etc. etc."[40]

Belletrists insisted that sociability must entail a distancing from the business of everyday life and preoccupation with self. Because taverns and coffeehouses served as venues for business as well as places of amusement, sociability sometimes demanded another resort. George Webb, Philadelphia's laureate of sociability during the early 1730s, recommended that Bachelor's Hall be built in suburban proximity to the town. There,

> Tir'd with the bus'ness of the noisy town,
> The weary Batchelors their cares disown;
> For this lov'd seat they all at once prepare,
> And long to breath the sweets of country air;
> On nobler thoughts their active minds employ,
> And a select variety enjoy.[41]

Webb mingled two traditions of representing pleasure: the urban tradition that stressed variety and social stimulation with the rural tradition of retired repose. Suburban sociability found fresh air and the avoidance of business encouragements to "nobler thoughts." *Batchelors-Hall* argued that a mental vacation into the realm of nobility was the most pleasurable refreshment available to men of affairs. The argument was a typical instance of what Michael McKeon has called the "rise of the aesthetic" in elite European culture.[42] Aesthetic experience entails the willing surrender of a subject's cares by transport into the irreality of some other condition. Whether imagining fairyland, utopia, ancient Rome, a pastoral field, heaven, hell, the tavern with perfect ale, or Bachelor's Hall, this other place insulated one from the immediate compulsion of necessity.

40. Benjamin Franklin, "Rules for Making Oneself a Disagreeable Companion," in Leonard W. Labaree et al., eds., *The Papers of Benjamin Franklin* (New Haven, Conn., 1959–), IV, 73.
41. George Webb, *Batchelors-Hall: A Poem* (Philadelphia, 1731), 8–9.
42. Michael McKeon, "Politics of Discourses and the Rise of the Aesthetic in Seventeenth-Century England," in Kevin Sharpe and Steven N. Zwicker, eds., *Politics of Discourse: The Literature and History of Seventeenth-Century England* (Berkeley, Calif. 1987), 35–51.

The ideal of sociability was to aestheticize social intercourse by marking it off in social and discursive spaces from quotidian affairs. In effect, sociable conversation had to be segregated. Shaftesbury identified wit as the discursive means by which mundane affairs were kept at bay and the market and street excluded from a company's concerns. Shared laughter, Shaftesbury said, would break the thrall of self-interest and care.[43] Many sociable companies employed additional means to make private society a haven from commerce and quotidian care: social legends of the salons and clubs, charters or "leges convivales" that prohibited the intrusion of certain concerns into the conversation of the company, special precincts or material environments such as the Apollo room or Bachelor's Hall that offered symbolic sanctuary. Of all these means, Shaftesbury most insisted on the primacy of wit. It constantly revived the sensus communis of friendly company. Its exercise prevented the reduction of conversation to the polite formulas that Swift predicted.

Shaftesbury's social aesthetics stands at odds with the two paradigms of the social organization of aesthetic experience that now dominate reflection — the community of the solitary reader and text and the society of the theatrical audience experiencing catharsis. Thus Hans Robert Jauss observes that the sociable person occupies a place in the theatrum mundi between the actor and sociological person ("homo sociologicus") in his or her role playing.[44] The actor performing a role enjoys a distance that renders his "playing the part" aesthetic.

This pleasurable distance does not exist in the performing of ordinary social roles, because habit or compulsion robs sociological man of any sense of the refreshing doubleness of his action. Aesthetic experience "thematizes role distance as man's possibility to experience his self through the doubling that role enactment occasions."[45] The experience of the sociable person more resembles that of the actor than that of sociological person. Yet the actor normally performs a role scripted by another. The polite conversation of a witty company may possess a prescribed quality, yet each participant in the talk is free to speak, quote, and recite as he or she wishes.

---

43. Shaftesbury, *Sensus Communis*, in Robertson, ed., *Characteristics*, II, 47–52.

44. Hans Robert Jauss, "Sociology and Aesthetic Role Concept," in Jauss, *Aesthetic Experience and Literary Hermeneutics*, trans. Michael Shaw (Minneapolis, Minn., 1982), 134–141. For a summary of the social applications of Shaftesbury's thought, see Lawrence E. Klein, *Shaftesbury and the Culture of Politeness: Moral Discourse and Cultural Politics in Early Eighteenth-Century England* (Cambridge, 1994).

45. Jauss, *Aesthetic Experience*, trans. Shaw, 134–141.

Thus the roles are improvised and necessarily subject to the constant adjustment that dialogue requires. As the examples of commedia dell'arte and jazz indicate, group improvisation proceeds by a more generalized vocabulary of gestures than the precisely mimetic indications of theatrical character.

A sense of how this generalized vocabulary worked can be had from George Webb's *Batchelors-Hall.* When Webb conceives of what the minds of his companions will turn to when they turn away from the cares of the busy town, he says they will "on nobler thoughts their active minds employ." Nobility was a concept that in the provincial world had wide semantic resonance, for it retained an ethical significance derived from the Greek τὸ καλόν, meaning that which was well formed in art or craft or well acted in human behavior. It also designated the titled class in European society. By metonymy those material objects, accomplishments, and mannerisms that typified the titled class became "noble." In sum, for the provincial merchants nobility was the "other" of an idealized metropolitan courtliness. Perhaps it captured the deepest ambition of some to procure enough wealth, power, and entrée to win a title and a place in court. But, more immediately, it meant the assumption of a style of conduct and thought.

The most distinctive thing about the conduct of "the world" that emanated from the court was the self-abstraction and stylization of its own social play. The court, the salons, the clubs, and the coffeehouses had in their own aestheticization displaced nobility from person and located it in manners and things. Belles lettres captured much of this manner for anyone to read: the tone of intimacy, the explicit cultivation of pleasure, the avoidance of didacticism, the easy use of pagan classicism, and the playfulness were stylistic marks available for emulation. In belles lettres even the provincial could see how sociability had transformed modes and manners. Wit had been made easy, learning was worn more lightly, compliment was made more friendly. These adjustments to the noble style made it less forbidding to would-be practitioners. Nobility transmuted by sociability became gentility. It retained the allure of the courtly and high, yet seemed more accessible to the aspiring citizenry.

Gentility and Taste

When People by their Industry or good Fortune, from mean Beginnings find themselves in Circumstances a little more easy, there is an Ambition seizes many of them to become *Gentlefolks:* But 'tis no easy

Thing for a Clown or a Labourer, on a sudden to hit in all respects, the natural and easy Manner of those who have been genteely educated: And 'tis the Curse of *Imitation,* that it almost always either under-does or over-does.

Benjamin Franklin here offered a critical commonplace of the period when he said that imitation was insufficient to learn gentility. Gentility entailed an internalization of manners and taste. Mere imitation was not enough. The ideal of conduct was a sociable *sprezzatura:* "The *true Gentleman,* who is well known to be such, can take a Walk, or drink a Glass, and converse freely, if there be occasion, with honest Men of any Degree below him, without degrading or fearing to degrade himself in the least."[46] Gentility consisted in mastering the fear of degradation so that one could be easy in public places with those of lower classes.

The public, for Franklin, was a place disturbed by social mobility and the convergence of classes. In such places gentility displayed itself as condescension, and lower-class aspiration as a willingness to emulate. If honest persons of lower rank enjoyed an unembarrassed communication with gentlefolks, the circumstances were ripe for the spread of gentility. The courtesy literature proposed that there was more to genteel behavior than easy comportment in public. Henry Peacham's *Compleat Gentleman* (1622) insisted that gentility resided in a range of accomplishments: book learning, horsemanship, skill at dancing, expertise with the foil, practical knowledge of music, draftsmanship, ability to cipher, talent at versifying, and aptitude at conversation. These accomplishments became matters of practical schooling in the West. An index of the importance of gentility was the proliferation of dancing masters, fencing instructors, and singing schools. In the provinces the dancing masters rose to be the most effective agents in the instruction of youth into manners.[47]

So important was the concern with the amelioration of manners among the aspiring classes in Britain and British America that it became a tenet of Whig ideology. Civility as much as wealth was promised by Britain's em-

46. Benjamin Franklin, "Blackamore, on Molatto Gentlemen," in J. A. Leo Lemay, ed., *Benjamin Franklin: Writings* (New York, 1987), 219. For a summary assessment of Franklin's attitude toward these issues, see Marc L. Harris, "What Politeness Demanded: Ethnic Omissions in Franklin's *Autobiography,*" *Pennsylvania History,* LXI (1994), 288–317.

47. Richard L. Bushman, *The Refinement of America: Persons, Houses, Cities* (New York, 1992).

pire of the sea. According to J. G. A. Pocock, the citizen of Britain's commercial empire was

> compensated for his loss of antique virtue by an indefinite and perhaps infinite enrichment of his personality, the product of the multiplying relationships, with both things and persons, in which he became progressively involved. Since these new relationships were social and not political in character, the capacities which they led the individual to develop were called not "virtues" but "manners," a term in which the ethical *mores* and the juristic *consuetudines* were combined, with the former predominating.[48]

Given the scope encompassed by manners, one can understand Franklin's insistence that gentility demanded something more than imitating well-mannered persons. Gentility entailed a consciousness that could not be transmitted by mechanical imitation. Instead, one had to cultivate an attunement to what was appropriate to a situation, a sensitivity for the qualities of persons and things, a critical judgment.[49] This attunement was called taste.

The problem of becoming genteel was that acquiring manners did not of itself give rise to taste. Tasteless persons could always mimic the dress and gestures of gentlepersons. These mock wits and would-be belles were favorite butts of stage comedy. Franklin's warning pointed to the temptation of the aspirants to gentility to be content with imitation in one's progress toward refinement. Yet red stockings, a sword knot, and an easy way with compliments constituted only the semblance of a beau. If taste could not be had by imitation, how was it acquired? Most readily by participating in the conversation of persons with taste until one had entered into the sensus communis of their expression. This did not mean gathering knowledge by precept. Rather, sensitivity to beauty and pleasure had to be heightened. An apperception of one's sensitivity made taste "conscious." The consciousness that taste endowed was not self-consciousness. Taste put one into accord with a style of expression. Beauty, if it were true beauty, for instance, was not personal; it was "natural" or "Attic" or "divine."

Aesthetic thought insistently discriminated between style and mode,

48. J. G. A. Pocock, "Virtues, Rights, and Manners: A Model for Historians of Political Thought," in Pocock, *Virtue, Commerce, and History: Essays on Political Thought and History* (Cambridge, 1985), 49.

49. Hans-Georg Gadamer, *Truth and Method*, trans. Garrett Barden and John Cumming (New York, 1975), 33–38.

using self-consciousness to demarcate.[50] That which was modish caught society by its peculiarity. It exalted novelty of manners and dress in order to make the "man of mode" conspicuous in the eyes of society. The self-obsession of the modish coxcomb was recognized by the term "foppery." The social construction of the fop is a subject of historical as well as aesthetic interest. While narcissicistically self-fixated, the fop sought to have his self-estimation duplicated by the indiscriminate admiration of society. His demand for general admiration precluded the desire for any particular experience of love. The fop appeared as an epicene figure, indifferent to certain potentials offered by the conversation between the sexes. In literature, especially in plays, the fop appeared at court, haunted the city salons, and strutted at Man's Coffeehouse; he was rarely spotted at the spas, the one arena where heterosociality was developing beyond the Platonism of the salon and the gallantry of court.

The Spas and the Sexes

England's spas burgeoned during the 1600s. Though they were "new towns," their growth did not depend on the usual forces of economic concentration around markets or transportation centers.[51] Bath, Epsom Wells, Tunbridge Wells, Buxton, and Scarborough throve because people began to take great stock in the hygienic benefits of "taking the waters," imbibing water from mineral springs as a tonic and bathing in warm springs as a restorative. As early as 1562, tracts were being published on the salubrious quality of the water at Bath. Dr. Lodowick Rowzee made similar claims on behalf of Tunbridge Wells. A gentry clientele began to congregate at Bath in the early 1600s; their good taste received royal endorsement when the Stuart queens visited after the Restoration.

The fashion for bathing began during the reign of Charles I, during which time public baths began to proliferate in London. The "bagnios" operated in districts known for fashionable nightlife. As the name suggests, the baths were a cultural importation from Italy, where a revival of Roman bathing had taken place in the 1500s as a recreational atavism. In England,

50. Dell Upton has made the most careful renovation of these critical categories in *Holy Things and Profane: Anglican Parish Churches in Colonial Virginia* (Cambridge, Mass., 1986).

51. Peter Clark and Paul Slack, *English Towns in Transition, 1500–1700* (Oxford, 1976), 33–36; Phyllis Hembry, *The English Spa, 1560–1850: A Social History* (London, 1990), 66–78.

the baths attracted a following for reasons other than a desire to relive the glories of the past. Washing encouraged the formation of an elite ethic of sanitation. Then too, the London baths became popular among certain men because they served as places of prostitution. Meeting a woman in the "stews" was one of the more lurid of town diversions during the latter years of the Stuarts.[52] Bagnios that strove to disassociate themselves from the skin trade made a point of advertising that men and women performed their ablutions on alternate nights. While trying to keep prostitution at bay, the spas nevertheless earned reputations as places of sexual adventure.

During the spring and autumn, baths were in season. Each locale had its constituency. Scarborough attracted its North of England and Scottish gentry; Epsom Wells, middling citizens from London. Bath drew the highest society from country and town. Tunbridge enjoyed a strong following among merchants, officers, and planters. During the seasons, the local inns swelled with a cosmopolitan array, ranging from three-generation gentry families with entourage to solitary adventurers and including a welter of marriageable persons of both sexes. Richard Ames, the poet and devotee of wine, observed of Islington Wells,

> Of either Sex whole Droves together,
> To see and to be seen flock thither,
> To Drink, and not DRINK the WATER, —
> And here promiscously they CHATTER.[53]

What to Ames seemed promiscuous chatter struck the majority of contemporary commentators as a strikingly new sort of conversation. The unique conditions of the spas placed a premium upon wit in the social commerce. Unlike the court, where the number of beautiful women and handsome men of fortune was limited, the resorts abounded with attractive persons. Something other than beauty or fine manners was required to attract notice in these hypercompetitive arenas of social display. William Byrd II, one of the beaux who haunted Tunbridge Wells, recognized in "Lady S" the new creature who came to power in the spas, the female wit:

52. For a European history of sanitation, see Georges Vigarello, *Concepts of Cleanliness: Changing Attitudes in France since the Middle Ages*, trans. Jean Birrell (New York, 1988). For English developments, see Roy Porter, ed., *The Medical History of Waters and Spas* (London, 1990). On prostitution, see G. S. Rousseau and Roy Porter, eds., *Sexual Underworlds of the Enlightenment* (Manchester, 1987).

53. [Richard Ames], *Islington-Wells; or, The Threepenny-Academy: A Poem* (London, 1691), 3.

Plautinas wit divinely draws,
Our adoration and surprize:
Her charms invite, her Conduct aws,
And wounds like Parthians as she flys.[54]

The emergence of wit as a significant feminine attribute during the late-Stuart period is attested in any number of writings. Tom Brown devoted many lines to "The Witty Woman" in his *Legacy for the Ladies; or, Characters of the Women of the Age* (1705), complaining that "no *Condition* can please her, without *Politeness*, because *Wisdom* and *Truth* are banished from her *Study*, which she wholly applies to the most received nice . . . Expressions." The playwrights were more sympathetic. One notices, for instance, the order of traits ascribed to Lucia and Carolina, Thomas Shadwell's heroines in the extremely popular *Epsom-Wells*: they are "Two young Ladies, of Wit, beauty and Fortune."[55]

Shadwell's representation of the talk between male and female wits at the spas reveals something of the new economy of polite sociability when questions of sexual desire intrude. Lucia rallies a witty beau named Rains:

> LUCIA: A man of wit and make love, leave off this foolish, old
>   fashion'd subject: I'd have all discourse between us tend to
>   something.
> RAINS: 'Tis as unseasonable for a young Lady not to entertain love, as
>   for a Judge or a Bishop to make love.
> LUCIA: Love is so foolish and scandalous a thing, none now make use
>   of any thing but ready money.
> RAINS: Methinks, ready Love is a pretty thing.
> LUCIA: But there are few in this Age have it about 'em.
> RAINS: I have as good a Stock, and am as full of love, Madam —
> LUCIA: That you squander it away upon every one you see, as a young
>   Prodigal newly of age, treats and pays reckonings for every body.

54. William Byrd, "A Poem upon Some Ladys at Tunbridge, 1700," in Maude H. Woodfin and Marion Tinling, eds., *Another Secret Diary of William Byrd of Westover, 1739–1741, with Letters and Literary Exercises, 1696–1726* (Richmond, Va., 1942), 248. There is some controversy about the dating of this poem.

55. Thomas Brown, *A Legacy for the Ladies; or, Characters of the Women of the Age* (London, 1705), 32; Thomas Shadwell, *Epsom-Wells*, in Montague Summers, ed., *The Complete Works of Thomas Shadwell* (1927; rpt. London, 1966), II, 97.

RAINS: How prodigal soever I have been, I am resolv'd to take up in my expences, and reserve all my love for you.

LUCIA: For me? I am as hard to be fixt as you: I love liberty as well as any of ye.

[III, i]

So much for the courtly discourse of Platonism. If beauty, as Waller argued in "Go, Lovely Rose," imbued women with the exchange value to exercise power in the commerce of society, then wit preserved a woman's liberty (her right to free trade) within the bourse. Lucia marshals wit to deflect those proprietary claims that beaux make in the name of love. Once the compact of love is entered into, both parties foreclose power, liberty, and beauty in the thralldom of mutual desire. The problem of love, as Shadwell and a host of notable readers of manners indicated, was that men often did not surrender their liberty in the compact. Consider the witty riposte of Aphra Behn's Amynta, "To Lysander, Who Made Some Verses on a Discourse of Loves Fire":

> Since then, *Lysander*, you desire,
> *Amynta* only to adore;
> Take in no Partners to your Fire,
> For who well Loves, that Loves one more?
> And if such Rivals in your Heart I find,
> Tis in My Power to die, but not be kind.[56]

Libertines "but with their Tongues Confess" love, not giving themselves wholly to its mutual consumption. Wit, according to Shadwell's Lucia, enabled a woman to exercise a measure of control over her consumption (whether by the "Fire" or in the social economy), by serving as a means to question the beaux' talk of love. To "love liberty," as Lucia does at Epson Wells, is to defer consumption. It may even challenge the economics of desire promoted by the new sociability. Aphra Behn's Amynta raised this possibility in "To Lysander, on Some Verses He Writ, and Asking More for His Heart then 'Twas Worth":

> Take back that Heart, you with such Caution give,
> Take the fond valu'd Trifle back;

56. Aphra Behn, *Poems upon Several Occasions* (1684), in Montague Summers, ed., *The Works of Aphra Behn* (1915; rpt. New York, 1967), VI, 196–197.

I hate Love-Merchants that a Trade wou'd drive
   And meanly cunning Bargains make.

.   .   .   .

An Humble *Slave* the Buyer must become
   She must not bate a Look or Glance.[57]

The consents worked between men and women should be conceived, not as a compact of constraints, but as a contract ensuring the same degree of liberty:

Be just, my lovely *Swain*, and do not take
   Freedomes you'll not to me allow;
Or give *Amynta* so much Freedom back:
   That she may Rove as well as you.

Amynta here sounds like a radical Whig free trader attacking a mercantilist male autarky. Behn might have been Tory in some aspects of her politics; not, however, in her economics.

Analogy between the new courtship talk and the language of commerce has been a favorite matter for comment among Marxist critics, particularly those wishing to illustrate Marx's dictum that the bourgeoisie reduces all human relationships to cash transactions. Shadwell's *Epsom-Wells* lends itself to the traditional sort of Marxist reading. Married folk display no sense of the sacredness of marriage. In the dramatis personae, Shadwell cues readers by identifying merchant husbands as cuckolds and wives as strumpets and whores. At play's end the suggestion that Rains might marry is treated as a joke. A wit observes, "One Fortnights conversing with us will lay such a scandal upon 'em [Lucia and Carolina], they'll be glad to repair to Marriage" (V, i). Lucia has agreed to accept Rains's attentions on trial, not with the prospect of a domestic future, but because his conversation might afford "a little harmless Gallantry" (V, i). The male and female wits are not enthralled with one another; marriage remains an unsavory option in the play's argument. The final agreement between Rains and Lucia is that the play of wit will continue indefinitely.

The possibility that conversation can be an open-ended exercise of social play is advanced by Shaftesburian aesthetics, yet Shaftesbury envisions this occurring only in private companies when sociability is grounded in friendship. It is commonplace to call friendship the glue of sociability for the permissions it grants enabling the "free conversation" upon which the

57. Ibid., 202–204.

health of the sensus communis depends. Yet when we turn to the conversation between the sexes, we discover something new about the friendly freedom of wit. The bonds of friendship preserve the freedom of conversation precisely because they entail a distance, a possibility of saying no. The compulsions of love permit no such possibility.

One historical importance of the emergence of the spa style of conversation lay in its demonstration of how friendship between the sexes could be rendered practical. When women exercised wit as well as men did, and often better, they could deflect or defer the claims of love. Beauty and wealth served only to incite desire and provoke these claims, whereas wit enabled women to speak the amiable no of friendship. Spoken within the social formulary of politeness, the witty no required the man to sublimate his desires in play. Earlier, the salons had attempted to permit a conversation between the sexes by sublimating desire in the symbols and language of Platonism. It elevated the patroness on a divine pedestal and expunged the body by a rhetoric of spiritual rapport, thereby giving sufficient distance between women and men to permit conversation.

These bonds of spiritual empathy, however, were no less absolute than those of common love; consequently, the Platonic love discourse could never wholly escape the suspicion that the sublime feelings shared by Platonic consorts simply masked more carnal attractions. Salon Platonism was the historical precondition for conversation of sexual wit, though spa wit dissolved the older idealism. The presumption in *Epsom-Wells* is that talk of Platonic love is a pretense. Lucia makes it a point of her wit when she twits Rains for the violence of his declarations of love: "Methinks 'twere enough to arrive at Platonick Love at first." She closes the exchange by observing, "This is no Age for Marriage; but if you'll keep your distance, we will admit you for a Couple of Servants as far as a Country Dance, or Ombre, or so" (V, i).

At this juncture we can investigate the utility of the language of trade for the spa style of wit. Negotiation in trade presumes sufficient self-possession that one can calculate one's interest in terms of another's desires to arrange something mutually beneficial. Circumspection is the rule. In wit, a similar circumspection governs one's judgment of the apposite words for a situation. If the agreements struck between members of the opposite sex could be negotiated through the symbols of trade, then the absolute claims in force between the sexes proclaimed by the Christian theology of love, the Platonic philosophy of love, the emerging biologism of natural philosophy, and the language of English jurisprudence might be displaced in favor of a discourse that permits the woman and man more leeway to act autonomously. The freedoms of friendship might be possible. The something toward which conversation would tend would become itself open for discussion.

The new conversation between the sexes did not go unchallenged. Reformed Christians condemned the worldliness and playfulness of spa wit and deplored its secular and antidomestic tendency. Social traditionalists on the left and the right anathematized female wit as an offense to male prerogative. The most powerful attack on the new-styled politeness came from the agents of the newly emerging print culture, the Grub Street authors. They made it the central target in their project to disrupt Whig civility.

The Profanations of Grub Street

We must recall the peculiar conditions that gave rise to the first hirelings of the press. Appearing in the 1690s, the Grub Streeters should be viewed as bastard offspring of the Glorious Revolution. Tom Brown, William Pittis, and Richard Ames were university men whose devotion to the Stuarts and the High Church denied them the patronage that would have been their due if the coup of 1688 had not taken place. William Fuller and Edward "Ned" Ward were ingenious persons, also Tories, who emerged from the tavern world by power of eloquence.[58] Daniel Defoe, after his failure in business, found himself drawn into the welter of press activity that the Tory hacks had fueled. Relegated to the margins by the Whig triumph, displaced from William and Mary's court and its ceremonious discourse of nobility, alienated from the society in which a Whig rhetoric of contract could suffuse the language of love, a society enabling women to exercise wit and display learning and city merchants and their wives to put on genteel airs — they felt little compunction to mouth the pieties of the era. Whiggery, whether polite or pietistic, provoked Grub Street's curse. Freed from prior censorship by the termination of the Licensing Act in 1695, the Grub Streeters vituperated so extravagantly that some earned

58. A brief prosopography of the Grub Street writers is included in Philip Pinkus, *Grub St. Stripped Bare . . .* (Weston, Conn., 1968). John Granthan Turner has argued about the programmatic incivility of Tory writing in "Cultivated Incivility and Restoration 'Wit,'" paper delivered at the Twenty-fifth Anniversary Meeting of the American Society for Eighteenth-Century Studies, Charleston, S.C., Mar. 15, 1994.

cropped ears, prison terms, and lockups at the pillory despite the increased freedom of the press.

To deride the polite conversation of gentlefolk, Tom Brown and Ned Ward fashioned a literature of the impolite. In poetry they combined Rochester's ribaldry with Samuel Butler's Hudibrastic doggerel to fashion their own rude verse. In prose they managed to capture on paper the "stupendious obscenity and tonitrous verbosity" of the swearing practiced by the fishwives of the Billingsgate market in London. Brown and Ward's Billingsgate prose, with its extravagant similes, brought into print the city's one oral form made to stop conversation. Verbal rant of such stupefying virtuosity did not permit reply; Grub Street's print version of billingsgate foreclosed dialogue.[59] A victim might: counter with a fusillade of curses, or condemn a Grub Streeter's execrations; or try to turn a deaf ear to the vituperation.

The novel extravagance of the Grub Streeters' manner can be gauged by comparing Rochester's "Tunbridge Wells: A Satyr" with Ned Ward's "Walk to Islington." Rochester's satire was a courtier's ironic comment on the attempts of would-be beaux and belles to ape genteel discourse, in the form of a sample of spa talk:

> Madam methinkes the Weather
> Is growne much more Serene, since you came hither:
> You Influence the Heav'ns — but shou'd the Sun,
> Withdraw himself to see his Rayes outdone
> By your bright Eyes; they wou'd supply the Morne
> And make a Day, before the Day be borne.
> With Mouth screwd up, conceited winking Eyes,
> And Breasts thrust forward — Lord Sir (she replyes)
> It is your goodnesse, and not my Deserts
> Which makes you Shew, this Learning, Witt, and Parts.
> He puzled, bites his Naile, both to display,
> The sparkling Ring, and thinke what next to say.
> And thus breakes forth a fresh: Madam, Egad
> Your luck at Cards last Night, was very bad;

59. Thomas Brown, "A Walk round London and Westminster, Exposing the Vices and Follies of the Town," in *The Works of Mr. Thomas Brown, in Prose and Verse*, 3 vols. (London, 1707–1709), III, 43. William Wycherly attempted to capture something of the extravagance of Billingsgate in his dialogue in *The Plain Dealer* (1676).

> At Cribbidge, Fifty Nyne, and the next show
> To make the Game; and yet to want those Two.
> Gad-Damme Madam, I'm the Son of a Whore
> If in my life, I saw the like before.[60]

The beau's oath reveals the crudity being papered over by cliché gallantries. The point of Rochester's satire is to show how déclassé the attempts at resort wit by lower-class aspirants to gentility were. The poem's true wit shows up the false wit of would-be gentlemen and ladies whose dullness emerges to reveal their true vulgarity.

Contrast Ward's sortie upon resort sociability. He does not allow the discourse even that status of pretense. The conversation that serves as climax of the tour of Islington takes place in a woman's water closet into which a beau has wandered by mistake. An anonymous beauty suffering from bladder control difficulties

>   had the Scurvey mishap
> To thrust open the door, and clap Arse in my Lap:
> Ads-wounds, said I, Lady Fair, as I'm a Christian,
> I never deserved from your Sex to be pisst-on:
> The Lady, surpriz'd at the Voice of a Man,
> Gave a Skip like a Squirril, and out again ran.
> Her Person denoted her of such a Genus
> I dare t'engage, she'd a Bum like a Venus:
> So soft, that I thought, I for ever cou'd feed on,
> Such Forbidden Fruit, like an Adam in Eden.[61]

Ward's doggerel exemplified Grub Street profanity. The dialogue of gentility has been degraded to the monologic jest of a male libertine. The social intercourse of the sexes has been debased into an accidental episode of urophilia. The female character has been reduced to either a squirrel or an arse. Classical learning has become the adornment of a bald rump, and Scripture a vehicle for imagining the pleasure of sinning eternally.

At another point in the tour Ward burlesqued the commercial metaphors in the courtship talk at the spas, anticipating the claims of mid-

---

60. Keith Walker, ed., *The Poems of John Wilmot, Earl of Rochester* (Oxford, 1984), 71–72.

61. [Edward "Ned" Ward], "A Walk to Islington," in *The Second Volume of the Writings of the Author of the London Spy* (London, 1704), 71.

twentieth-century Marxists that bourgeois courtship really negotiated a polite form of prostitution.

> We *Prattled* and *Tattled* tho' what 'twas we said;
> If you'd have me Discover, indeed I must fail you,
> I found by her Words I her Heart cou'd command,
> So quickly we settl'd the matter in Hand.[62]

By maintaining the proprieties of polite conversation with the reader, the speaker suggests the dishonesty of genteel discourse. What is repressed is the fact that it is not "her Heart" that is "the matter in Hand." In a separate prose portrait of Tunbridge Wells, Ward, in the guise of the London Spy, expatiated on the bargains struck at resorts:

> Maidenheads here bear an extravagant price, for a great lover of priority, gave fifty guineas for one at secondhand, thought he bought it for span new, but unhappily heard soon after, it had been sold for a hundred a fortnight before; and when he found himself cheated by his commodity broker, was forced to undergo the lash of the old proverb, A fool and his money were soon parted.[63]

The gist of Ward's argument is that the commerce of the spas did not differ from that of the city's stews; both were engaged in the flesh trade. The former merely pretended it was not.

Ward could at times manage a sarcasm about flesh equaling that of that later Tory, Jonathan Swift. For savage eloquence, few passages in eighteenth-century prose match the scabrousness of Ward's portrait of the sacred well of English gentility, King's bath at Bath:

> In this *Bath* was at least fifty of both Sexes, with a Score or two of Guides, who by their Scorbutick Carcasses, and lacker'd Hides, you would think they had lain Pickling a Century of Years in the *Stygian Lake*. Some has those Infernal Emissaries to support their Impotent Limbs. Others to scrub their Putrify'd Carcasses like a Racehorse. In one Corner was an Old Fornicator hanging by the Rings, Loaded with Rotten Humidity; Hard by him was a Buxom Dame, Cleansing her *Nunquam Satis* from *Mercurial* Dregs, and the remains of *Roman Vitriol*. Another, half cover'd with Sear-cloth, had more Sores than *Lazarus*, doing Pennance for the Sins of her Youth: at her Elbow was a Young

62. Ibid., 65.
63. [Edward "Ned" Ward], *The London Spy*, ed. Kenneth Fenwick (London, 1955).

Hero, supported by a couple of Guides, rack'd with Aches and Intolerable pains, Cursing of *Middlesex* Court, and *Beveridges* Dancing-School, as Heartily as *Job* the Day of his Birth. At the Pump was several a Drenching their Gullets, and Gormandizing the Reaking Liquor by wholesale.[64]

Here the flesh bargained for so zestfully elsewhere appears in its disgusting corruption. The duplicity of Grub Street narrations, their contradictions, and the instability of values point to the peculiar quality of its style of profanation. The imagery oscillates between the sacred and the debased, the beautiful and the ugly, the tasteful and the disgusting, the lovely and the lewd. Job with his unmerited sores must appear among the syphilitics in the King's bath. An antique goddess must be invoked by the sight of a girl's spouting hindquarters. Whatever is elevated, reputable, or the height of fashion must be yoked to the low and contemptible.

It is not the inevitable discovery of the low in Ward's writing that most fascinates in reading, for the low appears, almost mechanically, as some figuration of the flesh (the perishing *sarx* of Christian discourse), the monstrous (drawn from travel literature), the vicious (inverting the casuistical literature concerning the sins, particularly lust and gluttony), the lewd (imagined in the light of the new pornography of Pietro Aretino), the stupid (imitating the gulls in English rogue literature). The low is never unintelligible in Ward or Brown; it is always recognizable and always communicated according to one of the conventions named above. Billingsgate needed no interpretation. What fascinates in Ward, Brown, Richard Ames, and Pittis is the range of noble matters being debased. One could map the scope of Williamite reputability by Ward's desecrations. An index of the value attached to a place, condition, mode, or behavior could be adduced from the insistence with which Ward denigrated it from text to text. The spas and their conversation were hammered in Ward. Only the self-promotion of the metropolis inspired his vituperation in equal measure.

In the *London Spy*, he anatomized — flayed — Augusta (London), defaming the parks, bagnios, palaces, coffeehouses, hospitals, and fashionable parlors with such vigor that London's claim to be the center from which civility spread throughout the world became wholly questionable. For Ward and Brown the polite worlds of the spas and city were linked in their dependence upon commerce. Courtship talk, fashion, dress, luxury goods,

64. [Edward "Ned" Ward], *A Step to the Bath, with a Character of the Place* (London, 1700).

places at court—all hinged on the Williamite empire with its banks, merchants, lotteries, monopolies. The beau monde had lost its aesthetic distance from the world, for it had become too much a mirror for the self-interest of those who exploited the globe. The Grub Street Tories made a point of linking the metropolis with the empire upon which it depended through terms of mutual degradation.[65]

Ward was particularly trenchant as a critic of the sea empire, having himself briefly heeded the promise of metropolitan projectors that broken fortunes might be repaired in the colonies. He headed in the 1690s to the great engine of British imperial wealth, the West Indies. Instead of an Eden of commodity he found "the Dunghill of the Universe . . . the clippings of the Elements, the shameless Isle of Rubbish, confus'dly jumbl'd into an Emblem of the Chaos, neglected by Omnipotence, when he form'd the World into its admirable order." Ward's *Trip to Jamaica* (1698) sparked a literary rage for defamatory voyages, often anonymous, in which "the Comical Humours, Ridiculous Customs, and Foolish Laws, of the Lazy Improvident People the [fill in the blank]" were displayed. First the old island empire of the British Isles was defamed in *A Journey to Scotland* (1699), a *Trip to Ireland* (1699), *A Step to the Bath* (1700), and *A Trip to North-Wales* (1701). Then the Grub Streeters ranged wider: *A Trip to St. Helena* (1703), *A Trip to Germany* (1705), and *A Trip to Spain* (1705). Ward himself had followed his blast at the Indies with another assault on British America, *A Trip to New-England* (1699). There he showed that the plain-spun Puritan Whigs of Boston suffered from the same malady afflicting polite Whigs at the spas: "The Inhabitants seem very religious, showing many outward and visible Signs of an Inward and Spiritual Grace; But tho they wear on their Faces the Innocence of Doves, you will find them in their Dealings, as Subtile as Serpents. Interest is their Faith, Money their God, and Large Posessions the only Heaven they covet."[66] The whole world—that world that projectors claimed would be ameliorated by metropolitan arts and civility—received in Grub Street fantasy, as their portion in the imperial commerce, the vanity, hypocrisy, and cupidity of Augusta.

65. David S. Shields, "The Rise of Grub Street and the Williamite Imperium Pelagi," paper presented at the Annual Meeting of the American Historical Association, Washington, D.C., Dec. 27, 1992.

66. [Edward "Ned" Ward], *A Trip to Jamaica* and *A Trip to New-England*, in *The Second Volume of the Writings*, 161, 173–176; Howard William Troyer, *Ned Ward of Grubstreet: A Study of Sub-Literary London in the Eighteenth Century* (Cambridge, Mass., 1946), 16–28.

Within Augusta's cultural geography the Grub Streeters tended to identify with the tavern against the coffeehouse. Ward, a sometime tavernkeeper, Brown, an alcoholic, and Ames, author of *The Bacchanalian Sessions*,
saw the coffeehouse as the arena where the metropolitan world conversed
with the world at large and, therefore, as the necessary institution of commercial Whiggery. Tom Brown in "Amusement" no. 7 leads an American
Indian around London to show him the manners of the persons who im-
pinge upon his life and stops at the coffeehouse. There amid the "Miscel-
lany of Mortality" he specially notes the traders: "These are they that in-
veagle unthinking Animals into all sorts of extravagant Expences, and ruine
'em insensibly, under colour of *Kindness* and *Credit*." Brown pronounces the
talk so vain and self-interested that "*all speak*, but *no-body heard* or answer'd":

> Now they tell their several Adventures by Sea and Land; how they
> conquer'd the Gyant, were overcome by the Lady, and bought a pair of
> wax'd Boots at *Northampton* to go a wooing in. One was commending
> his *Wife*, another his *Horse*, and the third said he had the best *smoak'd*
> *Beef* in *Christendom*. Some were discoursing of all sorts of Government,
> *Monarchical*, *Aristocratical*, and *Democratical*; some about the Choice of
> *Mayors*, Sheriffs and *Aldermen*; and others, of the transcendent Vertues
> of *Vinegar*, *Pepper*, and *Mustard*.[67]

In this indiscriminate welter of talk only one discourse was sensational
enough to compel the attention of the multitude: news. In his comedy, *The
Humours of a Coffee-House*, Ward expatiated on the galvanic effect of news
on the caffeine crowd:

> I can give you such a piece of News from *Sadler's Wells*, of an Exploit
> perform'd there by an *Hibernian* Canibal, that will Operate as well upon
> a foul Stomach, as a Gallon of *Caruds Posset-drink*. But I won't venture to
> tell it you, unless you assure me first of your strength of Constitution,
> that no gentle Purgative will work with you.[68]

Ward's play burlesqued the sensationalism of news by exaggerating representations to the point of incredibility. Newswriters offer tales of floating

67. Thomas Brown, "Amusements Serious and Comical, Calculated for the Meridian of London," *Works*, III, 75, 77.
68. [Edward "Ned" Ward], *The Humours of a Coffee-House: A Comedy as It Is Daily
Acted . . .* (London, 1707). Ward cannibalized most of the scenes in this drama from his
Weekly Comedy, as It Is Dayly Acted at Most Coffee-Houses in London (London, weekly
installments, May 10–July 12, 1699).

islands off the coast of Ireland inhabited by miniature men who tended sheep "no bigger than *English Rabbits*, but very delicious Food; their Wooll being Cole-Black, and their Horns as White as Ivory." These fantastical accounts are linked with obsessively detailed recitations of the circumstances of discovery: the incredible and credible became interfused. These tidings excite the speculators in the crowd with thoughts of commercial exploitation. Ward's portrait showed that the extravagance of lying in news was matched only by the extravagance of citizens' credulity when their imaginations were excited by the prospect of future wealth. Ward's sketch of the pathology of the imagination in coffeehouses may be the best historical introduction to the international financial crisis caused by the bubbles (the frenzies of financial speculation) in England and France.

Despite the prescience of the Grub Street critique, it failed to dislodge the central and positive place that commerce assumed in the imagination of metropolitans and colonists who aspired to the graces and places of the beau monde. Commerce was simply the most efficacious means to pleasure and position for those who lacked breeding. None of the ideals of the earlier court society — nobility, Platonism, or virtue — could enable incorporation into the easy, sociable exchange of the gentility. Even the female wits delighted in confessing the place of commerce in the play of courtship. Mary Evelyn's *Mundus Muliebris; or, The Ladies Dressing-Room Unlock'd, and Her Toilette Spread* satirizes the ceremonies and accoutrements of the sex game by metaphorizing it as a colonial commercial venture, *A Voyage to Marryland*, as it were:

> HE that will needs to *Marry-land*
> Adventure, first must understand
> For's Bark, what Tackle to prepare,
> 'Gainst Wind and Weather, wear and tare.[69]

In a preface the publication of her portrait of a lady's dressing room is justified as instructions for the colonial adventurer:

> It is for direction of such as are setting out towards this Great and Famous Emporium (whether the design be for Miss or Marriage) what Cargo he must provide; not as Merchants do for *America*, Glass-Beads, and Baubles, in exchange for Gold and Pearl; but Gold and Pearl, and all

---

69. [Mary Evelyn], *Mundus Muliebris; or, The Ladies Dressing-Room Unlock'd, and Her Toilette Spread; In Burlesque; Together with the Fop-Dictionary, Compiled for the Use of the Fair Sex*, 2d ed. (London, 1690), 3.

that's precious, for that which is of less value than Knives and Childrens Rattles.

In Maryland there was no question that commerce would be the means by which the beau monde would be built. By commerce Maryland was connected with Marry-land. By commerce it could make itself over into Marry-land, provided that those other elements necessary to creating the space of gentility were present: the conversation of tasteful persons, a social zone insulated from church and state, the materials that made up the current image of fashionability, and instructions on what was currently fashionable. Literature could supply the first and last of these and contribute somewhat to the establishment of the second. Even Evelyn's burlesque glimpse of the city lady's dressing room supplied information that provincials might not get elsewhere. Would-be gentlewomen in Boston might well be intrigued by the wares on the table in that dressing room:

> A *Tea* and *Chocolate* Pot,
> With *Molionet*, and Caudle Cup,
> Restoring Breakfast to sup up:
> *Porcelan* Saucers, Spoons of Gold,
> Dishes that refin'd Sugars hold;
> *Pastillios de Bocca* we
> In Box of beaten Gold do see,
> Inchas'd with Diamonds, and *Tweeze*
> As Rich and Costly as all these.[70]

If provincials found themselves stymied by certain of the emphasized terms in the description, they could consult the "Fop-Dictionary, Compiled for the Use of the Fair Sex" appended to the pamphlet.

The greatest attestation to the power of the beau monde's images of civility was their capacity to incite emulation even when presented in humorous guise. The greatest evidence of the self-possession of the gentility was the beau monde's capacity to make itself a matter for wit, to make witty self-raillery the essential mode of conversation.

70. Ibid., 11–12.

3

Coffeehouse
and Tavern

William Penn recognized the greatest threat to order in his infant province. The unregulated activity of the public houses stimulated the growth of vice and looseness. The problem was not merely the corruption of manners. In England, coffeehouses and taverns had by 1680 become havens of sedition and heresy, places where ideas and actions challenging civil power and religion throve. The political opposition that would eventually oust the Stuarts from the throne gathered in the King's Head Tavern and in the political coffeehouses. The attempt of Charles II in 1675 to quash the political ferment in the public rooms by suppressing the coffeehouses resulted in so volatile an outcry from the citizenry that he was forced to rescind his order in a scant eleven days. Suppression by royal decree seemed a drastic measure — a sign of weakness in controlling civic life. It signified the king's failure to complete the full restoration of governmental order. Part of the crown's problem arose from the control that keepers of public houses exerted over their own licensing and other activities. The Society of Vintners, not the municipal authorities, licensed the London taverns. Policing the spaces became a problem. Penn did not allow a similar state of affairs to arise in Pennsylvania: the governor licensed taverns in Pennsylvania, and the Provincial Council regulated what could and could not take place on premises.[1]

1. Mary Maples Dunn et al., eds., *The Papers of William Penn*, 5 vols. (Philadelphia, 1981–1986), II, 151; Lawrence Klein, "Coffee Clashes: The Politics of Discourse in Seventeenth- and Eighteenth-Century England," paper given at the Annual Meeting of the American Historical Association, Chicago, 1991; Peter John Thompson, "A

Although Philadelphia in 1700 contained a number of houses that boasted the name "tavern," a number of these were alehouses, simple dwellings with a barrel of porter in the hall and two extra beds in the chamber for the use of guests. The Blue Anchor, where Penn spent his first night in the province, had measured a scant twelve feet by twenty-two. These were minor temples of vice, where prostitution, drunken disorder, and riot might break out; they did not trouble Penn's mind so much as those establishments accommodating the traders and cosmopolitans essential for the economic welfare of the colony. These persons posed two threats: they could subvert the economic health of the colony by organizing clandestine trade, and they potentially harbored an opposition. The establishments that loomed largest in his thoughts were Enoch Story's Tavern, the London (or Carpenter's) Coffeehouse, and the Pewter Platter Inn.[2] Despite Penn's best attempts to eliminate any advantage for a public house by fixing prices and products by law, these businesses managed to

Social History of Philadelphia's Taverns, 1683–1800" (Ph.D. diss., University of Pennsylvania, 1989), 128–149.

"WHEREAS it is most apparent that the multitude of coffee houses of late years set up and kept within this kingdom, the dominion of Wales, and town of Berwick-upon-Tweed, and the great resort of idle and disaffected persons to them, have produced very evil and dangerous effects; as well for that many tradesmen and other, do herein mispend much of their time, which and probably would be employed in and about their Lawful Calling and Affairs; but also, for that in such houses . . . divers false, malitious and scandalous reports are devised and spread abroad to the Defamation of his Majesty's Government, and to the Disturbance of the Peace and Quiet of the Realm; his Majesty hath thought fit and necessary, that the said coffee Houses be (for the future) Put down, and suppressed." A Proclamation for the Suppression of Coffee Houses, [Dec. 23, 1675], as paraphrased in William H. Ukers, *All about Tea*, 2 vols. (New York, 1935), I, 45.

2. Harold Donaldson Eberlein and Cortlandt Van Dyke Hubbard, *Portrait of a Colonial City: Philadelphia, 1610–1838* (Philadelphia, 1939), 10. The prospect of the tavern's becoming the haven for persons challenging authority troubled provincial governments throughout the eighteenth century. David W. Conroy, *In Public Houses: Drink and the Revolution of Authority in Colonial Massachusetts* (Chapel Hill, N.C., 1995), shows how Massachusetts taverns nursed an oppositional culture. Similar histories could be written for New York, South Carolina, and Georgia.

The antiquarians Benjamin Boggs and Mary Boggs in 1914 identified the following public houses as operating in Philadelphia during the first decade of the eighteenth century: the Blue Anchor, the Broadaxe, Carpenter's Coffeehouse, the Crooked Billet, Enoch Story's, the George, the Globe, the Pewter Platter, the Scales, Thomas Hooten's, the Three Tuns, the Tun, William Frampton's, and Whitpain's ("Inns and Taverns of Old Philadelphia," MS, Boggs Collection, Historical Society of Pennsylvania, Philadelphia).

build for themselves a clientele and level of capitalization that made them establishments on the London model. A photograph of the second London Coffeehouse (1753) from the 1850s suggests the grandeur of the largest provincial houses of resort (see Plate 2). Located on the corner of Market and First Streets, its multistoried, heavily windowed facade overlooked the city waterfront. In scale and finish it equaled any coffeehouse and all but the largest coaching inns in the metropolis — a fact adverted to in its name. That "the London" called itself a coffeehouse, and not a tavern, meant that it ascribed to itself the gentility and commercial spirit that attached to coffeehouses of the imperial center. By the turn of the century, however, names were not all they portended. "Tavern" had lost its earlier associations with upper-class consumption, the serving of wine rather than ale and the exclusion of the tramping classes. "Coffeehouse" retained something of its Restoration luster, still calling to mind a space devoted to free conversation, sense, and sobriety. Nevertheless, coffeehouses in London, in the provinces, and in the colonies now served alcoholic beverages and differed little in the services offered from large taverns.[3]

In Chapter 2, we touched on the cultural situation of metropolitan coffeehouses, and here we may recover in detail the cultural associations they evoked for Americans and transatlantic clienteles. Foremost was the suggestion of imperial commerce. Coffee was an important commodity in that commerce, imported from Turkey. When retailed, it was advertised by symbols celebrating its foreign origins; it was a signal demonstration of the pleasures obtained by England's globe-girding enterprise. During the last half of the seventeenth century, the beverage identified merchants and mercantilism. The greatest concentration of coffeehouses in London surrounded the Exchange, and the association between the metropolitan bourse and the coffeehouse stuck in the provincial mind. Thus Charleston, New York, Annapolis, and Norfolk each boasted an Exchange Coffeehouse.[4]

The earliest London coffeehouses vended the "liquor of the urn" to the exclusion of other beverages. Specialization soon gave way to diversification as new establishments reckoned that they could attract more trade

3. An indication of the lubricity of the terms "tavern" and "coffeehouse" is shown by the Exchange Coffeehouse in Norfolk, which alternately advertised itself as a coffeehouse and a tavern in the *Virginia Gazette* during the early 1770s.

4. Boston had Luke Vardy's Royal Exchange Tavern, site of the first Freemasonic gatherings in the city.

PLATE 2 Second London Coffee House, Corner of Front and Market Streets, Philadelphia. *Photograph, 1857, as rebuilt in 1750s. Permission of the Historical Society of Pennsylvania, Philadelphia*

with variety. Garraway's Coffeehouse introduced Chinese green tea to the public in the decade after the Restoration. Thereafter the monopoly of temperance was largely overthrown, and wine and spirits were added to the bill of fare.

A host of pictorial and verbal representations of London's coffeehouses may be abstracted to form a general description of the better sort of establishment: one entered into a common room on the ground floor filled with circular tables seating from five to eight.[5] In some houses booths line the sidewalls. Although these boxes could be reserved, at the tables one took a seat at any available opening. An egalitarian spirit reigned in the common room, as the verse regulations at Pasqua Rosee's testify:

> First, gentry, tradesmen, all are welcome hither,
> And may without affront sit down together:
> Pre-eminence of place none here should mind,
> But take the next fit seat that he can find:
> Nor need any, if finer persons come,
> Rise up for to assign to them his room.[6]

This egalitarian spirit did not extend to the penniless, for a penny cover charge was exacted. While the charge putatively paid for candles and the many newspapers dispersed through the room, it served in effect to keep the indigent out-of-doors. Nor, for that matter, did it extend to women. The homosociality of the coffeehouse came to distinguish its society from that of the tavern (more on this later). Indeed, the appositives in the first line well defined the "all" found in the Restoration coffeehouse: "gentry" socialized with "tradesmen." The coffeehouse was the space in which men of the propertied classes socialized with men of the commercial classes.[7] Only within this composite community were the laws of precedence waived. The rule of first-come, first-served governed in the contest to secure the best seat (near the fireplace, or near the windows if one had a foppish fastidiousness concerning tobacco smoke). The coffee urn occu-

5. *The Coffee Scuffle* (1662), *A Cup of Coffee* (1663), *The Character of a Coffee-House* (1665), *News from the Coffe-House* (1667), and *The School of Politicks* (1690) were highlights of this often anonymous metropolitan literature.

6. Aytoun Ellis, *The Penny Universities: A History of the Coffee-Houses* (London, 1956), frontispiece.

7. A third group, not mentioned, also injected itself into the company: professional men. Coffeehouses became the offices of physicians and quacks and a space beyond the Inns of Court where lawyers might converse with the world.

pied a place in an inner room on the ground floor. Most coffeehouses had multiple stories, the rooms on the second floor standing at hire for special uses. There was usually a back kitchen. If the coffeehouse sold tipples as well as coffee and tea, they were dispensed from a caged enclosure abutting a wall on the ground floor.

Because of their favor in the eyes of merchants and tradesmen, coffeehouses early on became dispatch points for letters. The transatlantic network of coffeehouses became in effect the collection and dispersion centers for a postal system operated by ship captains. The houses sometimes contained a rack of boxes in which letters were received for regular patrons. Even the degenerate coffeehouse-taverns of mid-eighteenth-century British America banked on a reputation for being postal centers, places privy to the newest news. Commercial men throughout the century continued to frequent coffeehouses, though their popularity in London waned. The provincial cities each had at least one and as many as three major coffeehouse–commercial centers serving as satellites of that colony's exchange, as business premises or places of vendue. Persons involved in transatlantic trade knew the London coffeehouses associated with the affairs of each colony. The habitués of Carpenter's London Coffeehouse in Philadelphia would have known the conversation of the Pensilvania Coffeehouse in Birchin Lane during the eighteenth century. In the decade 1701–1710 London contained the following commercial coffeehouses serving the American trade: the Antegoe in Finch Lane, the Barbadoes and Jamaica in Water Lane, the Carolina in Birchin Lane, the New England in the Minories, the Virginia in Birchin Lane, and the Jamaica in St. Michael's Alley. As one would expect, most of these were clustered around the Exchange.[8]

The clientele of these metropolitan coffeehouses was the intended audience for certain American writings. John Cotton's "History of Bacon's and Ingram's Rebellion" (1680s) has long troubled commentators because of its political ambivalence and its burlesque of both sides of the rebellion. This indeterminacy becomes understandable when we realize that the manuscript was probably prepared for the delectation of a merchant company at the Virginia Coffeehouse, a company whose interests coincided with neither Governor Berkeley nor Nathaniel Bacon's rebels.[9] Throughout the

---

8. The standard historical register of the metropolitan establishments is Bryant Lillywhite, *London Coffee Houses: A Reference Book of Coffee Houses of the Seventeenth, Eighteenth, and Nineteenth Centuries* (London, 1963).

9. Jay B. Hubbell suggested that Cotton's manuscript was prepared for a readership

provincial period, American cosmopolitans possessed a firm sense of which coffeehouses offered which sorts of company. Governor Jonathan Belcher in 1732 admonished his son in London against spending too much time at the New England Coffeehouse: "The Temple Coffe House, Dick's, or the Rainbow wou'd be much more to your advantage." "At Tom's Coffe House you have polite company, but at the New England ordinary." The governor recommended that his son contribute to the wit of the polite company by reading classmate John Seccomb's burlesque, "Father Abbey's Will."[10]

A number of writings survive from British America that suggest that some provincial coffeehouses emulated Dick's and the Temple by projecting themselves as cultural centers — "penny universities" generating polite conversation, belles lettres, and natural philosophy as well as news. The Reverend Louis Rowe's Latin chain epigram, "A Prospect of Chess-Play and Chess-Players, at the Coffee House New York" (circa 1735), is an unusually striking evocation of that metropolitan ideal, showing politicians, church musicians, ministers, lawyers, ship captains, and schoolmasters engaged in the most challenging of intellectual games. Rowe began the piece with a complaint about the scene — the abundance of argument and gossip, and lack of serenity, the jocularity without seriousness, and the unceasing talk.

> Nimis multum Stridoris et Rumoris,
> Nimis Parum Silentii et Tranquillitatis.
>
> Nimis multum de Lusu et Otiis
> Nimis parum de Negotiis
>
> Nimis multum de Loquacitate
> Nimis parum de Taciturnitate.[11]

---

of noncolonials. He thought the piece was intended for publication or for manuscript circulation outside the colonies because of the finish of the fair copy. He did not explore the manner in which an implied metropolitan readership shaped the values or rhetoric of the production. "John and Ann Cotton, of 'Queen's Creek,' Virginia," *American Literature*, X (1938–1939), 200.

10. George T. Goodspeed, "Father Abbey's Will," Massachusetts Historical Society, *Proceedings*, LXXIII (1961), 26.

11. Rowe's is the final poem contained in the appendix to "Poems on Several Occasions By Archibald Home, Esqr., Late Secretary, and One of His Majestie's Council for the Province of New Jersey: North America," Laing Manuscripts, III, 452, University of Edinburgh Library. Rowe apparently prepared the epigram here for Governor William Cosby.

Here is a picture that accords closely to Ned Ward's portrait of the masculine bustle of London coffeehouses. An even more elaborate view of coffeehouse society can be had from incidental remarks in the records of the Homony Club of Annapolis, which met in the Annapolis Coffee House during the early 1770s (Chapter 7).

Coffeehouses in eighteenth-century America more often alluded to certain cultural ideals than manifested them. In Philadelphia, perhaps to curry favor among the more temperate of the Quakers, Henry Flowers in 1703 suspended the sale of alcoholic beverages at the city's coffeehouse (Carpenter's establishment under new ownership). This experiment in atavistic specialization did not last the decade but might have contributed to the Philadelphia Corporation's adopting the place as the seat of city government. While certain establishments, such as the French and the Exchange Coffeehouses in Charleston, the Tontine in Boston, and the New York in New York City, loomed large in the civic life of their localities, few manifested any clear-cut alternative to the world found in the larger sorts of tavern, particularly the "city taverns" that became popular after midcentury. When cities such as Philadelphia or Boston regulated price and vendibles by law, the ability of a coffeehouse to distinguish itself by quality of fare or drink or by the economic level of the clientele was somewhat hindered, since law tended to repress any increase of prices.[12] Coffeehouse and tavern at the turn of the century suffered from a legally mandated promiscuity of patronage. The imperial placemen and the market girl shared space at the bar. Because of the promiscuity of company and conversation in these spaces, how could any order — whether of sober manners or gentility — be imposed?

To quell Penn's anxiety about the influence of public houses, legislation was drafted restricting their hours of operation. It was directed that no resident of Philadelphia could remain at a public house "longer than one whole hour at one time . . . unless at a meeting of business."[13] A general

12. Boggs and Boggs, "Inns and Taverns," 156; Thompson, "A Social History of Philadelphia's Taverns," 134–136, 156. Penn attempted to legislate away the alehouse by requiring all public establishments to provide accommodation for four. In 1706 the failure of this policy was recognized, and the legislation was altered to recognize a two-tier business, roughly equivalent to the tavern-alehouse demarcation that Peter Clark showed as traditional in England. The question remains whether the impetus for the revision came from the desire to license a clandestine system of cheap drink houses to improve the revenue.

13. "Laws and Orders for the Keepers and Frequenters of Ordinaries," in Jean R.

closing time of 8:00 P.M. was mandated for all premises. In London there existed no restriction on the duration of a citizen's stay on premises, and the legal closing times were something of a joke (one thinks of Hogarth's *Morning* showing the late-night clientele of Tom King's Coffeehouse spilling out into Covent Garden square and disturbing the maids going to sunrise church services). At the turn of the century 6:00 P.M. marked the surge of evening activities in the metropolis. In the major port city of his proprietary Penn allowed only two hours of operation during the prime evening business period before shutting down services. After the turn of the century, Philadelphia's Quaker-controlled City Corporation oversaw the enforcement of the law with an aggressive constabulary. In 1701 Penn's anxiety about the connection of the tavern set with illegal trade prompted the Council to order that "all inkeepers and keepers of public houses and ordinaries give due notice of all strangers coming to their houses to some neighboring magistrates." Restrictions on operating hours were circumvented by merchants' conducting their business late in the evening — business upon which the welfare of Pennsylvania depended. Circumvention of the law gave way in 1703 to direct defiance of Quaker control over public life. That this opposition took place in 1703 instead of 1693 may be explained by the shift in the religious composition of the merchant community from an overwhelmingly Quaker one to one with a substantial Anglican and Presbyterian membership. The young gentry who had adopted Enoch Story's Tavern as their meeting place inaugurated a tavern war against the constabulary and the city corporation.[14]

What sparked the outbreak of hostilities cannot now be determined. Perhaps it was the Quaker constabulary's brandishing against the public diversions at Story's the Great Law:

> Whosoever shall introduce into the Province or frequent such rude and riotous sports as Prizes, Stage-plays, Masques, Revels, Bull-Baiting,

Soderlund, ed., *William Penn and the Founding of Pennsylvania, 1680–1684: A Documentary History* (Philadelphia, 1983), 206–207.

14. Gary B. Nash, "The Early Merchants of Philadelphia: The Formation and Disintegration of a Founding Elite," in Richard S. Dunn and Mary Maples Dunn, eds., *The World of William Penn* (Philadelphia, 1986), 337–362. Enoch Story's Tavern was located on the corner of Market and Front Streets, contiguous to the Pewter Platter Inn. Its proprietor, Enoch Story, was the son of New York merchant Robert Story, who died in 1683. His widowed mother Patience married Thomas Lloyd of Philadelphia, a member of the governing council of Pennsylvania.

Cockfightings, with such like, being convicted thereof, shall be reported and fined as breakers of the peace, and suffer at least ten day's imprisonment at hard labor in the House of Correction, or forfeit thirty shillings.

Sometime in 1703 the vagabond actor Tony Aston visited Story's but did not perform in Philadelphia as he had performed in Charleston and the West Indies.[15] The constabulary might have intervened to prevent Aston's performance. Shortly after the actor's removal to New York, the denizens of Story's provoked the Quaker constabulary. A company of young gentry, including Robert Grace and Henry Brooke, "scour'd" the streets, offending public peace. Brooke later described the "false humour of our giddy club" as "The Bread, the Watch, the Windows, Doors or Tub." If these jests approximated those of the London rakes depicted in Shadwell's 1690 comedy, *The Scowrers*, then the Philadelphia beaux amused themselves by tipping over bread carts, assaulting the watch, breaking the few glass windows in town, "dunging and rattling" doors, and rolling unsuspecting citizens about Philadelphia's muddy streets in a hogshead. One night in late August 1703, the club members after protracted drinking exited Story's and were seized in front of the neighboring Pewter Platter "for raising a great disturbance and riot in the city at the dead of night." The seizure would have political consequences, for Henry Brooke, the queen's customs collector at Lewes at the mouth of the Delaware River, was a partisan of the Church of England and a vocal critic of the Quaker-controlled Assembly's policy of nonsupport in the War of the Spanish Succession. He was also a friend of the newly appointed governor John Evans, an ex-army officer in his twenties whose martial career predisposed him to a contempt for Quaker nonsupport of the defense of the colony. On September 1, 1704, constable James Wood and watchman James Dough entered the tavern after a fight at Story's about Evans's initiatives in forming a militia. They rounded up most of the young gentry in the colony; among those detained

15. Anthony Aston, "A Sketch of the Life, etc. of . . . Tony Aston," in *Church Music and Musical Life in Pennsylvania in the Eighteenth Century*, Publications of the Pennsylvania Society of the Colonial Dames of America, IV, 3 vols. (Philadelphia, 1926–1947), III, 13. The memoir makes no mention of a performance in Philadelphia, whereas accounts of other towns visited note the nature and success of Aston's theatrical offerings. The editor's speculation (III, 92–96) about what Aston performed at Story's is entirely fanciful. In the wake of the 1701 prosecution of a costumed Boxing Day revel at John Simes's tavern, it is highly unlikely that Aston would have risked arrest. The editor's dating of Aston's appearance in November is also incorrect; he probably appeared in Philadelphia in early summer.

were Sheriff John Finney, scrivener Thomas Gray, Joseph Ralph, and Billy Penn, the son of proprietor William Penn. "It is charged that Mr. Penn called for pistols to pistol the complainants, but none were seen. The keeper of the Inn, Enoch Story, was of the party but gave no hand and is detained for witness."[16] (Young Penn felt such disgust with the treatment he received at the hands of his coreligionists that he threw over the Quaker faith and returned to England repudiating his father's utopia in the wilderness.)

Two months later watchman Solomon Cresson provoked the climactic battle of the tavern war by invading Story's after hours to break up a revel. Among the company of gentry was Governor Evans, who thrashed Cresson, at which point the entire City Corporation appeared (mayor, recorder, aldermen) to wage war. Many were injured, including Evans, in the melee.

Governor Evans exploited the political tensions by staging a hoax in collusion with Henry Brooke in Lewes and Colonel John French in Newcastle. Orchestrating a series of dispatches from various points from the mouth of the Delaware northward to Philadelphia, Evans created the impression that the Spanish had landed and were advancing on the Quaker capital. Evans hoped to panic the Assembly into funding a defense force. Though the ruse didn't work, it created a popular anxiety about security that would remain a challenge to the Quaker peace policy long after Evans left office. The hoax solidified a cosmopolitan opposition to David Lloyd's Quaker party and to the proprietary interest. It also brought to public notice the first champion of polite urbanity in Pennsylvania. Henry Brooke became the most eloquent opponent of the simplicities and austerities of Quakerism.

Henry Brooke: The Poet as Agent of Urbanity

Pennsylvania's first belletrist was a scion of the baronets of Norton Priory in Chester, England. Like many younger sons of the lesser nobility, he received the benefit of an education but no property. If we may credit Henry's epigram, "Mariage for money," the Brooke family was strapped for cash: "D[ick], P[usey] and H[enry], three pu'ny boys, / (The dwindled Race of fine Sir Harry) / Are fruits best worthy of the joys / of such as tens

16. John F. Watson, *Annals of Philadelphia, and of Pennsylvania in Olden Time . . .* , ed. Willis P. Hazard, 3 vols. (Philadelphia, 1881), I, 327. Such rioting, Shadwell makes clear, had political purport. Scowrers were often sons of the Tory nobility and gentry, disrupting an emerging Whig urban civility.

of thousands marry."[17] Henry chose not to follow the lead of his older brothers in chasing after heiresses. Taking a degree from Brasenose College, Oxford, in 1693, he enjoyed metropolitan life for a period before emigrating to Pennsylvania in 1702 in search of a sinecure. Brooke's hope was to be appointed customs collector for Philadelphia or, failing that, Newcastle in "the three lower counties" (present-day Delaware). James Logan, Penn's deputy, appreciated the young gentleman's abilities, but Brooke's Church of England religion prevented appointment to the Philadelphia post. Newcastle's position was already occupied. Logan could only offer the collectorship at Lewes at the mouth of the Delaware River. Brooke accepted, assuaging his love of society with frequent trips to and protracted stays in Newcastle and Philadelphia. He quickly became the premier wit in the tavern circles up and down the Delaware Valley. A poet, twelve of his thirty-five surviving works proclaimed their origin in this sociable world by bearing the superscription "writ in company."

Impromptu composition in company became a mark of wit in the sociable world during the 1670s. Toasts, epigrams, and bons mots were the principle species of impromptu wit that came into fashion in the English spas as adjuncts to the conversation between the sexes. *Tatler* no. 24 supplied a history of the toast, recounting its emergence at Bath as a means of complimenting a woman. Like a spiced piece of toast in one's cup, the compliment was supposed to flavor a bumper. A company of wits organized themselves into a mock-chivalric order, the Knights of the Toast, honoring a woman to be the toast for the season. The knights vied with one another at minting distichs epitomizing the beauties of their candidates until preeminent excellence won the assent of the company. Then the toast

---

17. Henry Brook of Norton ("Sir Harry") was made baronet in 1662. He married Mary Pusey of Nottinghamshire and sired three sons: Richard, his heir, Henry, and Pusey. All were born before 1666 according to the register found in George Ormerod, *The History of the County Palatine and City of Chester . . .* , 6 vols. (London, 1881), I, 681.

This account of Brooke revises my speculative biography offered in "Henry Brooke and the Situation of the First Belletrists in British America," *Early American Literature*, XXIII (1988), 4–27. I now believe that the birth date of 1676 for Brooke (supplied by his friend, the Reverend William Becket of Lewes Town) is several years too late, a product of an aging man's vanity. Figuring Henry's place in the genealogy of the baronets of Norton Priory is complicated by the fact that Richard and Henry are recurring names in every generation of the family. I have also reconceptualized my view of the literary and cultural situation of Brooke, after a few further years thinking about the society of the Delaware Valley during the earliest decades of the century.

was engraved on a glass with a diamond and the woman accorded the honor of the Knights' accolade. At the springs and in London's drawing rooms the epigram returned to vogue by jettisoning studied ingenuity and cultivating an air of spontaneity. Creation on the spur of the moment in the pitch of conversation gave an epigram greatest effect, or quick composition in company, often in the frame of a contest among wits to treat a subject, was a sign of parts. As Charles Gildon observed in *The Complete Art of Poetry*, epigram took in all subjects of the greater and lesser poetry — praise, dispraise, and persuasion. Its virtues were beauty, point, and brevity, the essentials of polite diction. Impromptu epigrams were so intimately linked with their fashion at the spas that they went by the designation "water poetry" (John Taylor, one of the early geniuses of the impromptu, earned the sobriquet "the water poet").[18] More significant to our inquiry, the inaugural figures of British American belles lettres — the persons who adopted the polite mode from 1695 to 1705 and brought it to the New World — received their poetic baptism in the waters of the spas. William Byrd, "the first gentleman of Virginia," earned his laurels as a wit fashioning epigrams to the beauties of Tunbridge Wells. The Reverend Benjamin Colman, the single figure who marks the turn toward elegance in New England letters, traded epigrams with polite Christian ladies at Bath. Henry Brooke made his poetic task the reformation of the tavern's profane talk into a semblance of the polite wit of spa society.

Brooke's project was fraught with difficulty. In the masculine society of the tavern rooms conversation suffered from the degeneration of political debate into malediction, the debasement of wit into profane jest, and the reduction of talk into commercial negotiation. Brooke recognized the difficulty of reforming political debate, because he was no stranger to party passion. Yet he realized that the public spirit ultimately suffered when party loyalty stifled thought or when political debate became a duel of curses and hurrahs. Brooke injected thought into controversy by coining political epigrams. The piquancy that poetic wit bestowed on political critique may be judged by reading "On P: Painted in Armor and a Scarfe," an impromptu upon the most famous of William Penn's portraits, showing him at age twenty-two dressed in military gear:

18. Charles Gildon, *The Complete Art of Poetry*, 2 vols. (London, 1718), I, 150. Taylor's works were collected under the title *Aque-Musae: All the Workes of John Taylor the Water-Poet* (London, 1630).

Armo'r and Scarfe on P appear
As meant to guard him from his fear;
In vain the Painter try'd this Art.
The fears lye, under at his heart.[19]

The epigram performed on several levels: aesthetically, it asserted the superiority of poetry over painting in adducing truth. Painting represented surfaces; poetry revealed depths. The portrait operated only at the level of description; the epigram, at the level of interpretation. The poem interpreted Penn theologically, calling into question the Quaker doctrine that peace and solace were manifested internally by the spirit. Poetry illuminated Penn's interior and found fear in the heart, not an inner light of assurance. The military surface Penn displayed belied the inner turmoil. A psychological history was suggested: Penn in his youth imitated his father, Admiral Sir William Penn, in his externalization of conflict and aggression. But the enemy lurked within, and Penn turned away from his father's vocation. According to Brooke, Quakerism maintained a surface pacifism by transporting all conflict into the human interior; the heart became the battleground. Politically, the Quaker rendering of all conflict psychospiritual was objectionable to the extent that people were threatened by real, external enemies. When Governor Evans attempted to secure an appropriation for the military defense of the colony, in accord with crown and proprietary instructions, Quaker David Lloyd blocked the legislation and all attempts at gaining revenue. Lloyd indited a remonstrance designed to stir Quakers in England against the proprietor.[20] Thus, Penn was to discover his principal political enemies among those of "like heart," the "Friends" in Philadelphia — an irony that James Logan, Penn's secretary, drew to the proprietor's attention repeatedly in their official correspondence. In four brief lines Brooke revealed the abundance of meaning that eloquence could lend to complaint.

Not everyone in the tavern world possessed the ingenuity to appreciate Brooke's eloquence. Understanding the epigram depended on a knowledge of current politics, Quaker theology, and the aesthetic claims ad-

19. "On P: Painted in Armor and a Scarfe," 9. All of Brooke's poems quoted herein are taken from the MS collection, Commonplace Book, Peters Collection, Historical Society of Pennsylvania.

20. Roy N. Lokken, *David Lloyd: A Colonial Lawmaker* (Seattle, Wash., 1959), 133–161.

PLATE 3 William Penn in Armor. *Oil, artist unknown. England, 1660s. Permission of the Historical Society of Pennsylvania, Philadelphia*

vanced by the sister arts. Epigrams were, of course, a challenge to the wit of the hearer; but Brooke's epigram posed a challenge that only the most accomplished in the tavern world were prepared to meet. Yet it was precisely the elite, in Brooke's eyes, who stood in need of reformation. As a participant in the tavern war with others of the young gentry of the province, Brooke had contributed to the degradation of politics in Philadel-phia.[21] After 1704 Brooke repented his circle's scowring of the town and sought to turn his friends from the violence of their actions and profanity of their expressions. To this end he exploited the permissions extended by friendship to address certain of them individually, using the Horatian epis-tle as a prototype for candid, free expression. In 1705 he directed a verse letter to his club companion, Robert Grace, entitled "A Discourse upon Je'sting attempted in the way of Horace."[22] Brooke's task was to reclaim wit from jest. The difficulty of his task lay in the power of jest to satisfy the *sensus communis* of tavern society. Shaftesbury in *Sensus Communis* had observed that shared laughter established a firmer community of interest than any based on law or doctrine, for it proceeded from the free and voluntary coalescence of subjectivity. The jest, an expression capable of giving rise to laughter, possessed the power to call a society into being. In Brooke's eyes the danger of jest lay in the volatility of the community it created, for in jest liberty of expression became libertinism at worst or whimsicality at best. Jests created momentary diversions, whereas wit re-vealed a durable common sense among persons. Brooke's allegiance to wit required that he repudiate the means (libertine practical jokes — that is, jests) employed by his circle in the war against the city corporation:

A Discourse upon Je'sting attempted
in the way of Horace. —

I Prithee Bob! forbear; or if thou must
Be talking stil, yet talk not as thou do'st;
More matter; or less sound; for I protest
Against thy darling bosome Sin, a Jeast. —
Believe me, 'tis a fond pretence to Wit
To say what's forc'd, unnatural, unfit;
Frigid, illtimed, absurd, rude, petulant;
'Tis so, you cry, all this I freely grant:
Yet such were those smart turns of Conversation,

21. In this regard, the riot of Brooke's circle is descended from the upper-class agitation of the tory scowerers.

22. This is the sole text of Brooke's that survives in more than one copy. The second copy, "A Discourse upon Je'sting Attempt in the Way of Horace" is found in case 19, box 18, MS Collections, Historical Society of Pennsylvania. It seems to have circulated in more than one state, since a fair amount of textual variation is found between the copies.

When, late, our Kentish Friends, in awkward Fashion,   [10]
E'en burst with joy and I with Indignation. —
Oh how I loath that time! All all that past,
When fools or mad we scourd the City last;
All the false humo'r of our giddy Club,
The Bread, the Watch, the Windows, Doors or Tub;   {the Instruments
Or rageing Youth, that urg'd the' estravagance,   of so many
Or Easiness; the Bubble's Complaisance; —   silly Frolicks
These, tho' my Hate: (and these God knows, I hate,
Much more than Jones, or Story do debate;   {two squabbling
More than All shapes of Faction, Corporation,   disputative
Remonstrances, a Whig-and-Tory-Nation —   Quakers
Reviews, or Churches, in or out of fashion —
Examiners, Rehearsals, Observators;
Or Truborn Daniels unpoetic Satyrs,)   {The City officers
From wines inchanting pow'r derive excuse;   were (at that time)
But for a Man unpoison'd with the Juyce,   very rude and
T'indulge, whole precious days, in pun and prate;   impertinent
And sell rich Time at such an under Rate: to Strangers
This hath no show, no colour of defence,   and the Assembly
And wants so of wit, it fails of Comon-Sence.   had publish'd a
                                                      most odious Remon-
                                                      strance against a
                                                      worthy Governor

For Wit, My Friend — but you regard not me,
Regard our Dryden then; True Wit (says He)
Is true propriety of Sense and Words:
How litle to a Je'st this Rule affords:
Propriety of Sense is where a Tho'ght
Of Nature is a just, and faithful Draught;
Of Words, where with the tho'ght they so agree,
As fully to convey anothers Sense to me.
These are the sum of Wit: and mingle then
If due regard be had to How, and When;   [40]
To what, where, whome; by these directions steer,
By these, in time you'l speak, in time forbear.

Thus Dryden taught; and, as he taught, he Wrote;
Well chosen were his words, and just his tho'ght:
Yet, even this Dryden, once, a Gomez drew
A merry je'sting Soul, that talks like you
He's rob'd, he je'sts; Is cuckolded, jests on,   H. Brooke

Drag'd from his house by Ruffians; 'tis all one
Stil Gomez je'sts; He's sworn into a Plot;
A Good conceit must never be forgot: [50]
He's try'd, his death is counsel'd by the Priest: {the Spanish
What do's me Gomez then? e'en breaks his Je'st.   Fryer

But some may say, By'r favor, Knowing Sir!
Is this Old Gomez, this his character,
Gomez, the wealthy jealous Usurer?
Yes Gomez Sir! that wealthy jealous One
Is, to all that, A trifling rank Buffone. —

And what d'you think mislead a Wit so right?
Lured by some gay Conundrums treacherous light,
He struck upon your fatal rock; and strait,   [60]
The Poet sunk, to heighten the Conceit. —

But wou'd you learn the art of speaking well?
Read Congreve too, Consider Mirabel.
Why Mirabel has Je'sts! He has (I grant)
But they'r on Witwoud, stil, or Petulant;
And, yet, that Witwoud, give the man his due,
And Petulant, Je'st full as well as you.
Witwoud — the name's significant, beware;
And Petulant — ah shun the character.
But Mirabel instructs as he inveighs,   [70]
Gives beauty and a weight to all he says;
Starlike, he shines with native lasting light:
While, those, like meteors, skip before our sight;
Now they blaze out, and now again, 'tis Night.
Oh were that flowing courtly turn, aswel
Perused by him, as Easy! Mirabel   {Sir Charles Easy in
Wou'd, in all shining quality's Exell. —   Careless husband

By this True wit's distinguish'd from a Jest:
That must be lasting, and abide the Test
Of coming Ages; this a short-lived tho'ght   [80]
By Rodeney laughd at, and as soon forgot.   {the name of the
                                                         Gentleman at
And if you mind, a thing thats said with Art   whose house I
Convey's a calmer joy thro' e'ery part,   pas'd three days
Dilates the bosome, chear's the Vital Flood,   with my friend Bob

And heard again, and yet again, is Good;
But scarce provokes to laugh: yet that's the best
The brightest charme of your bewitching J'est;
Now 'tis discharg'd, and now, all voices chime
In clamorous joys; but that too fleeting Prime
Once o'er: it half offends the second time.   [90]
Thus tickling puts us in the laughing veine
But, if continued, changes that to paine;
While Gentle Hymens strong, yet serious play,
Tho' sighs, not smiles, the full content betray,
Gives solid joy's that but with life decay. —

But least my Rules fall short, or over-reach,
Turn we to Men, and let example teach.

Behold that Roof; beneath whose happy Square,
Lelius and Varro, an Immortal Paire,
By living Rules the neighbouring Youth refine;   [100]
Th' illustrious Patterns of this faint Designe.
Lelius and Varro: Two the brightest Stars
That Gild the Globe of Learnings Hemispheres.

Read them, as that has Men, this Books has read,
And follow in the glorious Path they lead.
Blest Path! the Guide to that eternal Spring
Where Learning and Goodsence in joyful Consort sing;
Blest Guides to all those sacred arts, that can
Make the good Scholar, or fine Gentleman.
Thou teachest to think well, to speak with ease,   [110]
And, that as useful art, To hold ones peace.
Thou teachest what's too litle, what enough;
How to begin, continue, and break off;
Hence, nothing comes from These that wounds the Ear;
For what is fit to speak, is fit to hear:
No cold insipid je'sts escape from These;
But Truths welldres'd, that both instruct, and please. —

Read them, and learn, by reading what you want,
That needful truth that Man's an Ignorant
(For stil the more our Understanding clears,   [120]
So stil the more our Ignorance appears.)

This Truth will teach you shame, humility,
Cando'r, goodnature, conscious modesty;
All med'cines for the Jesting-malady.

Dare to be Wise, let je'sts be Firmins Fame;   {an Old Punster
Erect your Mind; persue a nobler aime;
In short be your own Contrary: — and then,
You'l know what's to be Man, and how to live with Men.

Brooke's conflation of jesting with scouring, and his linkage of both to other things lacking "colour of defence" — faction, fashionable religion, and partisan periodicals — communicate the weight of his displeasure with the practice. The principal charge laid against jesting, however, is its abuse of time, not its cruelty, vulgarity, or triviality. The importance attached to "rich Time" is conveyed by the pointedness of the rhetoric, for the poet dresses the matter in the language of commerce, the species of talk in which value most inheres for a merchant such as Robert Grace: "sell rich Time at such an under Rate." The point is not that time is money, but that true wit, like common sense, is not simply for the moment. It must "abide the Test of coming Ages." Besides being repeatable and long-lived, wit must present an apposite and sufficient picture of nature in language. Citing Dryden, Brooke asserted the rule that wit must possess a mimetic propriety, "where a Tho'ght of Nature is a just, and faithful Draught." Jest, besides being the sort of humor that exhausts itself upon recitation, fails the test of mimetic propriety to the extent that it (1) evades the issue of mimesis by taking the form of a practical joke, or (2) violates it by resorting to puns, or (3) violates it by employing non sequitur.

Having admonished his friend by precept, Brooke presented positive and negative examples drawn from literature. Brooke recalled the character of Gomez in Dryden's *Spanish Fryar* as an instance of "a merry je'sting soul, that talks like You." This character suffers a bad fate while he "jests on." As a witty paragon Brooke enlists that most quotable and polite of characters, Mirabell. He "instructs as he inveighs, / Gives beauty and a weight to all he says." The instruction that Mirabell conveys is not moral; rather, like Brooke's instruction to Grace, it elucidates manners and taste.

Brooke's rhetorical strategy was well tuned to his audience. Politically, citing plays as paradigms of good manners asserted a sensus communis in opposition to the Quaker ethic of simplicity. The Quaker-inspired Great Law proscribed the theater as a pernicious influence on the public. Thus the politeness that Brooke wished to inject into the profane sociability of his companions did not surrender its sense of opposition to Quaker civic moralism. Whether plays had the interest of the forbidden or the charm of metropolitan fashion for Brooke's audience, they opened up a range of possibilities regarding roles. Brooke's argument testified to the power of metropolitan culture over the imaginations of a provincial elite attempting to settle on a mode of self-expression. At the end of "A Discourse upon Je'sting" Brooke affirmed that provincials could realize a self-ennobling transformation, by citing the characters of Lelius and Varro (Judge Mompesson and James Logan?) who

> By living Rules the neighbouring Youth refine;
> Th' illustrious Patterns of this faint Designe.

The importance of learning in qualifying Lelius and Varro as "illustrious Patterns" raises the questions, What is learning in the polite world, and, What is one supposed to learn? The former question can be answered directly: learning is that part of human discourse that bears repetition in perpetuity because of its truth. What Robert Grace has to learn, as the final line of the epistle declares, is how "to be a Man, and how to live with Men." Learning's truth gives an understanding of the self-limitation entailed in living in community, for "this truth will teach you shame, Humility, Cando'r, goodnature, conscious Modesty."

We must now remark some of the tensions that render Brooke's argument dynamic. Although his goal was to reform the conversation and action of a friend in the tavern world, his promotion of learning and the examples found in literary characterization injected the instruction of the print world into a local scene of living speech. While invoking the permissions of friendship, Brooke did not employ the most intimate form of persuasion, a heart-to-heart talk, to couch his admonition; rather, it was written with a focus sufficiently generalized that it might have an interest beyond its stated audience. Like the popular literature on the government of the tongue and like much of the belles lettres espousing polite sociability, Brooke's poem put literature in the service of future oral communication.[23] Yet, if wit truly was manifested in repeatability and discovered in the longevity of expression, was not writing, man's artificial memory, the aptest vehicle for wit, and was not the printed text, which combines writing's durability with multiplicity, a more rigorous test of wit's vivacity than repeating bons mots in the tavern common room?

23. For instance, [Cotton Mather], *A Christian Conversing . . .* ([Boston], 1709).

For Brooke the problem of the printed text was its indeterminacy of audience. The poet wished to transform the conversation of a particular set of people, the elite company he kept in the cities along the Delaware River. Brooke's resolution of the tension between the evanescence of conversation and the impersonal obduracy of print was to resort to manuscript communication. In private society the manuscript proved entirely serviceable to the task at hand — to provide a record of the spontaneous inspirations Brooke had "in company" or to script a performance in the clubroom and eventually to memorialize his part in the installation of belles lettres in Pennsylvania. In 1727, when copying out a collection of his works for the benefit of Varro (James Logan?), Brooke penned "A Dedication Designed to a Private Friend," testifying to the exclusive notice to which his art aspired:

> When I dye, as in short time I must,
> And moulder wth vile worms and roots to dust,
> My Name embalm'd in pure Castalian dew
> Shall live indear'd to the less Captious Few:
> At least, as are my fondest hopes, to you.

Brooke was not much removed in time or attitude from the court literary culture in which the manuscript was the privileged means of communication, capable of procuring immediate reputation and even immortality. The aristocratic disregard for print displayed by a Rochester or a Waller remained in force after the eclipse of the court by the club culture in the metropolis and the provinces.[24] The genius for profanation demonstrated by the Grub Street authors who served the press and wrote for the captious multitude did not impart a Castilian purity to the printed page. Indeed, the maledictive aura surrounding the products of the English press did not disperse until the final years of Queen Anne's reign, when the *London Spy* was supplanted by the *Spectator* as the monitor of metropolitan mores. Brooke embraced his poetic vocation at the turn of the century, when the press still labored under a vile reputation. Although Brooke's ample library attested to a reverence for the book, he, like Swift, was convinced that a historical turn had taken place, turning the press into the engine driving the declension of English letters. In Pennsylvania the muse the press served was a provincial replica of the hackneyed muse of Grub Street; only

24. For an analysis of the views of courtiers toward print, see Arthur F. Marotti, *Manuscript, Print, and the English Renaissance Lyric* (Ithaca, N.Y., 1995).

the "unpoetic Satyrs" of the almanac maker Daniel Leeds ("Trueborn Daniel") or Jacob Taylor were distributed.[25]

Brooke's nonchalance about the effect of the metropolitan print culture upon his literary immortality persisted until the advent of Alexander Pope, the figure around whom the London booksellers built the print culture of literary celebrity. Pope's celebrity commenced with *An Essay on Criticism* (1711) and grew with *Windsor-Forest: To the Right Honourable George Lord Landsdown* (1713) and *The Rape of the Lock* (1714). By 1717, he, at age twenty-nine, had sufficient eminence to warrant publication of *The Works of Mr. Alexander Pope.* Brooke recognized in Pope a phenomenon unprecedented in the world of letters, a figure whose centrality, reinforced by the metropolitan privilege of Britain's mercantile empire, had become so concentrated that he threatened to render all other writers mortal in the lists of fame and all other writings peripheral beyond mere provinciality. Like James Kirkpatrick in Charleston and Mather Byles in Boston, Brooke assuaged his anxieties about his place in the realm of letters by pledging his allegience to Pope and all he symbolized.[26]

On Reading Mr. Popes Homer. 1725.26

Eustathius, both Dacier's, Spondamus Thou[27]
With learn'd Remarks compel us to allow
The Poets Crown yet due to Homers Brow
Thou cheifly Pope (who to thy Countreys Fame)
Hast in thy English so preservd his Flame,
So painted every strong, or graceful Part,
So trac'd each speaking Figures wondrous Art,

25. One of the curious literary survivals of the earliest stage of Philadelphia's literary culture is a systematic satire of the literary abilities of the city's almanac makers, "The Diarist," Norris Commonplace Book, H.M. 164, Henry E. Huntington Library, San Marino, Calif. It might have been written by Joseph Norris, or perhaps Elizabeth Magawley as part 2 of "The Wits and Poets of Pennsylvania." It was published in *Leeds Almanac for 1735*, the sole copy of which is missing its title page and is mislabeled as being from 1733 in the New-York Historical Society. J. A. Leo Lemay discovered this item.

26. Austin Warren, "To Mr. Pope: Epistles from America," Modern Language Association of America, *Publications*, XLVIII (1933), 61–73.

27. Eustathius (fl. 1175–1200), archbishop of Thessalonica, was a renowned editor and commentator on Homer. The two Daciers were the classicists André and Anne Dacier; her translations of Homer into French were acclaimed. Jean de Sponde also produced an edition of Homer.

Each speaking Sound, (so full thy Numbers roll,
So warm thy Colours glow, so breaths the Whole)
As if that Poets Muse inspire thy Soul.
Sure no presuming Critic more will boast
Of Modern Bards, and Homer's glory lost;
(As Wotton saves, and plodding Bentley dreams
Mislead by vain Peraults mistaken Schemes.)
But taught by thee confess that rhyming Choir
So feebly squeak oppos'd to Homer's Lyre
That Priams Sages humbler notes as well
May be compared to Stentors loudest Yell;
Or Mars's bellowings at their utmost swell;
As well may Saccharissa's ribbon share
In Fame with that bright Zone, the Paphian Fair
Lent, with resistless charms the Queen of Air:
As well, may Hero's of the Modern Line
Hector, in strength, or Thetis Son outshine.

Brooke's is a poem about the means by which poetry lives. Set against the backdrop of the quarrel of ancients and moderns, the poem denies the efficacy of the attempt by Richard Bentley and the other academic partisans against the ancients to vivify the classic epic by means of scholarship. Their efforts simply confirm the eclipse of "Homer's glory." Only by a renovating reproclamation in the language of modern poetry can "Homer's Lyre" resound. Pope's reproclamation fused past with present, so that no "presuming Critic" could elevate the modern at the expense of the ancient. Pope's imitation resembled an act of poetic metempsychosis, assuming the genius of Homer, "As if that Poets Muse inspire thy Soul." Brooke's "As if" shows his sensitivity to the conditions that pertained in poetic immortality. The modern was not eradicated in the reproclamation of poetry—Helen's beauty is known in tension with the beauty of the modern paragon, Waller's Saccharissa. On the other hand, Pope's art shone with an atavistic glory that Homer's Lyre and Homer's Muse ignited. In sum, Homer's immortality was maintained by modern Pope. The immortality of poetry was revealed by ancient Homer. The power of Pope's language to vivify art was attested by Brooke in his imitation of the master's style.

For Brooke, Pope reigned as the master of modern letters, not because he was the main cog in the engine of the new print market, but, rather, because he possessed the greatest power to keep poetry alive. This power arose because Pope's English most eloquently articulated the beauty and force of the modern. If wit was, as Brooke insisted, that which was revealed in its repeatability, art gave the creations of wit sufficient eloquence to refresh a work with each subsequent experience of it. Pope revealed modern eloquence.

To claim that originality in subject matter held only modest importance in neoclassical aesthetics is to repeat a critical commonplace. To call attention to the extraordinary power accorded eloquence in poetic imitation, however, is to make a historical point that deserves repeating. The act of dressing a familiar subject matter in the most effective language available to the moment becomes the deed whereby a poet manifests mastery. For Brooke the exercise of this mastery was involved with his project to reform the conversation of the tavern world, redeeming talk from a mundane discussion of business. His poetic masterwork was an artistic retelling of a merchant's tale about a commercial debacle — a story that enjoyed currency at Story's in 1702. "The New Metamorphosis; or, Fable of the Bald Eagle" showed the path from mercantile tavern talk through politeness to art.

Tavern Talk Transfigured

Henry Brooke's services to British American literature would not be worth recalling if he were simply the literary equivalent of a provincial dancing master, an agent of civility teaching the tavern crowd to be polite. Nor would he demand attention if he were simply another neo-Roman acolyte to the muse of empire. But Brooke was a poet, a master of eloquence who could resolve the contradictions of his situation into art. "The New Metamorphosis" revealed the tension pervading Britain's commercial empire as no other work except Ebenezer Cooke's "Sot-Weed Factor" did. Like Cooke's poem, "The New Metamorphosis" was a doggerel tale about a greenhorn tobacco merchant's failed business venture. Unlike Cooke's poem, Brooke's ballad did not burlesque metropolitan legends about the degeneracy of the New World. Rather, it mocked the motives of British enterprise. Though an agent of Britain's commercial empire, Brooke knew the denizens of the London Coffeehouse, the Blue Anchor, and Story's too well to pay lip service to the mystique that patriot authors were creating about the English sea empire and its hero, the British merchant. The chauvinism of the imperial poetry prompted by the Anglo-Dutch wars and the proclamations about England's fated rise to commercial preeminence featured in books like John Evelyn's *Navigation and Commerce: Their Origin and Progress* (1674) ill suited the agents and sotweed factors at Story's Tavern (those persons whom Penn suspected of involvement with clandestine commerce).[28] One British hero provided the subject of Brooke's ballad.

> A Young Merchant by name Michael, but ordinarily call'd Michy by his Father, (a Leather dresser in Southwark) who I found at Philadelphia the Year of my Arrival; Having from his first sally to America, carried nothing home with him, but a bald Eagle, Had form'd that Adventure into a formal Tale, adorn'd with as many humerous incidents as his wit could devise: particularly, that of the wonder and big expectations of the women of the neighbourhood, when they saw him alight at his Fathers) Which, he never faild to tell over, as of't as a Stranger came into Company. After the twentieth hearing, or thereabts, I, one night proposed to have it turn'd into Verse; to refresh, by novelty of that a good story, almost stale, with often repeating; which, being accepted, on condition I undertake it; was the first Rise, and (I beg) may Excuse, of the foregoing Fable without a Moral.

Brooke's note certified that "The New Metamorphosis" was not a satire designed by a customs officer to ridicule traders; rather, the ballad rendered poetic a merchant's antiheroic self-understanding. By redefining mockery as self-mockery, the note underscored the tension between the grandiosity of metropolitan fantasy about what trade would bring and the self-deprecation of the person to whom the fantasy attached. The women of Southwark might have viewed the returning Michael as the conquistador of commerce, but Michael knew himself to be Michy who botched the deal and brought home the bird.

If indeed "The New Metamorphosis" originated in an oral tavern tale, then the poet so transmuted the tale as to be recognizable only on the most primitive level, that of incident. Narration, the sine qua non of fable, was displaced in Brooke's travesty. "He's gone; he's return'd (for his errand is not, / Or at least, the most part, any part of the Plot)" (57–58). By dispensing entirely with the story of Michy's enterprise in the New World, Brooke prevented the heroic rhetoric of the Virgilian quest from attaching to his representations. The antiepic drew attention to the epic's dependence on

28. For the creation of the literary mystique about commerce, see Margaret Anne Doody, *The Daring Muse: Augustan Poetry Reconsidered* (Cambridge, 1985), 281–285.

the machinery of narration, particularly the linkages of virtuous action and reward. In Virgil's place, Brooke substituted Ovid as a precursor. The substitution marked the poet's aesthetic acuity. In Ovid's *Metamorphoses* the schemes of reward and punishment are absurd. Arbitrary gods inflict extravagant changes upon humans disproportionate to transgressions. The inexplicability of supernal justice was repeatedly brought to the fore in the strange mutations wrought upon persons and things. In the human sphere irrationality reigns; whimsical emotion prompts persons to actions calling down the gods' incomprehensible justice. The supernatural derangement of schemes of reward and punishment puts commonsensical notions of causality into doubt.[29]

Common sense in the commercial world holds that enterprise will produce profit. When this expectation is inflated to a heroic scale, it becomes so extravagant that it transforms the enterpriser. America would be the alembic in which the base metal of an artisan's son would be transmuted into the gold of a merchant prince (the eagle perched on the returning Michy's arms is the emblem of royalty). Brooke burlesqued the expectations of greatness that prompted green youths to leave the towns of Britain to seek wealth and fame in the colonies. The argument of the travesty is baldly stated:

The New Metamorphosis
or
Fable of the Bald Eagle

THE ARGUMENT

Michy, the Hero of my Rhyme
Sent to the Golden World, to trade,
All spent and gone, Returns in time,
With a Bald Eagle, to his Dad.
The Neighbo'rs big wth expectation,
In shoals attend the Rareeshow.

All You of the West, No'th, Eastward, or South,
Who Gape, for a Ballad, at eye ear and mouth,

29. Brooks Otis, *Ovid as an Epic Poet* (Cambridge, 1970), anatomizes the antiepic elements of the *Metamorphoses* and speculates on their influence on Western intellectual history.

Open all, to a tale told a thousand times o'er,
But never adorn'd with gay Dogrel before.

In Southwark, renown'd for those eminent Schools
Of faith and good pay the Kingsbench and the Rules,
A darksome old Shed, now on crutches for Age
Held the reverend head of Peltander the Sage.
Long time this old Sire in the liberal Arts
Of scraping and saving exerted his parts   [10]
And each night in good straw, threw himself and his care
On the fleabitten breast of Membrana the Fair.
With tumbling together and heaven knows what,
A thing on two legs, call'd a Son, was begot.
So taper and small that some Authors protest
He wrigled his way from his Mother's right breast
But whether 'twas so, or the commoner way
Or, as one, from Ear, it beho'ves not to say
For us 'tis enough that the day he came out
He dress'd leather, told money, got drunk and what not   [20]
As indeed was it fit that one born to such feats
Shou'd ignobly be swath'd or lose time at the teats?
Besides it agrees not with what we're adoing
To suffer our Hero be too long agrowing.
This Worthy high Michy, a name so compleat
So fit, so fullmouth'd, so Heroick, and great,
That Pyrgopolinices, Bombardomachides
Orgoglio Pantagruel Roland Alcides
With all the tall Huffers that ever were written
To Michy compared are but names for a kitten   [30]
I'm amaz'd the dull writers neglected so long
A Name so well turn'd for Heroical Song;
But blest be the Muses it so was forgot,
And blest o'er and o'er that it falls to my lot;
Inspired, I scarce bear its impetuous sway,
And a Writer so help'd, what cannot he say.
And oh! had You seen, at a pun or a jeer
How he darted his tongue with an amorous leer,
Stretch'd his cheeks to a Cubit, and twinkled his eyes,
With me, you'd pronouce him as lovely, as Wise. —   [40]

Now so it fell out, by I know not what shifts
That Mich' gave his Daddy such hopes of his gifts
That all the gay gold he cou'd e'er rap or rend
With Michy to Sea for a venture he'll send
And having himself, with nineteen of his kin
To raise twenty good pounds pawn'd all to the skin;
And, withal, taken up, at unspeakable charge,
A Hopsellers coat of a sadcolourd serge,
With a gay Calimanco, the best you may swear
That Norwich cou'd boast, for 'twas made by the Mayor,   [50]
For a holyday vest; a special gray felt,
And ratling new breeks of an old weathers pelt,
A groat for the fob, woolen hose, russet shoen.
And dropping some tears for his gold, or his Son:
Brave Michy's cal'd in, he appear's, is made fine,
Scrapes a leg, goes abo'rd, and away for the Line. —

He's gone; he's return'd (for his errand is not,
Or at least, the most part, any part of the Plot)
He's ashoar, nobly mounted on that very beast   } He realy bought
He bought by the pound; a notable jeast!   a lean jade at 6s
They that ask, may be told it some leagues to the West. 4d and had
                                                          a very hard
                                                          bargain. —

But Michy draws near, and now 'ery Friend
May expect his approach at Southwark townsend:
The Streets are all lined with the Bands, as 'tis said,
Not those of the City, the Orange, or Red;
But those of the Rules, the Mint, the Kingsbench,
Kent-Street, Pickle-herring; the devil a Wench
That cry's my fresh Oysters, brooms, matches, or dill,
But see jolly Mich had a hearty good will.
Away then, in shoals — when lo! as they wish'd,   [70]
He enters in pomp, with a Bird on his fist.
Ah Sirs! if you're Wise, take example this day,
Fit out the Young Urchins, and pack 'em to Sea:
[See] there what comes on't. Why Michy! why Sirrah!
[I kn]ew You the dirtiest rogue in the Burrough;
Oh [———] how his Voyage has [———]
How the Young Knave is chang'd? why H'as got a clean [shirt]
My Watty for farthings must trudge with a link,

Had I sent him to Sea — I know what I think;
Here! Michy returns so rich and so fat, [80]
'Tis like he's too proud to take notice of Wat.
Who'd ha' thought twenty shillings so much cou'd ha' done?
Had I known't, I shou'd e'en ha' kept mine for my Son.
But bles'd be the loins that so richly were stow'd,
And happy the tripe that once held the dear load!
With joy my heart swels (like the Mother's) to think, —
When the bags are turn'd up, how the money will chink.
Oh Lud! what a glittering heap We shall see!
Alass my dear Watty! is none of't for thee?
Then the Bird, ay the bird, what a stately choice thing! [90]
To be sure tis for no less a man than the King. —
But thereby hangs a tale — for that bird is the glory,
The flow'r, and the cream, and the Gem of my story;
Not hatch'd from an Egg, but in fashion so strange
That not Ovid himself hath so wondrous a change.
Then, while the Young Knight's by the Rabble's adored,
Let's withdraw from his joy's, and inquire of the Bird. —

Now Mich was arrived at Antigua, Jamaica
Barbado's, Bermude, or the Lands of Tobaco,
And had frugaly laid his twenty good pounds [100]
In the best Oroonoke on American grounds;
His market soon made, and about to turn home,
He wash'd down his cares in all-sovereign Rum.
Night came, and 'twas time to retire to his lodging,
When lo! as Young Michy was thitherward trudg'ing
A Minion of Venus presents in his way,
And Michy was frail, and consent to stray;
But time and the place and the sum were agreed,
And my Gallant had all his affections cou'd need;
But his Mistress (poor heart) for demanding her pay, [110]
Was dismis'd, with a kick, and my Spark slunk away. —
Enraged with her wrongs, and dissolving in tears;
To Venus her Goddes, she offered these prayr's. —

Oh thou! that from Cyprian Idalium, or Paphos,
Art charm'd by our sorrows, and haste: thee to save us!
Oh thou! to whose great and mysterious Rites

We devote all our thoughts our days, and our nights,
Thou! from whom thy inspired learn that speech of the Eye
That appoints where and when, tho' the husband be by;
To talk love upon fingers, to tread without noise,   [120]
Bribe hinges and locks that they blab not our joys;
In vain do'st thou teach, in vain do we serve,
Thy bounties are scorn'd, and thy Preistesses starve.
Young Michy tho' wanton voluptuous and strong, —
— But what need of telling a Goddes my wrong?
Thou knows't all my griefs, oh some succour dispense!
And teach the bold Atheist to know his offence. —
So may thy realms flourish, new votaries rise,
And thy Altars stil glow with the last Sacrifice. —
She said, she was heard — and the Goddess exprest   [130]
In Oracular wise how she lik'd her request:
A fierce Bird of prey shall the preyer chastise.
But hast thou to his store, understand, and rejoyce. —

Away, as comanded, my Damsel do's speed,
And finds Michy at work on a hogshead of Weed,
When, behold! he turn'd pale, and the Nymph drawing near,
To inquire of the cause of so sudden a fear,
What he pack'd for Tobaco, oh wondrous to speak!
Was converted to talons, plumes, quills, and a beak;
The Leaves, flesh and entrails and feathers were grown,   [140]
The stems and the fibres, beak talon and bone;
These scattering parts reunite in one frame,
And what, now, was a weed, a Bald Eagle became:
The like wonder was wrought in the hogshead unseen,
Which sprung up in a Cloud and left nothing within. —

No sooner 'twas done, but the birds took their flight;
Save that one staid behind to give som'thing to write.
For this was the Bird that we left long before,
Perch'd, on Michy's right hand, at his Daddy's own door;
Where, we now shou'd go on to relate what was done,   [150]
But You'l guess how a Miser, receiv'd such a Son.
Besides, we've perform'd what we first did intend,
The tale of the Eagle; which now's at an end.
Other times we shall tread in our Knights other paces,

And sing how he won a fair Widows good graces:
But sure we deserve many thanks, the mean time,
Who've enrich'd a dull Story with delicate Rhyme.

Commercial failure numbered among the least poetic of subjects in the estimation of neoclassical critics; therefore, it demanded treatment as a travesty. Brooke rendered the quotidian plainness of a blown deal miraculous by vesting it with the supernaturalism of an Ovidian metamorphosis. The tobacco, which expectation foresees being turned to gold by means of exchange, is transmuted by divine decree into an eagle — Michy's sole take from his New World enterprise. Venus intervenes to turn Michy's profits into feathers because the young trader, violating the fundamental rule of commerce, failed to honor a contract. Venus proclaims, "A fierce Bird of prey shall the preyer chastise," and directs the wronged whore to witness the transformation of Michy's sotweed into bald eagles that fly away, except for one that serves as a reminder of his loss. The doxy's spectation of Michy's loss prefigures the inspection made by the street wenches and townsfolk of Southwark of the returning adventurer as he suffers public humiliation. The multitude witnesses the transformation of the eagle from a sign of Michy's pomp and wealth to a token of failure. The ballad suspends its narration at the point of Michy's reunion with his father, so the reader is left to "guess how a Miser, receiv'd such a Son."

By ending with the rebuke of the father looming, Brooke leaves the audience with the question, Whose expectation was it being exploded? Epic heroes have a quality of autodynamism; their actions are fundamental expressions of their desires. Michy is, instead, a vehicle of his father's desires and his townswomen's expectations. In a burlesque of classical legends of the genesis of heroes, Michy is shown being fleshed in conformity with his father's desires and formed in the likeness of his father's aspirations. The mythological conceit that the hero upon birth possesses the prodigious abilities of an adult found in the tales of the infancy of Hercules was travestied by visualizing adult abilities in terms of the ignoble commerce of townsmen. Peltander outfits his son to prepare him for his quest, yet Michy, the hero of commerce, is not autodynamic. He serves as agent of a company of backers; he performs another's commission. He must answer to authorities for the success or failure of the venture. When the additional weight of patriarchal authority is added to the burden of obligation, the full measure of Michy's subservience is plumbed.

Mercantilism, the economic system that organized Britain's commercial empire, allotted to the metropolis commercial advantages. Of the profits that accrued from trade, the surplus assigned to London outweighed that given to the colony. "The New Metamorphosis" offers a surprising gloss upon metropolitan privilege, by depicting how the merchants who ply the trade are haunted by the commission they carry from home. Even in the friendly haven of Story's Tavern the anxiety about fulfilling the expectations of father, commercial backers, and the citizenry proves so absorbing that, in a ballad about enterprise and reward, the bulk of the poem visualizes the scene at Southwark. The poem is an index of the psychic weight of London on the colonial enterpriser. Indeed, the sole glimpse provided of the New World is a sketch of the neighborhood of the taverns where Michy's fallibility is manifested in the transgression against the minion of the goddess of love.

The presentation of women in Brooke's antiepic deserves particular attention. Classical epic characteristically visualized the hero's quest ending with a woman's love, among other rewards. Indeed, the restoration of civil order consequent to a successful quest is signified by a marriage or a matrimonial reunion.[30] For Michy, the quasi hero of commerce, the prospect of female admiration was an incentive over and above Peltander's patriarchal directive. "The wonder and big expectations of the women of the neighbourhood" would presumably have resulted in the "consummation" of Michy's quest if he had been successful in his enterprise. In effect, any love of a woman won at the end of Michy's quest would be got by his New World wealth. Love would be reduced to a commercial transaction. In this connection it is interesting to note that, when Brooke represents the women of Southwark, they are all seen to be creatures of commerce themselves. "The devil a Wench / That cry's my fresh Oysters, brooms, matches, or dill, / But see jolly Mich had a hearty good will." But Michy forfeited the rewards to be had in Southwark by repudiating his bargain with another creature of commerce in the New World. He fails to honor a contract with a prostitute — "But time and the place and the sum were agreed" — and brings upon himself the wrath of the chief enforcer of the guild of women, Venus.

Brooke called his ballad a "Fable without a Moral." Although the poem is no apologue, since it lacks a closing admonition, the piece does offer a mock-moral economy. Michy's enterprise has failed because he denied that

30. Conversely, falling in love with a woman encountered during a quest often threatens its fulfillment — the dilemma of Aeneas for Dido.

the reign of commerce is all encompassing. Contract is sacrosanct. The gods enforce it; man, woman, family, and nation subserve it. To break the rule of commercial exchange is to suffer divine confiscation of one's goods, public humiliation, patriarchal punishment, and sexual ostracism. The Ovidian extravagance of these consequences provokes the willing restoration of disbelief, which is the effect of burlesque. The point was to make the tavern population see how absurd life would be if commerce, its preoccupation, were truly the prime directive of the universe.

Art does not simply counsel that the thralldom of conversation to commerce be broken; it worked as a counterspell dissolving the fascination that commerce exerts. The magic solvent was humor. Brooke's expertise with "gay Dogrel," his aptitude with the antic anapests of burlesque verse, showed him to be a master of the manner of low literature rivaling the giants of Grub Street. Unlike the Grub Street bards, however, Brooke applied doggerel to instructive rather than malicious ends. Rather than disrupt civility, Brooke used burlesque to suggest a standard of propriety. The difficulty of his accomplishment may not be readily apparent.

Doggerel according to neoclassical theory was that species of comic poetry that profaned nature by caricaturing it in ridiculous language. Because of the obtrusive effect of the language, which dominated plot (fable), argument, action, and character, it differed essentially from other species of comic poetry. It proved a critical problem precisely because plot and character were subordinated to the absurdity of language. Only when the object being ridiculed was by nature profane could the poem be critically justified — as satire. In practice, critics allowed only human character to be an appropriate subject matter in doggerel, and Samuel Butler's *Hudibras* was held up as the model of the genre. But critical provisos held little sway on Grub Street, and doggerel became the vehicle of malice. Ned Ward and Tom Brown did not hesitate to mock virtue and defame character. Brooke took doggerel back from malediction and turned it to instructive ends. Adding a tincture of learning (the Ovidian subtext) and elaborating an anti-heroic merchant's self-mocking tale into a total satire of commercial enterprise made the doggerel ballad both polite and instructive, if not moral.

Beyond Politeness

Brooke's poetry marked out a region of discourse apart from the austerities and simplicities of Quakerism yet distanced from the libertinism and profanity of the Grub Street literature. The poetry exploited the permissions of friendship to instruct companion readers about manners and taste; it wore its learning lightly; it demonstrated how eloquence made opinion witty, how wit aspired to lasting interest, and how social pleasure arose from polite conversation. As Brooke grew older, he realized making tavern talk genteel was not enough. During the 1720s he broadened the scope of his address to incorporate women into the polite conversation. Then, too, he began to look beyond politeness for the grounds of sociability. He became increasingly aware of the capacity of politeness to degenerate into surface agreeableness.

Brooke's attitude toward women has a biographical interest, since he remained a lifelong bachelor, content to reside in the household of the Reverend William Becket in Sussex County. Several of his poems, "Sylvio's Wooing," for instance, employ the persona of an aging gallant whose forays at love prove unsuccessful, prompting a casual attitude toward matters of the heart:

> Sylvio, on the Golden Shoar,
> Thus to Mira sued:
> Once, nor slighted, gave he o'er,
> Twice, tho' treated as before,
> Thrice; but then he sued no more;
> And, Prithee! who the devil wou'd?

Perhaps no poem in Brooke's canon captures the ambivalence about venturing beyond the tavern brotherhood to experience the pleasure of female company more than his impromptu written in Newcastle.

To my Bottle-friends

> The Wine and Company are good,
> Another flask, another hour;
> Such juyce is Wits peculiar food:
> And Wit's a Sociable Pow'r. —
>
> Who's stealing off? — oh! let him go,
> He's young enough to trust the Fair.
> But we, who Love's delusions know,
> Shall find it better to be here. —
>
> Kind Bachus aids each Manly bliss;
> Good humo'r, mirth, the song, the dance;
> But what hath Love, beyond a kiss,
> What, but a dozeing, drunken Trance?

Fond' hasty spark, when passion palls,
And Chloes charmes have lost their flow'r,
Will, one day, be the first that calls
Another flask, another hour. —

Fill then, and, wisely scorn the Boy:
What hath that Chit to do with Men?
At least, this interval enjoy
Til Beauty makes us Fools agen. —

The possibility of a beauty beyond that provided by the social bowl causes one to venture beyond the friendly circle to seek Chloe. Yet feminine beauty eventually loses its charms. Unless the companionship of a woman can compete with the good-humored, amusing conversation of male bottle friends, the relationship between the sexes is fated to falter.

Gentility, of course, promised the development of companionable qualities equivalent to those that made the tavern fellowship so pleasurable. The urge to be genteel fired the imagination of women who aspired to "the notice of the world." For a girl of middling birth, the amelioration of manners might mean an elevation in status. For the wellborn, it could enhance power in the social world. Brooke offered his bemused poetic advice to a typical would-be gentlewoman, Moll Annisseed, in "Molly Made a Gentlewoman." (The name well conveys the aspiration of a common townswoman — anise seed being the favorite herb with which to sweeten one's breath before going into company.) The poem, like Brooke's epistle to Robert Grace, begins with a pungent bit of satire before turning to advice:

Moll Annisseed with note as loud
And harsh, as singer in a Crowd,
Address, and diction of a rate
That makes thee famous Belensgate!
Complain's, That stays w[i]th tissue shining,
Silk of Damascus, persian lining,
Nor Chints, w[i]th Indian monsters gay
Her lustrings, modess nor poudesay;
Can save her from the Worlds neglect:
Ah Molly! do you want respect?
Sink that exalted Pipe a note,
Reform that harsh untuneful throat,
Clip yo[u]r harangues at either end,

And chuse such words as least offend;
Let every gesture, look, and Air
Speak you the Graces chosen care:
So may yo[u]r wishes find success
In Cantaloons; or homespun Dress.

Gesture matters more than surface, and graceful speech more than either in winning the world's "respect." Conversation remains the vehicle of advancement in the world. Until Moll has internalized a sense of grace, she will suffer the world's neglect. Once she has reformed her tongue, her motion, her air to the measure of taste, she will have manifested gentility so successfully that no surface can disguise it. One notes that Brooke does not suggest that such reformation is impossible for Moll. Instead, Brooke indicates that Moll's wish is worthwhile and points the path leading to its fulfillment. What in other hands would have become an antifeminist caricature, or an aristocratic put-down of the aspirations of the unrefined, in Brooke's becomes a true satire, a criticism whose point pricks the subject onto the way of correction. Even when Brooke's conversation with the opposite sex has a satirical edge, it confirms the woman's wish to have a place in the realm governed by belle esprit.

Supplying a poetic warrant for feminine participation in the polite world was in Pennsylvania something like providing an admission ticket to a ball that was not being held. As "Damon" remarked in 1729,

> That Man who is not Moved by the Restraints the Fair Sex are under at this Place, must be either a Morose Father, or a Jealous Husband: Here are no Masquerades, Plays, Balls, Midnight Revellings, or Assemblies to Debauch the Mind, or promote Intriegue; and yet the Fair one who admits an Innocent Familiarity with our Sex, and ventures a Mile out of Town for the Benefit of the Air, or Pleasure of Retir'd Conversation, is sure to suffer in her Character, by a Censorious Brood of Ditractors, and Calumniating Preciants.[31]

Under the critical scrutiny of pious Quakers the conversation of the sexes was an occasion of immorality. In a poem addressed to a female wit who had taken up residence in Philadelphia after a life in the metropolis, Damon envisioned a New World resort for politeness — the Pennsylvania version of the pleasure gardens at the English spas. But before such a utopia of sociability could exist, the people must be rendered more polite:

31. Damon, *American Weekly Mercury*, no. 494, June 26, 1729.

Would they be Open, Generous and Free,
This Place in time, a Paradise might be,
Did they allow what I prescribe to you,
Something to Pleasare (something is it's due)
They'd Taste Sweet Benefits that would ensue.

England thy every Grotto, every Grove,
Are Scenes of Friendship, and are Scene[s] of Love,
Thy Sons are Humble Subjects yet they'r Free,
But here's no Kingly Power — or Liberty:

What was it first that Polish'd Humanekind,
But Conversation Free and Unconfin'd,
Sweet Interviews, and Grateful Exercise,
Which open Hearted, Generous Souls Devise,
Are Life and Lungs of Trade and Merchandize.

Damon's hope is that mercantile sociability might project beyond the limits of private society to reform society at large. But the paradisiacal conversation that Damon envisions exists only in utopian futurity.[32]

Female wits might wait a long time before being granted the freedom to speak their minds openly. At least one female wit (perhaps the one Damon addressed) chose not to wait for such an uncertain eventuality. Elizabeth Magawley, a middle-aged widow residing on Joseph Jones's plantation in the Northern Liberties, took up her pen and began addressing the public in the pages of Andrew Bradford's *American Weekly Mercury*. In a droll essay Magawley challenged the male wits to explain the seeming uninterest of sensible men in women's company. Magawley makes the absence of a polite conversation between the sexes seem a matter of sexual deficiency. Such a challenge did not go unanswered. Joseph Breintnall and Jacob Taylor replied in print with a verse satire making out that Magawley was a middle-aged widow suffering Cyprian heat.[33] Magawley posed a greater challenge to male prerogative than simply twitting wits on their masculin-

32. By the 1790s the liberty of conversation among the sexes here envisioned as an ideal appears to be a practice in Philadelphia. Consider the opinion of Moreau de St. Méry that young ladies enjoy in 1796 "unlimited liberty." Kenneth Roberts and Anna M. Roberts, eds. and trans., *Moreau de St. Méry's American Journey [1793–1798]* (New York, 1947), 285.

33. *American Weekly Mercury*, no. 575, Jan. 5, 1730/1, essay discussed below at the beginning of Chapter 4; Joseph Breintnall and Jacob Taylor, "To Caelia," *American Weekly Mercury*, Jan. 26, 1730/1.

ity. If we are to credit Joseph Norris's manuscript satire, "On E Magawley's Pres[um]ing to Write," it would seem that Magawley set up a household devoted to the muses over which she presided:

> Here uncontrould yr dictates are Obey'd
> No Lordly Tyrant can your Laws invade
> But free and unconfind as tho[ugh]t you stand
> A Jointurd Widdow. At your own Command.[34]

Norris did not stint when picturing the ill effects of a free woman's poetic government of an estate:

> In this sweet Solitude this calm Retreat
> Your own pernassus, and the Muses seat
> A Wond'rous mansion spires above the Trees
> Crack'd all around, a passage for the breeze
> Here Gentle Zephers in soft murmurs play
> Doors Stairs and Windows from a long decay
> Join with the Roof and so admit the day
> A world of weeds on Every side is seen
> And distant Tussocks terminate the Green
> Thro' verdant meads the Christall Rivletts flow
> The Harvests Ripen, and potatoes grow —
> On Visionary Lawns the Muse Surveys
> Where bleating Lambs and Lab'ring Oxen graze,
> Delusions All — but One poor Cow appears
> With hunger Shrivelld and oppressd with years.

In his closing mock benediction, Norris wishes, "Sweet be your Rest untroubled yr repose / Free from the worst of all our plagues — the Beaux." Since the absence of worthy men was precisely the problem Magawley charged to Philadelphia society in her essay, Morris is inverting her reality as his closing trope.

Magawley replied to her male respondents with a systematic critique of their abilities, "The *Wits* and *Poets* of Pennsylvania," in verse.[35] The excellence of her own poetry served as one warrant of her authority to make

34. [Joseph Norris], "On E Magawley's Pres[um]ing to Write," Commonplace Book, H.M. 164, Huntington Library.

35. E. M., "The *Wits* and *Poets* of Pennsylvania, A Poem, Part I," *American Weekly Mercury*, no. 594 [592], May 6, 1731. For my analysis of this poem, see "The Wits and

such a summary judgment; another was the scrupulousness of her remarks. Instead of lambasting the wits and prompting another turn on the cycle of malediction, she opted for the unanswerable last word. Joseph Breintnall was commended for his diction and condemned for his prolixity. Jacob Taylor was praised for his boldness, blamed for his lack of correctness. George Webb, the would-be laureate of the province, received an accolade for the sublimity of his poetry on public affairs, then a rebuke for the bathos of his fantasy of masculine retreat, *Batchelors-Hall*. Of all the wits and poets of the province, only one received Magawley's wholehearted approbation: Henry Brooke. The terms of her praise well epitomized Brooke's service to making "the Town" more urbane.

> In Br[oo]ks Capacious Breast the Muses sit
> Enrob'd with Sense polite, and poignant Wit;
> His Lines run smoothly, tho' the Current strong;
> He forms with Ease, with Judgment sings the Song.
> As th' Awful Elm Supports the Purpling Vine,
> So round his Sense his sprightly *Wit* Entwines:
> Oh! would He oftner write, so should the Town
> Or mend their Tasts, or lay the Muses down;
> For after Manna, who would Garbage Eat!
> That hath a Spark of Sense, or Grain of *Wit*.

The responsibility of being the monitor of taste for a city in which he was not often resident forced Brooke to transmit his judgments in writing. He was only in company for a few short weeks every year. In these brief periods he exerted his power as archpoet, rebuking Aquila Rose for accepting patronage by serving as court poet for Governor William Keith, or castigating Alderman Joseph Wilcox for the stupidity of his public pronouncements and the grossness of his appetites. Yet Brooke could not, like Dryden at Will's coffeehouse, serve as the standing speaker for a *sensus communis*. Brooke could not preside over tavern society because of his duties at Lewes. But Pennsylvania society was well adapted to dealing with the written declarations of absentee authorities. Periodically Brooke dispatched satires attacking the degeneracy of letters and manners in the province. These include "An Invective agt: a Certain Brewer of Bad Ale and Worse Rhymes, in Part of Paymt for a Paltry Libel," "An Answr to a

Most Insipid Epistle, Beginning and Ending in Like Humble Meetre," a reply to a satire from Newcastle, and "Modern Politeness, 1726." This last evinced Brooke's critical development beyond an aesthetics governed by the imperative to sociability. In his satire of Young Dapper, Brooke questions the adequacy of politeness as the superintending ideal of character formation.

Modern Politeness. 1726

Young Dapper once had some pretence
To Mother Wit, and Common Sense;
And had he but apply'd those Parts
To Sciences, or useful Arts,
Religion, Med'cine, Law or Trade,
Lord, what a Figure had he made!
But all his Stars contriv'd in Spite
That he should only be Polite.
Only Polite, Whats that you'l say?
Observe him, and he'l show the way.   [10]
A Modish Suit, with Sword on Thigh,
A Wigg, and how to comb and tye;
To drink, to drab, to toast the Fair,
A brisk decisive tone and Air,
Are the first Rudiments: and these
Dapper acquir'd with so much Ease
As rather Nature seem'd than Art,
So sudden he commenc'd a Smart.
What follows next? to dance and sing;
Is that so difficult a Thing?   [20]
Not so to Dappers application,
Who boasts in each so good a fashion,
That He, who (as Epigram makes known)   {Memphis and Demophilus
So Daphne danc'd, and Niobe,   in the Anthologia
As that a Stock, and this a Stone
Hardly so lifeless seem'd as he;
Nor t'other celebrated Head
Who sing the Rival Screech Owl dead.
(Tho' Fame hath blabb'd their worth's so long)
Excell'd his manner, or his Song.   [30]
Must the Proficient read and write?

For reading, tis not so polite,
It spoils the Features; and beware,
A thog'tfull, or Scholastic' Air:
But easy writing, Or to write*   *see Wycherly
What any may with Ease indite
A flow of words dispos'd for Sound,
And Periods Numerous and Round:
The Subject trifling News and Chat,
Good sense apart, no matter what,   [40]
A dash of [——] here and There,   }
Have such a Charm for modish Ear   }
As merits Dappers strictest Care: }
And he (as Envy must confess)
Hath master'd with great Success.
So — but what Topicks for Discourse?
Oh Heaven's, how plenteous is the Sourse!
'Tis to have al the names by Rote
Of Lords and Commoners of Note,
To tell long Stories, wrong or right,   [50]
Of Robert's twain, the Peer and Knight.
Of Swifts inimitable Fancies;
And how his Highness bow's and dances.
On Church and Parsons to declame,
And call em by a filthy Name.
Praise Toland; sneer at Orthodox,   Hen Brooke
Creeds, Bubbles Mysteries and the Pox,   Anna Regina
Laugh at the City's awkard Pride,
And without Ear or Art decide
Betwixt Faustina and Cuzzone,   [60]
What gaming Ladies pledge for money,
What reigning Toasts in Order tell,
Who buys a Post, a Vote who sell.
Talk of the Play, the Opera, Park,
And what diversions there when Dark?
All these, and Twenty thousand more
Made but a part of Dappers Store.
How but a Part! pray whats the whole
Mark for he's reaching at the Goal.
His grand Ambition was in short,   [70]

To view the worst side of a Court.
He comes, he see's, and nobly fir'd,
Snatches the Palm so long desir'd,
Mounts the Professor's Chair, and thence,
With a becoming Negligence;
From Vulgar prejudice set free,   }
Ring's o'er the Changes on these Three,   }
Detraction, Bawdy, Blasphemy.   }
Oh! inexhaustible supply
Of wit, oh Fountain never dry!   [80]
Oh matchless Dapper! rising Name,
Consign'd to everduring Fame!
How surely did thy Stars contrive!
Thou'rt the Politest Thing alive.   Henry Bowman)

Beyond easy politeness Brooke asserted the need for a person to cultivate a social utility. "Mother Wit" and "Common Sense" nurture in a man of parts the public spirit. Brooke here endorsed a characterology combining politeness and social vocation. Doing so, he anticipated the conflation (some would say confusion) of the figures of the gentleman and the professional man that occurred throughout Europe during the course of the eighteenth century. Less prescient was Brooke's rebuke of Dapper's devotion to surface. Brooke suggested that "modern politeness" transgressed the original program of politeness by neglecting elements of self-cultivation that made a gentleman a worthwhile as well as agreeable partner in private society. Significantly, modern politeness eschewed an interest in reading.

Dapper's writing is worse than ornamental nothings. His compositions combine the beauties of the easy verse with a profanity once the preserve of Grub Street. They deal in "Detraction, Bawdy, Blasphemy." Dapper's modern politeness, which put eloquence in the service of malediction, inverted the politeness that Brooke introduced to Pennsylvania. Brooke reformed profane conversation by reshaping it in light of sociable wit of the spas. This wit founded a common sense more durable than invoked in a bawdy jest or a slander of the court. Yet, as Brooke's satire suggests, it was vulnerable to the infestation of metropolitan fashion. The sensus communis of true wit needed more than conversational repetition or preservation in manuscript to endure.

A problem of the Shaftesburian account (and Brooke's understanding) of sensus communis was a disinclination to see that it animated and informed institutions that would secure it into the future — the private society, the public press, the library, and the academy. To view sensus communis as having a practical effect in society was to conceive of it as rhetorical consensus rather than as an aesthetic community articulated in distinction to public affairs. Giambattista Vico in *The New Science* undertook the revision that conceived of sensus communis as framing the pathetic dimension of rhetoric.[36] Before Vico certain English writers developed a pragmatic sense of the power of sensus communis to found or reform institutions when elaborating the idea of "project." In Philadelphia it was the greatest student of Defoe's "Essay on Projects," Benjamin Franklin, who founded the Junto, the private society whose schemes did much to institute civilization in the city, by projecting the Library Company of Philadelphia, the American Philosophical Society, and the Philadelphia Academy.

Franklin founded the Junto in 1727, the same year that Brooke put down his pen. But one should not view 1727 as marking a historical succession in which the rhetorical conception of sensus communis eclipsed the aesthetic. The fundamental disparity between Shaftesbury's view and Vico's, Brooke's practice and Franklin's, would remain in force in Philadelphia, in British America, in Europe subsequently. Belles lettres would be bound for much of the eighteenth century to the Shaftesburian trajectory of sensus communis. The pleasure of polite literature would be experienced by an exclusive, charmed circle of gentlefolk who delighted in the nobility of sentiment and the beauty of eloquence. Yet Franklin and others who made rhetorical use of the beauties of literature had their influence on belles lettres. They made belles lettres institute civility in the public sphere.

36. The argument of John D. Schaeffer in *Sensus Communis: Vico, Rhetoric, and the Limits of Relativism* (Durham, N.C., 1990).

4

Tea Tables
and Salons

Henry Brooke refined tavern talk by importing wit and spa gallantry into male shoptalk and jest. Elizabeth Magawley had another project. She campaigned to remedy the frivolity and malice of women's conversation by injecting into it "masculine sense." Militating against the conventional wisdom that polite women's talk reveled in surface rather than substance and that polite women welcomed only men of surface — "Fools and Coxcombs" — into their company, Magawley, as Generosa, addressed the readership of the *American Weekly Mercury*:

I have observ'd of late, that our unfortunate Sex have been the Subject of almost all the Satyr that has dropt from your Pen for some Months past; I do assure you notwithstanding, that as I am your constant Reader, so I am your hearty Well-wisher: I am not sorry to find Vice or even Fooleries put in odious Colours; nor more Angry to see ill Women expos'd, than a Valiant Soldier would be to see a Cowardly one call'd Coward. But as there is an Insinuation in one of your Papers, which I think is entirely groundless: I hope you will Pardon me the Freedom of telling you it is. The Sum of the Charge is, *That Fools and Coxcombs are most acceptable to the Ladies.* The Word Ladies is an ambiguous Term, to which no single Idea can be affix'd; as in your Sex there are several Classes of Men of Sense, Rakes, Fops, Coxcombs, and down-right Fools, so I hope, without straining your Complaisance, you will allow there are some Women of Sense comparatively, as well as Coquets, Romps, Prudes, and Idiots. If you had said Fools and Coxcombs are most acceptable to Coquets and Romps I readily grant it: Men of Sense value themselves too much to be used as Tools, they cannot stoop to the little Fooleries impos'd on them by their imaginary Goddesses, and their Resentments are too strong to bear Contempt and Insults. As to the Women of Sense (if you allow any to be so) you will also own THEY are more delighted with Conversation of Men of Sense, than with that of Coxcombs or Fools, since the contrary takes away their Character of Sense. But Men of Sense are scarce Sir, very scarce indeed, and those few that are, are too proud or think their Time ill bestow'd, in the Conversation of Ladies. They very often Think for Want of Trial, that what I argue against is true: the Vulgar Error has impos'd even upon them. This is our lamentable Case, and what must we do? Must we resolve never to Converse with the opposite Sex, or go under the Reproach of favouring Coxcombs? It may be said that we love Fops and Fools, because we play with them, and so we do with Parrots, Monkeys and Owls; and if we cannot procure objects of Admiration and Esteem, we divert our[s]elves with those of Redicule and Contempt: But, Oh, Sir, if you knew the exquisite Pleasure that we Women receive from the Conversation of a Man of Sense; what Raptures we conceive upon the least Imagination of being belov'd by him, you will confess with me, that Coxcombs are merely indulged out of meer Necessity; and the ill success of Men of Sense, is owing to their want of Courage.[1]

Magawley indicated that the conversation of mixed company was controlled in large measure by the conversation of ladies. The coxcombs, fops, and fools who attended the ladies had such ephemeral standing that they could be equated with pets. The problem for Magawley was how to attract men of sense into a space dominated by women. Her method was to suggest that within the feminine company there existed women of sense worth communing with. Magawley's letter certified the existence of sensible women within the bon ton. Her sense was displayed in her critique of those feminine characters who appeared to dominate feminine conversation. She, in effect, declared her power over them by passing judgment upon them.

Magawley argued from the premise that *lady* was a term of such ambiguity in the polite world as to be meaningless until naming the sort of *lady*

---

1. Generosa [Elizabeth Magawley], *American Weekly Mercury* (Philadelphia), no. 575, Jan. 5, 1730/1. For my attribution of the essay to Magawley, see "The Wits and Poets of Pennsylvania: New Light on the Rise of Belles Lettres in Provincial Pennsylvania, 1720–1740," *Pennsylvania Magazine of History and Biography*, CIX (1985), 99–103.

in question. Her list of particulars — women of sense, coquettes, romps, prudes, and idiots — recalled the cast of female characters that peopled the Restoration stage, with the noteworthy exception that the woman of sense replaced the female wit. Who were these types? Except for the woman of sense, each was typified by distinctive behavior when acting in mixed company. The coquette marshaled beauty and grace to attract men for the gratification of her vanity; she flirted in the new arenas of competitive heterosociality to gratify her pride by provoking male contests. The romp breached common rules of civility to indulge her love of play; she exploited the new freedoms of mixed company to experience extravagances of diversion. The prude reacted against the new liberties of the spas and city parlors by insisting rigidly upon proprieties of conduct to the exclusion of all play between the sexes. The idiot played dumb, simpered, and flattered the vanity of males to gain attention. The vanities and perversities of these characters were mirrored in a cast of male characters — rakes, fops, coxcombs, and fools. When rake and romp or coquette and fop dominated the social stage, conversation suffered the vagaries of Vanity Fair. As a contemporary observer of the bon ton opined, vain women "speak to all they meet, tho' they have nothing to say to 'em: The Exteriour of Acquaintance is all they aim at."[2]

Magawley as early as 1725 might have criticized female vanity in the polite world. Widow R——lt had published in the *American Weekly Mercury* her "Dream," a poetic mash note to a beau. "A Lady" (most likely Magawley) rebuked the mindlessness of Widow R——lt's effusion. These were the offending sentiments:

2. Thomas Brown, *A Legacy for the Ladies; or, Characters of the Women of the Age* (London, 1705), 32. Lawrence Klein commented on Magawley's sense of the multifarious public identities attached to "lady" in "Women 'in Publick' in Eighteenth-Century England," Twenty-fifth Anniversary Meeting of the American Society for Eighteenth-Century Studies, Charleston, S.C., Mar. 13–17, 1994.

Compilations of generalized female characters in the Theophrastian mode were a staple of the English press during the period. One might compare Tom Brown's *Legacy for the Ladies*, which treats the following types: the wanton (the "romp"), the modest woman, the pretended godly woman, the religious woman, the witty woman, the prudent woman (the "prude"), the penurious housewife, the good housewife, the gaming woman, the diligent woman, the litigious woman, the quiet woman, and the self-lover (the "coquette"). In British America these sorts of characters were a staple feature of almanacs; see, for example, the verse portrait of a prude in *The Maryland Almanac for 1764* (Annapolis, Md., 1763), [5], or the coquette in Theophilus Wreg, *The Virginia Almanack for 1765* (Williamsburg, Va., 1764).

IN vain is all you speak, and all you Write:
What avail manly Charms, or manly Wit?
For at my Birth 'twas by the Fates decreed
That I should never lay aside my Weed:
'Till a tall Youth shall at a Ball be seen,
Whose Legs are, like the Spring, all cloath'd in Green;
A yellow ribbon ties his long Cravat,
And a large Knot of Yellow cocks his Hat;
With yellow Clusters dangling at his Knee;
This is the Man the Fates ordain for me.[3]

Mrs. R——lt as a widow could presumably lay claim to worldly experience,
yet she declared that fate's signature was written on the fashionable surface
of a youth. Green trousers (noted first), a ribbon, and a yellow topknot
have usurped the place of character and talent in her evaluation of men.
Show has assumed the mysterious weight of fate. Magawley countered the
widow's mystification of male surface by showing how it concealed a particularly shallow depth, an aging woman's venery.

Ribbons with Ornaments, Attire,
Were not your Ladyship's Desire.
These are external Graces, which
Could not your Passions so bewitch.
Your *Dream* of such fantastick Things
Was not what Frolick Nature brings:
She's warm with fervent Zeal for Man,
(Deny it, Madam, if you can).[4]

Fashion was no self-certifying glory; it signaled no worldly grace. Rather, a
beau's costumed luster reflected the plainest of natural desires, a widow's
yearning for the man beneath. The pretense revealed the poverties of
conversation without sense: if women's conversation were restricted to
matters of surface, it would foreclose communication with men other than
fops, ornamental figures dressed in green and yellow. The Lady's remedy
went unspoken: mixed company could be redeemed only if its conversation

3. Widow R——lt, "A Dream," *American Weekly Mercury*, no. 284, May 27, 1725.
The identity of the widow cannot now be determined. There was no widow Roosevelt
in Philadelphia or New York that can be immediately linked to this item. The poems
were not reprints of English pieces, so far as I can determine.

4. A Lady [Elizabeth Magawley?], "The Answer," *American Weekly Mercury*, no.
284, May 27, 1725.

were dominated by the interchange between men and women of sense. Later it would become the burden of Magawley's public writing.

By "Sense" Magawley meant intelligence married with sensibility; the term was opposed to "wit" in the lexicon of the day.[5] Magawley did not follow Henry Brooke in attempting to rehabilitate wit by making discriminations between true wit and false. She understood that wit, whether true or false, functioned as a device for shining in company or deflecting the particular attentions of others. In its former function it reinforced a culture of vanity; in the latter it prevented intellectual communion between persons. Sense and its ancillary faculty, sensitivity, could permit intellectual rapport. It was the promise of this rapport and the further promise that this rapport might lead to love that Magawley held out to men of sense as reason to venture into the domain of polite women. Men of sense, at least in Philadelphia, were distinguished by their nonparticipation in the contest and conversation of the sexes: they are few and "are too proud or think their Time ill bestow'd, in the conversation of Ladies." Magawley suggested that their reluctance to engage in mixed conversation arose from the fact that "Vulgar Error has impos'd even upon them." What was the "Vulgar Error?" It was the common caricature of female society.

5. *Sense* was one of the master terms of the critical lexicon of the period and consequently encompassed a wide semantic space. Its usage here was shaped by the opposition of *sense* to *wit* in the 1690s, wherein *sense* came to mean an "intuitive perception of consonance and propriety" (Samuel Johnson, describing Pope's intellectual character in the *Lives of the English Poets*), as opposed to a schooled capacity for invention and verbal play. *Sense* was linked to judgment, both moral and aesthetic, rather than to operations of will, memory, or imagination. In the act of literary creation it was associated with correction and refinement into a finished work of art. In reading it was the grounds of a proper understanding of a work. Benjamin Franklin explored the figure of "A Man of Sense" in a dialogue signed A. A. in the *Pennsylvania Gazette* (Philadelphia), no. 323, Feb. 11, 1734/5, and in Leonard W. Labaree et al., eds., *The Papers of Benjamin Franklin* (New Haven, Conn., 1959–), II, 15.

G. J. Barker-Benfield has provided a cogent definition of sensibility: "The word denoted the receptivity of the senses and referred to the psychoperceptual scheme explained and systematized by Newton and Locke. It connoted the operation of the nervous system, the material basis for consciousness. During the eighteenth century, this psychoperceptual scheme became a paradigm, meaning not only consciousness in general but a particular kind of consciousness, one that could be further sensitized in order to be more acutely responsive to signals from the outside environment and from inside the body. While sensibility rested on essentially materialist assumptions, proponents of the cultivation of sensibility came to invest it with spiritual and moral values." *The Culture of Sensibility: Sex and Society in Eighteenth-Century Britain* (Chicago, 1992), xvii.

Magawley's belief that women's sense would best be exercised in concert with male sense in the conversation of mixed company marked her as a salonniere, one of the earliest to proclaim her views in British America. Her understanding that the conversation of mixed company took place under women's superintendence conformed with the convictions of salonnieres since the establishment of the Parisian hôtels a century earlier. What is historically significant about Magawley's advocacy was her rhetorical stance. She knew that her ideal was threatened by another view of female society then in ascendancy. Though she calls this view a "Vulgar Error," it might better be characterized as a competing vision of feminine society and conversation in which fashion and play were means of exerting power. Magawley asserted the heterosocial sense of the salon against the fashionable gynarchy of the tea table.

Tea and Sympathy

Performing a literary archaeology of the institution of the tea table in British America is a difficult task. Although material remains of polite tea culture abound, written expressions of it do not. We have, instead, editorializing about it, satires of tea tables, and mock tea literature, for the emergence of tea culture became a flash point in the quarrel between the sexes that agitated English letters.[6] Males throughout the British Empire recognized the tea table as the critical institution in the assertion of women's presence in the emerging public sphere. Those who felt anxiety about the consolidation of women's power in Anglo-American culture attacked tea and its female devotees. Most writings from women about the tea table were composed as rejoinders to male censors. Since talk was the preferred medium of tea-table expression, we must recognize that the written sources treated below constituted only a portion of women's response. Yet sufficient material remains to recover the distinctive features of tea-table talk: its tone, its characteristic subjects, its social functions.[7]

6. It is instructive to note that one of the major salvos in the literature of the quarrel between the sexes, *The Challenge, Sent by a Young Lady to Sir Thomas ——, etc.; or, The Female War* . . . (London, 1697), a series of letters pro and con on "all disputable points concerning women," indicated that the defenses of female virtue and ability were composed by various London tea tables, some of which had been assigned the topics that they treated.

7. Before 1700, table talk — published collections of a person's bons mots, aphorisms, observations — was a genre recognized by English writers as characteristically

Recovering the discourse of the tea table transforms our understanding of significant early American texts, such as the journal of Sarah Kemble Knight, and alerts us to the development of a women's domain in the public sphere.

A literary-cultural archaeology of the tea table could be performed for several British American cities — Philadelphia, New York, Charleston, perhaps Annapolis — but Boston supplies the amplest documentation of the institution's spread. We know that tea's first importers there were Robert Vernon and the energetic ex-Londoner Benjamin Harris, who supplied stocks as early as 1680. We know that Zabiel Boylston sold it at his apothecary shop. We know it was served to Samuel Sewall on his ill-fated courtship visit to Widow Katharine Winthrop. Let us begin, however, with an analysis of the social workings of the tea table published by the Reverend John Adams of Boston and Newport in the *New-England Weekly Journal* in 1727:

> If you visit the Tea-Table of some few Ladies, (to speak genteely) you have good Manners, a civil sort of Impertinence, Remarks made with excellent Judgment upon the Fashions, the Position of some Gentlewoman's Headdress, or fine Lectures upon the Affairs of a House, the finest way to make Sowse and Jellies, with many more Particulars of the like Advantage and Instruction, and it is very well if you escape hearing a

---

French. When Tom Brown surveyed the genre in 1701, he could name only William Camden, Francis Bacon, and John Selden as English practitioners of the form, whereas the French literature boasted the names of La Rochefoucauld, Saint-Evremont, and La Bruyère and less famous collections. See [Tom Brown], *Laconics; or, New Maxims of State and Conversation* . . . (London, 1701). Although a British literature did emerge, it was often in the form of anecdotal filler in magazines. In British America even this impoverished form of table talk did not have much currency in print.

In the absence of a published table-talk literature in British America, journals supply the most ample record of conversation. The letters and journal of Philadelphian Anne Home Shippen (Livingston) during her courtship, marriage, and separation are a particularly rich deposit of talk, including the sole schematic diagram surviving from the eighteenth century of the seating arrangement of a group at tea. A new edition of this journal is needed to supersede Ethel Armes, ed., *Nancy Shippen: Her Journal Book: The International Romance of a Young Lady of Fashion of Colonial Philadelphia, with Letters to Her and about Her* (1935; rpt. New York, 1968).

At the end of the eighteenth century the forms of tea conversation were sufficiently conventionalized that Richard Johnson could publish *Tea-Table Dialogues* . . . (Philadelphia, 1789) as a model for would-be participants.

long Roll of your Neighbour's Faults, which either are not true, or if so would better be buried in Silence.[8]

Tea-table talk might have seemed impertinent to Adams — it did not speak of the world to come or heed Paul's ban on gossip — yet condescension could not entirely mask his interest. Adams and his friend Mather Byles were the politest of New England's native ministers. He could not help noticing that this female institution contributed to cultural refinement. Somehow the conversation conducted over steaming cups of Bohea nourished good manners and judgment. Somehow women were performing Amphion's task, creating civility with art.

Chat was the art of the tea table, a dangerous art in the eyes of many men. Chatting went beyond the pieties and homely maxims of proper feminine conversation. The most dangerous sort of chat was scandalous gossip, and a host of male monitors stuffed the provincial papers with warnings against it. Only one glimpsed the depth of gossip's challenge to male prerogative. Z. Y., a correspondent of the *New-England Courant*, saw that gossip constituted an alternative history, a different news, which broke the masculine monopoly on representing past and present. Gossip, he asserted, was "of no Use but among the most barbarous Nations, who want the Use of Letters to preserve the memory of their Actions for the Benefit of their Posterity."[9] Z. Y.'s yoking of gossip with incivility provoked "Bellona," a female wit, to write in its defense. The very act of publishing a defense in the *Courant* exploded Z. Y.'s hint that gossip was a function of female illiteracy.

> I wou'd have you to know, Sir, that some of us can handle our Pens as well as our Tongues, and it will be your wisest way to be quiet, or treat us with better Manners in the future."[10]

8. [John Adams], "Proteus Echo no. 29 [On Politeness]," *New-England Weekly Journal* (Boston), no. 31, Oct. 23, 1727. Proteus Echo was a name adopted by Mather Byles, John Adams, and Matthew Adams for their literary contributions to the newspaper. Besides appearing under this corporate name, each contribution was further identified by initials. The key to authorship of individual items in the Proteus Echo essay series is provided in no. 52, Apr. 1, 1728. Adams (1705–1740) was minister of the Congregational Church in Newport; see Chapter 7 for more by and about him.

9. Z. Y., [essay on gossip], *New-England Courant* (Boston), no. 111, Sept. 16, 1723. The standard study of the subject is Patricia Meyer Spacks, *Gossip* (New York, 1985); the sections on the eighteenth century are the strongest in the book.

10. Bellona, [a reply to Z. Y.'s remarks upon gossip], *New-England Courant*, no. 112, Sept. 23, 1723.

Having cast Z. Y. as the barbarian and challenged him to shut up or improve his manners, Bellona exposed the fear goading men to denounce gossip:

> We can tell who they are that pretend to a greater Authority than ordinary over their Wives, when they are out of the reach of the Broomstick, tho' they are Hen-peck'd at Home from Morning till Night, and dare as well die as claim the Breeches. We can discover, if we will, all the excellent Qualities you are endow'd with over a Cup of Drink with your Companions, and let the World see, that your Knowledge is as universal as that of Gossips, only with this Difference, that yours comes and goes with the Liquor, and theirs is always the Same.

Gossip could attack masculine arrogations of authority by revealing their pretentiousness. Gossip could tarnish one's image in the eyes of "the world," posing a present danger to the vain. Bellona extolled gossip as the antidote to vanity:

> The Ground would be presently too good for you to walk upon, if you were not told, that your Fathers were *Porters* or *Plough-joggers*.

Furthermore, gossip's exposure of spite and scandal among neighbors enabled people to maintain a proper circumspection in dealings with others. The gossip's tongue cut through pretense and ceremony to speak uncomfortable truths for the benefit of the world — something historians and gazette writers presumably were loath to do. Gossip was brash honesty, not false witness.

Some men believed that the censures of the tea table constituted a campaign against male privilege. Their resentment found expression in a 1722 letter by "Sisyphus":

> My Grievance proceeds altogether from the Insolence of an incorrigible *Virago* of a Wife, who (tho' she denies herself nothing to put her upon a Par with the best in the Town, as to outward Apparel,) thinks what is ordinarily worn by Porters good enough for me, who take all the Pains to support her Extravagance, which is such as causes Wonder and Amazement in all those who see her, particularly on those Days when she is disposed to attend the Weekly Lectures. Her Companions (who are not a Jot better than her self) are sure at every Visit not to miss of a Belly-full of *Tea*, whereas when I return from taking my Glass with my Friend (tho' not one bit beyond my Last,) my Ears are immediately fill'd with *Sot* and *Drunkard*, and other such like opprobrious Expressions, which

render my Life meerly burdensome. Thus does she insult me, having as well the Command of my Purse as Person: And as all our domestick Jars contribute only to make her worse and worse, I hope this publick Admonition will so sensibly touch her guilty Conscience, as to cause a Reformation.[11]

The satire abstracted the charges commonly laid against tea-table society in the faults of its representative, Sisyphus's wife: indulgence in fashion, resistance to male control, verbal aggressiveness (she echoed the time-honored charges of intemperance that tea drinkers level against the male tavern set), and attentiveness to the public scene rather than the domestic hearth. The keenest stroke of the satire was its final sentence. Sisyphus had to resort to "publick Admonition" because public matters were the only things that absorbed her. The wife had become the totally undomesticated woman.

What truth resided in the indictment of tea tables? Just this: they were interested in fashion; they were havens of gossip; they did encourage a feminine interest in the public sphere. These were not faults to the tea drinkers. Consider their regard for fashion. Fashion was not useless luxury; it was a means of asserting power in public. Flaunting a modish hat, a mask in the streets, or a whalebone petticoat commanded the eyes of the town upon the wearer's terms. The power to command another's gaze was a public power that women could exert so long as they dared to risk novelty and ignored the pulpit's frequent calls for female modesty. The tea table served several functions in regard to fashion: it could provide a venue for fashionable display, it could pass judgment on the tastefulness of a person's getup, and it could encourage a general interest in sartorial display. The tea tables, for instance, made the Thursday church lectures a weekly exhibition of finery. Long custom had made the period after the lectures a time of visitation for Christian fellowship among women. During the late 1710s it became the favored time for taking social tea. "Bridget Bifrous" explained in 1723:

The Time after Lecture on Thursdays until Sunset, I usually set apart to receive or pay Visits, agreeable to the *good Old Way* . . . I took a Walk to the House of a certain Lady of this Town, who is famous for much Reading, and some Learning: It so happened that I found with her three

11. Sisyphus, [letter complaining of wife and tea companions], *New-England Courant*, no. 35, Apr. 2, 1722.

Ladies of her Acquaintance, and not unknown to me; and when the customary Salutations were over, I took a Chair. . . .

. . . *Pretty* brought the Tea-Table, the Entertainment at which is well known to be cheifly Scandal: To keep up that laudable Custom, they did not omit to slander all their Friends and Acquaintences they could think of.[12]

Since women made their visits directly after lecture, there was no opportunity to change attire. Tea-table fashion became meetinghouse fashion. There were few better arenas for public display than the expansive visual spaces of houses of worship.[13] By filling the pews with ribbons and silk, the devotees of fashion were conducting a sortie into the camp of the enemy. Their progress can be measured in the swelling chorus of complaint in the public prints, as in an advertisement of 1721:

Whereas several of the Ladies of late have been observ'd to sit down in time of publick Prayer (a Posture very Indecent and irreverent in that solemn part of Worship,) and not only so, but to smile and play with their Fans, an Indication of criminal Carelessness, and unthoughtfulness of the awful Presence they are in. This, therefore, is to inform them, That unless they speedily reform, they must expect to be more particularly expos'd.[14]

The threat had little effect, since public exposure was precisely what the "Ladies" aimed at when sitting at prayer and fluttering their fans.

The church was not the only sanctum into which the devotees of fashion intruded. In May 1724, tea-table society invaded the courts: "At a Court of Admiralty held in *Boston*, for the Tryal of certain Pirates, a Company of

12. *New-England Courant*, no. 107, Aug. 19, 1723.

13. There were more than a few poetic appreciations of attractive women spotted in church composed during the colonial era. See Damon, "In the Afternoon at the P[res-byteria]n Meeting," *American Weekly Mercury*, no. 492, June 12, 1729; or Thomas Chase and Thomas Cradock's collaboration, "Baltimore Belles," admiring the charms of two ladies who sat in the pew in front of them; this verse stimulated a paper war with poets of the Tuesday Club, and supplies the subject of book III, chap. 6, of Dr. Alexander Hamilton's *History of the Ancient and Honrable Tuesday Club*, ed. Robert Micklus, 3 vols. (Chapel Hill, N.C.,1990), I, 152–160, where portions survive.

14. [Nathaniel Gardner, Sr.], [notice to irreverent ladies who flirt during church], *New-England Courant*, no. 8, Sept. 25, 1721. On the piece's authorship, see Joseph Fireoved, "Nathaniel Gardner and the *New-England Courant*," *Early American Literature*, XX (1985–1986), 226–227. Fireoved sees an element of burlesque in Gardner's ad.

Ladies of the first Quality attended during the whole Process, to the great Anoyance of his Majesty's good Subjects the Male Auditors, who were unmercifully squeez'd together [by] . . . the huge Bulk of the said Ladies Petticoats." What seizes attention in the complaints about female incursions into public spaces is the insistence that they were organized and deliberate. When a fire broke out near Oliver's Wharf in Boston in August 1724, the fashionable set was so quickly alerted that an "army of petticoats" arrived at the dockside before the firefighters; a Boston wag suggested that the women should be enlisted as replacements for the fire wardens.[15]

The movement of masses of genteel ladies out-of-doors marked another revision in the manners of the town. In London, alfresco promenades had been a feature of post–Great Fire city life. A woman's unchaperoned appearance at St. James's indicated that she was either a doxy or a mistress en route to an illicit rendezvous. During the 1720s and 1730s, park mores changed when London's tea-table society sought a more savory open-air venue for its public displays. Vauxhall Gardens opened in 1732, with its lantern walks, music pavilions, and tea stands to answer feminine demands. In British America's provincial capitals, women forced other innovations in the conduct of open-air diversion. The changes were not always welcomed. In Charleston in 1735, the Meddlers' Club rebuked women who chose to promenade on the Cooper River dockside while ignoring the orange gardens off Tradd Street.[16] The rebukes fell on deaf

15. [Ladies in the male auditory at the pirate trial], *New-England Courant*, no. 146, May 18, 1724; [concerning the forwardness of lady spectators at the fire near Oliver's Wharf], *New-England Courant*, no. 159, Aug. 17, 1724.

New York City constructed gardens with the same names and functions. For the improvement of the public spaces of provincial cities, see Peter Borsay, *The English Urban Renaissance: Culture and Society in the Provincial Town, 1660–1770* (Oxford, 1989).

16. "Says *Dick Haughty*, I can't help taking Notice of the great Concourse of People of both Sexes that assembles on the Bay almost every Evening: And I think as we are Meddlers, that that is a Topic worthy our Observation; for in my Opinion, it is a Custom that will never resound to the Honour of *Carolina*, and tends to promote Vice and Irreligion in many Degrees. And tho' it may be objected that the Heat of the Climate will not permit them to walk in the Day, and it can't but conduce to their Health to walk and take the air; yet I think there are many more fitting places to walk on than the Bay: For have we not many fine Greens near the Town much better accommodated for Air, than a Place which continually has all the nauseous Smells of Tarr, Pitch, Brimstone, etc. and what not, and where every *Jack Tarr* has the Liberty to view and remark the most celebrated Beauties of *Charles-Town*, and where besides (if any Air is)

ears. The orange gardens were turned into town lots, and Whitepoint Gardens, a riverside park, was built to suit female taste. In New York City, Governor William Cosby in 1732 constructed at his wife's behest "Very Pretty bowlling greens with a handsome Walk of trees Raild and Painted Just before the fort in t[ha]t Large Durty place."[17] The Cosbys resided at the fort; the green was intended as a promenade for the ladies of Mrs. Cosby's court.

The sway of the tea table over the female population at large became a matter of concern among the enemies of the beau monde. Once a new trick of manners or a new style of dress caught on with arbiters of fashion, country wives and the city commonality mimicked it. In 1723, "Dorothy Forecast," writing from Rehoboth in the Massachusetts hinterlands, explained that country women going to Boston assumed imperious airs because "the Simplicity of Dress and Manners which runs through most of our Country Towns, being accounted scandalous and ungraceful in *Boston*, they think themselves oblig'd to imitate the *Town Madams* in Pride and Extravagancy, to avoid the Scandal of being singular in Prudence and Industry." When the "Town Madams" began attending the Admiralty trials, a man complained that "every Custom taken up by *Ladies of Quality*, is presently follow'd by the Trulls and Gossips of the vulgar Herd." The specter of women exerting conscious control over feminine behavior disturbed more than a few, and fashion was the means by which a female urban elite formed a broad feminine sensus communis.[18]

Men, witnessing the power that women of fashion exerted over the imagination of their sex, began to condemn fashion as a symbolic form of emasculation. The diatribe of "Homespun Jack" against women's wearing hats (it was a usurpation of male "shape") sounded an alarm that Boston's

---

there's such a continual Dust, that I should think it were enough to deter any Lady from appearing, least her Organs of perspiration should be stopt, and she be suffocated." [Meddlers' Club III], *South-Carolina Gazette* (Charleston), no. 83, Aug. 30, 1735.

17. Abigail Franks to Napthali Franks, in Leo Hershkowitz and Isidore S. Meyer, eds., *The Lee Max Friedman Collection of American Jewish Colonial Correspondence: Letters of the Franks Family, 1733–1748* (Waltham, Mass., 1968), 24–27.

18. Dorothy Forecast, letter dated "Rehoboth, Nov. 20," *New-England Courant*, no. 121, Nov. 25, 1723 (there is more than a little likelihood that this was written by a male author using a female persona); letter, *New-England Courant*, no. 146, May 18, 1724; Elizabeth Wilson, *Adorned in Dreams: Fashion and Modernity* (Berkeley, Calif., 1987), 9–13. See also Barker-Benfield, *The Culture of Sensibility*, 173–190.

streets would "be fill'd with *Hermaphodites,*" as women fasted themselves to a boyish *"genteel shape."* Jack recalled Lucian's tale of the self-castration of Combabus and its imitation by men of the African court: emasculation as fashion. "Had this Custom prevail'd in the World, the notorious Fashion-Mongers among the Fair Sex, had met with a just Reward for their Extravagencies." Fashion disturbed traditional custom. Because custom preserved male prerogative, it was to be defended against modish innovation. Homespun Jack distinguished between fashions that were merely obnoxious and those that were dangerous. Anything that emphasized the distinction between male and female was tolerable; anything that attempted to overcome the distinction demanded resistance: "We may allow them to incommode themselves with their Hoop-Petticoats without parting with an Inch of our Prerogative; for we know to our Cost that they differ *widely* from the Breeches."[19] Brimmed hats on women, because they diminished the male advantage in height and mocked male profile, had to be knocked off.

Of the fashions that contributed to forming the new female gentility, none was so important as tea drinking itself. Hoop petticoats, hats, and ribbons might have been essentials in the equipage of a town madam, but without the tea party she would have been all dressed up with no place to go. How, then, did the taking of tea become the central rite in the new feminine mysteries? How did the oriental beverage come to be so directly associated with the taste of British and Anglo-American women? The chain of circumstances was roughly this: as England's empire of trade pumped more and more consumer goods into the metropolis during the mid-seventeenth century, a peculiar vogue grew up in affluent circles for strange beverages: first chocolate, then coffee, and, finally, in 1657, tea. Around coffee a new institution sprang up, the coffeehouse, which city gentlemen made their own. Men of like interest tended to congregate at particular premises. Quickly the coffeehouses became places of business for a population of entrepreneurs and jobbers. Heretofore business had been conducted at home. When men and men's work moved out of the house to coffeehouses, the ladies saw it as a blow to the integrity of the household and an attack upon female rights granted in the covenant of domesticity. In works such as *The Women's Petition against Coffee* (1674),

---

19. Homespun Jack, [essay on female fashion], *New-England Courant*, no. 138, Mar. 23, 1724. The fashion of hoop-petticoats provoked substantial comment in New England, particularly since Massachusetts whalers supplied the material used as stays. See *The Origin of the Whale Bone-Petticoat: A Satyr, Boston, August 2d, 1714* (Boston, 1714).

female wits linked the homosociality of the coffeehouse with the emasculating effect of "the Excessive Use of that Drying, Enfeebling LIQUOR."[20]

Women's embrace of tea must be understood as a reaction to the masculine infatuation with coffee and all that it implied. That women seized upon tea and not chocolate as their drink was due to the influence of Catherine of Braganza, the consort of Charles II. She made tea the novelty of the Stuart court, having learned the proper technique for brewing the liquor in her native Portugal. (Before the Restoration, coffeehouses served tea that had been brewed in cold casks where liquid and leaves steeped to a tannic syrup so bitter that it set one's teeth grinding.) Brewing tea was simple. One did not have to roast, grind, or percolate anything. Boiling water was poured over the dried leaves in a pot and allowed to sit until the infusion had taken on the desired color. The liquor was then poured through a strainer into ceramic cups. Tea could be prepared at home without great fuss. It provided elevation (the caffeine kick) without intoxication. Physicians approved it for a range of ailments from colds to fevers. Most believed it cured ague. Medicinal, flavorful, fashionable, and capable of domestic preparation, tea became the drink of choice among the female gentility.[21]

20. Wolfgang Schivelbusch, *Tastes of Paradise: A Social History of Spices, Stimulants, and Intoxicants* (New York, 1992), 78–86; Aytoun Ellis, *The Penny Universities: A History of the Coffee-Houses* (London, 1956), 88. The best feminist commentary on the gendering of tea is Beth Kowalski-Wallace, "Tea, Gender, and Domesticity in Eighteenth-Century England," *Studies in Eighteenth-Century Culture*, XXIII (East Lansing, Mich., 1994), 131–145. Kowalski-Wallace's account differs from mine in purpose and in evidence but makes the same point: tea was gendered as the result of specific historical circumstances connected with the structure of European court and mercantile cultures.

21. William H. Ukers, *All about Tea*, 2 vols. (New York, 1935), I, 43–45. A further impetus to the adoption of tea in the court was a 1666 entertainment held by Lady Arlington and Lady Ossory featuring tea shipped from The Hague. Ukers is the standard English-language history of tea, its trade and culture.

It may be that the cask brewing and storing of tea was dictated by the excise officers who administered the licensing and taxing of tea; 21 Car. II, c. 23, 24 placed a duty on every gallon of tea sold. This standard of measure might have required that coffeehouse-keepers produce and store tea in large volume.

The Dutch were the most influential early publicists of the medical benefits of tea. Nikolas Tulp [Dr. Nikolas Dirx], *Observationes Medicae* (Amsterdam, 1641), and Cornelis Bontekoe, *Tractaat van het excellenste kruyd thee* (The Hague, 1679), were widely circulated medical recommendations of tea, prescribing it for a range of ailments such as fatigue, gravel, gallstones, headaches, colds, ophthalmia, catarrh, asthma, indigestion, and constipation.

The question remains, How did circles of English women gather around the teapot? The court, where tea was popularized, was a mixed-sex society. When ladies served tea at home, they originally dispensed it to the mixed company of the drawing room or to the family. Sometime — the date cannot be determined precisely, 1690 will be suggested here — the tea cabals began to form. Why? Perhaps it was a cultural legacy of the Glorious Revolution, one of the practices imported with William and Mary's Dutch entourage. In Holland in the latter decades of the seventeenth century, circles of tea-drinking Dutch ladies gathered in taverns. If the women of England did adopt the Dutch model, they dispensed with the favored Dutch locale. Most English tea circles met in the parlors of town houses or country mansions. The early evening hour (6:00–7:00 P.M.) that became the favorite time for teas was also the prime hour for business in the coffeehouses in England.[22] The absence of men from the house afforded an occasion for women to be out and visiting among themselves. By the 1710s the tea table was a fixture of city life in Britain; it was the superintending agency in the spread of manners and taste among British American women by the 1720s.

Tea and teawares were costly in the early decades of the eighteenth century. The woman who had a set either possessed personal wealth or had a powerful say in the disposition of the household purse. In 1722, "Anthony Fallshort" laid out a sample budget for a "Journeyman Gentlewoman" in Boston. Of the £1,836.4.4 needed to set up in style, £257.3.11 went "To a Tea Table worth its Equipage, Sugar, Tea, etc.," the largest line item in the ledger, topping the cost of three silk suits (£101.11.7), a "fine Parrot" (£23), Knick-knacks (£124.8.5), 105 pairs of white gloves (£25.1.3), and a chambermaid's board and wages (£211.17.0). The £257 bought sugar, tea (Bohea sold at 24s. per pound in 1720), a teapot, slop bowl (strainer), cream container, tea canister, sugar container, tongs, teaspoons, cups, and saucers. It also bought the table upon which tea was served and the tea service displayed. The effects of such displays on the fancies of middle-class women became the butt of one of Benjamin Franklin's finer early satires, the letter of tradesman "Anthony Afterwit" complaining about his wife's consumer fetish:

22. Kit Chow and Ione Kramer, *All the Tea in China* (San Francisco, 1990), 15. The four o'clock tea time was an innovation of the early nineteenth century, attributed by legend to Anna, tenth countess of Bedford (Gilles Brochard, "Time for Teah," in Anthony Burgess, *The Book of Tea* [Paris, 1992], 161)..

My Wife being entertain'd with *Tea* by the Good Women she visited, we could do no less than the like when they visited us; and so we got a *Tea-Table* with all its Appurtenances of *China* and *Silver*. Then my Spouse unfortunately overwork'd herself in washing the House, so that we could do no longer without a *Maid*.

Her fit of acquisition worsened with purchases of a clock and a "fine pacing Mare." After a severe dunning for debt, Afterwit sold his wife's entire equipage when she was off on a social visit.[23]

Franklin was astute enough in his satire not to attempt to turn ladies of quality away from their favorite pastime. The target of his ridicule was women of the middling sort, the would-be gentlewoman who violated the codes of prudence and frugality that regulated middle-class morality. When writers attempted to destroy the fashionability of tea for a readership of gentlewomen, the rhetoric played to the readers' vanity.[24] The most insidious attacks were couched as medical advices, such as this front-page newspaper diatribe:

> *Tea* increases the Quantity of *Bile* in too frequent Drinkers of it. Now what Physicians call *Bile*, is a yellow Bitter, (and consequently hot) Liquor diffus'd about the Body. And underneath the fine *thin* skin of *Women's Faces*, where it communicates its ill-favour'd, dingy Colour, making Women, if they are of *cool* Constitutions, to look very *Pale*, or *Tawny*, or *Swarthy:* And if they are of *warmer* Constitutions, then it gives them *Red, Ruby, Plain looking Faces*, and *Red Noses*. Then the *Hot* Adust Quality of this *Bilous* Humour in their *Faces, dries up*, and *shrivels* their Skin, and thereby brings *Wrinkles* on Women's Faces, long before Age does. Hence Physicians call *Bile* the *Mother of Deformity*, and nothing increases

23. Anthony Fallshort, "Journeymen Gentlewoman," *New-England Courant*, no. 34, Mar. 26, 1722; Anthony Afterwit [Benjamin Franklin], letter, *Pennsylvania Gazette*, no. 189, July 10, 1732. For a historical treatment of tea consumption and status in Virginia, see Ann Smart Martin, "Teadrinking in a New Consumer World: A Case Study of Cultural Meaning," in "Buying into the World of Goods: Eighteenth-Century Consumerism and the Retail Trade from London to the Virginia Frontier" (Ph.D. diss., College of William and Mary, 1993), 319–354.

24. This is not to say preachers did not make direct denunciations on moral grounds: for instance, *Reflections on the Evil Consequences of Tea-Drinking* (n.p., 1760) (Evans 41869; no copy survives). As late as 1774, when halting the practice was a lost cause, a minister could still publish *A Sermon on Tea* (Lancaster, Pa., [1774]). But conversions of old opponents such as George Whitefield to the cause of the leaf decreased the number of Christian critics as the century wore on.

Bile more in Women's Faces than too frequent drinking of *Tea*. So that if Women would drink less *Tea*, they would Preserve their *Beauty*.[25]

Specious arguments could not stem the rising tide of tea or diminish its social cachet. Few believed that tea was the liquor of ugliness. As Rodris Roth has shown, tea drinking became a popular habit by midcentury, not limited to the tables of the elite. Foreign visitors to British America noted that a cup of tea had become "the country people's daily breakfast." Cheaper leaf and teawares had altered tea drinking from a luxury to a household commonplace. Concurrently, the coffeehouse and coffee suffered a decline in popularity. Men in increasing numbers became tea drinkers, particularly gentlemen who wished entrée into the drawing rooms of genteel women. Some — George Washington, for instance — grew quite avid in their devotion to the leaf. Attendance at tea was frequently the sole noteworthy event recorded for days on end in Washington's diaries during the deliberations on the Constitution.[26]

Given the richness of contemporary testimonies to the cultural influence of the tea table and the wealth of material objects that survive from the circles, the paucity of literary remains of the tea table is striking. No substantial transcription of the women's conversations has survived from the period when the cabals rose to power, perhaps in part because talk had greater vivacity and pointedness than transcripts of talk.[27] The formality of most forms of literary work stood at odds with the spontaneity of talk. Even when read aloud, any essay, tale, or poem longer than an epigram smacked of artificiality in the heady breeze of scandal and repartee. Informal literary modes — impromptus, epigrams, and anecdotes — were better suited to tea-table communication, the sort of stuff "writ in company." It is

25. *New-England Weekly Journal*, no. 537, July 19, 1737.

26. Rodris Roth, "Tea Drinking in Eighteenth-Century America: Its Etiquette and Equipage," *Contributions from the Museum of History and Technology*, United States National Museum Bulletin no. 225 (Washington, D.C., 1961), 84. Donald Jackson and Dorothy Twohig, eds., *The Diaries of George Washington*, 6 vols. (Charlottesville, Va., 1976–1979). Read through any stretch of vol. V or VI when Washington is in Philadelphia.

27. Kathryn Zabelle Derounian, *The Journal and Occasional Writings of Sarah Wister* (Rutherford, N.J., 1987), 53–54. Sarah Wister (1761–1804) attended Benezet's Quaker's Girl School, where she met Deborah Norris, one intended reader of the journal. She was known to her friends and appears in the journal as "Sally." A "sample of female conversation" from the town madams who invaded the audience of the pirates' trial in Boston is included in Kitchen Stuff's account, *New-England Courant*, no. 146, May 18, 1724.

noteworthy that *The Journal of Madam [Sarah Kemble] Knight*, the one masterwork of British American literature seemingly prepared for the delectation of a tea table, is liberally sprinkled with such verses. Madam Knight had unusual expertise as a writer, having worked as a scrivener in Boston. Legend also speaks of her running a writing school. If anyone was equipped to intrude a script into the tea table's continuum of talk, it was she. In the final entry of her 1704 journal of travels through New England, she wrote of recounting the "story" of her "transactions and travails" to her "Kind relations and friends." That is, she read her journal aloud to a company—not unusual in the English-speaking world of 1704. Thomas Wright's 1693 play, *The Female Vertuoso's*, a satire on a London society of women, featured a scene in which a visitor read a journal of travels through the English countryside to the company; the implication was that such readings were the latest metropolitan fashion.[28]

Sarah Kemble Knight's narrative featured all of the signal concerns of the new female sociability. The urbanity of a "lady of quality" was evident in every witticism about the rudeness of the country between Boston and New York City. The wilderness that Knight bemoaned was, not the pagan forest that haunted the Puritan, but the incivility of the countryside and the deficiency of village people in speech, dress, manners, and material. As befitted a connoisseur of sociable talk, Knight had an acute ear for conversations heard along the way. Talk was a social marker, revealing one's true standing on the index of gentility. Thus "Bumpkin Simpers" and "Jone Tawdry" on a fashionable ribbon:

BUMPKIN: Its confounded Gay I Vow.
JONE: Law, You, its right Gent.
BUMPKIN: Do You, take it
JONE: 'Tis dreadfull pretty.[29]

The itinerant tradesmen and goodwives of New England in no way yielded to their Cockney counterparts when it came to bumptious phraseology.

28. Sarah Kemble Knight, *The Journal of Madam Knight*, in Wendy Martin, ed., *Colonial American Travel Narratives* (New York, 1994); Thomas Wright, *The Female Vertuoso's: A Comedy, as It Is Acted at the Queen's Theatre, by Their Majesties Servants* (London, 1693). In the play Sir Maurice observes, "The women of Old did not read so much, but lived better, Housewifry was all the Knowledge they aspired to; now adays Wives must Write forsooth, and pretend to Wit with a Pox."

29. *Journal of Madam Knight*, in Martin, ed., *Colonial American Travel Narratives*, 66. I have recast into dialogue form.

Fashion mattered for Knight. When she encountered the truly sumptuous in New York City, her descriptions of the dress and jewelry were precise and detailed:

> The English go very fasheonable in their dress. But the Dutch, especially the middling sort, differ from our women, in their habitt go loose, were French muches wch are like a Capp and a head band in one, leaving their ears bare, which are sett out wth Jewells of large size and many in number. And their fingers hoop't with Rings, some with large stones in them of many Coullers as were their pendants in their ears, which You should see very old women wear as well as Young.

Her consciousness of the material condition of people, particularly the layout, finish, and furnishing of their houses, manifested a worldly-mindedness characteristic of the city madam or "Journeyman Gentlewoman" of Boston. Finally, Knight's pride in venturing into public spaces where women commonly did not go showed that she championed the great enterprise of the tea tables, projecting female presence in public places and affairs. One is tempted to attribute her defamatory wit to the spirit of tea-table gossip, but there were more direct models for her journal's arch manner.

Grub Street's literature of defamatory travels had obtruded upon the attention of Bostonians in 1699 when Ned Ward published *A Trip to New-England*. This account and the related books were narrated by a figure whose gentility was offended by the crudities of life in inhospitable lands. Knight's journal, because of the sex of the narrator and because of her cultivation of a comic resignation in the face of travail typical of the picaresque heroine, possesses more interest than most works in the genre.[30] Yet it runs absolutely true to form in organizing all perceptions around the opposition of gentility to crudity. Here the values of the travel writers and the denizens of the tea table coincide. Yet this coincidence must be understood as incidental—a function of Grub Street and the tea table both realizing that the cultural moment was characterized by a redefinition of social and cultural hierarchy in manners and style. Knight attempted to reinforce the canons of civility and propose the centrality of women in making public space polite. Her writing enlisted the power of women in

---

30. Concerning the picaresque persona of Madam Knight, see Kathryn Zabelle Derounian-Stodola, "The New England Frontier and the Picaresque in Sarah Kemble Knight's Journal," in Derounian-Stodola, eds., *Early American Literature and Culture: Essays Honoring Harrison T. Meserole* (Newark, Del., 1992), 122–131.

the task of publicizing urbane manners and fashion. It organized women behind an interest in wielding a form of public power. Grub Street, conversely, burlesqued the enterprise of cultural hierarchy by making all "others" so uncivil that their monstrosity beggared belief.

In Boston the tea table was successful in great measure because its cultural projects were limited and practical. By the 1730s women had access to a range of public spaces theretofore restricted. They had succeeded in forming a widespread feminine interest in fashion and its material manifestations, an interest that would subvert the old sumptuary customs and lead to a demotic form of gentility — respectability. They had organized a network of polite circles that by conversation policed the reputations of members of the genteel classes; scandal could be said to have a punitive power upon violators of social convention equal to Christian admonition. There were, however, limits to the influence of circles organized primarily among women. Men still determined politics, dominated the arts, and determined much of the exercise of commerce. Polite women with a will to power saw the necessity of conversing with men in order to influence them, and prescient women, such as Elizabeth Magawley, understood that the sorts of men attracted to the feminine conversation practiced at the tea table were not the sort most worth influencing. Magawley's strategy was twofold: to reform the tea table to make it more interesting to men of affairs, and to draw men of sense into the company by extending the promise that conversation with women would be to their advantage. Her task was to supplant the tea table's reputation for gossip with that older promise, sounded in French courtesy literature: Conversation with women gives polish to men, rendering them more polite and therefore more socially effective. Salons had given French women a hand in affairs of state by incorporating men of affairs into a conversation superintended by women.[31] Magawley would make a salon of the tea table.

There were problems in translating French cultural practices into British and British American conduct.[32] Whereas sexual allure contributed to the charm of society and became a dimension of the aesthetics of social

31. See Dena Goodman, *The Republic of Letters: A Cultural History of the French Enlightenment* (Ithaca, N.Y., 1994).

32. It could be argued that a salon wholly on the French model did not exist in America until Anne Willing Bingham's in Philadelphia in the 1780s and 1790s. Wendy A. Nicholson, "Making the Private Public: Anne Willing Bingham's Role as a Leader of Philadelphia's Social Elite in the Eighteenth Century" (master's thesis, Winterthur Program, University of Delaware, 1988).

play in France, in Britain it threatened the contractual basis of voluntary association. Reason and law, the governing directives of British society, were threatened by the personal power exerted by charming women. A political aphorism of 1702 observed, "The reason why Women have a greater share in the government of France, than they have in that of England, is, because France is a Government of Men, and England a Government of Laws, the former they know how to manage, the latter they are not bred to understand."[33] The dilemma facing women like Magawley was which promise to make in order to entice men into the female company. Intellectual stimulation? The possibility of love? The possibility of a rapport that encompassed both mind and heart? And what end did the incorporation serve? To project power in affairs of state? To learn those principles of law and government that women were not bred to understand? To cultivate oneself by improving sense? The pleasure of varied and worldly company? One thing is certain: the salon in Britain and British America, when it did come to fruition after the 1750s, made the cultivation of sense the overriding concern in the conversation of mixed company, just as it made the tutelage of sensibility the ruling passion of sisterly communication. The hallmarks of the bluestocking would be moral earnestness, a concern with education that verged on didacticism, a turn from oral to written communication, and the elevation of feminine sympathy into a political principle.[34]

This advance did not mean the total eclipse of tea tables peopled by gossips, romps, and fashionable idiots. They remained fixtures of the cultural scene in British America throughout the colonial period. In 1773 John Trumbull made "The Progress of Coquetry, or the Adventures of Miss Harriet Simper" the third of his immensely popular satires of American manners in *The Progress of Dulness*.[35] Yet their dominion over elite women's society and conversation had been broken. The sort of transformation of feminine conversation that Magawley had advocated was sufficiently advanced by the 1760s that a provincial woman could demystify the attractions of an English spa for a female friend without being prudish or insensible to its pleasures. Elizabeth Graeme, a seasoned Philadelphian of

33. [Brown], *Laconics*, 28.

34. For the cultural program of the English bluestocking set, see Sylvia Harcstark Myers, *The Bluestocking Circle: Women, Friendship, and the Life of the Mind in Eighteenth-Century England* (Oxford, 1990).

35. [John Trumbull], *The Progress of Dulness, Part Third* . . . (New Haven, Conn., 1773).

PLATE 4 Francis Hopkinson and Elizabeth Graeme. *Drawing by Benjamin West. Philadelphia. Permission of the Historical Society of Pennsylvania, Philadelphia*

twenty-four, visited Scarborough in September 1764, sampled the diversions of the resort, and passed judgment in a letter whose tone of bemusement conveyed more sense than any censorious rebuke of the bon ton.[36]

To Miss Betsy Stedman in Philadelphia: giving her an
Account of the Movements of one Day as spent by people of
Fashion in the full Season at Scarborough

Dear Betsy since your Friend at last;
Thro' various Scenes of Life hath past;
How spend in haste for you to know
May please some moments as they go.

When chamber Clocks at Eight do chime
Your Maid informs you 'tis the Time
To Rise; and for the Bath prepare
And breath the Sea Salubrious Air;
Close in a *House* by Horses drawn
You view the beautys of the Morn
First darting thro a pane of Glass
Enough for Phoebus Rays to Pass.
Disrobd of Cloaths in flannel Dress;
Each Beau and Bell the Waters press!
Return and Chat with sprightly Glee,
O'er *Coffee*, *Chocalate*, and *Tea*:
The Breakfast past to *Deards* we run,
To cheapen Toys but purchase none;
Then saunter up and down the Room,

36. Graeme went to England in the company of the Reverend Richard Peters. She recorded her impressions in a journal that circulated among the literati of Philadelphia upon her return. Certain of the poetic portions of the journal were copied into the "Poemata Juvenilia." The text of her epistle derives from this collection. The journal was lost sometime at the beginning of the nineteenth century. Its remnants include an anecdote published in the *Universal Asylum and Columbian Magazine* (March 1791). A more extensive section — ten MS pages in all — was copied by Milcah Martha Moore into her commonplace book preserved at Haverford College, now edited by Catherine La Courreye Blecki and Karin A. Wulf: *Milcah Martha Moore's Book* . . . (University Park, Pa., 1997).

This poem and all subsequent verses by Graeme are taken from the major surviving compilation (made in 1793) of her early work, "Poemata Juvenilia," Library Company of Philadelphia, MS 13494.Q.

And laugh of every weight or Gloom.
Then leaving of the Rooms above;
We talk of *Friendship*, *Wit*, and *Love;*
Just as the present Whim prevails;
For judgment Seldom turns the Scales,
By three we make a Shift to dine
Oh how ones hurryd here for Time!
Be sure the Coach is at the Door!
Precisly at the Stroke of Four!
Then off we Skim to reach the Ground;
Where Grooms; and Racers hem us round;
One bet on Beaumont one on Spinner
A third Swears Angel shall prove winner;
This point discussd; for none will yield
We turn our Cars and View the Field;
The Coursers Start and reach the *goals*
While Hope and Fear usurp the Souls
That warmly feels the Joyous Race
And Stak's their Mony on the Place.
Now Crys and Oaths are heard around
Aplauss or Murmurs quick rebound;
The Victor Gay the loser Sad;
Some Sullen seem; while others Mad
Fly from the Turf dejected Home
With empty pockets pensive roam.
We then return where China's Leaf;
Composes every female Grief;
(If Griefs we have) but Forms so fair
Can harbor no ungentle Care!
So say the Men! they little know;
How 'oft we taste the Cup of Woe.
The Gay *pompoon* and *Negligee;*
Are hurryd on before the Tea;
We join the Rooms and then advance;
With pleasure to the sprightly Dance;
Now this Nymphs Shape, and that ones air
Amanda's Face and Chloes Hair
Must stand the Test of Female Knowledge
As some New Book at Oxford's College:

Partys divide to Crib or Whist
Something to chance we all must risque;
Here fashion Rules with Tyrant Sway
Who will not Bow should keep away,
Return and Sup, and laugh, and Sing;
And make remarks on every Thing:
In this one point we all agree
That Granby's nobel Generous Free.
This Scene of Dissipation o'er;
We dream on all we saw before.

And think you now my dearest Bess
A Moral may be drawn from this?
When opening on Lifes early dawn
All Nature seems a flowing lawn;
O'er spread with Sweets, bedeck with smiles
That 'oft our weary Steps beguiles;
With Vigor too we join the Chaice
Tho' often Losses by the Race;
Then try some new amusment o'er }
And drain from Fancy all her Store }
Old Age dreams what is Saw before.}

Graeme's moral is subtler than any pious commonplace: the danger of giving oneself over to the fashionable world lies in the exhaustion of one's fancy. Glutting oneself with the world's sensations consumes vitality; the pursuit of amusement expends psychic and physical energy. After the sensations have all been experienced, one's subsequent life is devitalized. Fancy turns backward, recycling old stimuli. One loses the capacity to approach the future creatively. Without using the word "dissipation," Graeme illustrated how one's substance or energy wasted away through continual dispersion in a way that would permit anyone with medical knowledge to venture a symptomology.

Graeme's argument possessed an element of rhetorical guile. Reiterating the strictures of the pulpit on the fashionable world would, no doubt, have appeared a sort of mindless pharisaism to Betsy Stedman, a young provincial woman smitten with the romance of metropolitan fashion. To claim that immersion in the chase foreclosed one's worldly future, rather than one's otherworldly future, had the force of novelty. The genius of Graeme's "Account" lay in its simultaneous evocation of the pleasurable commotion of resort life and the suggestion that all the activity produced little enduring benefit. Stedman would not doubt that she was receiving a true representation of the beau monde. Yet part of the truth communicated in the account was that, like the stakes race that occupied Scarborough's attention during the afternoon, the pursuit of fashionable diversion rewarded pursuers arbitrarily. Consider how many of Graeme's activities seem fruitless: she goes shopping, but does not buy; she attends the race, but only witnesses the wins and losses; she promenades, dances, joins the card tables, talks of friendship, wit, and love, but attracts no friend or lover. "We" seem caught up in a whimsical play of gestures lacking substance or certitude. Consider the passage on the tea table, that most familiar institution of feminine sociability. First, it appears as the place of consolation (presumably from losses at the stakes), then as an enclave of beauty that grief cannot trouble. Then, reacting to this gallant fiction, it sounds as female opinion, declaring that men know little of women's woe: whereupon Graeme suggests a cause for male ignorance, flashing back to a scene of women costuming themselves for tea, seemingly to fulfill the male stereotype of the tea table as the realm of gaiety.

Such variety of guises prevents any simple response to the tea table. Graeme's representations of Scarborough complicate the task of moral judgment by never letting matters be illuminated long by the light of preconception. Never are Graeme's criticisms of resort society simply prejudices fleshed into caricatures. Instead, they emerge from a reflective engagement in the talk and play of the town. Her disquiet, the moral turn of her thinking, shows up the vaporousness of spa talk. Graeme finds relationships among men and women "whimsical." Because the resort lacks a moral sense, judgment ceases to be a function of human care, becoming an instrument of malice. Where does one see judgment in Scarborough? Only when women were subjected to the feminine gaze in the assembly rooms. Then a woman's competitors in the grand display passed judgment on her attractiveness.

Graeme's judgment is not malicious, for in her censoring of the scene she invariably includes herself as a participant in the town's vanities. By using a plural first-person pronoun through the poem, Graeme fulfills the first requisite of moral inquiry, undergoing self-trial before censoring others. "We" operated amorphously in the poem, encompassing at times the whole of the fashionable company, the fashionable women, and even incorporating the intended reader, Betsy Stedman. By including herself as the subject of judgment, Graeme avoided the problem of appearing a self-righteous censor. She remained identified with the other actors participating in the "we." The bonds of fellow feeling were maintained in this manner of judgment.

Because the fashionable world itself did not instruct one in this sensible mode of fellow feeling, the question arises, Whence did Graeme derive her sense of judgmental perspective? How was she equipped by education and experience to be able to stand at that point both complicit and judgmental that marks bemusement? To answer this question we must turn to her earliest poetry, the compositions that mark her intellectual and aesthetic development.

The Garden of Sensibility

Elizabeth Graeme was the most conspicuous of a community of women poets who circulated writings through the Delaware Valley during the latter half of the eighteenth century. The daughter of Dr. Thomas and Anne Diggs Graeme, Elizabeth grew up in a polite and learned gentry household. Her father had come to Pennsylvania as an attendant to Governor William Keith (a physician and placeman). He used his position to secure substantial property — including Keith's house — and secure a place in the Anglican elite. Elizabeth's circle of friends and relations included the Moores of Moore Hall, the Stedmans, the Willings, and the Abercrombies. These gentry families practiced the rites of hospitality, visiting one another's country houses and town houses. Graeme Park, in the Philadelphia suburb of Horsham, was one of a number of exurban mansions that became outposts of gentility on the English "big house" model.[37]

---

37. The study of the women poets of the Delaware Valley was pioneered by Pattie Cowell in her ground-breaking collection, *Women Poets in Pre-Revolutionary America, 1650–1775: An Anthology* (Troy, N.Y., 1981). The community included Susanna Wright, Deborah Logan, Annis Boudinot Stockton, Elizabeth Graeme Fergusson, Hannah Griffitts, Rebecca Moore, and Deborah Pratt Ruff during the colonial period. It expanded greatly in the post-Revolutionary era.

Susan Stabile is presently completing a Ph.D. dissertation at the University of Delaware about the institutional organization and discursive character of their exchange: "American Women Writers of the Middle Colonies, 1770–1820."

On Graeme, see Simon Gratz, "Some Material for a Biography of Mrs. Elizabeth Fergusson, *née* Graeme," *PMHB*, XXXIX (1915), 257–321, 385–409, XLI (1917), 385–398; Chester T. Hallenbeck, "The Life and Collected Poems of Elizabeth Graeme

The young women who learned to write in these settings articulated a self-understanding that displayed a remarkably consistent symbolism. All assumed neoclassical cognomens. All identified a pastoral landscape as home. The felicities of this home were invariably contrasted to the vanities of the city. "Emilia" (Annis Boudinot) offered the usual counsel:

Leave the towns deceitful noise
Its peagentry and pride.[38]

"Felicia" (Deborah Pratt) complained that she was

Tir'd of the noise and folly of the town,
Shock'd to see Sin so bold, and Virtue flown;
(For virtue now, neglected, hides her face,
And Vice, in gaudy garb, assumes her place—
What pleasure then can be expected there.)[39]

This contempt for the city is explicitly suburban: the advantages of town life (conversation, friendship, sociability) are at hand in these rural places because of their proximity to population, on which their fortunes de-

---

Ferguson" (master's thesis, Columbia University, 1929); Martha C. Slotten, "Elizabeth Graeme Ferguson: A Poet in 'The Athens of North America,'" *PMHB*, CVIII (1984), 259–288; Mark Reinberger, "Graeme Park and the Three-Cell Plan: A Lost Type in Colonial Architecture," in Thomas Carter and Bernard L. Herman, *Perspectives in Vernacular Architecture*, IV (Columbia, Mo., 1991), 146–154.

38. Annis Boudinot, "An Invitation Ode to a Young Lady in New York from Her Friend in the Country—New Brunswick May the 22nd, 1752," in Carla Mulford, ed., *"Only for the Eye of a Friend": The Poetry of Annis Boudinot Stockton* (Charlottesville, Va., 1995), 71. Annis Boudinot Stockton, the eldest daughter of Elias Boudinot and Catherine Williams, was born July 1, 1736, in Darby, Pennsylvania. Her father was a silversmith and merchant whose interest in mining and manufactures caused him to resettle in New Brunswick. She married Richard Stockton of Princeton sometime in late 1757 or 1758. At the Stockton mansion, Morven, she established a literary salon that lasted into the post-Revolutionary era. When the Continental Congress moved temporarily to Princeton in 1783, she served as hostess, establishing a prototype for the republican court. She composed poems throughout her life.

39. Deborah Pratt, "Felicia to Marcia, 1765," Deborah Pratt Ruff Notebook, Manuscript Collection, American Antiquarian Society. Deborah Pratt was daughter of tavernkeeper Henry Pratt III and Rebecca Claypool and the sister of painter Matthew Pratt. For her biography, see William Sawitzky, *Matthew Pratt, 1734–1805: A Study of His Work* (New York, 1942).

pended. Here is none of the anxiety expressed by the truly rusticated — that sense that Susanna Wright had when removing to the wilds of Conestoga,

> From all the social world estrang'd
>   In desert wilds in woods
> Books and engaging friends exchang'd
>   For pendant rocks and floods.[40]

The suburban countryside possessed a number of cherished features:

> A pleasant cottage on a rising ground,
> A fertile soil, kind neighbours all around;
> Thick shades and murm'ring brooks within our view.[41]

Nature's benignity appeared so undisturbed that the landscape appeared as a garden. This garden, with the labor of its creation and maintenance rendered invisible, seemed a Horatian place of achieved civility. Only Rebecca Moore discovered in the landscape a tiller of the soil, an ideal yeoman producing peace and plenty (no Thomsonian laborer suffering the depredations of insects, intemperate weather, and the vicissitudes of markets). Rebecca, daughter of Judge William Moore and Lady Williamina Wemyss, had grown up in Moore Hall, the fieldstone mansion dominating the Schuylkill River at Pickering Creek in Chester County, Pennsylvania. Her father had an Oxford education (supposedly), a twelve-hundred-acre estate, a pew at St. David's Church, Radnor, and a contentious spirit, often provoked by the Quaker party in the Assembly. Her mother, kin to the third earl of Wemyss, possessed a forbearance in the face of political tumult born of a Jacobite heritage. It would serve her well, particularly when Judge Moore and Provost William Smith were imprisoned for their political activity. Rebecca would marry her father's prison companion, Provost Smith, shortly after his release in 1758, and would preside over Smith's Philadelphia household, where the Schuylkill Swains met and experimented with

40. Susanna Wright: "The following lines were written in the year 1726 by Susanna Wright on removing from Chester County to the banks of the Susquehana — the spot where the Town of Columbia now stands," J. Watson Notebook (Am 301), 501, Historical Society of Pennsylvania. The current interest in Wright's work was stimulated by Pattie Cowell, "'Womankind Call Reason to Their Aid': Susanna Wright's Verse Epistle on the Status of Women in Eighteenth-Century America," *Signs*, VI (1980–1981), 795–800.

41. Pratt, "Felicia to Marcia, 1764." The echo of John Pomfret, *The Choice* (London, 1700), is striking.

poetry, oratory, and painting.[42] Rather than labor, the garden harbored play or contemplative pastimes such as reading, conversing, and reverencing the Creator. More than anything else, nature seemed the garden of friendship, where companions learned new depths of sympathy and virtue. Deborah Pratt's brief invitation rang all the changes of the symbolism:

1762. To Marcia

Come, Marcia, from the noisy town,
    To sylvan scenes repair,
Where you and I'll together roam,
    And breathe the wholesome air.

With earliest birds we'll cheerful rise,
    And adoration pay
To the great Ruler of the skies,
    Who guides us through the day.

We, in the sultry noontide hours,
    Will seek the coolest shade,
Or, in sweet smelling jes'mine bow'rs,
    We'll calmly sit and read.

And when with reading we have done,
    We'll take our ev'ning walk,
To view the glorious setting sun,
    Or of our Friends to talk.

Then with the sun we'll go to rest,
    But first with rev'rence pray
We may with balmy sleep be blest,
    And crown'd with health each day.

Thus we'll our happy hours employ
    In friendly acts of peace,
And taste each pure and heav'nly joy
    That conscious virtue gives.[43]

Here nature was a sensorium of modest pleasures. Its ordered and elemental cycles inculcated a sense of divine and moral regularity into its inhabit-

---

42. Rebecca Moore, "To My Ever Dear Miss Graeme Moore Hall June th. 28 1756," in Graeme, "Poemata Juvenilia."

43. Pratt, "1762. To Marcia," Deborah Pratt Ruff Notebook.

ants. Lacking human want, the fatigues of labor, history, or the vanities of urban life, it was an experimental haven for the heart, where, undisturbed, young persons might explore the possibilities of friendship and social joy. The wholesomeness of this garden preserve existed in specific tension with city life (competitive, vain, energetic, immoderate), with commerce (the agitations of the "vulgar few in trade, / Whose minds by miser avarice were sway'd" [Pratt, 1765]), and with eruptions of history into the countryside such as the Seven Years' War.[44] It was also disturbed by the immoderate passion of men. Besides being pastoral, suburban, and sensible, besides being the expressions of a leisure class, the poetry of the country house was overwhelmingly sisterly. Friendship prevailed only where dispassionate reason, religion, and a trusting sympathy reigned. Men obtruded passion, wit, and love into this rural preserve such that their presence was problematic unless it was confined to wishes about the ideal partner or to a metonymic presence in books. (Milton, Thomson, Isaac Watts, and Edward Young were always welcome in the garden.)

Elizabeth Graeme's development as a poet is marked precisely by her working out the problem of male presence in the garden of female sensibility. From the first, her overriding concern in poetry was exploring her affective response to society, debating the degree of emotional commitment to persons in it. Her earliest verses were all in speculative forms: dream visions, wishes, declarations of ideals—all projecting desiderata for social interaction. In her first surviving poem, "A Dream," the nymph "Friendship" visits her and provokes a psychic crisis about her feelings for "Strephon." Should the dreamer withdraw with Friendship, or stay and risk "some Danger if I made delay"? This verse was followed by a reflection, "On the Preference of Friendship to Love," in which she claimed that

> Friendships Steady Flame as far;
> Out shines that transient Blaze
> As Mid Day suns a glimmering Star.

In poem after poem, "Laura" opts for moderated emotion. The presence of men in her world raised the issue of passion and its uncontrollability. In "The Maids Choice" the poet-maid "Rossella" specifies the qualities a youth must possess "To Suite Rossellas Heart":

---

44. Deborah Pratt, "To Miss Becky Jennings, of Bermuda, on Her Making a Curious Cabinet and Hat," ibid.

His Passions should be guided,
　　By Reason's ruling Hand;
And with Good Sense provided,
　　Rossela to Command.

In "The Choice of Life," Graeme uses the popular "ingredients of contentment" formula popularized by John Pomfret to visualize an ideal existence. Her original version of the poem declared that contentment could be gained only if she could "strip rough passion of its force / Nor let it intervene." The danger lies in subjective feeling. Toward the end of her life, Graeme struck out these lines, indicating instead that contentment "must be a work of time / to give the world up by degrees / and pleasures to resign." The world, not subjective feeling, is the great hindrance to happiness in the mind of the experienced salonniere.

Graeme reconceived the problem of passion in "A Pastoral Dialogue between Damon and Alexis." The poet observed in a note, "This little piece took its rise from a dispute, pasing one Evening in Company; whether the feeling or insinsible Minds were the happiest this Life." Alexis suffers from an overly sympathetic heart, feeling the woes that afflict his neighbors. Damon practices a brand of stoicism, remaining unmoved by the pleasures and woes of others while enjoying a constant philosophic calm. Alexis rejects Damon's philosophy as a type of mechanical living on so narrow a plan as to dwindle man to degeneracy. In turn, Damon rejects Alexis's "universal love" because it necessarily subjects him to the dominion of gloom, given the fallen condition of the world. He punctuates his argument with a hypothetical case:

Ther's Sylvia gay whom you adore;
And of that lov'ly Maid think more;
Than if you were possessed of all,
The Wealth that fills this earthly Ball;
Was she to drive you from her Sight;
Your Day would turn to gloomy night;
You would your wretched Fate deplore.
And Seek some foreign distant Shore.

Damon then commends Strephon, who

　　cares not if his Nymph denys;
He scarcly gives an hours pain
He trys some other Fair to gain.

Strephon's equanimity is derived from the philosophic knowledge that "thousands round are equal fair" and one could be as pleasing as another. Alex counters with a vision of the intensity that life takes on in the light of feeling. When he looks upon Sylvia, for instance, his "Soul seems mounted in my Eyes." He concludes:

A kind and Sympathizing Breast
With every Social Virtue blest;
Is beyond Wit, or Eloquence
Or the smooth Rhetoric of Sense;
For Pleasure allways gathers Force;
When true Benevolence is the Source.

Graeme uses this vision of life as emotional force to convince Damon and convert him from stoicism. Sympathy not only binds society into virtuous and pleasurable community but vests individual life with meaning. Its meaningfulness stands opposed to wit, eloquence, and talk about sense. The last bears noting; sense has value only in practice, not as a theoretical construct or a topic of conversation. "A Pastoral Dialogue" marked a turn toward feeling in Graeme's thought. Poverty of feeling attached to the shallow sociability of wit and also to the philosophical dispassion of stoicism. Love, which had been rejected in earlier poems for its passion, was here rehabilitated as an especially meaningful form of "sympathy." The new commitment to emotional intensity coincided with Graeme's blooming romance with William Franklin that would culminate in an informal engagement in 1757. It would be a relationship that would teach the poet the wisdom of Damon's warning; for, when the relationship fell apart in 1758, she experienced the dejection of a "wretched Fate" and overcame it only after she sought a "foreign distant Shore."

Their courtship in winter of 1757 was negotiated in verse. An exchange of poems counterposed the competing languages of wit and sense, friendship and love, domesticity and sociability, working toward a mutual understanding.

A Song Wrote by a Young Gentleman to a Young Lady

1.
With pleasure have I pass'd my days,
    And every Minute blest:
No anxious wish disturbed my Ease,
    Nor sigh distroy'd my Rest.

Thus void of Care my Hours have flown,
For still I found my Heart my own.

2.
I listend to the *Syren* voice;
 By Musicks Art improv'd;
The *Syren* could not fix my Choice;
 The Song alone I lov'd.
Thus void of Care my Hours have flown
For still I found my Heart my own.

3.
But now O *Love!* I own thy Reign
 I find Thee in my Heart;
I know yet bear the pleasing pain
 For *Laura* threw the Dart
Laura's too powerful Charms have shown,
My Heart is now no more my own.

4.
I often praisd a handsom Face,
 Extol'd a sparkling Eye,
And Safe examind every Grace
 Without one real Sigh.
Thus free from Care each hour hath flown,
For still I found my Heart my own.

5.
Sweet Innocence and sprightly Wit,
 With strength of Reason joind;
Thoughts that an Angels Tongue might fit,
 Enslave my Heart and Mind.
Laura's too powerful Charms have shown
My Heart is now no more my own.

6.
I heard, I saw, I felt the Flame,
 For *Laura* smild and spoke;
Oh *Cupid* take some other aim
 Or my poor Heart is broke;
To *Laura* let the Dart be thrown
And make her Heart no more her own.

Laura responded two days later:

The foregoing Song answerd by a Young Lady

1.

Ye *Virgin Sisters* of the Grove!
   Attend the plaintive Song,
And know the sly encroacher *Love*
   For Reason is too strong;
For former boasting I find vain
And dread the links of *Cupids* Chain.

2.

I laugh'd at *Strephon's* lively air;
   Was pleasd with *Colin's* Wit;
Politeness fell to *Thyrsis* share;
   Yet none my Fancy hit.
Nor of them thought a single Hour
But made a jest of *Cupids* power.

3.

Young *Damon* came in Friendship drest
   At first spake not of Love;
With Freedom we our Thoughts exprest
   And talked of Powers above,
Of what was Right, and just, and true,
But my own Heart I little knew.

4.

The Wiser set saw the pretence
   And told me I was wrong;
They spoke Experience backd by sense
   I deemd my Heart too strong!
For I was pleasd to boast my Friend
Nor thought *Love* was at th' End.

5.

There's various Reason to be seen,
   which make it wrong to join
Tho' Warm Affection Steps between
   I will the Youth Resign;

Oh may he ever happy be!
In loving, or forgetting me.

6.
In paths of *Wisdom* may he tread
   And *Virtue* prove his Guide!
In *Honours* School be nicely Read!
   Goodness his only pride!
Nor long in distant Climes remain
But meet with *Laura* once again.

These were public declarations, employing the cognomens by which William Franklin (Damon) and Graeme (Laura) were known in polite society. Franklin's poem accompanied a letter to "Betsey" urging her to throw off the influence of an unnamed parson (Richard Peters? William Smith?). "[Have] a WILL of your own; and then I am sure it will not be in the Power of either D——ls or Parsons to keep us asunder." Franklin's song (with an opening pun on his name) testifies to the fixity of his own will in loving Laura. It offered as evidence a contrast between his indifference to the charms of other women and his subjection to Laura's charms. Neither physical graces nor musical ability (frequently noted female "charms" in courtship verse) was grounds for the attraction (the barbs of Laura's "dart"), but rather mental and spiritual power. Franklin seemingly appropriated the privileged terms of Laura's poetry and used them to stake his claim upon her heart. Echoing her language suggested that he, too, recognized what was truly valuable and was therefore a soul mate. When Laura replied, she remarked that their conversation about what was "Right, and Just, and True" first drew her into friendship. But Laura insisted that such talk was pretense when it led to overtures of love. In 1750s Philadelphia a woman and a man reenacted the conflict that had troubled mixed conversation since Platonism usurped the dialogue of the sexes during the 1630s. Only friendship (Platonic love) permitted philosophic communion; love entailed so personal an interest in one's partner in conversation that no sublimation of thought was possible. Hence Laura faced an either-or: either she had to reject the claims of love and preserve the possibility of talk "Right, and Just, and True," or she had to surrender the conversation to the compulsions of mutual interest. She opted for "Reason" and for saying no. Her concluding phrases indicated that this rejection of Franklin's claim did not entail a rejection of his company; she wished that they would meet again and, presumably, reactivate their conversation on its old footing.

Both verses have a dual audience: the individuals to whom the lyrics were addressed and the participants in polite society. Graeme invokes the *"Virgin Sisters* of the Grove" particularly, presenting her reply as instruction in the problem of conversing with young men. Those of "the Wiser set," or more experienced members of Philadelphia's gentility, are also commended for their "sense" of what was happening when Damon and Laura perambulated. When eligible persons in society were courting, the exact nature of their relationship was a public matter. Engagements were formally declared so families would not be disturbed by further suits and petitions for marriage. In courtship, the declaration of choice became the equivalent of a commercial bid with ramifications for all unmarried persons. If a bid were accepted and an engagement declared, then the arbiters of polite reputation — "the Wiser Set" of city matrons — ensured that conversations with persons of the opposite sex were put under the strictures of rigid propriety. The good opinion of these persons had influence that extended well beyond the city parlors. At the same time that Franklin courted Graeme, Benjamin Y. Prime was forced to resign his post as tutor at the College of New Jersey for allowing his poetic conversation with Annis Boudinot to display too much warmth after she became betrothed to Richard Stockton.[45] Though the action against Prime was initiated by a college rival, it succeeded because the rival successfully raised the question of the tutor's reputation and the college's.

By rejecting the claim of love, Laura informed other eligible women that both she and Damon remained at liberty. In one sense it reasserted her connection with the *"Virgin Sisters* of the Grove." Her profoundest explorations of friendship throughout her career were addressed to female correspondents, the first being Rebecca Moore (Sylvia), with whom she exchanged poetic epistles in 1755 "at the time of the Indian War." Against the disorders of a state at war, Laura championed friendship as typified by her relationship with Sylvia:

> Friendship's a Theme much spoke of, little known
> Love, Innocence with her Togethers flown;

45. Carla J. Mulford, "Annis Boudinot Stockton and Benjamin Young Prime: A Poetical Correspondence, and More," *Princeton University Library Chronicle*, LII (1990–1991), 231–266.

To some lone Hermits Couch and moss grown Cell
Watching the Midnight Lamp and solemn Bell;
Perhaps beneath some rural Cottage shed;
The blest Companions has for refuge fled!
Tird with pursuits; and Sick of Crowds at Court
Where herds of Mankind do with Smiles resort:
At first fair Friendship they did entertain
Till Selfish interest broke the twisted Chain
Interest that Charm which like a Magic Wand
Will every former gentle Tye disband:
Heaven grant no jarring passions may divide
My dearest Sylvia from her Laura's Side;
So when we go the World may Join each name
Nor Mention my Miss Moore without her Graeme.

Stripping away the commonplace imagery of retirement, we encounter two points in Graeme's argument: the subordination of love and innocence to friendship, the peril that interest poses to friendship. We have already seen how love and interest interact to imperil friendship and philosophy in Graeme's thought; here we see the more conventional notion of interest as the selfish passion of persons engaged in the contest for precedence found at court. Because of the gentility's concern with familial advantage, marriage among young persons of the upper classes caused love to become involved with the contest for precedence.

One of the mysteries of Graeme's career is the reason for her breakup with Franklin. Graeme's writings suggest that a contributing factor could have been her ambivalence about committing herself to him. We learn in a letter from Franklin after the breakup, "London Octr 24, 1758," that he had attempted to marry Graeme privately before leaving for England. She had not consented.

> We were not engag'd to each other. . . . On the contrary we mutually promis'd that in case of any Change of Sentiment, or that either should think the Obstacles to our propos'd Happiness insurmountable, to give immediate Notice of such Change or Opinion. Its true, as Mrs. G. was so condescending as to say she would consent to her Daughter's waiting for one Twelve month to see if Matters could be settled agreeable to our Inclinations, I look'd upon myself as engag'd to her during that Time; and no Consideration on Earth should have induc'd me to think of

marrying another—Nor do I believe that, as long as she remain'd single, and I had Reason to think her Affection for me continu'd, aught but dire Necessity would have suffer'd me to entertain the least Thought of giving myself to any other Woman.[46]

We do not have the letter from Graeme that caused the rupture, but from Franklin's reply we know that two reasons were broached in the letter: her displeasure at receiving little or no correspondence from him and his active participation in antiproprietarial party politics. Writers sympathetic to Graeme have suggested that Franklin's attentions to another woman provoked the break and that he jilted her. There is nothing of this in his letter, and the tone suggests that Elizabeth Graeme initiated the split. The consequences of the rupture are less in dispute: Franklin married another and would reap the reward of his politicking, appointment as governor of New Jersey. Graeme went into a five-year funk overthrown only by her visit to England and social success there. When she finally did marry (an unsuccessful two-and-one-half-year liaison with Henry Fergusson), she did so privately with no prior notice to friends or family.

Graeme's return to Philadelphia in 1765 inaugurated her reign as the presiding female genius of the Delaware Valley. Her success in England, particularly her recognition by Laurence Sterne, renovated her sense of esteem and her ambitions as a writer; she began translations of Fénelon's *Télémaque* and the Psalms. Yet revitalization of her art was most pungently registered in her widely circulated English travel journal, a witty survey of manners and mode that includes her contact with Sterne, of which only fragments have survived. The bemused verse account of fashionable life at Scarborough evokes the spirit of the journal. Back in Philadelphia, she symbolically separated herself from town diversions by establishing her salon at Graeme Park in the rural countryside north of Philadelphia. Yet the sort of conversation she practiced there after 1765 differed from the sisterly confidences of her youth. To the good sense of her youth was added a cosmopolitan scope of interest and wit. The presence of wit is the principal stylistic signal of the transformation wrought by Graeme's experience in England. The place of wit in Graeme's poetics shifts. No longer was it an expression of unfeeling vanity employed in arenas of polite con-

---

46. Gratz, "Some Material for a Biography of Mrs. Elizabeth Fergusson," *PMHB*, XXXIX (1915), 263–267.

test; rather, it had become a vehicle of judgment useful in gaining a perspective on the foibles of the world and deflecting the claims of passion. Assuming wit armed Graeme with a self-assurance in mixed company that allowed the sorts of liberties of conversation that marked the Parisian salons. When the Reverend Nathaniel Evans, one of the talented circle of litterateurs nurtured by Provost William Smith at the College of Philadelphia, began paying court to Laura at Graeme Park, presenting himself as the new Damon, Laura knew how to cool his ardor:

Since I esteem your bliss so great,
IN PENNANCE YOU WILL CHOSE A MATE,
And tell me — "I may share your fate!"
The scheme is good, I must confess,
If you have bliss, to make it less!
Yet take a hint, before resolv'd,
And in the *dragging chain* involv'd.
While youthful joys around you shine,
Haste not to bend at Hymen's shrine;
Let friendship, gen'rous friendship, be
The bond to fetter you and me,
Vestal, Platonic — what you will,
So virtue reigns with freedom still.
But if, in matrimonial noose,
You must be bound — and have a spouse;
The faithful rib that heav'n shall send,
I'll fondly greet, and call her friend.[47]

Wit — here seen as raillery — becomes the guarantor of friendship, as important to maintaining the free conversation of friends as sympathy. Elizabeth Graeme's education as a woman of letters can be seen as an intellectual journey proceeding from the moral earnestness of English sense to a discovery of the social utility of wit as a means of maintaining liberty.

47. The exchange between Evans and Graeme was published in Nathaniel Evans, *Poems on Several Occasions, with Some Other Compositions* (Philadelphia, 1772). Evans wrote "An Ode, Written at G——me Park" and "Some Lines out of Mr. Pope's Eloise to Abelard"; Graeme replied with "A Parody on the Foregoing Lines, by a Lady, Assuming the Name of Laura"; Evans replied with "An Epistle to Laura, on Her Parody," and Graeme supplied "Laura's Answer," which in turn provoked "To Laura, in Reply to the Above." The quoted verse comes from "Laura's Answer," 152–154.

The conjunction of sensibility with wit distinguished Graeme's mature art. It also distinguished the art of Graeme's great appreciator, Laurence Sterne. Most important, it distinguished the conversation of that institution that most effectively fulfilled women's potential in social exchange, the salon.

5

Rites of Assembly

Some scenes of sociability in British America depended more on ritual action than on conversation: Sunday socials, holiday feasts, court days, horse races, card parties, and balls. All such occasions took place regularly, and all reasserted the already constituted character of a community. In the vocabulary of the age, they were ceremonies of "complaisance." Persons performed conventionalized roles that secured them in a traditional communal identity. By performing these rituals, individuals and families projected their status in society. Like games, certain rites were occasions of competition; persons, in accord with strict rules, asserted their mastery over play. In the British American colonies, where no long-standing aristocracies commanded automatic deference, social rites (and social games as preparations for these rites) to assert status became critical to self-understanding. They took on peculiar weight because of the lack of signs that fixed one's place in the social hierarchy in the Old World. In Europe titles, blood, offices, and good breeding established one in the scheme of things. Merchants and talented persons of the middling orders exerted energies to secure offices and titles, marry into the blood, and acquire the habiliments of good breeding. Aristocrats made exertions in regard to spouse and house to establish a "super-eminency" in society or state. British Americans, lacking titles, scant of blood, and possessed of few offices, established their social place by material markers and by taking part in social rites of complaisance to display the degree of one's good breeding.

In the American colonies refinement of manners, graces, polite accomplishments, and fashionability of dress and equipage were measured against a metropolitan standard. The occasions when aspirants to reputation gathered to assert their quality and undergo judgment had Old World origins. Even when certain sociable rites — the barbecue, for instance — sprang up in a New World setting as creole novelties, they were understood in light of traditional Old World patterns. Actor John Singleton's poetic description of a 1767 barbecue in Barbados viewed the occasion as a Theocritean rural feast peopled by African servitors and amorous planter couples. The neoclassical diction underscored the point that "behaviour decent, and polite address" adorned this open-air repast:

> The sable cooks, with utensils prepar'd,
> Their sev'ral stations take, and crackling flames
> Enkindle; not with bellows, but with lungs,
> Expert at blowing culinary blasts.
> Whilst Cuffee, Lovelace, Talliho, and Sal,
> With viands stor'd, the loaded baskets bring:
> This a variety of herbage holds,
> And that the solid sav'ry meat contains,
> The well cramm'd turkey and the rosy ham;
> Nor is the mellow cheese forgot, of taste
> High relishing, when silver-tipp'd black jack
> Or tankard bright, fam'd Calvert's porter holds,
> With flow'ry head high tow'ring o'er the brim.
> The destin'd shoat on Ethiop's shoulders swags,
> Grunting, as to the rural shrine he's brought:
> Here one beneath a load of liquors bends,
> Cooling sherberts, and various dainty wines;
> Another the capacious bowl conveys,
> With sacharissian loaf; the spirit fine,
> From choicest cane distill'd, mellow'd by age,
> Within its glassy rounds alluring smiles;
> Nor does the neighb'ring brook refuse its aid,
> In mingling with the juice of yellow fruit,
> Lemon or Lime, which in contiguous groves
> Upon the loaded branches fragrant hang.
>
> . . . .
>
> The smoaking BARBECUE in sight appears,
> Escorted by a train of sable guards,
> Wafting its favour tow'rds the jovial board,
> All nicely brown'd and crisp. Transported they

View it approaching with an eager eye;
For the keen wholesome air, that gently breathes
Along the bubbling stream and fans the vale,
A never-failing appetite creates.

Now all prepare; and one, with dextrous hand,
And knife of keenest edge, the shoat dissects.
The choicest bits each for his fair procures,
And all his care bestows to see her pleas'd.
Behavior decent, and polite address,
These festive scenes adorn: Not like to those
In famous city off, when Lord-Mayor's feast
Calls forth the well-fed alderman.[1]

Against the egalitarian disorders of the London lord mayor's feast, Singleton asserted the decency and good order of the Barbadian barbecue framed in terms of a civil naturalism. What attracts the notice of a late-twentieth-century reader of the passage are the constituents of good order here: a class of Africans who serve but do not consume, a class of Barbadians who consume and play, a class of planter youths who demonstrate their decency by a proprietary attentiveness to their female favorites. Singleton's description was profoundly traditional; it asserts propriety and civility of the Barbadian social rite and makes its innovations seem more ancient and proper than the sociable practice of London.

One feature of the description commands particular notice—the displacement of conversation from the center of sociability. Conversation possessed a potential to lead persons away from a sense of commonality to something peculiar; consequently, the sorts of talk that predominated in rites of complaisance tended to be formulaic—indeed, at times to be ritual proclamation—toasts, compliments, pleasantries, anecdotes, jokes, and bets. In societies as dynamic (unformed) as those of the colonial port cities, the impulse to secure one's place in a traditional order was strong but fraught with difficulties. Brandishing signs of class, rank, profession, religion, or organization membership became the task of all who had found a secure place or who aspired to a secure place in the social hierarchy. A social rite served as a semiotic case—a frame that presented certain signs of rank,

1. John Singleton, *A General Description of the West Indian Islands . . . as Far as Relates to the British, Dutch, and Danish Governments . . . from Barbados to Saint Croix, Attempted in Blank Verse* (Barbados, 1767), 19.

place, profession, politeness, talent, and beauty to mark those in power. The periodic repetition of such occasions provided opportunities to maintain appearances: to be richly dressed despite rumors of reversals of fortune or to show that the ravages of disease had not disfigured one. When one failed to appear or when one's show could not disguise the decline in one's status, beauty, health, or ability, these occasions registered the failure that gave contrast to the sheen of success. Gossip was a social barometer supplying a moment-by-moment commentary on the rise and fall of reputations. Gossip's mutability, however, proved unsatisfactory for those who wished to register their reputations in memory. Writing, portrait painting, and even music supplied more durable registers of one's attainments. Talk was incidental in conserving reputations; music, literature, and fine arts were central. Artistic expressions might serve as elements of a rite, as convivial songs did at a club dinner or an alderman's feast, as hymns did in worship, or odes did on state occasions; or they might memorialize the victor of the race and the belle of the ball.[2] As elements of ritual, song and dance were instruments determining who belonged (who knew the words, the tunes, the steps) and who excelled in performance. When a dancing master named a piece "Mrs. Hodges her Minuet," he certified a woman's preeminence on an occasion; at every ball under the dancing master's direction, the tune, when announced, would recall the moment of Mrs. Hodge's triumph. Dedicated songs and odes proclaimed the hierarchy of beauty and wit, serving as the memory of the provincial "world."

Forms of private society that depended on conversation found themselves in tension with ritual aesthetic culture. The tea table and the salon, because they advanced the liberties of conversation, countered complaisance. The salon stood in peculiar relation to rites of complaisance. The ideal of sororal sensibility espoused by Elizabeth Magawley and other salonnieres opposed the vanities of society. Yet the power of social rites to bestow status and the regard of the world was such that they, not salons, were the predominant institutions of heterosociality during the colonial era. To secure a reputation in the world, women participated in the card

2. The scholarship of Richard Leppert about the role of musical performance in sociocultural formation in Europe is particularly pertinent to the issue raised here, particularly in *Music and Image: Domesticity, Ideology, and Socio-Cultural Formation in Eighteenth-Century England* (Cambridge, 1988). Also pertinent is Thomas Crawford, *Society and the Lyric: A Study of the Song Culture of Eighteenth-Century Scotland* (Edinburgh, 1979). For British American practice, see John Barry Talley, *Secular Music in Colonial Annapolis: The Tuesday Club, 1745–56* (Urbana, Ill., 1988), 45–64.

parties and assembly balls that consolidated a status quo. Sensibility clashed with worldly aspiration in these theaters of ambition, and most violently at the one social rite generally deemed as being for the delectation of ladies, the ball.

At the Ball

Balls were complex entertainments featuring dancing and any of a number of subsidiary pastimes — musical performances, cards, an evening repast (usually a light "cold collation"), conversation, and perhaps a demonstration of the latest dance steps.[3] During the eighteenth century, several sorts of balls were commonly held. For splendor, state balls eclipsed all others. Sponsored by colonial officials, often in public places such as statehouses, courthouses, the executive's mansion, or a tavern, state balls celebrated the birthdays of the reigning king and queen, the installation of colonial executives, colonial anniversaries, or the winning of great victories. Most of the actors in public life — officials, professional men, merchants, large tradesmen, ship captains, and their spouses — received invitations; members of the lower orders participated in a related event, usually a

3. The literature on British American dance is not ample. By far the largest body of work consists of practical guides to dancing. For a bibliography of practical dance, see Robert M. Keller, comp., *Dance Figures Index: American Country Dances, 1730–1810* (Sandy Hook, Conn., 1989). The best introduction to the English background of provincial dancing is Shirley Spackman Wynne, "The Charms of Complaisance: The Dance in England in the Early Eighteenth Century" (Ph.D. diss., Ohio State University, 1967). Jennifer Kaye Lowe Martin, "The English Dancing Master, 1660–1728: His Role at Court, in Society, and on the Public Stage" (Ph.D. diss., University of Michigan, 1977), is valuable for its insights into this central figure in the culture of gentility. Norman Arthur Benson, "The Itinerant Dancing and Music Masters of Eighteenth-Century America" (Ph.D. diss., University of Minnesota, 1963), is more useful for its treatment of musicians than for dancing masters. Kate Van Winkle Keller, "John Griffiths, Eighteenth-Century Itinerant Dancing Master," in Peter Benes, ed., *Itinerancy in New England and New York*, Dublin Seminar for New England Folklife, 1984 (Boston, 1985), 90–111, is the best portrait of a dancing master currently in print. Judith Cobau's manuscript, "The Precarious Life of Thomas Pike: New World Dancing Master," has also aided my understanding of the world of social dancing in a port city greatly.

Birth night balls were particularly important rites and might have been instituted in provincial centers under court sponsorship as a feature of the Restoration's attempt to build a monarchal mystique around Charles II. Besides the ball, the lighting of bonfires and distribution of money to the poor were features of the events in England, Ireland, and America.

bonfire or an illumination and procession. Less splendid, yet still the occasion for elegant self-display, were the public assemblies. Sponsored by a society of subscribers or by dancing schools, these balls took place periodically (weekly, fortnightly, monthly, or so) in taverns, theaters, or, later in the century, in assembly rooms. Private balls sponsored by important families took place in city residences or in country houses. Attendance at a state ball could be had by paying admission or by receiving an invitation from the organizing committee. Assemblies, too, levied an admission, and strangers could attend provided that they could secure the sponsorship of one of the subscribers. Participation in private balls was by invitation only.

State balls were expected to be lavish and elegant affairs, with free-flowing wine and revelry lasting well past midnight. Thus Lieutenant Governor William Gooch complained of having to spend one hundred pounds on a birth night ball shortly after assuming office in Virginia. The literate population had a firm notion of the ingredients of an elegant revel, for the *Virginia Gazette* published accounts of at least thirty-three balls in England during the period 1736–1780.[4] Of the fifty-five notices of balls held in Virginia, the most extensive described a "Grand Entertainment" held in July 1746 by the government of Virginia at the Capitol to celebrate the outcome of the Battle of Culloden:

> In the Evening, a very Numerous Company of Gentlemen and Ladies appear'd at the Capitol, where a Ball was open'd, and after dancing some Time, withdrew to Supper, there being a very handsome Collation spread on three Tables, in three different Rooms, consisting of near 100 Dishes, after the most Delicate taste. There was also provided a great variety of the choicest and best Liquors, in which the Healths of the King, the Prince and Princess of Wales, the Duke, and the rest of the Royal Family, the Governor, Success to his Majesty's Arms, Prosperity to this Colony, and many other Loyal Healths were chearfully drank, and a Round of the Cannon, which were remov'd to the Capitol for this

4. Thad Tate, "Information on Eighteenth-Century Social Events for Use in Connection with Governors' Conference Party," Jan. 15, 1957, 2, Central Files, Colonial Williamsburg Foundation; Lester J. Cappon and Stella F. Duff, *Virginia Gazette Index, 1736–1780*, 2 vols. (Williamsburg, Va., 1950), I, 49–50. English masquerades, because of their reputation for wickedness, were also noted frequently. There is, however, no indication that a masquerade was ever held in British America, so it would be problematic to apply Terry Castle's insights in *Masquerade and Civilization: The Carnivalesque in Eighteenth-Century English Culture and Fiction* (Stanford, Calif., 1986) to the American scene.

Purpose, was discharg'd at each Health, to the Number of 18 or 20 Rounds, which lasted 'til near 2 o'clock. The whole Affair was conducted with great Decency and good Order, and an unaffected Chearfullness appeared in the Countenances of the Company. All the Houses in the City were illuminated, and a very large Bon-fire was made in the Market-Place, 3 Hogsheads of Punch given to the Populace; and the whole concluded with the greatest Demonstrations of Joy and Loyalty.[5]

Men invariably organized state entertainments, presided over the change of diversions, and did whatever public speechifying or toasting was required. Most balls, state or otherwise, followed an agenda (or, as Dr. Alexander Hamilton termed it, the same "common and thread bare method"): musical concerts took place first, if offered, and then dancing would commence. An evening's dancing entailed four or five dances, after which a meal was served. (It was considered an innovation to offer cake on a buffet for consumption during the dancing.) If the number of dancers was large, the company would be organized into sets. The Philadelphia Assembly standardized the number of couples in each set at ten, and the composition of each set was determined by a male dancer's order of arrival at the event. Ladies would draw for their places, with one place reserved for the director's discretion. Each set performed a specific type of dance, though for variety a march might be introduced. Sets were re-formed when the type of dance changed; later in the century the sets remained intact, and the lead woman could call the dance to be played. The first set, usually a minuet, showcased grace and gentility. In this set one established one's standing as a dancer. Judgments would be passed immediately on the sidelines and among other dancers. At evening's end a verdict would be rendered and reported in letters, diaries, and gossip. A typical comment: "I think a Mrs. Cuthbert (formerly Mrs. Blair, a Daughter of Dr. Eustis of New York) made the best appearance as a Dancer." Later sets became less graceful and more energetic — first reels, then country dances, climaxing in southern balls in the jig, a dance then believed to have been borrowed from African American slaves.[6] Andrew Burnaby reported on this usual climax

5. Quoted in Tate, "Information on Eighteenth-Century Social Events," 4.

6. "To Regulate the Dances," in Joseph P. Sims, *The Philadelphia Assemblies, 1748–1948* ([Philadelphia], 1947), 12, 22. Lynn Matluck Brooks, in "The Philadelphia Dancing Assembly in the Eighteenth Century," *Dance Research Journal*, II, no. 3 (Spring 1989), 3–5, documents the method of arrangement and behavior of the sets for the 1780s and 1790s. Quote in Tate, "Information on Eighteenth-Century Social Events,"

of Virginia balls in his travel journal for 1759: "A gentleman and lady stand up, and dance about the room, one of them retiring, the other pursuing, then perhaps meeting, in an irregular fantastical manner." To cosmopolitans unused to the increasingly syncretic dance practices of white Virginians, the jig seemed "sociable, but . . . looks more like a Bacchanalian dance than one in a polite assembly." In the eyes of a cosmopolitan, provincials might contrive new forms of sociability; they could not give rise to new forms of politeness, which were determined solely by metropolitan standards of civility. One risked one's reputation for grace to the extent one entered into the spirit of the jig. As Nicholas Cresswell observed of a 1775 ball featuring jigs in Virginia: "Here was about 37 ladies dressed and powdered to the life, some of them very handsome and as much vanity as is necessary. All of them fond of dancing, but I do not think they perform it with the greatest elegance."[7]

Women were the contestants, and men vied to be arbiters of the contest. Women sought a reputation for beauty, grace, and accomplishment at balls. They were at the center of attention vying for preeminence in the eyes of the assembly. Talk at balls most avoided formula when it commented upon performers and their performance. Loquacious Scribble's wry commentary on the Tuesday Club ball of 1745 aptly suggests the relationship of talk to feminine display:

> There were danced many minuets, country dances and Jiggs, and there was as much bowing, cringing, complimenting, Curtsying, oggling, flirting and Smart repartees, as is usual on such occasions, and The Reverend Mr Sly, tho the gravity of his Cloth, would not permit him to dance, yet he made by much the Smartest figure, in Squiring the Ladies, comparing them, as they stood in a row, to the milky way, and telling them, that he hoped, most of the young Ladies in the Ring, were travelling fast, towards that same Galaxy or milky way, and abundance of other droll witty and facetious repartees, puns, dowble entendres, and gallant Sarcasms passed, 'till that Gentleman, being called upon, by a

---

3. On the African-American element of the jig, see Marshall Stearns and Jean Stearns, *Jazz Dance: The Story of American Vernacular Dance* (New York, 1979).

7. Andrew Burnaby, *Travels through the Middle Settlements in North-America, in the Years 1759 and 1760 . . .* , 2d ed. (1775; rpt. Ithaca, N.Y., 1960), 26 (in a footnote, Burnaby likens the dance to the trescone of the Tuscans, which he observed on a trip to Italy); Nicholas Cresswell, *The Journal of Nicholas Cresswell, 1774–1777* (New York, 1924), 52–53.

lady to dance; he pretended to step aside alittle for his hat and gloves, but took care to abscond, and not make his appearance again that night upon the dancing Stage.[8]

The Reverend Mr. Sly's activities suggest the desideratum for men at balls: to be recognized by the ladies as the modern Paris. Men competed in witty combat to win the role of judge. Success in the contest meant being recognized by the women as the one who truly knew grace and beauty. Success for women took several forms: receiving the kudos of the judge, attracting a bevy of suitors, triumphing over a particular rival, winning the heart of a particular gentleman, or capturing the interest of the company by declaring a favorite. For those women who had shone in the contest, there existed a desire to certify the verdict and fix it in public memory. To satisfy this desire, young gentlemen fashioned the evening's compliments into durable verses that circulated among the gentry or were published in local newspapers.

The form, a survey of beauties, derived from seventeenth-century English "water poetry." The survey presumed that all the beauties of a locality were present at a ball and that the description constituted a comprehensive evaluation of feminine grace for that place and time.[9] The convention for this form dictated that the description serve as a mirror and that the poem be addressed to the ladies. The author's purpose was to cement his reputation as both a gallant and a man of parts with the local female population, not to provide a spectacle of female pulchritude for the delectation of male

8. Dr. Alexander Hamilton, *The History of the Ancient and Honorable Tuesday Club*, ed. Robert Micklus, 3 vols. (Chapel Hill, N.C., 1990), I, 193–194.

9. Surveys or prospects of beauty marked an evolution from the impromptu toasts dedicated to the various ladies at the spas in that an author, instead of the entire company of men, provided all the versified compliments. The various male companies, or knights of the toast, that formed at the resorts passed judgment in concert on the best epigram; and the best epigram determined who would reign as the season's belle. The provincial poets who surveyed the beauties of a state or assembly ball attempted to capture in their verses the verdict of the room rather than rendered a determination by fiat.

At times the geographical organization of these surveys gave rise to arguments concerning the comparative beauty of the women at various localities. W[illiam] S[hervington], *The Antigonian and Bostonian Beauties: A Poem* ([Boston, 1751?]), presented the most elaborate British American comparison. Shervington was governor of Antigua at the time of writing, so the argument had the utility of cementing his reputation among the female gentility of the island.

companions.[10] Success as a poetic arbiter of beauty consisted in giving the broadest possible satisfaction to the ladies being represented. Consequently, liberal attention to the merits of the women on view, an ample stock of complimentary adjectives, and an ability to discriminate that quality upon which a lady prided herself—form, face, gracefulness of movement, and sense—ensured the satisfaction of the audience. Joseph Shippen presents a capable example of the mode, winning for him a lifelong reputation as a poet in Philadelphia.

Lines written in an Assembly Room

In lovely White's most pleasing form,
    What various graces meet!
How blest with every striking charm!
    How languishingly sweet!

With just such elegance and ease,
    Fair, charming Swift appears;
Thus Willing, whilst she awes, can please;
    Thus Polly Franks endears.

A female softness, manly sense,
    And conduct free from art,
With every pleasing excellence,
    In Inglis charm the heart.

But see! another fair advance,
    With love commanding all;
See! happy in the sprightly dance,
    Sweet, smiling, fair M'Call.

10. The titles of these poems advertised the audience; for example, "To the Ladies at Boston in New-England," *Boston Gazette*, no. 622, Nov. 19 [29], 1731. I've found only two examples of the survey-of-beauties form with an obviously male readership intended: John Thomas, Jr., verse epistle to his cousin, dated "West River [Maryland], May the 13th, 1759," MS 1970.2, Maryland Historical Society, Annapolis; [Charles Woodmason?], "Black Mingo Girls, Sung at the St. John's Hunt, 1753," MS, South Carolina Historical Society, Charleston. Given the number of salacious tavern songs circulating in eighteenth-century America (the most ample collection is contained in the Hugh McConnel commonplace book compiled at Fish Kill Landing from 1777 to 1788, MS 6329, Alderman Library, University of Virginia, Charlottesville), one is tempted to speculate that narrative is more essential in the formation of a male pornographic aesthetic than is descriptive representation.

Each blessing which indulgent Heaven
    On mortals can bestow,
To thee, enchanting maid, is given,
    Its masterpiece below.

In Sally Coxe's form and face,
    True index of her mind,
The most exact of human race
    Not one defect can find.

Thy beauty every breast alarms,
    And many a swain can prove
That he who views your conquering charms,
    Must soon submit to love.

With either Chew such beauties dwell,
    Such charms by each are shared,
No critic's judging eye can tell
    Which merits most regard.

'Tis far beyond the painter's skill
    To set their charms to view;
As far beyond the poet's quill
    To give the praise that's due.[11]

If one were to lay a critical charge against Shippen's verse, it would be that the poem inadequately measured the scope of beauty's power. Sally Coxe's preeminent ability to inspire universal love among men was, after all, a limited sway. The sovereignty that women sought in their display was

11. Joseph Shippen, "Lines Written in an Assembly Room," in [Thomas Balch, ed.], *Letters and Papers Relating Chiefly to the Provincial History of Pennsylvania, with Some Notices of the Writers* (Philadelphia, 1855), lxxii–lxxiv. The women being described in the poem are Ellinor White, Abby Willing, Polly Franks, Katharine Inglis, Margaret M'Call, Sally Coxe, and two daughters of Benjamin Chew.

Joseph Shippen (1732–1810) was the second son of merchant Edward Shippen of Lancaster, Pa. A graduate of the College of New Jersey (Princeton), he joined the provincial army, rose to the rank of colonel, and distinguished himself in the capture of Fort Duquesne. In 1762 he was appointed secretary of the province of Pennsylvania. He married Jane Galloway (herself a verse writer of note) of Maryland in 1768 and moved his expanding family in 1773 to Chester County, where he farmed. From 1789 until his death, he served as judge of the Lancaster court. His cognomen in the literary world was Annandius.

not limited to men; they wished a dominion over women as well. All eyes must testify to admiration if a woman's triumph were to be total. Shippen had forgotten the lesson of the Cavalier poets — that the sovereignty of beauty was best metaphorized as an imperial political dominion over "the world." The fantasy was that a woman's domination of an assembly at a provincial center was not spatially limited by the four walls of the ballroom; it radiated throughout the globe and throughout history mastering space and time in an epiphanic glory.[12] Contestants in other parts of the world would be conquered as well. The superlative poet fed this fantasy, making its vanity excusable by making its ambition plausible. The author of "The Belles of Barbados" (1738) excelled all other poets in his skill at plying the imperial metaphor:

> *Britain* long reign'd pre-eminent in Charms,
> And *British* Eyes subdued, like British Arms;
> Till wide, at length, her Conquests spread, and far,
> She gain'd new Colonies — the Crop of War!
> Then peopled Places which her Valour won,
> Freezing in Snow, or broiling in the Sun.
> Soon the created Settlements grew strong,
> And greatly vied with those from whom they sprung;
> Dar'd with their Mother-Isle themselves compare,
> Their *Sons* now valiant, and their *Daughters* fair.[13]

The poet then named the reigning belles of London, indicating how each suffered eclipse by a Barbadian counterpart. The critical moment in this transit of Venus occurred when the metropolis's preeminent beauty, "Famed Egerton," yielded her mastery over the world and the age:

> Youthful BLENMAN shall inherit all
> Thy Beauties, and a gazing World inthrall,
> Shine at a Court, and sparkle at a Ball;
> She'll be (inspir'd, the Poet may presage)
> As once thou was, the Beauty of her Age.

12. The global consciousness of the poem confirms the central contention of Jeffrey H. Richards, *Theater Enough: American Culture and the Metaphor of the World Stage, 1607–1789* (Durham, N.C., 1991).

13. "The Belles of Barbados" (Saturday, Dec. 16, 1738), in [Samuel Keimer, comp.], *Caribbeana: Containing Letters and Dissertations, Together with Poetical Essays on Various Subjects and Occasions*, 2 vols. (London, 1741), II, 293–296.

Having dramatized for the realms of beauty Machiavelli's historical thesis about colonies' eclipsing the mother countries, the poet then reflected upon other means by which women asserted dominion — by art and by inspiring love.[14]

Of all arts, the one that animated the ball was music. It was the soul of the dance. Its power was akin to beauty's though addressed to the ear rather than the eye. One New York poet of the 1730s commented on the assault on the senses that a man experienced at an entertainment:

> Music has Power to melt the Soul:
>   By *Beauty* Nature's sway'd,
> Each can the Universe controul,
>   Without the other's Aid.
>
> But here together both appear,
>   And Force united try;
> *Music* inchants the list'ning Ear,
>   And *Beauty* charms the Eye.
>
> What Cruelty these Powers to join!
>   These Transports who can bear!
> Oh! let the Sound be less — divine,
>   Or look, ye Nymphs, less fair.[15]

A woman could lay claim to music's power variously: by performing artfully in song or on a musical instrument or by demonstrating her attunement to music by the gracefulness and enthusiasm of her dancing. The dancer, as the resonator of music's power, sometimes laid a proprietary claim on pieces of music greater than that of the musician-composer. Thus of thirty-eight pieces in the John Ormsby manuscript of minuets compiled in Annapolis in 1758, twelve were named by their dedications to women,

14. Niccolò Machiavelli in *Discourses upon Titus Livius* advanced the thesis that colonies based upon imperial settlement would supersede in strength and wealth the imperial center, for the wealth that the metropolis reaped from imperial enterprise would subject it in the course of time to debilitating luxury.

[Joseph Browne], *The London Belles; or, A Description of the Most Celebrated Beauties in the Metropolis of Great Britain* (London, 1707), is the model text of the metropolitan prospect-of-beauties literature. Some London descendant of Browne's poem probably supplied the Barbadian with the list of current reigning beauties in the metropolis.

15. "Written at a Concert of Music, Where There Was a Great Number of Ladies," *New-York Gazette*, no. 427, Dec. 31, 1733.

six of whom were Annapolitans (fourteen were identified by composer).[16] By performing music, a woman could appropriate music's power more directly. Consider the extent of that power, as measured by the celebrant of the "The Belles of Barbados":

> *ORPHEUS* cou'd give (for such is Musick's Force)
> Motion to Woods, and stop a River's Course;
> From *Pluto*'s Realms *Eurydice* recall,
> And sweet *Amphion* build the Theban Wall;
> To both superior, beauteous BIGNAL charms,
> Not savage Breasts, but human Hearts, disarms;
> Harmonious Sounds thrill gently from her Throat,
> Dwell on her Tongue, and sweet every Note.
> Musick with Beauty join'd — What Breast can bear
> A Voice so charming! in a Nymph so fair!

The craft of this passage lay in its argument: the legendary potency of Orpheus and Amphion was exercised on objects, beasts, and mythological beings — all of which are lesser entities than humans in the hierarchy of being. Therefore, Bignal, by moving human hearts, manifested superior power than that revealed in mythology. She exercised a mastery over nature because she moved the ruler of nature, man. Since her art worked in conjunction with beauty, she wielded double power over the human heart, a power that could not be resisted. The woman's power to compel the human heart led the poet to a discussion of the ultimate means by which women exerted their dominion, by inspiring love:

> LOVE is a Passion, which by slow Degrees,
> Like Opium, lulls us into seeming Ease;
> Drunk with the stupifying Draught we lie,
> And, lost in gay deluding Visions, die.
> Fantastick State, alas! we hug our Chain,
> And doat upon the Authors of our Pain
> With eager Steps pursue, whene'er they fly,
> And fondly play with Darts by which we die;

16. The Ormsby book of minuets is reproduced in Talley, *Secular Music in Colonial Annapolis*, 279–305. The local dedicatees: "Miss Chase, her Minuet," "Mrs. Gunning's Minuet," "Mrs. Hamilton's Minuet," "Mrs. Hodges her Minuet," "Mis Hopkisson's Minuet," "Mis Churchil's Minuet." Printed books of the 1790s by American dancing masters retained the practice of including numbers dedicated to local persons.

So Africk's raging Sons to Phoebus turn,
Adore his Rays, and in adoring burn.

What shall we make of the extravagance and ambivalence of the poet's imagery? Love's power here was not benign, but a compulsion toward self-destruction on the part of the loving subject: the annihilation of normal consciousness with opium, the surrender of circumspect liberty by the chains of slave masochism, the loss of life itself with the self-immolation of superstitious sun worshippers. These images of abnegation possessed a curious intimacy for a Barbadian audience. Who better knew the global drug market than Barbadian sugar planters who participated in it? Who better knew the chains of slavery than those who locked the shackles? Who possessed greater anxiety about the native beliefs of Africans than those who attempted to eradicate them? The poet's complicity in this economy of power stood revealed when he called the women who inspired such abjection "the Authors of our Pain." In one phrase the double-mindedness of the author — his identification with the woman as master and male devotee as victim — revealed the paradox of love, that power relations in the West Indies colored the emblems of beauty; that the leisure for art and time for love were purchased (as poets Alexander Pope and James Thomson charged) by the labor of slaves and the imperial market for drugs, stimulants, and luxuries.

In a way, the poet could not escape the contradictions of the workings of beauty, art, and love at the ball. The ritual enacted at the ball was a contest, and contests invariably give rise to questions concerning the grounds of someone's preeminence or the nature of someone's triumph. The author of the "Belles of Barbados" was sufficiently sensitive to the ramifications of the contest of the ball to realize that it had to be framed in terms of the power relations between the metropolis and the province. Despite the poet's insistence that Barbados eclipsed London in its beauty and accomplishment, the problem of dominion (whether of the empire, the economy, or the heart) could not be repressed, and the uncertainties of the status of Barbadians' power or powerlessness erupted in his consideration of that one emotion that humans identify most with benevolent community, love.

Norbert Elias has argued that the court was an arena of competitive display wherein great families asserted their glory through conspicuous consumption. Dynastic glory (a sort of vanity for the family) led persons to bankrupt themselves in building projects and in acts of largesse — trying to curry the favor of the king and, perhaps, secure a place that could replenish the family's exchequer as cash hemorrhaged from it. Perhaps the ball should be considered in the refracted light of this model. The contest at the ball served self-love, or dynastic love, rather than fellow feeling. Women were the actors in a theater of cultural power in which the collection of graces, accomplishments, and suitors became the means of asserting preeminence. Lacking a king or executive with sufficient authority to reward this self-love fully, women discovered triumph in the contest by creating a sensation in the community of actors—a success ratified by the local oracle, the poet. Provincial balls, however, were unlike European courts in that glory could not be found in innovation of manners or dress. Because the acclaim of the community signaled triumph at the ball, success had to be won by beauty, accomplishment, and riches already intelligible to the assembly. There was none of the creative self-fashioning practiced by courtiers in the self-projection of the ball. Rather, one excelled by making oneself the most perfect and stylish embodiment of metropolitan canons of taste. The terms of the contest are most vividly revealed in an episode at a ball in Barbados about 1709.

> There are 2 Gentlewomen in this island of the best rank that have ever endeavoured to outvie one the other as well in housekeeping housewifery, and above all in makeing a figure in this little world One of these ladyes bought her a Charming Manto and Petticoat of brogade Silk the richest that ever came to this Island, this she appear'd at a ball in where the other lady was, wth such a pert air that increased Envy in the other Lady, The Emulator went all over the town and to every shop to furnish herself wth as good a Silk, but the Country could not afford such another or come anything near it, but this Lady learning where the other Lady bought her Silk went there where there was a remnant left of Some Yards which she bought wth the same trimming that the other lady had, and with this she privately made a petticoat for her Negro woman that waited on her and Contrived an Entertainment for the other Lady to appear at in all her glory where she likewise came waited upon by her Negro woman with this petticoat on, which when the other lady saw she fell into a fitt, went home and unrobed herself, and has appeared in nothing but Norwich Stuffs ever Since.[17]

17. Thomas Walduck to James Petiver, Nov. 23, 1710, Sloane MS 2302, British Library.

This anecdote, composed by the merchant Thomas Walduck, can be read as a moral fable concerning vanity or as a reflection on the problems of determining social rank in new colonies. The moral of the anecdote is straightforward: the vain shall be humbled. What the anecdote has to say about rank in Barbados is less transparent. We are presented with a social world in which traditional markers of rank such as title, blood, and hereditary estate have been replaced by material symbols of elite style. Barbados enjoys nothing of the country complacency of an English gentry. Rather, its lack of the traditional markers of hierarchy has caused rank to become a result of competition. The most aspiring women assert their social preeminence in two arenas: the domestic sphere ("housekeeping housewifery") and the hospitable world of plantation balls and routs. At the ball, competition becomes particularly intense because of the face-to-face confrontation of rivals before the eyes of "this little world." The silk brocade mantle and petticoat is a potent symbol of high style because of its fineness, its rarity, and its exoticism. It possesses a metropolitan luster (London warrants the fashion for silk clothing) and an oriental mystique. It manifests the power of the British Empire of trade, for it has come from around the globe to adorn the enterprising in the plantations. A problem, however, attends those who found their status on commodities symbolic of elite style. Commodities are movable property and, unlike blood, title, or entailed estate, can be put in the hands of those who in all other respects are incongruous possessors. The incongruity here is acute, because the brocade is used to dress a slave; the power symbol is attached to a person rendered déclassé by two unambiguous markers of subordinate social status in the islands: skin color and chattel servitude. Thus the competition for rank becomes curiously ironic in the anecdote. Regardless of the effective hierarchies of colonial status, whether master-slave, European-African, or propertied-unpropertied, elite plantation women expend their energies striving for a preeminence that comes from being the sensation of the ball. We see fashion not as an indicator of class so much as a vehicle for asserting precedence within a class. Furthermore, the evanescence of fashion underscored the occasional character of precedence. Because it was the contest and not the result that was preserved in the reenactments of a ball, the competitors sought from writing a means to fix the results as firmly as the ball fixed the ritual contest. Thus we can account for the almost compulsive recording of actions at balls in verses, newspaper accounts, and letters: writing provided what the balls could not, the promise of enduring reputation.

Not every ritual contest in Western culture proved so subject to the changes in fashion or fortune. Certain contests involved less of chance and circumstance and more of experience and skill. An interesting comparison could be drawn between the ways in which card games and games of literary skill became, during the seventeenth and eighteenth centuries, rites of initiation into mastery by marking a progress in an art. Such a comparison would show how cards themselves turned from play based on chance to play based on skill and how experience in play served both sociability and self-cultivation. It would also show how similar institutions and methods mediated an individual's striving for mastery and reputation in society and art.

Card Games and the Muse

In August 1753 William Franklin dispatched a song to a circle of young ladies summering with Eliza Graeme in Horsham, north of Philadelphia. At twenty-two, Benjamin Franklin's son was then one of the illustrious city bachelors and served as their spokesman in this communication. The message was conventional: "We sigh and burn / While all our hopes are your return." Yet Franklin wished to distinguish himself and his friends from the multitude of sighing and burning beaux that addressed the ladies of the day, so he particularized the disturbances caused by the ladies' absence:

> Sometimes to kill a tedious hour,
>   We venture at *piquet*
> Yet even there we feel your pow'r
>   And know not how to *Bett*
> For *Cupid* laughs at our mistakes
> We lose our money for your Sakes.[18]

This was not a crass confession that affection had balked the efficient collection of winnings. The young ladies were sufficiently well versed in town diversions to understand the implications of the bachelors' card play. If gambling had truly been the bachelors' interest, they would have been playing one of several games of chance — basset, brag, poque, twenty-one, or gleek. But the beaux played piquet, the loneliest of the sociable card games, which paired off players in bouts of strategy. Piquet was the favorite

---

18. William Franklin, "A Song," in Elizabeth Graeme Fergusson, "Poemata Juvenilia," MS book, fol. 16, Library Company of Philadelphia.

game of lovers and married couples (much as contract bridge was during the 1950s). That bachelor contended with bachelor, that both were incapable of fixing attention on play, told the young ladies that the gentlemen had other partners in mind. Here the commonest sort of vers de société testified to the importance of cards as a symbol of social interaction. Because the card table was the altar of sociability (more card tables survive from eighteenth-century America than any other item of furniture), every polite lady and gentlemen knew its catechisms and rites. Even nonplayers realized the importance of the games to conversation, courtship, and conviviality. As Dr. Johnson confessed: "I am sorry I have not learnt to play at cards. It is very useful in life: it generates kindness, and consolidates society."[19]

Dr. Johnson's genealogy of influences should be reversed and revised: sociability generated kindlier forms of card play, which, in turn, consolidated society. In the history of play, the seventeenth and eighteenth centuries saw the development away from chance-based (aleatoric) gambling games pitting individuals against the turn of the cards to competitive (agonistic) games in which the skill of various players is displayed in a contest with others and with chance. The former discouraged conversation; the latter depended upon it. Piquet for two players, hombre for three players, and quadrille for four players came into being in the European royal courts as expressions of an urge to compete within the frame of socially negotiated contracts. These were bidding games that worked by the taking of tricks. To violate the contracts meant to transgress the grounds of society. When Alexander Pope composed a poetic fantasia on the disruption of a game of loo in "The Rape of the Lock" (1711), he could depend upon a genteel audience that would accept the connection between social transgression and the breakdown of play. That same audience could, conversely,

19. David Parlett, *The Oxford Guide to Card Games* (New York, 1990); Benjamin A. Hewitt, Patricia E. Kane, and Gerald W. R. Ward, *The Work of Many Hands: Card Tables in Federal America, 1790–1820* (New Haven, Conn., 1982), 15; James Boswell, *The Journal of the Tour to the Hebrides . . .* , in George Birkbeck Hill and L. F. Powell, eds., *Boswell's Life of Johnson, Together with . . .* , V (Oxford, 1950), 404. This observation, recorded by Boswell on Nov. 22, 1773, marks a change in attitude. In *Rambler* no. 15, Johnson spoke vehemently against gaming, and in no. 80 observed, "It is scarcely possible to pass an hour in honest conversation, without being able when we rise from it, to please ourselves with having given or received some advantages; but a man may shuffle cards, or rattle dice, from noon to midnight, without tracing any new idea in his mind." Samuel Johnson, *The Rambler*, ed. W. J. Bate and Albrecht B. Straus, II, in *The Yale Edition of the Works of Samuel Johnson* (New Haven, Conn., 1958–), IV, 59.

see the amelioration of society in the refinement of sociable games. In 1728 Lord Folkestone's coterie at the Crown Coffeehouse reformed the play of whist to create a challenging strategic game requiring good memory, sympathetic partnering, and psychological acumen. To excel at whist one had to learn to cooperate as well as compete. More than any other card game, whist promoted kindness and consolidated society. The creators of whist discovered the "ludic principle" celebrated by the historian Johan Huizinga: free play requires a framework of universally understood and accepted game rules.[20] Most card games mutated rapidly and gave rise to dozens of local variants and much uncertainty concerning the methods of play. From the first, the whist coterie encouraged the uniformity of their game, codifying and distributing rules, protocols, and model strategies of play. Edmond Hoyle, composer of the *Short Treatise on the Game of Whist* (1742), became the Moses of the playing rooms.

The practice of cards and the practice of literature shared several structural similarities during the eighteenth century: both developed personal skill in competitive exercise (agon made both player and artist); both constrained the ambition of the competitor, making him or her perform before a social tribunal; play and art took place within highly regulated conversations. These regulations permitted strangers, including strangers of the opposite sex, to interact with one another with a minimum of uncertainty. One could limit one's remarks to game matters, or one could employ the pauses over play to display one's personality. Simultaneously, one could demonstrate one's skill as a player and as a wit.

20. Parlett, *The Oxford Guide to Card Games*; Johan Huizinga, *Homo Ludens: A Study of the Play-Element in Culture*, 2d ed. (Buenos Aires, 1968).

Although certain historians (John M. Findlay, *People of Chance: Gambling in American Society from Jamestown to Las Vegas* [New York, 1986], foremost among them) stress the growth of gambling during the eighteenth century, what is most significant is how gambling becomes increasingly socialized and theatrical. The lottery, that characteristic gamble of the era, emblematizes the socialization well, since an entire community is enlisted in the play of chance. The growth of gambling clubs—White's and Almack's being the most famous—also marks the movement away from the solitary encounter with fortune suffered by the player of a traditional aleatoric game. Thomas M. Kavanagh, *Enlightenment and the Shadow of Chance: The Novel and the Culture of Gambling in Eighteenth-Century France* (Baltimore, 1993), well captures the confluence of cultural and intellectual currents of the postcourt culture of France and the conspicuous contest for display, wealth, and speculation.

When our topics are spent, and the talk's at a stand,
We have instant relief if we take cards in hand;
They afford us much matter as dealing we sit,
To remark on, and show off our judgment and wit.
Very strangers that had not before ever met,
By the time a game's over quite intimate get.

Because artful talk had less of chance in it than success at cards, a witty coup could outrank the victory of play.[21]

Beyond the momentary applause of the whist table lay a more substantial regard — reputation. Just as master players imposed system on the vagaries of play, the master wits made an art of the play of language. This art took conversation progressively away from the verbal improvisations of the table to writings. For those to whom wit and letters mattered, literary games supplanted cards as the preferred form of play. Mastery was marked by success at ever more sophisticated forms of wit. One usually began one's progress in wit with the common (often recited) jest. When jokes grew stale or clashed against more pungent witticisms, then one was forced to improve or suffer humiliation. From jest and pun the tyro passed to riddle, then to crambo, then to impromptu. Mastery meant that one could mint an epigram extemporaneously in the face of one's rival, that one could memorialize occasions easily in verse, and that one could ply one's pen fearlessly in a paper war.

The Sphinx's Challenge

The interest of the riddle lies in the breadth of its challenge. There is no preliminary restriction on who may respond to a riddle except that imposed by the language of utterance. The Sphinx made only one discrimination when it asked what walks on four in the morning, two at noon, and three in the evening: those who had the wit to answer correctly, and those who failed. The riddle itself decides who belongs to the dull commonality and who to the charmed circle of the ingenious. The lack of prejudice in address and the implicit possibility that it might elicit one's ingenuity have made riddles widely popular throughout history. Their poetic com-

21. Q., "On Cards, after Winning," *Lady and Gentleman's Pocket Magazine of Literary and Polite Amusement*, I (1796), 127. The permissibility of trivial conversation at cards remained an object of comment throughout the century; see Almeria, "On Cards," *Monthly Magazine, and American Review*, I (1799), 188–191.

pression of possibilities into the ambit of a sentence, their metaphoric quality (which Aristotle commended, "for something is learnt"), gave them a worth that required preservation in writing.[22] Consequently, many ancient riddles have lived on to challenge the wit of successive ages and to measure the ingenuity of modern persons against that of the ancients. A collection of such riddles was among the first of English printed books, Wynkyn de Worde's *Demandes joyeauses* (1511), and thereafter the form enjoyed a particular prominence in print. Because riddles spoke to a wide audience, all who regarded themselves something more than witless, they invoked a general public. They could be considered the citizenship exam for membership in the republic of letters.

Given the intimate connection between the riddle and writing, there is a historical aptness that the first enigma to be published in a British American newspaper was the following, submitted by a "fair Correspondent" to the *South-Carolina Gazette* in 1731/2:

A Riddle

Who dare affirm my Pow'r is weak,
Whilst I instruct the Dumb to speak?
And, what's confess'd a greater Deed,
Bestow new Life upon the Dead!
The Things most valu'd here below,
To me, their Preservation owe.
Things past, with me, as present are;
And thousand Fancies that ne'er were.
Nay more, in my capacious Womb,
Are treasur'd up Events to come.
Futurity I penetrate,
And shew the dark Designs of Fate.
Thoughts never utter'd I can tell,
Imaginations can reveal.
Each Syllable I can repeat,
In all the Volumes ever writ.
Estates I give to whom I please,
Transferring that Man's Land to this.
I'm conversant the Earth throughout

---

22. Aristotle, cited in Tony Augarde, *The Oxford Guide to Word Games* (Oxford, 1984), 1.

From splendid Court to humble Cott.
I ratify the Leagues of Princes,
And Mine, their solemn Treaty's Fence is.
My Birth no human Skill can trace,
But, that I'm not of heav'nly Race,
Is easily discern'd by this,
In me, both Truth and Error is:
And tho, my Counsel he, that takes,
Shall certainly avoid Mistakes;
Yet whoso follows all I say,
Perplex'd in endless Doubts shall stray.[23]

As one of two answers to the riddle indicated,

"The Pow'r of *LETTERS* can't be weak,
When they instruct the Dumb to speak."[24]

The powers of articulation and reanimation in the riddle have been meta-phorized in terms of the transhistorical potency of the female body. The living character of letters is further communicated by a conventional de-vice of riddling: personification of address in which the object asks to be named.

Casting a conundrum in verse or elaborating a riddle into an enigma supplemented the pleasure of the challenge. As *Delights for the Ingenious* observed, "A wellpenned enigma, artfully contrived, wherein truth walks in masquerade, and where a delicacy of thought and beauty of expression shines throughout, is one of the most agreeable and delightful entertain-ments." In effect, the enigma challenged one to be polite as well as inge-nious. Nonetheless, poetic dress was an accidental feature of the riddle, for the essential elements remained the images employed to convey the mys-tery. These images could work their claim in prose as well as verse, and, for every fancy-dress enigma that survives from the eighteenth century, half a dozen conundrums in plain prose exist. Some of these, such as the Tuesday Club conundrums of 1749–1750, verged on jest with their punning "letter wit": "Why is a good Clergiman like a pair of Clogs?" Answer: "Because he

23. "A Riddle," *South-Carolina Gazette*, no. 3, Jan. 22, 1731/2 (interpolating changes in punctuation from *Pennsylvania Gazette*, no. 186, June 19, 1732, where it was re-printed, with omissions).

24. "Answers to the Riddle in Our Last," *Pennsylvania Gazette*, no. 187, June 26, 1732.

helps to save Souls — Soals."[25] Others grew so elaborate as to verge on allegory. The enigma, with its double premium of wit, however, merited special respect, for it pointed to a level of accomplishment that could earn reputation. The ingenuity of knowing the answer, for instance, was insufficient to merit notice in replying to an enigma. One had to imitate the riddler by casting one's answer in verse. Consider the opening lines of M. B.'s reply to the *South-Carolina Gazette* enigma on writing:

> Hail! great Instructor of Mankind,
> By whom the Dumb convey their Mind
> *Homer* and *Virgil*, dead so long,
> By thee revive and shine in Song.
> Those Things we Mortals value most,
> Without thy Aid would soon be lost.
> 'Tis by thy Force Things past appear
> The same as if they present were.[26]

While M. B.'s reply required no great skill, since the order of the argument was dictated by the riddle and the imagery was a matter of elaborative reiteration, he did attempt to show that he belonged to the company of the polite as well as of the ingenious. The recitation of the totemic names, Homer and Virgil, indicated precisely which of the "dead" mattered in the world of letters. Indeed, M. B.'s belief in the power of letters exceeded that of the riddler; for, while she characterized the representational force of letters to be analogical, M. B. claimed, "Things past appear / The same as if they present were."

The conversation set in motion by the riddler describes a community of ingenuity and politeness. No other criteria for inclusion on the newspaper page had bearing — not rank, not education, not gender, not birth, not age, not location (the riddler was Carolinian; both respondents were Pennsylvanians). The abstract community of accomplishment instituted on the periodical pages was what came to be known as the republic of letters. But to appear in so public a state, one had to be practiced in art. One must have managed the passage from prose riddle to enigma by acquiring an ability at versification. This was gained in private, in one's study, or in private so-

25. [Nathaniel Crouch], *Delights for the Ingenious* . . . (London, 1684); cited in Augarde, *Oxford Guide to Word Games*, 16; Elaine Breslaw, ed., *Records of the Tuesday Club of Annapolis, 1745–56* (Urbana, Ill., 1988), 193.

26. M. B., "Hail! Great Instructor of Mankind," *Pennsylvania Gazette*, no. 187, June 26, 1732.

ciety, perhaps by participating in that most fashionable of literary games, *les bouts rimez*, or its English cousin, crambo.[27]

Crambo

If games can be viewed as the signatures of cultures, then crambo might well be the identifying mark of the culture of sociability. Greatly popular in the colleges and salons where gentlefolk honed their abilities as conversationalists and writers, crambo required a company of at least four to play — the more participants, the more interesting the result. Play commenced with a person's writing a single line of tetrameter verse. The paper was then passed to the right, where the next person had to compose spontaneously a complementary line, creating a rhymed couplet, then add an additional line for the next person to complete as a couplet. If the meter was botched, the rhyme bungled, or the sense of the poem disrupted, the player was cashiered from the circle, joining the ranks of the dull on the sidelines. As the poem grew in length, the circle shrank until only the proficient participated. Drawing the poem to a close often proved difficult, requiring logical ability as well as wit. One can gather something of the challenge that the game posed by studying the product of an evening's play. Composed by members of the Phinphilenici Club of Harvard circa 1750, the poem evinces an interesting self-consciousness concerning poetic creation.[28] It begins with a statement of the obvious — the fact of their being assembled. What follows is a communal struggle for inspiration:

A Crambo at Friendship Hall

Come friends, since we are met together
And it is dusty dusty Weather

27. In the French version of the game participants are given in sequence paired end rhymes for which they must supply a coherent couplet; the next player must continue the sense of the poem, taking his assigned end rhymes and forming a couplet that connects logically with the previous. An example, composed by Elizabeth Graeme ("Laura") and Nathaniel Evans is included in the posthumous collection of Evans's writings, *Poems on Several Occasions, with Some Other Compositions* (Philadelphia, 1772), 157–159.

28. The Phinphilenici, or "Fifth Day Club," organized in November 1746. Its members included Robert Treat Paine, Edward Wigglesworth, Nathaniel Appleton, Jr., Abijah Thurston, and later Cotton Tufts, Joshua Green, Samuel Haven, and Ezekiel Dodge. Stephen T. Riley and Edward W. Hanson, eds., *The Papers of Robert Treat Paine*, I, *1746–1756* (Boston, 1992), 22.

Dont let us mourn our present Fate
Tho' we're oblig'd to set up late
Nor let us weep the Punch is out
But Crambo briskly pass about
Let us some Topick for Discourse
In wit and Rhime show all our force
Give every line its genuine strength
And Joy stretch its utmost Length   [10]
Pray what's the Reason that some lines
Were scant of sense and short of Rhymes
Tis surely but for want of Brains
Nor have we ever spar'd our Pains
But constantly have well Endeavour'd
To have our Thought from Nonsense lever'd
Tis sure because the muse is dull
Or Else because the Moon is full
Or rather Phebus won't assist us
Or else because no Lass has kist us   [20]
Or else because Our Subjects Dry
Or we can't tell the reason why
But since Apollo and the Nine
To smile upon us doth incline
I believe we had better go to bed
And clear the Vapours from the head
There sleep till morning guilds the East
And so Apollo's fairly pleas'd
Which by the day is not so civil
Tis Using of him like the Divil   [30]
But Phebus self must now expect
To lose his former great Respect
For sure we term his Godship's Reign
I would not have him tho' Complain
Because he has us'd us very Ill
Which us'd to Invoke the Quill
Come then o Quill attend my Verse
And we thy Praise will then Rehearse
The Bird from whince you Claim the fource
That stems the Waters liquid Course   [40]

To us a pattern gives of singing
And lite our Tympana a Ringing
Hence tis our lines so roughly sound
Like Ploughs harsh grating on the ground
And hence our verses are so silly
Therefore lets go to Bed say will ye
No not before the Poems Ended
The Goddess Dulness is depended
And she'll assist us if none else will
To Rhyme me as well as Beaux and Belles will   [50]
Beside we've just got in the Mood ou't
And all of us shall have the good ou't
Happy beneath her easy reign
Weel lead our lives and pass her Chain
And Joyfull in our Ignorance
To stupid Pleasures well advance
But least we spin out too much Brains
Weell haste to End our Doggrell Strains
Methinks weve made a mighty Pother
All over this nor that nor tother   [60]
But that is what we often do
When we to Crambo make a shewe
Come then lets ease our painfull Skulls
Lest we should prove a Pack of Fools
And be an Honor to our Goddess
Whose humble servt. Every Toad is —[29]

A humorous feature of the Harvard crambo is its incorporation of the mistakes into the poem. Usually a circle of players laughed down errors and struck botched lines from the manuscript. But here a short-metered line, such as 10, stands. Furthermore, criticism was incorporated into the poem, not operating as extratextual ridicule (see lines 11–12). The poem, then, must always be compensating for vagrant moments, wresting "Thought from Nonsense," as one player succinctly put it. Consider the eruption of the first-person request to go to bed in line 25, interrupting the line of

29. "A Crambo at Friendship Hall," Robert Treat Paine Papers, Massachusetts Historical Society, Boston, not printed in vol. I of Riley and Hanson, eds., *The Papers of Robert Treat Paine*.

thought about Apollo. It takes the effort of the two following players to tie the request into a line of development that permits the Apollo theme to be reinstated. The first-person plural is reestablished two plays further on.

"A Crambo at Friendship Hall" is literally the speaking of the *sensus communis* of a private society. More than that, it shows how the play of individual voices is a corrective to taste and a guide to art. The poem's suggestion that Apollo's reign is ended by their collaborative creation points to an interesting ambivalence concerning the nature of authority in the sociable world. While the canons of classicism — "his Godship's Reign" — operate in the sunlit world at large, in the nocturnal confines of "Friendship Hall" the company humorously recognizes its art to work at a distance from the nine's exalted music. Toward the poem's end the sovereignty of "the Goddess Dulness" is confessed:

> Happy beneath her easy reign
> Weel lead our lines and pass her Chain.

Confessing the rule of Dulness was disingenuous, for the effect of playing crambo was to sharpen the powers of invention, to undergo the double critical scrutiny of one's own judgment and that of the circle and to witness the felicity of wit practiced by those in the company more gifted in verse writing. In short, it was an education in verse making compressed into half an hour, an introduction into Apollo's court. Because of the liminality of the art performed in crambo — its position intermediate between the realms of Dulness and Apollo — it was treated with fond disrespect by poets and critics who had mastered the techniques of their art. A would-be wit who published a performance with commonplace end rhymes would be termed a "Crambo scribe." The implication was either that a writer had made a premature appearance in public or that the wit of the writer suffered from arrested development. Crambo was an apprentice exercise, a middling step on the *gradus ad Parnassum*.

The Contest of Wit

One virtue of crambo was that it introduced one into social competition yet maintained the collaborative circumstance found in conversation. In effect, it introduced one fully to the notion of social contest wherein the aspirant for reputation matched skill with worthy opponents before a select audience with the prospect of a decisive determination of superiority, judged according to generally accepted rules. Although such contests spurred the male company in collegiate halls to greater fluency of wit, those that took place in heterosocial situations possessed an additional competitive dynamic, since success might have more immediate consequences than earning the regard of an audience.[30] Scant evidence exists for literary competition pitting woman against woman before a mixed audience (female artistic competition seems to have been restricted to musical performance until the end of the century), but contest among males appears common in mixed companies. The association of such contests with the polite world was so strong that Samuel Keimer, when starting up the *Barbados Gazette* in 1731, instead of using the frame of a club, chose to evoke the polite plantation as an introduction to the pleasurable society whose conversation would be distilled in print. Because of its detailed picture of a hospitable scene of heterosocial literary production, the first issue will be quoted at length:

> I send you enclosed, by Leaves of the Parties concerned, two Copies of Verses which were lately composed at a Gentleman's House in the Country, where a Set of Friends of both Sexes were met, purely to pass away a few Days agreeably.
>
> As these Lines afforded the Persons then present a good Deal of Mirth, it is to be hoped they may give at least some Amusement to your Readers; for whose Sake, I have here added a short Relation of that little Contest which occasioned them. And, because the Authors think it improper to have their own Names inserted, I shall call the One *Freeman*, and the other *Truelove*.
>
> ONE Morning at the same House, *Freeman* having got up very early to take a Turn in the Garden, the fresh Air has such an Effect, that, at his Return, he found his Appetite very craving; but, unluckily for him, none of the Ladies were come down to direct the *Tea-Table*.
>
> In this melancholy Situation he bethought himself of an Expedient, which was to write an humble Petition, set the Hardship of his Case, and praying Relief in the Premises, etc. and got it conveyed to the Hands of the Fair. The Event answer'd his Wishes, for they immediately came down Stairs, and regal'd him with a good Breakfast. This Favour and a

---

30. William Patterson's undergraduate poem, "The Belle of Princeton, Betsey Stockton, Written at the College of New Jersey, 1772, and Read before the Cliosophic Society," was an instance of such a competitive poem; its sequel, "A Satire on Betsey's College Suitors," takes his opponents to task. W. Jay Mills, ed., *Glimpses of Colonial Society and the Life at Princeton College, 1766–1773* . . . (Philadelphia, 1903), 109–125.

full Meal chang'd *Freeman*'s Fast into a Thanksgiving; for he directly wrote a Copy of Verses expressing his Gratitude, and inscribed it to the Ladies, who honour'd it with their Approbation.

An Account of his Success, as well as the Verses themselves coming soon afterwards to *Truelove*'s Hands, he was fired with the strongest Jealousy imaginable; he attacks them at once, calling them *Hungry Lines*, and insinuated that they merited no better Reward than a *Slice of Bread and Butter*. This occasions a Challenge in *Poetry*, which is instantly accepted. The *Time*, the *Place*, *Judges*, and *Conditions* are presently agreed to; one whereof was, That the *Subject* should be given to the Candidates by the *Judges* immediately before they entered upon their Tryal of Skill, in Order to prevent either of them from becoming *Plagiary*.

The long expected Day at last came; the Competitors repair'd to the Place appointed, with great Impatience and Curiosity to know the THEME. *Freeman*, we were told, upon the Road shewed the greatest Uneasiness: *Suppose*, says he, it should be a Sugar-Cane, I have him there! In *short, if it should be a* Whale, or a Flying-Fish, *an* Elephant, *or a* Musketo, he declared himself *in utrumque paratus*. Nor was his Antagonist without his Anxieties. However, when *Freeman* arrived, he presently craved *Over* (to use his own Phrase) of his Opponent's Trunks, Papers, and Pockets; when, unhappily, *Bishe's Art of Poetry* was, upon a strict Search, found at the Bottom of *Truelove*'s Trunk, where he confessed it had been convey'd as his *Corps de Reserve*.

THE *Theme* was then given, which to their mutual Surprize and Concern (being quite unprepared for one so extraordinary) was *themselves*. Each was to write a *Satyr* or *Panegyrick* upon the other, as should best suit his particular Genius. This done, they were conducted to their respective Apartments, and were there kept like Cardinals in the Conclave, upon the Election of a New Pope. I cannot here omit telling you of an Imagination I then conceiv'd, that *Freeman*, instead of *Phoebus* or the *Nine*, had invoked the Goddess *Cloacina*, from the Place he chose to compose his Piece in, which, you must know, was the *Necessary House*.

THE Candidates being left to their Contemplations, the whole Company amused themselves with an Expectation of Pleasure from the *Performances, Countenances,* and *Behaviour* of the *Poets* when they should make their Entry: But I assure you, the Reality far exceed our utmost Conceptions. The Ladies too employed some Part of this Time in preparing a Laurel to adorn the Brows of the happy Bard to whom the Prize should be decreed, to which was affix'd this Motto in Capital Letters, DETUR DIGNIORI.

The Parties, having finish'd their Labours, were admitted, and presented them to the Chairman sealed up, who read them audibly, beginning with *Freeman*'s, which was first delivered. They were then order to withdraw, and the Court, upon a Division, determined the Competition in Favour of *Truelove*. But it is not easy to conceive, much less describe the various Passions, the Hopes and Fears, the Jealousies, by which these Candidates, on their being called in, were agitated, and which indeed were artfully protracted by the Manner in which the Chairman gave Judgment; who, upon the Occasion, expatiated largely on the Merits of the respective Pieces, and kept their Hopes alive to the very last, even till the fatal Sentence was pronounced. Immediately the Conqueror was crowned by the Ladies, to the great Satisfaction of himself, and the no less Mortification of his Adversary.

I SHALL only farther observe, That this cruel Defeat was borne by *Freeman* with an uncommon Presence of Mind, attended with a decent Submission to the Decision of the *Judges*. On the other Hand, *Truelove* shewed himself not at all elate, tho' highly pleased with his Success, and the Honours consert'd on him. The Court also, not being in the least conscious of Partiality, did consent to the Publication of their Performances; which, should they, in any Degree, contribute to the Diversion of your Readers (as I before hinted) I shall have my Ends, and you, I hope, will find your Advantage, as they may be the Means of promoting hereafter some more ingenious Attempts of a Tendency as innocent.[31]

The obvious points need be touched on only briefly. The ability to write poetry inspired male jealousy because in female estimation wit is desirable; for a sexual rival the only counter to a display of wit is to respond with more pungent wit; an audience composed largely of women passes judgment on the contest.

The ceremonious character of the contest deserves consideration. The company has been formed into a court, understood in its traditional sense — the retinue of authority. Truelove's challenge and the appointment of time, place, adjudicators, and conditions suggest the code duello, but the archaism of the narrator — "Tryal of Skill," "*Corps de Reserve*" — point to a less

---

31. *Barbados Gazette*, no. 1, Nov. 20, 1731, in [Keimer, comp.], *Caribbeana*, I, 1–6.

deadly and more aesthetic combat, the tournament. The medieval dress of the contest aestheticized the business of sexual assertion, making it agreeable by distancing it in time. The image of the contestants isolated "like Cardinals in the Conclave" further amplifies the theme of the sublimation of sexual jealousy into more socially acceptable "passions." Superimposed upon the medievalism is a classical imagery. By making the contest doubly archaic in its trappings, the combat is rendered playful rather than traditional. The more ceremonious the contention, the more artificial the proclamation of victory, the more the "Tendency" of the combatants is rendered "innocent."

The most diverting circumstance of the contest is the choice of poetic subject. By making the rival the subject of one's verses and by offering the choice to praise or satirize him, the court has ensured that the jealousies firing the challenge cannot be evaded but must themselves be thematicized and controlled by being dressed in acceptable language. Both contestants chose to combine the praise and satire in verses that commence as mock panegyric but close with undisguised malice. The winning verses prevailed because of the ingenuity of its mock-panegyric strategy. Since Freeman had distinguished himself as an actor in recent plantation theatricals, Truelove burlesqued his character by praising all the masquerade qualities he assumed on the stage:

> O Happy Freeman, who, with Spear and Shield,
> Has gain'd Renown on many a sham-fought Field.
> In softer Gallantries you topp'd your Parts,
> And, with rich Buskins, captivated Hearts.
> Each Scene, your well adapted Talents grace,
> Old Aunt's quaint Voice, and Gibbet's rueful Face.
> In You, sage Leontine essays to dance,
> Rough Oswald trips un Gentilhomme de France.
> A Well rais'd (at) rehears'd in Cato's Cause,
> Once from reluctant Envy forc'd Applause.
> And Prologue, fram'd for Thread-bare Stroler's Gain,
> Shew'd you a Master of the Plaintive Strain.
> Your Hungry Lines, with which you made such Sputter,
> Won, from the fair, some Tea, and Bread and Butter.
> Thus far triumphant, matchless in these Isles,
> You've stood above the Criticks Frowns, or Smiles.

Your Peerless Deeds, when sung in Grubstreet Lays,
May swell your Memory with lasting Praise.
Then stop your Muse, let cautious Shame prevail,
Lest on your Tomb, you fix some pointed Tale:
This was a Hero, without Sense to know it;
Spite of himself and Stars, he would turn POET.

To have made sense of the poem one had to have been able to decode the allusions. In order to accomplish this, one must have already been a member of that cultivated circle that attended the theatricals and seen Freeman as Old Aunt in *Sir Courtly Nice*, Gibbet in *The Stratagem*, the sage philosopher of *Theodosius*, and the Saxon General in the *Royal Convert*. Truelove engages audience members by recalling their own devotion to the muses. Knowledge of an allusion was a token of membership. Although the original manuscript reinforced the exclusivity of the company, Keimer's published version, which provided explanatory footnotes, was a window into the mysteries of the beau monde. Keimer even took the unusual step of suggesting to the readership the identities behind the writers' cognomens: Freeman was "Mr. J——n," and Truelove was "Mr. F——y." We can see in Keimer's treatment of the contest the newspaper acting to mediate reputation—to change the terms of renown from the charmed circle of friendly intimates to the general reading public interested in examples of politeness and gentility. The narrator helped to make the contest of more than local interest by his humorous deflation of the contestants' abilities as poets. Seeing one contestant hide a schooltext on poetry writing, the other worrying over subject matter, and both laboring in tedious solitude to produce their verses made them more aspirants to art than adepts. By so doing, the narrator placed the contestants on a footing more nearly equal to that of the interested reader than if they had been accomplished poets. The narrator at the same time suggested what accomplishment entailed—a knowledge of the techniques of verse in need of no schooling, sufficient learning to be able to treat most common subjects, and fluency of inspiration. When Freeman or Truelove could, like Henry Brooke in Philadelphia, compose spontaneously in company, or like William Byrd in Tunbridge Wells, mint epigrams impromptu, then he could claim the title of wit.

Once someone had mastered play, had worked through the gradations of skill in prose and verse, and had gained supremacy over the field, one was potentially a dangerous person, particularly when at large in the world. The master wit — a John Wilmot, a John Wilkes, an Alexander Pope — could become a monster of malice whose irrepresible genius brooked little restraint. The master gamester, such as a Charles James Fox, a Topham Beauclerk, could become the ruin of a hundred family fortunes. A virtuoso of politeness, say Barry St. Leger, could ravage a hundred hearts with his graces. Their fame came at the cost of resentment, fear, and, at times, social persecution. Mastery, that mastery that transcended the received conventions and presented itself in a novel genius, was best tolerated when it was insulated from society at large. Only Pope, of the above-named, was so confident of his power that he would project himself free of the protections of private society. Wilmot, Wilkes, Fox, Beauclerk, and St. Leger all flourished under the veil afforded by the most insular of the social institutions, the club. In British America, masculine society, particularly that of the most accomplished and powerful men, embraced the club as the institution in which their ingenuity could enjoy free play and their competitive spirit exercise beyond those limits set by the rites of assembly.

6

The Clubs

Social clubs constituted havens of play and free conversation in which the sorts of expressions most troublesome to church and state could be voiced, whether with seditious plainness or, more artfully, as travesty. In the second-story rooms of taverns and coffeehouses public opinion achieved its fullest scope of liberty by voicing criticism as wit.

The clubs meeting in the coffeehouses, rather than the coffeehouses themselves, were the crucial institutions in expanding the scope of public expression.[1] Club discourse differed from the promiscuous parley of the common room. The third earl of Shaftesbury identified club discourse, oxymoronically, as the speech of "private society." A society's private quality, for Shaftesbury, consisted in a shared sense of humor as well as a common conscience; the privacy of private society inhered as much in a "freedom of raillery" as in the liberty to express the promptings of conscience. Shaftesbury argued that "a freedom of raillery, a liberty in decent language to question everything, and an allowance of unravelling or refuting any argument, without offence to the arguer" were the sole conditions that enabled conversation to become both speculative and agreeable.[2]

1. In British America one does not encounter examples of coffeehouses whose client base became so specialized that they went private, making the premises a clubhouse. In British America clubs always form within coffeehouses or taverns. In London there are several instances of coffeehouses mutating into private societies—such as Almack's or Boodle's clubs.

2. Anthony Ashley Cooper, third earl of Shaftesbury, *Sensus Communis: An Essay on the Freedom of Wit and Humour* . . . , in Shaftesbury, *Characteristics of Men, Manners, Opinion, Times, Etc.*, ed. John Robertson, 2 vols. (London, 1900), I, 49, 53. Pt. 1,

The freewheeling conversation that Shaftesbury celebrated arose "only of the liberty of *the club*, and of that sort of freedom which is taken amongst gentlemen and friends who know one another perfectly well." Although the free play of conversation might be a product of friendly society, Shaftesbury believed that friendly society came to exist only by the exercise of such free play. Communities of interest and fellow feeling were invoked by wit, for the most authentic sensus communis was that established by spontaneous shared laughter in response to a joke. General laughter brought into the open whatever implicit consensus existed in a company, revealing to friends, acquaintances, and even strangers their shared attitudes. The successful common room joke was the first step in the formation of a private society. Shaftesbury's most influential essay, *Sensus Communis: An Essay on the Freedom of Wit and Humour* (1709), envisioned a process of social formation and refinement empowered by the free conversation of private societies engaged in witty thrust and parry: "We polish one another, and rub off our corners and rough sides by a sort of amicable collision. To restrain this, is inevitably to bring a rust upon men's understandings."[3] As the name of the Society for Promoting Virtue and Knowledge, by a Free Conversation (1730–circa 1747) of Newport, Rhode Island, suggests, the fruits of discursive liberty were not limited to social polish and mental acuity. Virtue, the totemic force in whose name republicans dared to criticize the prevailing schemes of power, was the product of the free play of wit.

What threatened to restrain the free play of wit? The church in its attempts to govern the tongues of individuals. The state in its attempts to preserve its authority to rule.

How did clubs insulate themselves from the interference of church and state? Margaret C. Jacob is suggestive. Secrecy protected freethinking, and clubs adopted and adapted guild mysteries to keep their proceedings hidden. (Thus, in the transformation of Freemasonry from a "practical" to a "speculative" society, a guild mystique was mutated into a club discipline.) Rules of silence, schemes of penalty, and oath-taking rituals all featured in club practice. Yet clubs also forestalled interference by dispensing publicity about themselves. Two sorts predominated: one emphasized a symbolism that projected the innocence and charitability of private society; the other conveyed a symbolism of frivolity that projected the impertinence, ridicu-

---

sect. 5, explores the distinctive modes of locution of "common society" and "private society."

3. Ibid., 45, 53.

lousness, and triviality of private society. The former strategy was followed by conventicles, academies, and societies for useful knowledge.[4] The latter strategy, adopted by many social clubs, was probably the more historically effective in expanding the public's capacity to voice opposition. Some private societies (the Freemasons, for instance) employed secrecy *and* both strategies of publicity to protect themselves. Printed works, manuscripts, table talk, and street processions promulgated public, or exoteric, images of clubs sufficiently innocent, ambiguous, or ludicrous to forestall the intervention of the state.

Societies that insulated themselves from legal coercion with the duplicities of wit could not deflect the animosity of pious Christians, who recognized that clubs, by making heretical ideas and dangerous doctrines a matter of play, denied the potency of the categories of good and evil, orthodox and unorthodox. Wit and freethinking challenged the seriousness of God's decrees and the theonomy that directed conscience in its judgments against the sinful self. Even so sociable a Christian as Jonathan Swift engaged in the campaign against "The Wits," whom he styled "the Atheists of the Age."[5] Orthodox assessments of the clubs and club wit were astute. With the same spirit of travesty that prompted Laurence Sterne and his circle to dress up as monks and perform mock black masses in Medmenham, clubmen burlesqued heretical creeds and dangerous doctrines for the frisson of audacity. Consider how Dr. Alexander Hamilton, secretary of the Tuesday Club of Annapolis, Maryland, could both affirm and deny neo-Epicurean materialism:

> I deny that the members of this here Club were in the least degree Philosophers . . . or lovers of Science, but, were more properly Philogasters, or lovers of their Belly, For I never yet heard that Luscious eating and drinking, was any one of the Seven liberal arts and Sciences, but

4. Margaret C. Jacob, *The Radical Enlightenment: Pantheists, Freemasons, and Republicans* (London, 1981), has exhaustively explored the protections that secrecy offers. For the cultural significance of the conventicle, see Stephen Foster, *The Long Argument: English Puritanism and the Shaping of New England Culture, 1570–1700* (Chapel Hill, N.C., 1991), 20. For the academies, see Peter France, *Politeness and Its Discontents: Problems in French Classical Culture* (Cambridge, 1992), 57–64.

5. Jonathan Swift, "Ode to the Athenian Society," in Harold Williams, ed., *The Poems of Jonathan Swift*, 2d ed., 3 vols. (Oxford, 1958), I, 19. For an account of the Christian war against the wits, and Swift's part in particular, see Roger D. Lund, "Strange Complicities: Atheism and Conspiracy in *A Tale of a Tub*," *Eighteenth Century Life*, XIII, no. 3 (November 1989), 34–58.

rather one of the many beastly appetites or lusts, that men are subject to, *ergo*, in whatever case these Longstanding members were Philosophers, they were none in this. As to Epicurus . . . how Idle it is to think, that Luscious eating and drinking, soft lying, Laziness, and an excessive Indulgence of venereal pleasures, could be Ingredients in this Philosophers System of happiness must appear, when we reflect, that he knew as well as we do, that these excesses constantly bring with them, gouts, Rheumatisms, Sciaticas, gravels, Scurvies, poxes, toothakes, colics, boils, blotches, Scabs, and all the plagues of Pandora's box, which are accompanied with pain, rack and torment Inexpressible.[6]

Hamilton's mock jeremiad (prompted by the introduction of iced cake into the club's repasts) confronts his reader with several questions. Did the members practice Epicureanism, or merely Philogastrism? Did they manifest a philosophy, or disguise a common appetite in philosophic dress? Then the reader must decide, Which is the more reprehensible thing to confess — being a neopagan materialist philosopher (that is, an atheist) or a person made incapable of philosophy by a mindless devotion to appetite? The matter is further complicated because Hamilton employed a somatic analysis of the Epicurean-materialist sort to point out to club members the presumably familiar effects of Philogastrism. The membership would thus seem to have included philosophers (at least Hamilton himself) and Philogasters. The playful ambiguities of the mock jeremiad deflected any serious charge made against the club by Christians and moralists. What rhetorical weight could charges of turpitude have if the group in question already denounced or confessed its sins so extravagantly?

For the clubs, entertaining the possibility that the impulse for private society lay in the guts rather than the brains could be liberating. Club conversation predicated on common appetite rather than on common belief or interest could speak at a playful distance from public pieties, unconstrained by the authority of church and state. Joseph Addison sketched the sort of liberties consequent from grounding fellowship on appetite: "Our Modern celebrated Clubs are founded upon Eating and Drinking, which are Points wherein most Men agree, and in which the Learned and Illiterate, the Dull and the Airy, the philosopher and the Buffoon, can all of them

---

6. Dr. Alexander Hamilton, *The History of the Ancient and Honorable Tuesday Club*, ed. Robert Micklus, 3 vols. (Chapel Hill, N.C., 1990), I, 171. The Tuesday Club operated from 1745 to 1756.

PLATE 5 The Whin Bush Club. *Drawing by Dr. Alexander Hamilton. Annapolis, 1750s. The History of the Ancient and Honorable Tuesday Club, Garrett 1; The John Work Garrett Library of The Johns Hopkins University*

bear a Part."[7] Society grounded on shared appetite offered the broadest potential for human participation. The common table promised amiable conversation spiced with the greatest variety. A willingness to entertain both philosopher and buffoon, Epicurean and Philogaster, in the sensus communis distinguished the club as an institution. The playful indeterminacy of club conversation stood at odds with the solemnities of state, the dogmas of the church, the zeal of the sects, and the passions of the parties.

Much of the playful spirit derived from the clubs' consciously maintained tension between the sensus communis of the private circle and prevailing civil myths or myths of the state. The celebration of appetite publicized in club names such as the Beefsteak Society, the Cheshire Cheese Club, the Calve's Head Club, the October [Ale] Club, and the Homony Club parodied the Hobbesian theory that society arose from the suppression of individual appetite in obedience to a principle of self-preservation.[8] Rather, the clubs discovered the origin of their society in the friendly bibulousness of ancient table fellowship:

> In the earliest ages of the world, it is supposed, that Clubs consisted as they do now, of Certain Select knots of men . . . that met together, either in the field, or under covert of a tent or house. It may be conjectured with some Show of probability, that the first societies of this sort, assembled in some Cave or grotto, or in some thicket or grove, hence we may derive the origin of the ancient Rural or Sylvan Deities, of Pan, the Satyrs, Bacchus, Silenus, and their followers, who were probably Jolly drunken Club Companions, but this was before the Cultivation of arts and Sciences, when men were barbarous and unpolished, and, by these Clubs, it is thought, they were first Civilized, and taught the use of arts and Arms, Love, dress and the bottle, hence the members of these early Clubs were deified, and those Satyrs, were nothing but the first beaus.[9]

Hamilton's mythical archaeology of clubbing burlesqued both skeptical speculations on the origins of the gods and Hobbesian myths of the origin of the state. Hamilton parodied the archaeological myths employed by

7. Joseph Addison, [About Clubs], *Spectator*, no. 9., Mar. 10, 1710/1.

8. The best general introduction to British private circles remains Robert J. Allen, *The Clubs of Augustan London* (Cambridge, Mass., 1933). For Scottish circles, see Davis D. McElroy, *Scotland's Age of Improvement: A Survey of Eighteenth-Century Literary Clubs and Societies* (Pullman, Wash., 1969). No adequate history of British American clubs exists.

9. Hamilton, *History of the Tuesday Club*, ed. Micklus, I, 38–39.

philosophical historians of religion and politics. Philosophical explanation often consisted of an "inferential recovery" (Hamilton would substitute "suppositious tale") of the archaic origin of a concept or scheme of belief. Hamilton caricatured the contemporary Scottish skeptical renovation of euhemerism, the ancient supposition that the histories of sylvan deities were mythical accounts of the careers of human beings. By identifying the conviviality of ancient gods-who-were-not-gods as the model of modern sociability, Hamilton's doubling of the demythicizing showed up the fantasy element in archaeology. His ambiguity exposed the two sorts of vanity characteristically inscribed in the archaeology of cultures — the fantasy of the returned glory and the fantasy of civilization's stage-by-stage rise to the achieved present. Was the club the atavistic second manifestation of the community of ancient gods that gave rise to civilization? Or was the club the culmination of that civilizing begun in the rudeness of ancient agricultural life? The two possibilities contradict each other. The seeming inability to determine in favor of either possibility renders them both incredible.

Hamilton's burlesque of Thomas Hobbes was more general. Hobbes, the great champion of state power, had realized the danger that the proliferation of private societies within the state posed to state power. In *Leviathan*, Hobbes had complained that "the great number of corporations which are as it were many lesser commonwealths in the body of a greater, [work] like worms in the entrails of a natural man."[10] Hobbes denied the legitimacy of private societies that were not warranted by laws common to all subjects. His requirement of a common law sanction for private society, had it been made the legal doctrine of the state, would have hindered the proliferation of associations. Yet Hobbes's requirement was never enacted in law, and private society could thus claim for itself the sanction of perpetual custom, the foundation of common law. Hamilton's portrait of a friendly circle of sylvan deities invoked the antiquity of convivial fellowship. Social revelry was presumably so long-standing a custom that it had been inscribed in ancient mythology. What matter if the myth be an ancient fiction, so long as it was ancient?

Hobbes was prescient in seeing that private associations would arrogate to themselves rights and liberties that would challenge the sovereignty of the state. From the 1650s onward, private societies increasingly claimed for themselves autonomy; indeed, they mocked the state by assuming the

10. Thomas Hobbes, *Hobbes's Leviathan, Reprinted from the Edition of 1651*, ed. W. G. Pogson-Smith (Oxford, 1967), 256–257.

character of commonwealths. The play politics of private societies, such as James Harrington's Rota Club, could verge at times on practical experiments in utopia, at other times on sedition. The more "projecting" (to use Daniel Defoe's term) a private society, the greater the need for insulation from state, church, and street.[11] How did the clubs clear a protected space for themselves? By myth, by symbol, and by contract. At the beginning of the seventeenth century, certain societies began a self-projection and image management: the Scottish Freemason corporations reorganized under the Shaw statutes into a network of lodges, elaborating a hermetic mythology from the Old Charters, instituting the rite of the Freemasonic Word, and generating an increasingly speculative Freemasonic symbolism.

The political organization of the Scottish Freemason lodges was particularly ingenious. They constituted themselves both as corporations (civic organizations recognized by charter) and as lodges (autonomous, self-governing entities).[12] This dual constitution vested them with a political ambiguity that they amplified by their rule of secrecy, ensuring the maximum liberty to do as they wished.

The lesson of the lodges was not lost on contemporaries. In London, a group of young gentlemen adapted the strategies of legislation, secrecy, and mystagogy to their society, forming the club that stood as prototype

11. The Rota was formed in 1659 as a political debating society. The members gathered around an oval table at the Turk's Head Coffeehouse, New Palace Yard, London; they included Cyriac Skinner, Sir William Petty, John Milton, Andrew Marvell, and Harrington. The name derived from the club's maintenance of a rotating executive; all points of controversy were decided by ballot. Harrington's *Oceana* derived much of its content from the conversation of the club.

D[aniel] Defoe, *An Essay upon Projects* (London, 1697), distinguished voluntary associations that prosecuted programs of public works from those whose activities were undertaken primarily for the delectation of the membership. The former had to take care not to seem a junto manipulating civic life; therefore, public perception of the club's doings had to be managed. Anthony Collins, the freethinker, elaborated on the disparity of image and actuality in projecting societies in his distinction between exoteric (publicly intended) and esoteric (privately intended) expressions. The various strategies of self-imaging fall into two categories: those predicated on secrecy and those predicated on burlesque. Secret societies restricted public access to the conversation of the membership; burlesque societies flooded the public with accounts (often specious) of their whimsical doings. The Kit-Kats (whose secretary Jacob Tonson assumed the mystic name Bojac to twit the public's hunger for the mysteries of private society) is the prime example of a burlesque projecting society.

12. David Stevenson, *The Origins of Freemasonry: Scotland's Century, 1590–1710* (Cambridge, 1988), 6–18.

for all subsequent English, Scottish, and Anglo-American clubs. Meeting at the Devil and St. Dunstan's Tavern, Ben Jonson's Apollo Club became the model of metropolitan sociability. Like Scottish Freemasonry, the Apollo possessed a dual constitution. On one wall of the meeting room under the bust of Apollo appeared the god's oracle:

Wine, it is the milk of Venus
And the poets' horse accounted:
Ply it, and you all are mounted.
'Tis the true Phoebeian liquor,
Cheers the brains, makes wit the quicker,
Pays all debts, cures all diseases,
And at once three senses pleases.
Welcome, all who lead or follow
To the oracle of Apollo!

On the opposite wall in Latin appeared the *Leges Convivales*, the humanly contracted rules governing the conduct and conversation of the club.[13] Thus the club was both a "natural society" — that is, a society "founded in natural Appetites and Instincts" (to use Edmund Burke's phrase) — and a contract polity, a society organized by the consent of the membership.[14] A third scheme of authority was the charismatic rule of Jonson over his "poetic sons," who made up the majority of the membership. The reign of Jonson (in effect, absolute rule) was empowered by the social obeisance to genius. The myth of Apollo's aegis, exercised through the power of wine, suggested the arbitrary rule of genius by recalling the irrationality of the antique gods in Apollo's call to serve appetite. The myth of Apollo's court further suggested a familial frame for authority in the club, with daughter muses replaced by Jonson's poetic sons. The figuration of the polity as a family headed by a potent and just father anticipated Sir Robert Filmer's

13. Ben Jonson, "Over the Door at the Entrance into the Apollo," in Jonson, *Poems*, ed. Ian Donaldson (London, 1975), 372, ll. 12–20; Jonson, "Leges Convivales: Quod Felix, Faustumque in Apolline Sit," ibid., 370. The laws became well known in Alexander Brome's poetic translation, "Ben Jonson's Sociable Rules for the Apollo," ibid., 371; and Michael Drayton, "The Sacrifice to Apollo" (1619), in J. William Hebel, ed., *The Works of Michael Drayton* (Oxford, 1961), II, 357–358. For the arrangement and function of the "Oracle" and "Leges" in the clubroom, see Percy Simpson, "Ben Jonson and the Devil Tavern," *Modern Language Review*, XXXIV (1939), 367–373.

14. Edmund Burke, *A Vindication of Natural Society . . .* , ed. Frank N. Pagano (Indianapolis, Ind., 1982), 14.

Patriarcha (1680) rather than John Locke's *Two Treatises of Government* (1690). Yet we should not ignore the most distinctive aspect of this triple manifestation of authority: the figurations are patent fictions. The "one omniscient and almighty God" of Christianity did not warrant society; rather, Apollo, the creator-creature of poets, did. Jonson was not the father of his "sons"; he just said he was. The archpoet's fiat did not mandate matters absolutely in the club, for his rule was restrained by the impersonal dictates of the *Leges Convivales*. Divine right, patriarchy, and absolute rule, the three traditional props of untrammeled executive power, were all de-realized in the aesthetic play of the club. The club set itself at a parodic distance from the traditional authority structure of the state. It is from this perspective that Harrington and Locke, members of later clubs, would critique the theory of structure of national authority. Both had firsthand knowledge of contract societies and their possible modes of operation when they wrote their political programs. Harrington tested his propositions in conversation at the Rota, Locke in his "academy."

The effectiveness of publicity in protecting clubs can be seen in the public response to the activities of the King's Head Club (or Green Ribbon Club). Organized by the first earl of Shaftesbury in London in 1680, the club advertised itself as a friendly society yet directed much of its energy to organizing pope burnings and popular demonstrations in London.[15] Even though several members were connected with Monmouth's Rebellion and the Rye House plot, the tincture of innocence so colored the public sense of sociability that even so extreme a critic of the Whig program as John Dryden indicted the club, not for practicing sedition, but for playing at it:

> These Gloomy, Thoughtfull and on Mischief bent,
> While those for mere good Fellowship frequent
> Th' Appointed Clubb, can let Sedition pass,
> Sense, Non-sence, anything t' employ the Glass;
> And who believe in their dull honest Hearts,
> The Rest talk Treason but to shew their Parts.[16]

15. Organized by Shaftesbury, the club met at the King's Head Tavern, London. It earned its sobriquet, the Green Ribbon Club, by the identifying token worn on clothing during street disturbances. It lasted from 1680 to 1685, when it dispersed after the dissolution of the Exclusion Parliament. There is some debate whether Locke was a member.

16. John Dryden, "The Second Part of Absalom and Achitophel, a Poem," in James Kinsley, ed., *The Poems and Fables of John Dryden* (London, 1962), 257.

Dryden could not know that the King's Head Club would serve as the model for a century of mug clubs, scowrers, and liberty gangs that would convert the streets of the metropolis and the colonial port cities into political theaters. From 1683 on, the public mischief occasioned by clubs' projects directed official attention increasingly away from the seditious writings of associations to the clubs' sponsorship of misbehavior in the streets: the clubs directed the thoughts and words of the people. The word *mob* first appeared in English in descriptions of the actions of the King's Head Club.[17] The public and public opinion were expanding from the exclusive preserves of the coffeehouses to the open air of the cities.

In British America, complaints about club-sponsored political mischief began to be voiced in the aftermath of the Glorious Revolution. Richard Coote, earl of Bellomont, for instance, as governor observed their influence in New York: "Cabals and clubbs . . . are held dayly at Colonel Fletcher's lodgings (from whence I have as great reason to believe) false reports and rumors are spread about the City and province, whereby mens minds are disturbed, and an odium cast upon the Government."[18] The nocturnal riots of Henry Brooke's club in 1703 Philadelphia should be seen as instances of political agitation. The young gentry at Enoch Story's Tavern combined to counter the power of the Quaker City Corporation. Their club was in effect a political party or, in the parlance of the day, a faction. In its schemes we see how private society's projects could challenge the integrity of the state. The extramural activities of clubs posed the most immediate challenge to state power; consequently, political theorists focused their attention on the politics of the street, treating issues such as the right of assembly, rather than on the private speech and action of groups. Thus, the right of free association would not be at issue in the First

17. On Nov. 17, 1680, "the Rabble first changed their Title, and were called *the Mob* in the Assemblies of this Club. It was their Beast of Burthen, and called first *mobile vulgus,* but fell naturally into the Contraction of one Syllable, and ever since is become proper English" (Roger North, *Examen* . . . [London, 1740], 573, also quoted in *OED*). Scowrers were young gentlemen who disturbed the peace of the City for pleasure or politics. Their deeds are portrayed in Thomas Shadwell, *The Scowrers: A Comedy* (1691), in Montague Summers, ed., *The Complete Works of Thomas Shadwell* (London, 1966), V, 79–150. Mug clubs were political clubs that met in London alehouses during the reign of Queen Anne. Their members came largely from the artisan class.

18. "Governor Bellomont Describes Factionalism, 1698," in Michael G. Hall, Lawrence H. Leder, and Michael G. Kammen, eds., *The Glorious Revolution in America: Documents on the Colonial Crisis of 1689* (Chapel Hill, N.C., 1964), 129.

Amendment, because it did not pose an immediate threat to the pubic peace, and it was a right that was presumed, regardless of whether a club constituted a faction. One could reread James Madison's "Federalist No. 10" with added nuance when keeping in mind the distinction between the external and internal activities of clubs — their public projects and their private proceedings.

> There are two methods of curing the mischiefs of faction: the one, by removing its causes; the other, by controlling its effects.
>
> There are again two methods of removing the causes of faction: the one by destroying the liberty which is essential to its existence; the other, by giving to every citizen the same opinions, the same passions, and the same interests.
>
> It could never be more truly said than of the first remedy, that it was worse than the disease. . . .
>
> The second expedient is as impracticable, as the first would be unwise. . . .
>
> The latent causes of faction are thus sown in the nature of man; and we see them every where brought into different degrees of activity, according to the different circumstances of civil society. . . .
>
> The inference to which we are brought, is, that the *causes* of faction cannot be removed; and that relief is only to be sought in the means of controlling its *effects*.[19]

One can adduce from Madison's comments why the First Amendment asserted a right of assembly and not a right of free association. For Madison, human nature endorsed the liberty of association that gave rise to faction: no constitution could counter the human love of society with any hope of success. Free association was thus one of the perpetual rights of humankind presumed in the Ninth Amendment. What was at issue — what had to be addressed in the Bill of Rights — was the scope allowed the public effects of human combination. Could the politics of faction-led mobs be permitted? Yes, provided that the attacks against persons and property that had characterized street politics since the days of the King's Head Club were eliminated. The First Amendment granted a right of popular demonstration in the streets, so long as the demonstration remained peaceable and could be construed as a public petition. Thus the Constitution's right of assembly

19. [James Madison], "The Federalist, No. 10," in Jacob E. Cooke, ed., *The Federalist* (Middletown, Conn., 1961), 58.

recognized the expanded practice of public criticism that the clubs had nurtured in privacy and then projected beyond the coffeehouse walls.

In Madison's justification of a right of assembly that incorporated the expression of public political partisanship in opposition to constituted powers and in his presumption of a right of free association standing behind assembly rights, we confront a theoretical proposal, not a legal doctrine. In subsequent decades a right of association had to be specified in law to authorize the formation of trade unions; in previous decades authorities were not so mindful of the distinction between agitations in the streets and sedition spoken in private company. Either was grounds for arrest if the authorities chose to be zealous in upholding the public peace. It was in the face of this threat of invasive coercion that clubs constructed their various hedges.

Behind a variety of barriers, clubs asserted their autonomy, insulating themselves and their discourse from the claims of the state. Similarly, clubs constructed protection from the intrusions of religious authority, sometimes in several layers. Many clubs instituted rules of secrecy. Certain clubs evaded religious controversy by legislating prohibitions on religious contention in the club conversation. As the *Leges Convivales* counseled, "Let none of us be mute, or talk too much; / On serious things or sacred let's not touch." The Tuesday Club's Gelastic Law required the membership to laugh down anyone making direct reflections on matters of church or state. The Jewish Gentleman's Club of Newport, Rhode Island, laid a penalty of four bottles of good wine if members swore or made heated comments about synagogue matters.[20]

On the epistemological level, religious truth—a truth grounded in the revelations of the spirit—was countered by an epicurean insistence that appetite governed human action and interaction. Kit-Cat pie, the rare roast beef of Britain, or Maryland hominy grounded community in the reality of the human senses. As William King, laureate of the Beef Steak Society, wrote:

Chimeras from the poet's fancies flow:
The cook contrives his shapes in real dough.

Furthermore, in the conscious cultivation of a taste for a wholesome native dish, the membership developed a government of appetite that trained one

20. "Alexander Brome's Translation of the *Leges Convivlaes:* Ben Jonson's Sociable Rules for the Apollo," in Jonson, *Poems*, ed. Donaldson, 371; Elaine G. Breslaw, ed., *Records of the Tuesday Club of Annapolis, 1745–56* (Urbana, Ill., 1988), 7–8; "A Club Formed by the Jews, 1761," *Newport Historical Magazine*, IV (July 1883), 59.

in simplicity and virtue. Charles Wallace, laureate of the Homony Club of Annapolis, wrote in 1773:

> Luxury, begone I say,
> Homony shall rule tonight;
> Gluttons, Epicures away,
> Homony puts all to Flight.[21]

In the Homony Club, human will had the capacity to govern the appetites of the flesh.

A second and more conspicuous symbolic departure from the mandates of religion was the systematic acknowledgment of pagan mythology instead of biblical legislation as the superhuman warrant for society. Consider again the allegorical painting displayed in the meeting room of the Bow Bell Club in Barbados we first viewed in Chapter 2. It showed "Men societated together Some eating some drinking and dancing and playing upon Musick full of Variety of Exercise. Over head the Gods, looked down upon them Smileing—The Moral shews that when men are met together through an Innocent design, Heaven above are well pleas'd as we poor mortals below."[22] It was, not Jehovah, but the pagan pantheon that condoned sociability, for the gods took pleasure in food, wine, and physical play.

There was something bookish in the identification of antique deities as the sponsors of clubical sociability. The Olympians were known only by texts that survived from the classical era, and college-educated males were the chief celebrants of Apollonian brotherhood. Even in the American academies, where the task of inculcating right doctrine in the New World dominated self-understanding, there emerged a welter of student secret societies cultivating pagan symbolism. Before Phi Beta Kappa organized at William and Mary in 1776, the F.H.C. society oversaw a generation of conviviality there. The Philomusarians met to reform learning and manners at Harvard, the Linonians organized their private library at Yale, and the Cliosophical Society battled the American Whigs at the College of New

---

21. [William King], *The Art of Cookery: In Imitation of Horace's Art of Poetry* (London, [1708]); Charles Wallace, "Homony Club Ode," Homony Club, Loose Papers, Gilmore Collection, Maryland Historical Society, Baltimore.

22. Thomas Walduck to James Petiver, Nov. 12, 1710, Sloane MS 2302, British Library, London.

Jersey (Princeton).[23] The nurseries of Christianity in British America by the 1720s harbored cults of the muses promoting pagan learning. They indicate the extent to which a secularized culture of gentility had emerged to offer an alternative to the various religious establishments in the colonies.

Did the clubs founded on wit challenge religious orthodoxy? There can be little doubt that the liberties of conversation explored by the clubs were at odds with the demands of faith. Did the clubs practice sedition? One must be circumspect when making claims about their subversiveness, for subversion implies a programmatic and active opposition to a prevailing state of affairs. Only the so-called projecting clubs (the nuclei of factions or parties) could be said at times to be seditious. Most clubs engaged in political controversy privately and indirectly. Politics in the clubs were more often performed through a parodic prism. The primacy of wit, the pursuit of pleasure, and the exercise of an all-encompassing raillery subordinated any political ideology to a social praxis of free conversation. Perhaps it is best to view the clubs as havens of alternative possibilities where Radical Republican or aesthetic or pagan or libertine or materialist positions might be exercised experimentally, protected by an exoteric symbolism that presented the doings of the club as play.

The Brotherhood of Fish

Although the literary remains of the Tuesday Club of Annapolis (1745–1756) afford the most extensive and provocative view of the play of British American clubs at statecraft, religion, and the arts, writings surviving from other private societies demonstrate the vitality and range of clubical experiments.[24] In Philadelphia the urge to serve appetite, mock imperial politics,

23. For an assessment of the politics of undergraduate literature, see Leon Jackson, "The Rights of Man and the Rites of Youth: Fraternity and Riot at Eighteenth Century Harvard," *History of Higher Education Annual*, XV (1995), 5–49.

24. For discussions of the character of the Tuesday Club writings, see J. A. Leo Lemay, *Men of Letters in Colonial Maryland* (Knoxville, Tenn., 1972); Robert Micklus, *The Comic Genius of Dr. Alexander Hamilton* (Knoxville, Tenn., 1990), 141–222; and my review article of Robert Micklus's edition of *The History of the Tuesday Club*, "The Tuesday Club Writings and the Literature of Sociability," *Early American Literature*, XXVI (1991), 276–290. I have not undertaken a particular analysis of Dr. Alexander Hamilton's Tuesday Club writings and Hamilton's *Itinerarium* in terms of the development of discursive institutions, because the issue has been treated exhaustively in Wil-

and enjoy rural recreations gave rise to the fishing companies — social societies that met biweekly at clubhouses on the banks of the Schuylkill from
May to October, angling, feasting, and performing state ceremonies.

One suspects that the idea for the fishing companies came from organized fox hunts. Yet all formally chartered hunts in British America (the St.
John's Hunt Club in South Carolina and the Gloucester Fox Hunting Club
in Pennsylvania, for instance) postdate the earliest of the fishing companies
by twenty years. The British hunts do not seem exact models, for they operated by custom rather than contract and did not exercise raillery or conversational liberty. One intriguing Old World antecedent for the Philadelphia fishing companies was the Scottish Fishing Company, a commercial
entity that controlled river fisheries yet also promoted a guild sociability.
Significantly, none of the four Pennsylvania companies advertised European ancestry. Their documents insisted that they were sovereign states or
chartered political entities. In order of founding, the important societies
were the Fishing Company of the Colony in Schuylkill (later the State in
Schuylkill), founded in 1732 and seated at Eaglesfield, the estate of William Warner, a mile above where the Fair Mount Water Works would be
erected; the Fishing Company of Fort St. David's, founded about 1750 at
the Falls of the Schuylkill and incorporated into the Colony in Schuylkill in
about 1795; the Mount Regale Fishing Company that flourished in the
early 1760s at Peter Robinson's Tavern near the falls; and the Liberty Fishing Company that enjoyed a brief existence in the 1770s but whose grounds
cannot now be determined. The oldest of the societies, the Schuylkill
Fishing Company, still exists.[25]

The Colony in Schuylkill was formally organized in October 1732. It
might have begun as a political practical joke. In late summer of that year,

---

son Somerville, *The Tuesday Club of Annapolis (1745–1756) as Cultural Performance*
(Athens, Ga., 1996).

25. [William Milnor], *Memoirs of the Gloucester Fox Hunting Club, near Philadelphia*
(Philadelphia, 1830), 2–5; Archives of the Schuylkill Fishing Company, 1732–present,
Manuscript Collection, Historical Society of Pennsylvania. A 1670 broadside of the
membership of the Scottish Fishing Company has been reproduced in microprint,
Goldsmith's-Kress Library of Economic Literature, no. 1932, Research Publications.
A minutebook for the Fort St. David's Fishing Company covering the years 1753–1769
is included in the Schuylkill Fishing Company Archives. A membership list of the Mt.
Saint Regale Company is found in the Shippen Papers, Historical Society of Pennsylvania. Notices of their activities are found in the private correspondence of a number of
significant Pennsylvanians of the period, particularly of the Chew family.

Thomas Penn, one of Pennsylvania's proprietors, arrived from England to exercise a more direct hand in the colony's affairs. Pennsylvania's would-be laureates greeted him in the local newspapers with odes lauding his rule in conventional court panegyric. They pictured a countryside animated by the proprietor's nurturing power. The rivers appeared as courtiers jockeying for proprietorial favor:

> I hear your Rivers boast,
> But *Del'ware* hopes to gain your Favour most,
> For his good Service every Moment shown,
> To wash the Banks of this your rising Town:
> *Schuylkil* some Part would in your Favour claim,
> And in some sort his Service is the same;
> His winding Stream, his Hills, and every Grove
> Humbly present their Service and their Love.[26]

Another laureate, Thomas Makin, further dramatized the riparian tribute. The Delaware offers

> various Fishes,
> And may afford Thee seasonable Dishes.
> *Bass, Pike, Chub, Roach, Perch, Sun-Fish, Ele and Pout,*
> The Regal *Sturgeon* and the Beautious *Trout.*[27]

After the fish have volunteered themselves to Penn's service, the "Indian Nations" appear, who

> With Presents will their Homage pay to Thee,
> In Testimony of their Loyalty.

Against this symbolism of obeisance before proprietorial prerogative the Schuylkill Fishing Company projected its identity. First, it claimed that the Schuylkill Colony's land right was equal to Penn's, for it devolved from the Leni-Lenape chiefs (the Club House, called "the Court," was said to be erected on the spot where the interview between Penn and the chiefs took place). Indeed, Tammany, the chief, whose motto was "Kawania Che Kee-teru" ("I am master wherever I am") and who granted the land around the

26. [Joseph Breintnall?], "Congratulatory Verses, Wrote at the Arrival of Our Honourable Proprietary," *Pennsylvania Gazette*, no. 195, Aug. 21, 1732.

27. T[homas] M[akin], "On the Arrival of the Honourable Thomas Penn, Esq: One of the Proprietors of the Province of Pennsylvania," *American Weekly Mercury* (Philadelphia), no. 659, Aug. 17, 1732.

Schuylkill to William Penn, became the club's tutelary spirit. Toasts were drunk in his honor. His motto was blazoned on the club arms. In club fantasy, Tammany deeded the land to their fishing colony, not to Penn. The Fishing Company was quite pointedly a contract society, claiming to operate under an ancient charter, and not a proprietary entity. It elected its executive and other state officers out of the membership. Clockmaker Thomas Stretch unanimously won election as first governor in October 1732, being reelected annually until 1765, when infirmities compelled his retirement. The General Court comprised the governor, the five members of the assembly (at times in the 1740s supplemented by three counsellors), sheriff, coroner (who examined the catch), and secretary. Payment of a tax was the requisite for voting.[28]

The civic unanimity of the society contrasted directly with the squabbling in Pennsylvania, particularly concerning the colony's participation in military enterprises. Pennsylvania could not manage its own defense because of Quaker pacifism, the Quaker-controlled Assembly repeatedly voting down the formation of colonial militias. Despite the fact that a number of the Fishing Company's members were Quakers, the society contributed a thirty-two-pound cannon for the battery of the Association, the private militia organized by Benjamin Franklin for the defense of Pennsylvania during the War of Austrian Succession (King George's War). The artillery

28. [William Milnor], *An Authentic Historical Memoir of the Schuylkill Fishing Company of the State in Schuylkill* . . . (Philadelphia, 1830), 17–18, 29; Nicholas B. Wainwright, *The Schuylkill Fishing Company of the State in Schuylkill, 1732–1982* (Philadelphia, 1982), 1–2. From 1732 to 1748 the myth of an Indian land grant dominated club history. With the erection of the club's "Court House" on the estate of William Warner, there emerged a second mythology in which Warner became "Baron Warner, lord of the land," the proprietor and the colonists rent payers (the issue of the Penn family's due as proprietors and the extent of their cash support of the colony were much in the air because of the question of defense). Thomas Stretch paid "three fresh sun perch" as one year's rent for the colony's domicile to Warner. Tammany became an icon in the club world of British America, particularly among groups that promoted whig principles. See Joseph White Norwood, *The Tammany Legend* (Boston, 1938).

Son of clockmaker Peter Stretch and Margery Hall of Leek, Staffordshire, Thomas Stretch (1695–1765) immigrated to Philadelphia in 1702. The family was Quaker. The family shop was on the corner of Front and Chestnut Streets, where Peter and Thomas enjoyed great success as craftsmen. Thomas built in 1753 the famous case clock used in the Pennsylvania State House. Beatrice B. Garvan, "Peter Stretch (1670–1746)," in *Philadelphia: Three Centuries of American Art*, Bicentennial Exhibition, Apr. 11–Oct. 10, 1976 (Philadelphia, 1976), 15–16.

piece was installed on the river below Society Hill in November 1750. During the Seven Years' War, the Colony in Schuylkill created its own mock navy: Pennsylvania could not police its shores and keep them free of privateers because of a reluctance to issue warrants for military action.[29] The Colony in Schuylkill had issued the following general warrant in 1744:

> WHEREAS great quantities of rabbits, squirrels, pheasants, partridges, and others of the game kind, have presumed to infest the coasts and territories of Schuylkill, in a wild, bold and ungovernable manner; THESE are therefore to authorize and require you, or any of you to make diligent search for the said rabbits, squirrels, pheasants, partridges and others of the game kind, in all suspected places where they may be found, and bring the respective bodies of so many as you shall find, before the Justices, etc. at a general Court to be held on Thursday, the fourth day of October next, there to be proceeded against, as by the said court shall be adjudged; and for your or any of your so doing, this shall be your sufficient warrant. Witness, myself, the twenty-ninth day of September, in the twelfth year of my Government, and year of our Lord, one thousand seven hundred and forty-four.
>
> THOMAS STRETCH

The warrant was properly ratified with the impression of the colony's state seal. To understand the pirate subtext of the warrant, one must recognize that Pennsylvania did not contribute to the War of Jenkins's Ear (1739–1742), an imperial adventure against Spain's New World colonies that had as its excuse the suppression of the piratical Garda Costa (a seagoing militia) in the Atlantic trade routes. When Jenkins's Ear gave way to King George's War in 1744, Spanish privateers raided the Delaware River.

The martial zeal of the Colony of Schuylkill was exceeded by the Fort St. David's Fishing Company. This government viewed itself primarily as a British imperial garrison. Its seventy-by-twenty-foot clubhouse was styled a citadel. Its members pledged not to "send or cause to be sent any am-

---

29. Wainwright, *The Schuylkill Fishing Company*, 7–8; "An Act for the Support of the Navy in Schuylkill, and for Better Regulating the Fishing Company," 1760, Schuylkill Fishing Company Archives; an imperfect transcript is included in Milnor, *Authentic Historical Memoir*. The navy was a collection of fishing skiffs. Isaac Warner, Thomas Mifflin, Anthony Morris, Jr., and Clement Biddle were noted militant Quakers. Biddle raised a company of Quaker volunteers and served as their commanding colonel throughout the Revolution. The cannon currently stands outside The Castle, the surviving clubhouse of the State in Schuylkill.

munition, warlike stores or provisions to any of his Majesty's Enemies." Furthermore, the citizen must notify the governor or Council of any "treason and traitorous conspiracies which you shall know to be contriving against his Majesty or any of our faithful allies." The government (seven assembly members, four inspectors, two burgesses, two sheriffs, two admirals, two captains, and two coroners presided over by a governor) issued mock legislative levies for war, including fifteen thousand pounds for "the assistance we owe our good friends and allies the Mohawks."[30]

Certain of Fort St. David's citizens were officers in the Association.[31] It is difficult to determine at times whether the quietism of Pennsylvania's Assembly or the bellicose talk of the Associators was being parodied in the company's proceedings. In a speech in April 1760, Governor William Vanderspeigle fulminated against sugar trees and Cherokees in the same burlesque declamation:

> Divers unwieldly sugar trees have sometimes of their evil disposition with a design to Interrupt the peace and quiet of this Colony come down Schuylkill and taken possession of our Government rocks. It shall be lawful to attack or sett upon the trees, with axe, fire or saw and other destructive weapons. . . . [I request that] 300 men be forthwith raised in this Colony, — clothed, accoutred and paid the expense of this Government, to act in conjunction with his Majesty's regular troops against our perfidious and cannable enemies, the Cherokees and all their adherents, and further, all expenses arising by this Act shall be paid out of the Duties arising on Shad Fish taken and exported from this Colony.[32]

Vanderspeigle's mock-gubernatorial address to the Assembly offered something more than the genre's usual anti-imperial satire. He, after all, captained the Philadelphia Company in the Association. No quietist, he! Yet he could burlesque his own beliefs as well as the ritual petitions of governors to assemblies for financing defense, the usual butt of governmental satire. The capacity to mock one's official role and rhetoric was the signal permission

30. 1755 oath, Minutebook of the Fort St. David's Fishing Company, Schuylkill Fishing Company Archives; Joseph Patterson Sims, *The Fishing Company of Fort St. Davids*, Historical Publications of the Society of the Colonial Wars in the Commonwealth of Pennsylvania, VII, no. 4 (1951), 6–7, and reprint of oath, 9.

31. This was the second, or reconstituted, Association, formed at the outset of the Seven Years' War.

32. Address of Governor Vanderspeigle, April 1760, in Sims, *The Fishing Company of Fort St. Davids*, 11.

granted persons in clubs — the most refreshing recreation for public men in a world in which one's gestures were increasingly fixed into ideological positions. Freedom of raillery gave rise to aestheticizing one's political stance.

The question remains whether the play of these clubs permitted such latitude of opinion that political identity itself was overcome. The Mount Regale Fishing Company, a group of some sixty persons largely drawn from the colonial executive (including the Penn brothers, James Hamilton, William Allen, and Benjamin Chew) and large merchants (Robert Morris, Thomas Willing, and Joseph Shippen among them) survived the Stamp Act agitations but dispersed upon the Revolution, its membership dividing between loyalty, neutrality, and patriotism. Conviviality seems to have been destroyed by the invasion of public controversy into the society of persons most interested in the political order of the colony. In contrast, the Schuylkill Fishing Company and the Fort St. David's Company, whose members were less involved with ruling the province, displayed a unanimity in opposition to Britain, providing much of the leadership of the Light Horse of the City of Philadelphia, and survived the war.[33]

It may be that societies that formed a *sensus communis* in opposition to state publicity possessed an integrity that permitted their community to weather civic crises. Certainly, the more profoundly a person was implicated in the political establishment of a country or colony, the more the conversation of the private society providing a haven of play for that person had to be demarcated as a distinct zone of activity. The elaborateness of the symbolic equipment around Freemasonry, the Tuesday Club, or the State in Schuylkill should be seen as the creation of a discursive fence that marked unequivocally the bounds of interest and play. The Mount Regale Fishing Company did not, so far as can be ascertained, employ any symbolism asserting its separateness, sovereignty, or liberty. Perhaps it ordained its dissolution by not insulating the brotherhood from its members' public interests. Trusting solely to the common pleasures afforded by baked perch, Madeira, and beefsteaks in butter to ensure amity in a company was dangerous; for, while appetite surely grounded pleasure, one's pleasure could rarely be reduced to appetite. Perch had to be sauced with conversation and play. The conversation and play had to liberate the members from business, necessity, and care; to do so it had to dissolve the bonds of business, necessity, and care by laughter, amusement, or both.

The importance of social recreation in competitive commercial and

33. Wainwright, *The Schuylkill Fishing Company*, 16.

political cultures was so great that appetite and art, conversation and ritual were put to the service of formalizing a practice of good fellowship. If the food and drink were satisfyingly sumptuous, the art sufficiently amusing, the conversation refreshingly free, and the ritual reassuring, even public political animosity might be held at bay in private society.

The muses served to amuse in the fishing clubs in unusual ways. The Colony in Schuylkill and the Fort St. David's Society erected clubhouses — frame structures that served as banqueting halls, chambers of state, and, in the case of the Fort St. David's Society, a museum. (Curiosities of nature and objects of virtu collected by virtuosos were popular among the Western elite during the late seventeenth century, and strange objects from about the world were registers of the scope of imperial sway. If relics were included, a collection might symbolize the virtuoso's mastery over historical time as well as space.)

The Fort St. David's museum thus served as a mirror to the club's identity. A mock-imperial garrison, the fort displayed portraits in the 1760s of George III and Queen Charlotte, weapons, and a hog in armor. All the fish and fowl of the subject territory were displayed: "Dolphins, Curious Lizard, Curious Wasp Nest, Shark's Jaws, Shark." The mounted birds included a black duck's head, a summer duck's head, a "Sprigg Tail Duck," a goldfinch, sparrow, bluebird, and an owl "excelling all others." Britain's victories in the Seven Years' War made the fort particularly conscious of its place in a global scheme of empire during the early 1760s. "The acquisition to the Crown of Great Britain is so great and the Glory to the nation so remarkable that it will be remembered and handed down to future ages. This has given us a new Empire with Emence Riches and proclaims our Sovereign George the 3d the greatest Monarch on earth, beloved by his subjects and the Dread of Nations." To testify to this new scheme of empire, the collection took on an international flavor: "1 Virgin's Foot from Teneriff, 240 years old," "1 String of Nuts from Guinea," "1 Elephant's Tooth."[34]

Of greatest interest to visitors was the fort's collection of Indian curios. The membership developed a cult, parallel to that surrounding Chief Tammany in the Colony in Schuylkill, about King Hendrick of the Mo-

---

34. "The Schuylkill Records," Minute Book of the Fort St. Davids Fishing Company, 1763 entry, Schuylkill Fishing Co. Archives; Address of Governor Vanderspeigle, October 1763, in Sims, *The Fishing Company of Fort St. Davids*, 13.

hawks.[35] His portrait (painted by William Williams) was displayed next to that of George III on the fort's wall. In 1755, shortly before his death in the Battle of Lake George, King Hendrick visited Fort St. David's for a convivial feast. The brotherhood embraced the sixty-five-year-old warrior. (This was the occasion when the club levied fifteen thousand pounds in Fort St. David's currency to assist the Mohawks.) Thereafter in the fort records, the interests of the fishing company were identified with those of the Mohawk federation; their enemies among the tribes became the fort's enemies. The walls of the fort displayed Indian weapons, snowshoes, pipes, and clothing.

Because much of the Fort St. David's membership was Welsh and recognized the particularities of ethnic identity in the fort's name, the club's celebration of and fascination with Mohawk identity possesses peculiar interest.[36] How much of the provincial Welshman's sense of peripherality in the British imperial enterprise was being expressed in role identification with the Mohawks? Did Hendrick's character as the noblest of the hunter-warriors offer an ideal of ethnic primitivism that served as an antidote to Welsh assimilation into Britain? Or was it the acculturation of the Welsh into polite British society that gave the membership sufficient aesthetic distance to mock the hot rhetoric of imperial warmongers? (Remember — politeness stood counterpoised to valor in Western societies.) Perhaps both tensions are at work, placing the Society at Fort St. David's at a distinctive intellectual remove and so capable of mocking the voice of warmongers, ventriloquizing Mohawks, and ridiculing Quaker pacifists. Whatever the case, the varieties of ridicule developed in the Colony at Schuylkill and the Fort St. David's Fishing Company as amusements offered a distinctive solvent to the solemnities of imperial rhetoric. In the wake of the Paxton uprising of 1763–1764, when public pamphlets were rife with the talk of Indian threat and backwoods insurrection, Phineas

---

35. Wainwright, *The Schuylkill Fishing Company*, 13.

36. During the early 1730s, Philadelphia had a "Society of Ancient Britons" — a Welsh club that might have provided the nucleus of the Fort St. David's membership. Because the first records date from and take up in 1753, the origin of the club is obscure. Welsh members of Fort St. David's included William Clampfer, Evan Evans, William Hopkins, John Howell, Samuel Howell, James James, Thomas James, John Jones, Jonathan Lewis, Edward Milnor, Benjamin Morgan, John Morris, Morris Morris, Samuel Morris, Samuel Morris, Jr., and William Peters. Yet most of the later membership were not ethnically Welsh.

Roberts, coroner of Fort St. David's, burlesqued the public fulminations with a mock petition:

> That the late insurgents at Germantown did maliciously and wickedly intend to monopolize your imperial dignity and power, burn, ravage and destroy your Dominions and Territories, plunder your loyal subjects of their estate and property, tomahawk, butcher and put to death some of your private accursed faithless and inhuman savages; whereupon your petititoner, as in duty bound, raised the posse comitatus hue and cry and went to the Governor upon the Court House by means whereof all the sturgeon, catfish, old wives and eels in Schuylkill were associated, mustered, armed and warlike equipped and thereby prevented the Evil Designs and assuaged the just vengeance of the said insurgents. For which mighty and glorious action which will everlastingly contribute to the public good, may it please your Excellency to immortalize the name of your petitioner either by gibbeting, hanging, drawing, drowning or quartering him and his posterity will ever pray.[37]

In this farrago, combining phrases from all sides of the Paxton controversy with the club's fantasy of military fish, the language of enmity became nonsense. When talk of war became nonsensical, the practice of brotherhood became possible.

The Practice of Good Fellowship

On Saturday December 22, 1770, "some Gentlemen, Inhabitants of the City of Annapolis, having Thought it an eligible scheme to form a Club, or meeting to promote the ends of Society, and to furnish a rational amusement for the length of one Winter evening in a week, There did meet at the Coffee house in the said City."[38] The company was initially composed of seven persons: John Lookup, Robert Couden, Dennis Dulany, John Hall, John Clapham, Reverdy Grieslyn, and William Deards. All were men of affairs; they reserved the time of their gathering to the season when public business and harsh weather kept them in town. One of the company, Den-

---

37. Sims, *The Fishing Company of Fort St. Davids*, 19.

38. "Records, etc. of the Homony Club, Instituted the 22nd of December, 1770," Dreer Collection, XV, 10, Historical Society of Pennsylvania. Entries from the record book will be identified by both meeting date and folio number. A body of loose papers (poem copies and compositions performed during the club meetings) is preserved as Homony Club Loose Papers, Gilmore Collection, Maryland Historical Society.

nis Dulany, had been an honorary member of the Tuesday Club, the premier private society in the city during the 1750s, and had ample experience of the pleasures of institutionalized sociability. He and Reverdy Grieslyn were probably the moving forces in forming the new club. Dulany was a bachelor and forty years old at the time of the club's founding. The company's membership requirement stated, "This Club shall consist of seventeen members and no more, such members residing in Annapolis with their wives (if married) and if not married, they must be Forty years of age or upward." All the original members seem to have been regular attendees at the Annapolis Coffeehouse. "The purposed end of these Gentelmens meeting being well known to each other [presumably from conversation], and being manifestly the same, they soon came to a resolution of electing a President for that night, that they might proceed with the greater order to establish on a good and permanent foundation, the club." Grieslyn was elected first president. Within moments of his occupation of the presidential chair, someone moved that "certain Rules should be drawn up, which being implicitly conformed to, would inevitably lend to the well governing of this Club."[39] Like so many of the private societies of the century, this club understood itself as a self-governing contract society, organized with hierarchical offices and ruled by law.

"The Laws of the Homony Club" prefaced the society's minute book. The final code contained eighteen laws, few of which were novel. The seventeen-person limit imposed on club membership in law 2 was unusual in that it was not determined at the outset, but evolved during a period of expansion, following the Ciceronian directive that the members in a sodality be restricted to a number that permits the participation of all in conversation without confusion. The six offices (president, secretary, advocate general, master of ceremonies, poet laureate, and secretary of foreign affairs) in law 3 suggest that practical considerations of governance did not determine the organization of the society so much as play. The poet laureate and master of ceremonies were posts of a court requisite for the ritual of a state, as advocate general and secretary of foreign affairs were in sovereign states.

Thus the Homony Club was another manifestation of that species of private society that constituted a mock state. It even adopted a political innovation of that most famous of English state clubs of the previous

39. Law no. 2, "The Laws of the Homony Club: Revised and Corrected in Jany 1774," *Records*, 2; Saturday, Dec. 22, 1770, 10.

THE LAWS OF THE HOMONY CLUB
Revised and Corrected in January 1774

1st   That this Club shall meet on the first Saturday in November annually, and continue to meet every Saturday following, between the hours of five and six in the Evening, until the last Saturday in March inclusive; at the Coffeehouse in Annapolis and no where else.

2nd   That this Club shall consist of seventeen members and no more, such members residing in Annapolis with their wives (if married) and if not married, they must be Forty years of age or upward.

3rd   That this Club, for the better regulation of The Society, shall elect among themselves monthly a President, a Secretary, an Advocate General, a Master of Ceremonies, a Poet laureat and a Secretary for Foreign Affairs.

4   That This Secretary shall have the honour of sitting on the Presidents right hand, The Advocate General on the Presidents left hand, and the master of Ceremonies at the bottom of the Table, where he shall act as Vice-President.

5   That it shall be the duty of The Secretary to enter up the Records of the Society, so be particularly careful of and to be acccountable to the Club for them.

6   That all the Members shall be elected by Ballot, not less than three negatives to exclude, and no Ballot unless nine members be present.

7   That any Gentleman desirous of being a Member, shall signify such his desire to the Club in writing, such application being backed by a Member at the reading of it.

8   That such applications being approved, the Person applying shall be ballotted for the following Club night, and if elected, be admitted the Club night following that, the Secretary giving him notice of his Election.

9   That the Club shall have power to elect Eight honorary members, and no more, such honorary members not residing in Annapolis, (save in the case of the present supream magistrate). To be elected according to the mode and form above prescribed to the ordinary members.

10th   That The said honorary members shall be subject to the common laws of The Society and shall enjoy the same Privileges, except the power of voting for any member, or for any Officer, nor shall they be Eligible for any Office whatsoever.

11th   That any members shall be impowered to invite one visiter on any one night except on the night of election of Officers, such Visiter not living in Annapolis, nor permitted to pay his Club on his first Visit.

12   That the games of Whist and Bacgammon shall be allowed to be play'd before Supper for any sum, not exceeding ½ a Crown, that they shall be quitted immediately upon Supper's being declared on the Table by the Waiter, without any money being paid or received on account of any such game then depending; nor shall any game be play'd upon any account after Supper.

13   That The first Toast given by the President shall be
                    Prosperity to the Homony Club
          the last, — Wives and Sweet Hearts
          and any member presuming to give a Toast with the least indecent Allusion, shall be reprimanded by the President for the same.

14   That The President, Secretary, or any important Officer being absent, an Officer shall be elected for the night, and the night considered the same as if he did attend.

15   That the President shall have full power to confer the honour of Knighthood on the master of Ceremonies for the time being.

16   That at ½ after 10 oClock it shall be at the Option of the President to call for a Bill; a last Bottle, and to adjourn the Club.

17   That no new Law shall be made, nor any old Law repealed, altered, or suspended the same night on which the motion is made for such new Law, Repeal, alteration, or suspension, but that the same shall be considered on a future night.

18   That any member absenting himself four nights successively from the Club, and being in the City — not detained by ill health, nor giving or sending an Apology on the fifth night, such member will be looked upon no longer as one of the Society, and be expelled accordingly.

century, the Rota, by rotating persons out of office in monthly elections. Law 15, reserving to the president the power of conferring the title of "knight," suggested that, despite the rotation of office, he possessed the customary and ancient prerogative of dispensing state honors.[40] The formality and durability of the club as an institution was reinforced by the requirement that a written record be kept of the proceedings, that a written code of laws govern its activities, and that application for membership be made by written petition. The most unusual of the club laws (the one that affords the most telling glimpse of the immediate circumstance of club activity) was law 12, directing, "That the games of Whist and Bacgammon shall be allowed to be play'd before Supper for any sum, not exceeding ½ a Crown, that they shall be quitted immediately upon Supper's being declared on the Table by the Waiter, without any money being paid or received on account of any such game then depending; nor shall any game be played upon any account after Supper." Here the club legislated a fundamental distinction between the modes of play in which it engaged. Before supper the amusement of the coffeehouse common room — gaming at cards — could be indulged, provided that the members accept one stricture, a top limit on wagers; thus the good order of the clubroom extended into the common room in the play of the club members. The common meal operated as a rite of transition. After dinner the play of the club would be of a more exclusive and imaginative sort. In the privacy of their room, surrounding their club table, they would play at society.

The meal was important to the identity of the club because the club's identity derived from an item that was invariably included in the repast, that humblest of native foods, hominy. At the first meeting, "the last order that was positively agreed to was with regard to the name by which this Society should be distinguished, when it was determined by a great majority to call it by the name of *The Homony Club*." We should note that it was not the method of governance or the love of rational amusement that

40. One peculiarity of club play was its fascination with feudal ranks; after sociability became institutionalized outside courts, the courts could be satirized by mocking them in archaic dress. The superseded ethic of masculine valor and knighthood was revived in play — beginning with the "Knights of the Toast" at Bath in the latter decades of the seventeenth century. The Tuesday's Club's John Bullen (alias Sir John Oldcastle) was made club champion and knight in an outbreak of martial spirit following the defeat of the pretender in 1745. See Hamilton, *History of the Tuesday Club*, ed. Micklus, I, 228–229.

distinguished the club from the mass of other societies in the clubical world; the laws and ends of society were pretty much the same. Rather, it was the nature of their shared appetite, their common passion for hominy, that gave them identity.

Here we come upon a paradox of clubbing: love of society, in itself, never was sufficient warrant to form a club, for love of society was innate in all humankind. There had to be something more that called an aggregation of persons into community. Private society precipitated out of the general commerce of the world because a number of persons discovered in themselves some common passion over and above a love of good fellowship. As Addison suggested, more often than not this common passion was an appetite. Whatever this common passion was, it was by nature irrational; thus, the creation of clubs must be understood as an aesthetic practice, an activity directed by affections and the desire for pleasure. What is striking was the number of Anglo-American clubs that recognized the aesthetic grounds of their being by emphasizing the irrationality of their commonality in club identity.

As early as 1709, Ned Ward, in *The History of the London Clubs; or, The Citizen's Pastime*, drew attention to the oddity of club identity, surveying the doings of the Lying Club, the Yorkshire Club, the Thieves' Club, the Beggars' Club, the Broken Shop-keepers' Club, the Basket Women's Club, the No Nose Club, the Beaus' Club, the Mollies' Club, and the Quacks' Club. He termed these "unlawful Societies or Clubs" because each group consolidated an identity in a common passion for a vice (the Yorkshiremen are cheats, the Basket Women drunks and tatlers, the No Nose set syphilitics, the Mollies sodomites) *and* because they constituted societies without the authority and regulation of the state. He designated the "Lying Club" the pattern of all such organizations, for lying "is the Spring and Fountain from whence all the rest have their very being." Fiction was the foundation of club identity because club community always grounded society on desires, wishes, and imagined interests. An ardent Tory with a Hobbesian regard for the authority of the state, Ward sought to mark the lurid "unlawful" extreme that the aesthetic constitution of clubs might allow: an urban world populated by sovereign societies of vice.[41] It is against the Grub Street popular imagery of rake gangs, secret juntos, sodomitical

41. [Edward "Ned" Ward], *The History of the London Clubs; or, The Citizen's Pastime* (London, 1709), pt. l, [7]; George Justice, "Characters and Clubs: Representations in

brotherhoods, and outlaw guilds that the clubs brandished their publicity about "rational amusement" and the "rule of law." But Ward, despite his Tory paranoia, understood and conveyed an essential truth about the burgeoning world of private society: one must look beyond the social contract to the common ruling passion to understand what private societies meant. The ruling passion was for amusement—for distraction from quotidian affairs by deceits, wonders, fictions, or play.

Amusement arose in the playful tension between irrationality and rationality—the mental back and forth between appetite and thought—the state of nature and the political realm. The Homony Club, like many a mock state, fixed upon the gaps between appetite and law, desire and duty, as the conceptual spaces for its play. Even in the mystification of hominy, that humble southern dish of lye-processed corn, one sees the tensions vibrate. Jonathan Boucher, an honorary member, in a mock remonstrance insisted that the etymology of hominy derived from the Greek ὁμόνοος, "which literally signifyes *Unanimous:* so that our American word *Homony* in this sense applyd to our Club, may be meant to intimate that we are a Club of men of *like minds*."[42] The humor of the bogus etymology lay in the favorite pastime of the club, engaging in frivolous civil prosecutions of various of the members for slights of the club's decorum and laws. The bulk of the Homony Club records consisted of transcripts of mock trials and poetic odes to hominy. So the life of the club oscillated between civil strife and ceremonies of poetic communion in cooked corn.

Two sorts of disturbance regularly occupied the club's judiciary: toasts violating the club's decorum, and secretarial misprisions regarding the keeping of the club records. In the former instance, a member gave a toast ("Four hams on a Spit!" for instance) that was a double entendre (a metaphor for copulation). The advocate general prepared charges, and the toasted delivered a defense protesting his innocence. These defenses afforded ample occasion for rhetorical posturing, experimental self-characterization, and parody of legal forms. Verdicts, delivered by vote of the company, were arbitrary. Feminist analysts of the text, following Eve Kosofsky Sedgwick, might note that this playful trial of smutty sloganeering was predicated on a symbolic sharing of a woman's body, confirming the feminist thesis that clubical homosociality was symbolically constituted

---

Early London Periodicals," paper delivered at the Twenty-sixth Annual Meeting of the American Society for Eighteenth-Century Studies, Tucson, Ariz., Mar. 3, 1995.

42. Records, Saturday, Mar. 12, 1771, 69.

over a woman's body.[43] Yet even this amusement in feminine flesh is treated as a joke, as fat, middled-aged bachelors muse how the possibility of concupiscence could be imputed to them, for age and disposition have redirected fleshy appetite away from the woman's body to hominy.

Hominy itself was subjected to playful destabilizations as a subject in the club odes. At times hominy supplanted women in a love lyric:[44]

Verses in praise of Homony humbly addressed to
The Honorable John Lockup Eqr President, and the other
worthy members of the Homony Club by
Thomas Jennings — Poet Laureat

1
Henceforth I'll banish every pain,
My fancy's fix'd on thee;
Nor other food my heart shall gain,
But wholesome Homony.
Thy flavour does such pleasure give,
Thy taste, so sweet to me;
Without Thee I could never live;
Deprived of Homony.

Or maybe the feminine analogue was maternal:

2
If fate shall tear thee from my heart,
How shall I lonely stray;
In dreary dreams the night Ill waste,
In sighs the silent day.
I never can so much virtue find,
Nor such good humour see,
Thy sons exceed all Humankind,
When round their Homony.

Whichever, she manifested a native, not a foreign virtue, and thus possessed both patriotic and natural features:

43. The thesis of Eve Kosofsky Sedgwick, *Between Men: English Literature and Male Homosocial Desire* (New York, 1985).

44. Thomas Jennings, "Verses in Praise of Homony Humbly Addressed to the Honourable John Lockup Esqr. President, and the Other Worthy Members of the Homony Club" (October 1772), Records, 132–133.

3
No foreign Dish shall fire my heart,
Ragout, or Fricasse;
For they can ne'er such sweets impart,
As good boiled Homony
'Tis this that like the morning sun,
Gives Joy and Life to me;
Oh! may we long enjoy our Fun
And eke our Homony.

Likewise, a spiritual dimension, with the conventionalized feminine qualities of contentment, peace, and health:

4
Contentment here invites to Joys,
And Peace hath blessed the Scene;
No jealous Fears or rattling Noise,
Disturb our Bliss serene;
We're pleased to see each Brother's Glee,
And hail his rising Fame;
We wish him Health and Homony,
Can Courtiers say the same?

Which puts the poet in mind of the divine powers who condone and promote sociability:

5
Ye Pow'rs That smile on social Love,
And in such Pleasures share,
Ye who our friendly Mirth approve;
Long, long each Brother spare;
Preserve each Members wonted Charms,
These Charms so dear to me,
That they may live secure from Harm,
To eat their Homony.

The brothers, having consumed homony and partaken of its virtue, assume its power of attractiveness and capacity to inspire pleasure. Its charm becomes theirs. They charm one another in social love.

When appetite wears such changeable features, it loses its stability, becoming mystery rather than a common possession of like-minded men.

The question arises, Is like-mindedness as much a fiction as hominy/ unanimity? Is one function of the legal play of the club to explore how difficult it is to base society on commonalities and unanimities? Is the practice of ridiculous clubs such as the Tuesday, the State in Schuylkill, or the Homony to parody political philosophy when it has become so obtrusive in the debate over the powers of empires and states? This possibility becomes particularly powerful when the memberships of these clubs are considered. Consider the Homony. Among its members and honorary members were the governor of Maryland Robert Eden, the ex-governor Horatio Sharpe, council member and commissary general William Fitzhugh, secretary to the province Daniel Dulany, Jr., placeman William Eddis, and the mayor of Annapolis Lloyd Dulany. It also included persons who were conspicuous in the patriot cause, William Paca and Thomas Jennings. The political tensions outside the clubroom were, it would seem, relieved in camera by a parody of the rule of law.

In one memorable trial the club secretary Anthony Stewart is prosecuted for leaving the club minute book unattended for five minutes on a coffeehouse table in the presence of two members. In his plea in defense, Stewart performed a rhetorical coup by momentarily enlisting a truth in his mock defense, a metacomment upon the club's judicial performance:

> But that I well know the foul fiends, Envy and malice can never find admission within these social walls, I really should have suspected them to have been employed in drawing up this aggravated Charge against me, I observe however every where but too evident marks of the interposition of another little Daemon hardly less mischevious, I mean Wit: It was Wit that suggested first, the idea of fastning an accusation on me, It was Wit that found matter of guilt in my innocent name, and unless this impartial Court shall be graciously pleased to exclude the little spiteful Wichin, how evidently engaged in the service of the Prosecutor (as she and I are well known never to have been on tolerable terms) from any further share in this Tryal, it is easy to foresee how it must end.[45]

Stewart confessed the truth that Shaftesbury first glimpsed, that the ruling passion that moved the clubs was a common love of conversational liberty, a love served only by the exercise of wit. The attraction of the play of wit was such that political opponents could meet at a common table and amuse themselves by travestying the struggle that was being enacted daily in their

45. Jan. 30, 1773, Records, 164–173.

offices. Such potent demonstrations of the power of wit to abstract persons from ordinary senses of duty and necessity show why wit has always been feared and reviled by persons who saw it as subverting all sincere feeling and disrupting the authentic bonds of care and commitment to religion, state, community, class, or family.

7

The College,
the Press, and
the Public

On the Continent one of the powerful models for clubs was the college. Indeed, academies of love, music, poetry, dancing, and joviality proliferated in Italy and France: after-images of the colleges making up the universities of the new humanism, the great centers of intellectual adventure in late-Renaissance Europe. The humanist centers, such as Padua and Parma, did not simply lend Platonist professors to the early salons. They projected an ideal of collegiate life that atavistically saw the academy as a convivium of philosophers. The classical vision of an Epicurean band, a brotherhood of honest and learned men, imbued college life with mystique while renovating academic study. The classicism of the humanists led to their distinguishing learning from religion. The range of ancient philosophical inquiry gave the modern academics a model for the scope of free inquiry. Once graduated from the colleges, former students hungered for a further taste of adventurous conversation and so formed circles in imitation of the colleges, calling them academies. Shaftesbury derived much of his sense of the potentialities of the sensus communis from his youthful visits to the private Academia degli Investiganti and the circle of Giuseppe Valletta. (He loved Naples so profoundly that he returned there in 1713 to spend his final days.)[1]

---

1. That was the ideal that Mr. Sociable pointedly rejected in the 1690 conversation in the suburbs (above). The doings of the academies suffuse the account of Italian literary activity from the sixteenth through the eighteenth century supplied in the classic history, P. L. Ginguené, *Histoire littéraire d'Italie*, 2d ed., 14 vols. (Paris, 1824–1835). Perhaps the modern account most familiar to American historians is Giorgio

Shaftesbury's encounter with the private academy points to the unusual predicament of intellectual life at the end of the seventeenth century; increasingly, the work of thought was being performed by institutions outside the universities. The English-speaking world did not differ from Italy, France, or the Netherlands in this regard. Not only did the coffeehouse seduce the student with its promise to study "the world," but a panoply of learned bodies had come into being, ranging from the Royal Society to informal networks of botanists and seed collectors. In England, the university suffered a division of purpose, making it a site of intellectual turmoil, as new humanists sought to renovate classicism while pious Christians sought to make the colleges laboratories of reformed Christianity. The institutional struggle drove some men out of Oxford and Cambridge in search of venues more propitious for conversation and inquiry. In the universities, learning became a contested term, with some divorcing it from religion, others identifying it with religion. This contest was horrendously amplified by the political divisions of the seventeenth century. Humanist Oxford became a Royalist camp. Puritan Cambridge suckled the Commonwealth. This antagonism placed a political onus on both, tainting truth with political interest.

The reason that the infant Harvard College chose "Veritas" as its motto was not that it was a commonplace boast of the academy; rather, truth had become an issue in a world of politicized universities. Harvard mirrored Puritan Cambridge, though with the difference that it exercised a monopoly over the learned world in New England that was scarcely challenged before 1700. Despite its dominion over the learned world, Harvard during the latter decades of the seventeenth century experienced intellectual tumults that eventually led to its transformation.[2] One dimension of this change has not been studied well: the reorganization by students of their society and conversation. European initiatives in natural and moral philosophy caused Harvard to rethink its curriculum. While the faculty drove the intellectual transformation of the college, undergraduates spurred a change in manners. During the 1710s and 1720s, they imported the styles

---

Spini, *Ricerca dei libertini: la teoria dell'impostura delle religioni nel seicento italiano*, rev. ed. (Florence, 1983), which treats the role of the academies in the spread of freethinking during the sixteenth century.

2. Norman Fiering, *Moral Philosophy at Seventeenth-Century Harvard: A Discipline in Transition* (Chapel Hill, N.C., 1981).

and forms of urban sociability into the college, organizing private meetings and clubs.

Among undergraduates there was little agreement about what elements of sociability should be featured in student companies. Some sought liberty of conversation, politeness, and joviality; others, fellow feeling and mutual aid. By the 1720s these diverse aims divided undergraduates into groups of those that took the coffeehouse companies as models and those that looked to conventicles. The former — the Tell-Tale Club (founded 1721) and the Philomusarian Club (founded 1728) — justified their existence by parroting the rhetoric of the Whig Reformation of Manners movement. The latter — the Society of Young Students (founded 1719) and the Young Men's Meeting (founded 1724) — pursued mutual aid in cultivating holiness. Both sides justified their activities by declaring themselves to be remedies for a prevailing degeneracy at Harvard College. They disagreed about the nature of Harvard's problem.

The Society of Young Students intended to revive a spirit of piety that had fallen away at the college. It saw contentiousness and malice troubling undergraduate life and vowed to suppress "all manner of Disagreing, strifes, or Quarrellings, with one another." Members met twice weekly "to Edifie, Encourage, and Excite one another in the ways of Holiness and Religion."[3] At meetings members admonished one another, prayed, and worshiped. Perfecting themselves, they would serve as a light to the society about them. Their society's method resembled that of the central institution of the Puritan movement, the conventicle, or private religious association. Its form, however, drew from the contractual associations of Williamite England. It was more regular than the conventicle, having a societal covenant and bylaws, and its membership was more homgeneous. Cotton Mather and other champions of religious renovation would call the evolved form of Christian association the "private meeting."

The Tell-Tale and Philomusarian Clubs worried about cultural rather than spiritual degeneration. The 1728 prospectus of the Philomusarian brotherhood lays out the complaint.

Whereas the Honourable and Laudable Designs (viz The Promotion of Learning and Good Manners) for wc This Illustrious Academy was founded Have Been of Late Subverted And Not Only So But Conversa-

3. William C. Lane, "A Religious Society at Harvard College, 1719," Colonial Society of Massachusetts, Publications, *Transactions*, XXIV (1923), 309–313.

tion, which is The Basis of Friendship The fundamental Principle of Society The Great Prerogative of Mankind and Every Way Adapted to the Dignity of Humanity, Is Now att A Very Low Ebb, The Necessary Consequence of Which is The Decay of Learning and Civility, Moreover, On The Contrary Vice and folly Are In Their Zenith and Meridian and Gild the Hemisphere of The Muses wth Meteors Whose false Glare is By Many Mistaken for the Refulgent Stars of Wisdom and Virtue. To be Brief, Vice is Now Become Alamode and Rant Riot and Excess is Accounted The Heigth of Good Breeding and Learning — In Order Therefore to Stem That Monstrous Tide of Impiety and Ignorance wch is Like to Sweep All Before it and for Our Mutual Advantage and Emolumt The Subscribers Have Thought fitt to Engage In The Following Combination As We are Sensible That Next to Religion Learning Claims The precedency.[4]

Piety was lauded, but the humanist heritage of the Philomusarian credo can be seen in the distinction made between learning and religion. (The brotherhood's self-identification as lovers of the muses advertised that their allegiance lay with the classical revival animating European culture.) The "dignity of humanity" rather than the glory of God moved the Philomusarians to combine. They worried that manners, good breeding, and learning were being determined by forces in the world other than themselves. The club's diatribe against vice "Alamode," riot, and excess echoed the verbal war that Whig coffeehouses waged against Tory taverns in the metropolis. Yet the Philomusarians reverenced the worldly motive animating many mercantile tavern fellowships — "Our Mutual Advantage and Emolumt." Nowhere was the spirit of the clubs confessed more plainly than in the Philomusarians' answer to the degeneracy of learning and manners. Reforming "Conversation" would strengthen friendship and encourage "Civility."

The calls for piety coupled with civility and for virtue coupled with good manners echo the language of the Whig social engineers of the 1690s who attempted to reform urban manners. Yet a strong distinction must be

---

4. Julius H. Tuttle, Constitution of the Philomusarian Club, ibid., XVIII (1915–1916), 79–84. There were ten members: Philemon Robbins, Benjamin Viall, Samuell Porter, James Diman, Stephen Emery, John Sparhawk, Henry Hale, Caleb Rice, Comfort Carpenter, Jonathan Cotton. Viall died before establishing a career. All the other members, except Hale and Rice, became ministers (Old Light to a man). Diman was the only member to publish.

drawn between the Philomusarians' program and that of the Society for the Reformation of Manners. The English reformers were intent upon disciplining the unruly lower orders. The Philomusarians were intent upon making themselves and their peers more illustrious, learned, and mannerly. The 1720s undergraduates of the Tell-Tale circle and the Philomusarian brotherhood were proposing a middle path between Grub Street libertinism and a dogged, homespun piety. The design was to make society both religious and polite. Their project was not limited to the club memberships, or even to Harvard College. In the end, the partisans of polite Christianity would aim at the transformation of all New England culture. They would use pulpits, conversation circles, manuscripts, and the public prints in their effort. Certain of them — Mather Byles, John Adams, and Joshua Gee — would bring into prominence an urbane, cosmopolitan style of Christian conversation that would eventually provoke reaction by evangelical New Lights who reviled it as worldly "Old Light."

The century's troubling divide between politeness and piety first became an open rift in the ideological distancing of Harvard's undergraduate clubs from the private meetings. The Philomusarian brotherhood owed much philosophically and politically to the Restoration clubs. It, like the clubs, was a self-governing sodality. Unlike the college in which it existed, the Philomusarian brotherhood was a contract, not a chartered, society. It derived authority for its existence from the mutual agreement of the members, not from the granted permission of an existing state or power (it did not seek legitimation from the college president or faculty). The stated grounds for associating — mankind's prerogative of friendship — invoked a politics of sympathy rather than Hobbes's contract of self-preservation. Yet, like political societies formed out of the state of nature, private society required a covenant, or code of *leges convivales*, to ensure that the free conversation of friends did not suffer from the instabilities of feeling that troubled friendships. The Philomusarians ratified a constitution regulating their conversation during the four evenings per week appointed for meetings. The document mandated the times of meeting (Monday, Wednesday, Thursday, and Friday), the purpose for assembling (conversation), the content of conversation (some point of learning), the format of proceedings ("Once A Week By Turns Every Member Shall Choose Some Topick Suitable to his Genius From whence He Shall Expound Make Some Poem or Raise Some Discourse or Chain of Argument"), the tenor of discourse (no railing or laughing allowed), the condition for membership (one must be a lover of learning), the privacy of discourse, and the punishments (fines) befalling those who violated the club directives.[5] Of particular interest is the requirement for secrecy. In a manner analogous to the Order of Freemasons, the Philomusarian Club would transform the conduct of a larger society yet perform this transformation through hidden means. In theory, the invisibility of designs forestalled opposition.

The opposition the Philomusarians anticipated came from two sources: the college establishment and the contingent of students organized to renovate Harvard's piety. Freedom of conversation posed a problem for the establishment, for it led invariably to the introduction of raillery and wit into discourse. The target of raillery and wit would invariably be college authorities and procedures. The Philomusarian's prohibition of railing and laughing thus was a hedge against faculty interference. The earlier Tell-Tale Club had experimented with the liberties of inquiry in a series of essays treating questions like "whether there be any standard of truth."[6] This was a bold query in an academic foundation that took as its motto "Veritas." The Philomusarians, too, challenged the existing order. Their announced goal was, not self-improvement, but the reformation of a "subverted" academy. Shaftesbury's contention that virtue, learning, and civility were products of conversational liberty lurked behind the Philomusarian assumption that refurbished conversation would be the means of overcoming the college's degenerate manners and learning.

One does not have to look hard to find fugitive expressions of free conversation, samples of talk or writing that went beyond the legislated decorum of the club. The customs, rites, and procedures of Harvard were subject to raillery. Targets included the competition for academic precedence, rote memorization in teaching, even the ideal of learning itself — ridiculed as the stuffing of a boy's brains with dead languages and ancient wisdom. Three generations before Philip Freneau had "The Indian Student" abscond from Harvard ("Where learned men talk heathen Greek, / And Hebrew lore is gabbled o'er" rather than submit to the thralldom of learning, an undergraduate wag composed "A Letter to a Gentleman, in Answer to a Latin Epistle, written in a very obscure Hand":[7]

---

5. Ibid.

6. The manuscript is in the Harvard University archives. For a description of its contents, see William C. Lane, "[The Telltale, 1721]," ibid., XII (1908–1909), 221–224.

7. Philip Freneau, "The Indian Student; or, Force of Nature," in Fred Lewis Pattee, ed., *The Poems of Philip Freneau: Poet of the American Revolution*, 3 vols. (Princeton, N.J., 1902–1907), II, 371–374 (1788 version of the poem); [John Seccomb], "A Letter to a

At Ten this Morn, Dear Friend, *Your most,*
Receiv'd your Packet by the Post,
Kiss'd the out-side, broke up the Seal-o,
And promis'd Fi'pence to the Fellow,
Then try'd to read — But hah! what is't?
O vile! the Language of the Beast!
Chinese? or *Syriac?* — Let me see, —
——*Amice selectissime*——
Magick! of which thy old Acquaintance
Knows not a Page, or Word, or Sentence,
But stands with Horror Half a Headful,
And cries, O terrible! O dreadful!

Published anonymously in the *New-England Weekly Journal* (the author was John Seccomb, class of 1728, who had often been in trouble with the college for misbehavior), the epistle operated on two levels: to the common reader, the one whose Latin was so lame that *"Amice selectissime"* seemed a scrap from the black mass rather than "Dearest friend," the letter posed a conundrum as obscure as the Latin missive that provoked it. The poet cued the commonest reader to alarm and forestalled any indignation at ostentatious learning by raising the possibility that a writing's unintelligibility portended danger.[8] What if one had received a message in the "Language of the Beast" and could not read it! Writing could simultaneously reveal one's ignorance and peril. For the select readership of Cambridge scholars, a different possibility stood revealed, the vain show of a fellow student brandishing his learning by sending a Chinese or Syriac epistle to expose the poverty of another student's school Latin. Seccomb burlesqued the Faustian competition for academic preeminence among the undergraduates in which the acquisition of magical power required the mastery of the language of the beast — that is, the world history of writing.

Gentleman, in Answer to a Latin Epistle, Written in a Very Obscure Hand," *New-England Weekly Journal* (Boston), no. 93, Dec. 30, 1728. The attribution of authorship to Seccomb is based on a vision-essay in no. 95 that refers in thinly disguised fashion to Seccomb's recent disciplinary difficulties at the college. Seccomb's most famous comic verse is "Father Abbey's Will," the parody testament of the college's sweeper.

8. The custom for correspondence among literary undergraduates was to begin and end an epistle with Latin tags. See the correspondence among William Downes, Samuel Haven, Samuel Quincey, Ezekiel Dodge, and Robert Treat Paine from the 1740s and 1750s in Stephen T. Riley and Edward W. Hanson, eds., *The Papers of Robert Treat Paine*, I, *1746–1756* (Boston, 1992).

Only the printed book contained the pages, words, and sentences of power by which New England boys might become learned doctors like that damned, late master of the University of Wittenberg.[9]

Seccomb's sardonic view of the vanity of collegiate learning required a double perspective: he had to be intimate with the polyglot stuff of the schoolbooks, and he had to have a vantage sufficiently removed from learning to see it as strange, indeed ridiculous. In "A Letter to a Gentleman" we see a discursive consequence of importing one institution, the club, into another, the college. A capacity to satirize from within emerged. A haven of liberty and levity was won within a society whose purposes were disciplined and serious.

In the eyes of others Seccomb's *jeu d'esprit* was idle mockery, a vanity worse than the vanity it purported to satirize. In the eyes of pious brotherhoods, it could be seen as an instance of the malice that troubled the college. The 1719 meeting of the Society of Young Students (merely the best documented of a series of such associations over the course of the century) had made unanimity a goal of its fellowship: "We will live in Love, Peace, and Unity, with One Another." Thomas Robie, in *A Sermon Preached in the College* (1721), told the meeting that the students' task was to enact the ideals of Christianity and learning that had brought the college into being.[10] By making of words a work they would find a common cause and do God's will on earth as it is performed in heaven.

For the religious meeting the truth had already been spoken; the task was to enact the truth by finding methods to put it into practice. No exercise of conversation would give rise to *veritas* or virtue; at best it could only aid in an understanding of the truth already revealed. The society's relationship with language revealed the meeting to be an institution of another order than a club. Its institutional antecedents were, not the coffeehouse or guild, but the conventicle. More distantly, it descended from ministerial meetings of the 1580s (the classes) that had given rise to Puritan practical divinity.

During the 1580s, small meetings of Essex clergymen (many of them Cambridge University graduates who would eventually teach and minister

---

9. Mastery of the book is signified by writing passages out in one's own hand or reproclaiming its contents in speech.

10. Thomas Robie, *A Sermon Preached in the College* . . . (Boston, 1721). Robie (1689–1729) was an alumnus of the college and widely known for his *Almanack* published in Boston from 1708.

to the first New England immigrants) collaborated to develop a Reformed practical piety. Many of the practices deemed typical of Puritanism — spontaneous communal prayer, the keeping of spiritual diaries, group exposition of Scripture — emanated from the experimental practices of these circles. When laymen and laywomen began to form meetings for the same experimental purposes in imitation of the classes, the conventicle was born. As Stephen Foster has argued, the conventicle became the crucial institution of the Puritan movement, the engine that performed the purification of the people.[11] Both men and women belonged to conventicles, and membership was drawn usually, but not invariably, from the membership of a congregation. The meetings were not bound by the protocols of Sunday worship, and great experimental latitude was given to creating methods to increase the holiness of the members. Here women (Anne Hutchinson, for instance) could expound Scripture, and persons could sing spiritual songs expressing concerns not spoken in the Psalms.

At the end of the seventeenth century the conventicle began to transmute into the religious meeting. Perhaps mirroring the increasingly particularized social formation in Western urban centers, groups of Christians began organizing by sex, age, profession, and interest rather than by neighborhood or congregation. Although prayer groups might have existed among the Harvard graduates as early as the 1670s, women's prayer meetings and young men's societies proliferated after the turn of the century. Cotton Mather recognized the change and sought to instruct the movement. In *Bonifacius* (1710) and in *Religious Societies* (1724) Mather extolled the good works that could be accomplished by "Young Men Associated." Besides providing a vehicle for mutually monitoring one another's walk with God, the religious society could project the practice of piety into society at large by replicating itself into an archipelago of pious circles: "Let every person in the *Society*, look upon it, as a special task incumbent on him, to look out, for some other hopeful *Young man*, and use all proper pains, to engage him in the resolutions of godliness, until he also shall be

11. Stephen Foster's investigations into the social ethic of Puritanism and its institutional manifestations are the most powerful historical portrait of the conventicle and its cultural work: *Their Solitary Way: The Puritan Social Ethic in the First Century of Settlement in New England* (New Haven, Conn., 1971); "English Puritanism and the Progress of New England Institutions, 1630–1660," in David D. Hall et al., eds., *Saints and Revolutionaries: Essays on Early American History* (New York, 1984), 24–26; *The Long Argument: English Puritanism and the Shaping of New England Culture, 1570–1700* (Chapel Hill, N.C., 1991), 16–24, 96–98, 135–136, 145–147.

joined unto the *Society*. And when a society shall in this way be increased unto a fit number, let it *swarm* into *more*; who may hold an useful correspondence with one another."[12] The emphasis on works linked Mather's young men's societies with the conventicles and ultimately with the classes.

What connected the religious meeting with the Philomusarian brotherhood was a projecting spirit. In both groups reforms were not limited to their memberships. Both aspired to change college society and even (if we are to believe Thomas Robie or Cotton Mather) society at large. In this, the societies might have been imbibing Harvard's governing myth: that it would provide the great men of Zion, that it would be the lampstand of the public spirit, that it would be the temple of fame in the New World. Both groups understood themselves to be actors in the public arena, and both saw the college and the press as vehicles enabling their projection into a larger world.[13] Indeed, if one mark distinguished the college societies (and here I include other colonial colleges as well) from clubs, coffeehouse circles, and salons, it was their prerogative to publish.

Printing came to British America in the service of the Scriptures when the Reverend Joseph Glover had conveyed the first press to New England primarily to print an Algonquian translation of the Bible. The government licensed the machine, but its chief employments would be academic and evangelical. Glover settled the press in Cambridge in 1638, shortly after

12. Cotton Mather, *Bonifacius: An Essay upon the Good*, ed. David Levin (Cambridge, Mass., 1966), 68. Mather makes a distinction between these societies for young men and "Reforming Societies" (treated in chap. 11). The latter imitated the Societies for the Reformation of Manners that came into existence in 1690s England. Envisioned as a social mechanism for controlling the vice and profaneness of the lower classes, these societies promoted the ratification of laws imposing control upon unruly elements in the cities and towns. Whiggish in spirit, the Reformation movement attacked Tory libertines as well as the urban mob. Its program is laid out in *Proposals for a National Reformation of Manners Humbly Offered to the Consideration of Our Magistrates and Clergy . . .* (London, 1694).

13. Consider some imprints by members of the Society of Young Students: William Balch (class of 1724), *A Publick Spirit . . .* (Boston, 1749); [Jonathan Bowman], *Remarks on the Result of an Ecclesiastical Council, Which Met at Dorchester . . .* (Boston, 1774); Simon Bradstreet, *A Pleasant Brother Lamented . . .* (Boston, [1755]); Marston Cabot, *Christ's Kingdom . . .* (Boston, 1743); [Benjamin Church], *An Elegy to the Memory of . . . George Whitefield* (Boston, 1770); David Hall, *The Vast Importance of Faithfulness . . .* (Boston, 1745); Jedidiah Jewet, *The Necessity of Good Works . . .* (Boston, 1742); Thomas Prentice, *Observations Moral and Religious . . .* (Boston, 1756); Josiah Smith, *Success a Great Proof . . .* (Charleston, S.C., 1770). Twenty-six persons belonged to the society; one did not survive to graduate; fifteen of the members became clergymen.

the founding of the college; Harvard received the print fonts as a direct benefaction. Eventually the Reverend John Eliot did produce the Indian Bible. For his efforts he would stand foremost in the lists of fame of any New Englander in the republic of letters — except perhaps his chief publicists, Increase and Cotton Mather.[14] No Harvard undergraduate who entertained ambitions ignored the example of those "great men in Zion" who had won fame by plying the press. The student exploited his privileged proximity to the press as early as possible. Typically, he demonstrated his polymathy by preparing the Cambridge almanac and his wit by minting an elegy.

During the 1710s and 1720s the culture war between the pietists and cosmopolitans of Harvard was played out in elegies and critiques of elegy writing. The two camps fought for ownership of Harvard's memory, attempting to set the conditions of fame. More significantly, they attempted to define the community — the public — that would register the renown of Harvard's sons. The pietists invoked the public of holy New England and the world of dissenting Christianity; the model for their expression was the plain elegiac verse of John Danforth (Harvard, 1677).[15] The cosmopolitans spoke to a British imperial public and were cognizant of the world republic of letters; their aesthetic model was an elegy composed by Benjamin Colman (Harvard, 1692) upon the death of college president Samuel Willard in 1707.

Elegy and the College Cult of Memory

The elegy, while capable of instructing readers on the gravity of death and the brevity of life, on its most primitive level was a means of memorialization. It testified to the worth of an individual, recommending that the person's memory be preserved by posterity. To enroll the community in its act of memory, the elegy amplified the community's self-regard, identifying it as the place whence great persons emerged and for whose benefit they labored. Usually printed in a broadside format, arrayed in double

14. George Parker Winship, *The Cambridge Press, 1638–1692* . . . (Philadelphia, 1945), 6–21; Ola Elizabeth Winslow, *John Eliot, "Apostle to the Indians"* (Boston, 1968), 137–147.

15. Thomas A. Ryan, "The Poetry of John Danforth," American Antiquarian Society, *Proceedings*, LXXVII (Worcester, Mass., 1968), 129–193; Astrid Schmitt-von Mühlenfels, *Die "Funeral Elegy" Neuenglands: Eine gattungsgeschichtliche Studie* (Heidelberg, 1973).

columns beneath a woodcut memento mori icon, the elegy adorned the sides of the casket during the funeral procession. In rural districts the printed elegies were collected and displayed in households. "Nor is there one Country House in Fifty which has not its Walls garnished with half a Score of these Sort of Poems, (if they may be so call'd,) which *praise the Dead to the Life*, and enumerate all their Excellencies, Gifts and Graces." The memories of 171 worthies were embalmed in elegy during the first century of New England verse, according to Harold Jantz. Significantly, university men (graduates of Cambridge, Oxford, or Harvard) composed 126 of these elegies; 91 of the subjects were university men. While it was claimed by one critic of 1722 that "there is scarce a Plow-Jogger or Country Cobler that has read our Psalms, and can make two Lines, jingle, who has not once in his Life at least, exercised his Talent this way," the predominance of college men as composers of surviving texts indicates that the sons of Harvard effectively exercised control over the public memory to keep recollection of their own alive.[16] With wonderful economy the young scholar won his fame for "parts" (that is, wit and accomplishment) by celebrating the ability of one who went before.

The parochialism of the collegiate cult of memory provoked criticism by the cosmopolitans of Harvard (undergraduates and alumni) well before Franklin's Silence Dogood voiced her criticisms in the *New-England Courant*. "Letter wit," "plain style," typological clichés, and the dogtrot metrics of the traditional elegy signaled artistic poverty for the cosmopolitans. When the capable mannerist poet, the Reverend Nicholas Noyes (Har-

16. William J. Scheick, "Tombless Virtue and Hidden Text: New England Puritan Funeral Elegies," in Peter White, ed., *Puritan Poets and Poetics: Seventeenth-Century American Poetry in Theory and Practice* (University Park, Pa., 1985), 290–297; Hypercriticus, essay on New England elegies, *New-England Courant* (Boston), no. 67, Nov. 12, 1722; Harold S. Jantz, "The First Century of New England Verse," American Antiquarian Society, *Proceedings*, LIII (1943), 219–508. No doubt substantially more were written than Jantz collected; my point, however, concerns the institutional circumstances of survival for those he did discover.

Nicholas Noyes (1647–1717) graduated from Harvard in 1667. He served as pastor at the Congregationalist Church at Haddam, Conn., and later Salem, Mass. Noyes's ability as an elegist can be seen in his 1708 elegy on the Reverend John Higginson, published in Cotton Mather's *Nunc Dimittis . . .* (Boston, 1709), 1–8. Jantz believed Noyes to have been author of a manuscript poem on his younger colleague at Salem, the Reverend George Curwin, found in the Curwen MSS, Peabody Essex Museum, Salem, Mass. It would have had to have been written during the twenty days between Curwin's and his own death.

vard, 1667), died in 1717, twenty days after the expiration of his younger colleague at the Salem pulpit, the Reverend George Curwin (Harvard, 1701), the Reverend Samuel Phillips (Harvard, 1708) responded with a lamentation that for mechanical sentiment and halt prosody could represent the nadir of the Harvard elegy:

> Behold and see what *Death* has done;
> For We by Death seem near Undone:
> Not long ago as Happy were
> As most that Breath in Common Air,
> In Mr. NOYES and CURWIN too,
> *Both Learned, Faithful, Wise also:*
> But now alas! from hence *Each one*
> To his *Eternal Home* is gone.

> EACH Life and Death *we'll Meditate;*
> And so *God's* Praises Celebrate.
> Of Mr. *Noyes* men truly say
> That *Few so Great* liv'd in his Day:
> His *Parts* and *Learning* shone so Bright,
> Who could not see them wanted *Sight.*
> He in the *Tongues* was skilled well;
> But's Skill in th' *Hebrew* did Excel.
> And by his Pains and Diligence
> Of Arts the *Master* did Commence.
> I shall be Blam'd if I pass by
> His *Skill in English Poetry;*
> Which men admire and justly too
> For's Lines are *Reg'lar, Plain and True.*[17]

Not everyone admired the painful and diligent regularity of Phillips's tribute. Peleg Wiswall (Harvard, 1702), a merchant turned schoolmaster, took offense that the memory of so fine a poet as Noyes should be dressed in death with this drab a shroud of verse. Wiswall made his own address to the deceased poet:

> Poor man what makes you look so sullen,
> Alas! instead of decent woollen

17. Samuel Phillips, *An Elegy upon the Deaths of Those Excellent and Learned Divines, the Reverend Nicholas Noyes, A.M. and the Reverend George Curwin, A.M. the Pastors of the First Church of Christ in Salem* [Boston, 1717], 2.

Which every English man's allowd
To dress himself in humble shroud
One of Appollo's little flirts
Has wrapt us up in doggrel shirts.
Cicero tho a heathen brute
Could not have had the heart to do't.
For tho the living saints he dressed
In bearskins, yet he let them rest
When under ground in decent vest.
But Phillips, worse than he ten times
Has Hugd our *Tails* with beastly rhimes
And makes us look like porcupines
Whilst waiting for Elesian chimes.
Old Father Noyce drops tears of brine
And says there's truth in every line
As witness this pen of mine.
And as for Mr. Curwen too
He says that every word on' tis true.
And each do pray in humble *wise*
That Phillips ne'er may elegize
On any Wight but hog or bear,
Or flock's that claws or bristles wear
And cease to tear the tender buff
Of Saints, with this his homespun stuff.[18]

Wiswall's satire employed two strategies of symbolism. Behind the imagery of the shroud operated a mercantilist presumption that English linen was superior to native homespun. To the extent that one believed oneself deserving of the linen "Which every English man's allowd" in death — that is, to the extent that one embraced English rights and privileges — then one disapproved of the rough treatment given the Reverend Mr. Noyes by shrouding him according to local custom. The animal imagery connected with Phillips's "homespun" recalled the London view of the colonies as

18. "Mr. Wiswell NEngland School-master on Samuel Phillips of Andover, His Verses on Mr. Noyce-1718," MS, Poetry Collection, Bentley Papers, American Antiquarian Society, Worcester, Mass. Peleg Wiswall (1682/3–1767) was infamous as a merchant for selling a shipload of rancid fish to Lisbon when it was besieged. He served as master of the North Grammar School from 1719 until illness forced him to resign in 1767.

wildernesses awaiting the full effects of civilization. Then, recalling that earlier imperial civilization, Wiswall indicated that pious plainness, regularity, and truth treated the poet's memory with an incivility that no pagan Roman would have endured. Ciceronian neoclassicism was the literary equivalent of fine linen while New England pious plainness was a barbaric animal skin. Thus linking London sensibility with literary neoclassicism, Wiswall attacked the parochialism of Harvard's and New England's ownmost form of poetic expression.

By twitting Phillips's lack of neoclassical polish, Wiswall challenged the conventional disavowal of pagan equipment in the Reformed Christian elegy. Instead of the pastoral, the New England elegist traditionally cleaved to scriptural precedents, chiefly to David's lamentation over the loss of Jonathan as the exemplary expression of grief and appreciation of life. In the verse introduction to Amos Throop's *Elegy Occasioned by the Pre-Mature Death of Mr. Joshua Lamb, Once Student of Harvard College* (1723), an admirer of Throop's artistry observed,

> His well Instructed Song was all Divine,
> Nor lack'd the Inspiration of the Nine:
> He suck'd no *Pegasus* nor fed upon
> The fancied Dew of Pagan *Helicon;*
> These are but Whimsies: Some Seraphick Fire,
> Had warm'd his Breast, and Tun'd his Heavenly Lyre.
> With bitter Accents and Pathetick Groans
> To mourn the Loss of one of *Harvard*'s Sons.[19]

The disavowal of ancient fictions, fancies, and whimsies in the New England funeral elegy was made in the name of the third of those qualities that the Reverend Mr. Phillips praised in the poetry of the late Reverend Mr. Noyes, truth.

The pietists cultivated biblicism, employing typology to link the subject's life to the fount of truth, Scripture. In the hands of a poet imbued with mannerist wit, such as Benjamin Tompson, the types, analogues, and allusions could achieve a virtuoso profusion. In the hands of a lesser poet like Samuel Phillips, the comparisons could be commonplace. Pious poets also performed character analyses in light of Christian virtues and vocations. They frequently made political points by presenting a death as a sig-

19. J. R., reply to Hypercriticus, *New England Courant*, no. 82, Feb. 25, 1723, quotes the poem, which does not survive.

nificant judgment on a declining community. Rarely present is the classical furniture so conspicuous in seventeenth-century elegies by English university men. Urian Oakes's *Elegie upon Thomas Shepard* (1677), with its comparison of Shepard to Leonidas, is a rare, perhaps unique, seventeenth-century Harvard employment of classical allusion. Even this verse wore its classicism loosely. The heart of Oakes's elegy was the tribal mourning found in every other example of the art.[20]

Neoclassical aesthetics and a metropolitan sensibility came to the Harvard elegy like a thunderbolt in 1707, when the Reverend Benjamin Colman published his poetic masterwork, *A Poem on Elijahs Translation, Occasion'd by the Death of the Reverend and Learned Mr. Samuel Willard*. Colman, born in Boston in 1673, had learned Latin at the famous school of Ezekiel Cheever and graduated from Harvard in 1692. After taking a master's in 1695, he shipped to England, was seized by pirates, and imprisoned by French Catholics as a Protestant minister at Nantes before securing his freedom. Virtually destitute, he boarded gratis in the house of Thomas Parkhurst, the foremost bookseller among the English Dissenting community. He became romantically attached to Elizabeth Singer, a poet who took the name Philomela, but did not marry her. Receiving ordination in England, he was called back to Boston in 1699 to minister to the Brattle Street Church, a society with marked cosmopolitan inclinations. A personable man with a talent for diplomacy and blessed with an Addisonian eloquence in the pulpit, he struck champions of the old way as a threat. Increase Mather complained that he lacked a studious and pious demeanor; he was "a raw and unstudied youth . . . of a very unsanctified temper and spirit."[21] Mather might have been seeing in Colman a manner new to New England but all too familiar from his stay in the London in the early 1690s, a "worldly face" — politeness. Instantly Colman's congregation became the center of a new style of polite Christianity, and his person became the lodestar of that contingent within Harvard that craved metropolitan polish yet did not wish to go over entirely to Anglicanism and worldliness. Colman's synthesis of politeness and Reformed Christianity provided a middle way for those embarrassed at homespun yet uncomfortable with courtly finery.

20. Karen E. Rowe, "Prophetic Visions: Typology and Colonial American Poetry," in White, ed., *Puritan Poets and Poetics*, 59–62; William Scheick, "Standing in the Gap: Urian Oakes's Elegy on Thomas Shepard," *Early American Literature*, IX (1974–1975), 301–306.

21. Ebenezer Turell, *The Life and Character of the Reverend Benjamin Colman, D.D. . . . .*, ed. Christopher R. Reaske (1749; rpt. Delmar, N.Y., 1972), introduction, x.

Benjamin Colman's *Poem on Elijahs Translation* marked out a way metropolitan neoclassicism could be combined with the local purposes of the elegy. The poem was conservative in its typological identification of Willard with Elijah, as the forebear of a generation of prophets, but advanced in its use of devices of the sublime to evoke prophetic power.[22] For the classes of prophets schooled under Willard's direction at Harvard, the poem's argument epitomized the cyclical renovation of memory that was the obligation of each generation of college elegist:

These *beauteous Sons* were the blest *Prophets* pride,
Under *his Wing* they *bloom'd*, and flourisht by his Side;
Paid him a Reverence profound and true.

Novel for New England was the illustration of how Willard manifested prophetic power in his proclamations, inspiring sublime transport in his student auditors:

To *them* His *Lectures* on the Holy Law,
Sublime they were, new *Mysteries* they saw:

22. [Benjamin] Colman, *A Poem on Elijahs Translation, Occasion'd by the Death of the Reverend and Learned Mr. Samuel Willard* . . . (Boston, 1707). The political interest of the poem lay in the fact that Colman, a son of Harvard who earned the suspicion of New England's ecclesiastical potentates by seeking ordination and "finishing" in the metropolis, won back their admiration by composing this elaborate celebration of Harvard's deceased president. (Colman would later be offered and refuse the presidency.)

John Saffin of the older generation wrote of the poem:

As to yor Epiecedium on the Exaltation of the Reverend and my Ancient and much Endeared Friend Mr Samll: Willard Decd: I have Severall times Read it with much Delight and Satisfaction; . . . the Subject you treat on is Sublime: in all Respects: not Onely to the first Super Eminent person (Recorded in Sacred Writt) but allso in a great Measure to the second on whome it doth Tacitly, yet Emphatically poynt at; wch Sublimity of the Subject. is (in my Opinion) a great Advantage to one of Apollo's Votaries to Expatiate himself, and Soare Aloft, without danger of burning his wings: or Icarus like fall Down into the Abiss of Infamy.

So, you have therein tun'd yor Song a Note above Ela; I mean yor Towering Phansey Flys above the Common pitch of the Capacity of Ordinary Readers; and have (in my weak Apprehention) given yor Poeme a vesture suitable to the nature and Eminence of the Theme you Insist upon: wch Doth Adorne Poetry: Viz To be Elligant, Emphaticall, Metaphoricall, and Historical.

Caroline Hazard, ed., *John Saffin His Book (1665–1708)* . . . (New York, 1928), 170. Commendations from Mather Byles and Nathaniel Gardner, Jr., survive from the younger generation.

Like Him with Heav'nly Light and Joyes Inspir'd,
Their ravisht Minds the *Sacred Deeps* admir'd.

. . . .

They Sang of the *Transfigur'd Saviours Rayes,*
What *Fav'rite Saints,* from Heav'n it self, to gaze;
On *Glories* yet Unknown; and *Talk* of High
Mysterious Truths; into which *Angels* Pry,
And pass in Transports *Immortality.*
They Sang his *High Ascent,* and *Gifts* Ineffable,
The Cloven Tongues of Fire on Pentecost that fell,
And what *Great Type* shou'd all these Wonders *Figure* and *Foretell.*[23]

The passage vividly dramatized the tension between the written and the spoken that pervaded student life at the college. The written law comes alive in Willard's lecturing. The prophet's living words inspire the youths to sing. The singing conveys a divinity transcending mere significance: the transfigured Savior, the ineffable gift, and mysterious truth, the Type of types. Singing gives voice to the breaking open of what was written into a something greater. And yet Colman's written verse somehow captures that transported sense.

The collapse of the distinction between the presence of the inspired spoken Word and its written representation in an event of poetic epiphany was the great aspiration of the literature of the religious sublime. Armed with this aspiration, a generation of writers arose in Colman's wake to take New England poetry beyond what was regular, plain, and true.

The Religious Sublime

In 1674 Nicolas Boileau-Despréaux translated the late-classical tract, attributed to "Longinus," Περὶ ὕψους (*On the Sublime*), into French as *Traité du sublime,* bringing to international attention a way of evaluating literature in terms of effect rather than form. Its analysis of the psychological response of a reader experiencing scenes of grandeur immediately challenged the dominion in criticism of Aristotle's and Horace's analyses of the forms and production of literary works. It revealed a new mode of classical thought about communication — one singularly useful to Christian evangelists, for it suggested to artists several means of imbuing their works with the power to seize the reader's imagination. Boileau warned elsewhere that

23. Colman, *A Poem on Elijahs Translation,* 7, 8.

there was no technique of writing sublimely, nor any "sublime style" of poetry. Nevertheless, a plentitude of writers, evangelicals, and humanists began creating a literature featuring a topology of sublime scenes — mountain crags, volcanos, storms, Arctic wastes, battles, primeval woods, jungles, and so forth, recycling scenes found in Longinus. Christian authors grasped certain possibilities raised by *On the Sublime*, defying Boileau's dictum that there could be no such thing as a sublime Christian poetry. The English critic John Dennis countered that the scenes most capable of inspiring sublime feelings were those representing supernatural actions; furthermore, the most sublime supernatural happenings appeared in the Scriptures, because the Bible claimed for its representations ultimate truth, whereas fiction and mythology presented things that only might be true.[24] Consequently, modern writings evinced the greatest sublimity when they fitted supernatural aspects of the biblical proclamation to the reader's imagination. Abraham Cowley's biblical odes, Milton's *Paradise Lost*, Sir Richard Blackmore's *Creation*, and the religious poetry of Elizabeth Singer Rowe and Isaac Watts constituted something of a literary canon of the religious sublime by the time Mather Byles declared the ambition of his generation of Harvard poets in "Written in Milton's Paradise Lost" (1727):

> Could I command the Harmony, the Force,
> The glitt'ring Language, and the true Sublime
> Whose mingled Beauties grace his glowing Lays,
> Then should my Lines glide Languishingly slow,
> Of thundring roar, and rattle as they sleet.
>
> .   .   .   .
>
> Thus with ambitious Hand, I'd boldly snatch
> A spreading Branch for his immortal Laurels.[25]

Sublime power materialized in poetry when language gave mimesis so great a verisimilitude that representations became presences. When the distinction between word and thing collapsed in a moment of poetic epiphany, the reader assumed the poet's enthusiasm. All the passion inherent in the act of inspiration became the reader's property.

24. David B. Morris, *The Religious Sublime: Christian Poetry and Critical Tradition in Eighteenth-Century England* (Lexington, Ky., 1972), 63–76; Nicolas Boileau-Despreaux, *L'art poétique*, in Boileau, *Oeuvres complètes*, ed. Françoise Escal (Paris, 1966), 173; John Dennis, *The Grounds of Criticism in Poetry* (London, 1704), 259–271.

25. Mather Byles, "Written in Milton's Paradise Lost," in Byles, *Poems on Several Occasions* (Boston, 1744), 25.

The religious utility of sublime poetry lay in the aid it rendered to religious conviction. One's confidence in the promises and warnings of the divine oracles would be strengthened if supernatural conditions seemed actual — if art could supply a foretaste of heaven's glories or scald the sinner with a heat that anticipated the eternal burning. In particular, poetry might assist conversion by enlivening in readers the terrors of justification when a seeker comes to understand his or her personal sinfulness and liability for death, an understanding that is a precondition to adoption by God. Roger Wolcott observed how

> Despair by Representing
> Eternity fill'd with Tormenting,
> By Anticipation brings
> All Eternal Sufferings
> Every Moment up at once
> Into actual Sufferance.[26]

Mental processes such as Wolcott describes were, as in the title by Cotton Mather, *Perswasions from the Terror of the Lord*. In the transports of feeling occasioned by art, preaching, or closet devotion, persons could "Antedate the *Day of Judgment*, and Represent it Livelily unto themselves in the *Revealed Circumstances* of it; and Suppose themselves *Pleading* for their *Everlasting Life* before the Tribunal of God." The linking here of the affective transport of sublimity with "perswasion" showed that the Harvard cosmopolitans absorbed Longinian doctrine into their traditional understanding of rhetoric, rather than into theology. A Harvard commencement thesis of 1653 insisted, "Rhetorica est affectuum hortus." Since sublime persuasion occurred by a pathetic rather than a rational appeal, it was a mode that produced the most fertile results in the "garden of emotions." The decisive intellectual development at Harvard during the seventeenth century was the elaboration of the role of the affects and passions in moral philosophy. Rhetoric converged with moral philosophy when one asked, How does one make homiletics more effective by making sermons speak more directly to the listener's heart? At issue was the extent to which affections (the dispositions of the heart) were tractable to reason or to the judgments of conscience. The story of the Fall and common sense held that affections could be moved to willful passion by the promptings of

---

26. Roger Wolcott, *Poetical Meditations, Being the Improvement of Some Vacant Hours* (New London, Conn., 1725), 14.

imagination. By binding imagination with reason in eloquence, the vagaries of the affections might be constrained. Poetry's value arose from its character as the most vividly affecting form of eloquence. A 1647 commencement thesis formulated the coappropriation of poetry and the affects: "Poesis vividos affectus tum postulat, tum paret."[27]

Injecting the sublime into the rhetorical understanding of how poetry worked highlighted imagination's role in perception and communication. The cosmopolitans of the 1720s made a further extrapolation: poetry, as the most exquisite precipitate of imagination, supplied the most acute and pleasurable acquaintance with the workings of one's soul: "The Soul seems to be let into its proper Element, and finds an Employment suitable to its Nature and Faculties. . . . Every Power is waken'd into a Delightful Exercise, and there arises in the Soul, such exalted Pleasures as are little Inferiour to an Extasy." Matthew Adams took the analogy between poetry and spirituality to the limit that Reformed Christian discourse would allow: "There is something in these Entertainments which bears so near a Resemblance to our Souls, that I have been sometimes ready to conjecture, That our Poetical Capacity will follow us into the other World, where the Anthems and Hallelujahs of the Blessed, may be finely adapted to gratify this Appetite of our Nature."[28]

Adams's extremity lay in his willingness to conceive of the sublime effect of poetry apart from the world experienced by the senses. Conventional wisdom held that imagination worked by manipulating sense impressions in such a way as to compel one's affections and move the will to a passionate response. Adams's vision of a poetry so otherworldly as to be a resonance of the soul risked a notion of unmediated divine inspiration. The other important New England poets who embraced the religious sublime in the 1720s—Mather Byles, John Adams, and Benjamin Colman's daughter, Jane Colman Turell—did not forswear the mediation of the imagination, and all evoked sublime "elevation" in verse by carefully rendering sensate images. The poets located the poetic speaker at the nexus of a panoramic field of sensation. Consider Mather Byles's "Conflagration" (1729), an imaginary representation of the sublimest of moments, the day of doom:

27. Cotton Mather, *Perswasions from the Terror of the Lord: A Sermon concerning the Day of Judgment* . . . (Boston, 1711), 27–28; Theses, Harvard College, commencement, 1647, 1653, reproduced in Fiering, *Moral Philosophy at Harvard*, 32, 35.

28. Matthew Adams, Proteus Echo no. 36, *New-England Weekly Journal*, no. 38, Dec. 11, 1727.

Deep groans the Earth, at its approaching Doom,
While in slow Pomp the mighty Burnings come.
As when dark Clouds rise slowly from the Main,
Then, in swift Sluices, deluge all the Plain,
Descending headlong down the Mountains sides,
A thousand Torrents roll their foamy Tides,
The rushing Rivers rapid roar around,
And all the Shores return the dashing sound.[29]

The mass of modifiers shows how the new literature of the religious sub-lime subordinated narration to description. The old-style plainness and regularity of, for example, Michael Wigglesworth's *Day of Doom* have given way to elaborate diction and rhythmic complexity. Note Byles's interruptions of the iambic meter with spondees (imposed accents) to provide a linguistic correlative to the disruption of creation. Another sound-sense device employed in the passage is the alliterative concatenation of consonants to convey the sensate overload of the Last Days. These devices became hallmarks of the sublime style. Anyone who wished to pump up a scene, regardless of whether it warranted elevation, could use these devices. The Harvard cosmopolitans were quickly joined by would-be practitioners of the sublime.

These Writers, to avoid the Imputation of low and flat, blow up every Subject they take in Hand beyond its natural Dimensions; and nothing will please them that is not big and boisterous, wild and irregular. They wonderfully delight in Noise and Clamour; a Rattle of Words, and an Extravagance of Imagination, they look upon as the Perfection of Rhet-orick; and are Transported beyond themselves, at the Tumult and Con-fusion that bellows through a Hurricane of Nonesense. In short, that which Men of this Turn applaud as the Master-piece of good Writing, differs from the *true Sublime*, as a Boys artificial Kite, wadling among the Clouds at the End of a Skein of Pack-thread, does from the natural Flight of an Eagle, towering with steddy Pinions up the Skies, and bearing full upon the Sun.[30]

Byles illustrated the false sublime by quoting a contemporary paean to Boston's Beacon Hill: "How does it shoot up its inconceivable Pinnacle into

---

29. Mather Byles, "The Conflagration," in Byles, *Poems on Several Occasions*, 100.

30. L [Mather Byles], Proteus Echo no. 3, *New-England Weekly Journal*, no. 5, Apr. 24, 1727.

the superior Regions, and blend itself with the cerulian circum-ambient Ether! It mocks the fiercest Efforts of the most piercing Sight, to reach to its impenetrable Sublimities." The fault of such bombast lay in the disparity between the subject and its manner of representation. A poetic predisposition to wax enthusiastic about things, no matter how insignificant, resulted in bathos if not modulated by a sense of affect appropriate to the scene. To counteract the poet's psychological propensity to effusion, judgment and taste had to work in concert with inspiration. The Harvard cosmopolitans of the 1720s appointed themselves monitors of taste and the enforcers of judgment. The imperative to bind the sublime to revelation led Byles to rebuke writers who used the mode to convey the impressiveness of natural scenes, despite the warrant of classical example. In his epigram "Written in the Blank Leaf of a Poem intitled Aetna," Byles denigrated one poet who viewed a volcano as essentially a natural phenomenon:

> That first of Beauties in your Numbers shines,
> You suit your Theme with correspondent Lines.
> As sounding Etna thunders from below,
> And Smoke, majestick, hovers round its Brow,
> While its tall Head shines with eternal Snow:
> Each various Scene your answ'ring Lines unfold,
> So rough you write, so cloudy, and so cold.[31]

Aetna was cold because it seethed with no holy fire.

Although the poets of the religious sublime might have made the sensate world seem the medium of divine power, they did so in a manner at odds with earlier Christian poets. The old New England poets excited wonder at violations of the natural order, "remarkable providences," rather than at the design or the regular workings of nature. The cosmopolitans of the 1720s learned from Sir Isaac Newton's "messianic science" to experience the sublime emotions — terror, wonder, awe — when apprehending the design of creation itself. Because of its concern with epitomizing the design of nature, the sublime poetry of the 1720s tended to be philosophical and descriptive rather than dramatic and narrative. Yet it was not a poetry devoid of activity: indeed, it was absorbed in visualizing three moments of action: the coming into being of creation, the scintillation of divine power in the created order, and the dissolution of nature. The

---

31. Mather Byles, "Written in the Blank Leaf of a Poem Intitled AEtna," in Byles, *Poems on Several Occasions*, 98.

method of the more philosophical apocalyptic of the 1720s poets merits particular notice. It consisted in an inversion of the principle of *concordia discors*, the harmonizing of discordant elements in creation, of much Christian humanist writing. A humanist couplet, "Here in full Light the russet Plains extend; / There wrapt in Clouds the blueish Hills ascend," reconciled antithetical images and harmonized ideas as opposed as horizontal and vertical by means of syntactical parallelism and rhyme. A couplet from an apocalyptic scene by John Adams displays a similar opposition of horizontal and vertical—"A sudden Earthquake rush'd along the Ground / And Nature leap'd, and quiver'd at the Sound"—but it performs a *discordia concors*, as it were, the dissolution of a harmonious order.[32]

There is a sense in which all sublime poetry of the philosophical sort was apocalyptic in that it never simply described the mechanism of nature, but traced the design and then collapsed it into the divine force that caused it to be and could cause it to cease to be. The religious sublime represented nature only to dissolve it and discover the divine power animating it; in this it differed from the poetry of physicotheology. The poetic model for this new picture of the sublime order of the universe was Sir Richard Blackmore's *Creation*. It represented the whole of nature as an expression of God's creating power. The poem is ordered as a regress, taking one from the present array of nature back through the Creation to that primordial moment before form became manifest, when "dark and undistinguished" chaos felt God's "Creating Might."[33] Then the force of God's might stood most immediately revealed. According to Blackmore, in the encounter with God's unmediated power, writer and reader "feel animating fires" and

32. The couplets are from Alexander Pope "Windsor-Forest," ll. 23–24; John Adams, "Revelation," in Adams, *Poems on Several Occasions, Original and Translated* (Boston, 1745), 124.

33. Richard Blackmore, *Creation: A Philosophical Poem, in Seven Books*, in *The British Poets*, XXVIII (Chiswick, 1822), 129.

Blackmore, a Reformed Christian, Whig, and enemy of the school of wit, was widely admired among the literati of New England. Cotton Mather commended his poetry as a model for Harvard's graduates in *Manuductio ad Ministerium* . . . (Boston, 1726), 43. John Adams paraphrased the 104th Psalm in Blackmore's style in *New-England Weekly Journal*, no. 33, Nov. 6, 1727. Jane Turell (1708–1735), the daughter of Benjamin Colman and wife of the Reverend Ebenezer Turell, was a prolific poet who circulated manscripts among the Boston and Harvard literati. Examples of her serious poetry, including her appreciation of Blackmore, were collected in [Ebenezer Turell], *Memoirs of the Life and Death of the Pious and Ingenious Mrs. Jane Turell* . . . (Boston, 1735), 81. Her witty verse does not survive.

experience a spiritual epiphany. The cognitive procedure laid out in *Creation* became fixed in its imitations: the poet asserted the connection between the sensible order and divine power; the poet surveyed the natural order; once its design had been intuited, a turn occured, and the order was shown to be a transparent vehicle of God's power; the poet encountered godhead in a climactic moment of feeling and insight.

It is difficult to conceive of an experience more at odds with the mood of polite sociability than that captured in the poetry of the religious sublime. Indeed, in the London literary battles of the 1690s, the sublime aesthetic stood diametrically opposed to wit. Richard Blackmore and John Dennis attacked the profanity of wit and the vulgarity of the stage, championing what they termed "sense." The paper war smoldered unresolved until the advent of Pope, who stood as the heir of both Dryden and wit, yet avowed sense. Pope's ability to encompass religious sublimity (in his "Messiah" for instance) and wit ("The Rape of the Lock") suggested that the disjunction between elevated sensation and social pleasure was not absolute. Certainly the American cosmopolitans of the 1720s attempted to diminish this disparity by reconceiving sociability in light of a sublimely created order. By presenting human relations as structured by the affects and by showing the order of society to be a species of natural order, New England thinkers rendered society sublime. The Harvard cosmopolitan John Adams composed "On Society," a three-canto poem on Blackmore's model, arguing the thesis that society was the divinely ordained coappropriation of disparate entities in creation. Finding society's archetype in the mysterious interbelonging of the persons of the Trinity, Adams discovered a similar binding power in the ethology of wild animals and the relations of human beings. For Adams the interest of society, and its problem, lay in the history of human relationships. They had been holy in their design, but sin had distorted their primordial purity. Originally human society had several modes of relationship, most importantly friendship and love.

> Mankind, alike (by Nature equal) tend
> In social Laws, and social Joys to blend;
> Or manly Friendship, or the softer Ties
> Of sighing Lovers, or the Marriage Joys,
> With all the Bands of humane Life, derive
> From that Propension which our Passions give.[34]

34. John Adams, "On Society," in Adams, *Poems on Several Occasions*, 27.

Adams, unlike a number of Christian belletrists, countenanced the possibility of female friendship. "Manly friendship" did not prevent "fair ones . . . with fairs ones join'd," nor did it imply that female passion was directed wholly toward the end of creating the family, unless the heart were corrupted by sin. Familial affection for Adams differed from other social modes only because parents project a tincture of self-love onto offspring, since children resemble their procreators.

Canto 2 of "On Society" developed the permutations of love. It identified lust as the principal distortion that sin effected in heterosociality. It also distinguished between the love characterized by the intoxication of fancy — "The shady Picture mocks our Hopes with Air / Nor fill them with the Substance of the Fair" — and true love, in which "Esteem and Vertue feed the just Desire." The binding of desire within esteem, a form of care that entails a just valuation of the desired object, yokes love to reason. It also renders love fixed and durable, because care grounded on a sense of the justness of the beloved's desirability binds affection with both imagination and reason.

The affective organization of true love mirrored the structure of sublime experience. Just as true love demands that judgment discover a reason for desiring the desirable so that affection may bloom as esteem, a sublime transport in the face of nature requires that reason apprehend something of the suprahuman majesty of nature's design before one can give oneself over to elevation and awe. Reason is prior to the imaginative realization of divine power. In friendship, reason manifests particular prominence:

> Here Reason rules with indisputed Sway,
> And makes the subject Appetites obey;
> Its powerful Beams melt Softness all away:
> For Softness sinks the Vigour of the Mind,
> As Edges loose their Force the more refin'd.
> [P. 2]

In Canto 3's celebration of friendship Adams provided his most vivid portrait of social felicity. After supplying the desiderata of the ideal friend (a sketch owing much to John Pomfret's anatomy of the boon companion in "The Choice"), Adams envisioned a life roaming hillsides studying nature with this comrade. Demi-Newtons, they would philosophize themselves into sublimity together:

On Nature's Work by gentle Steps to rise,
And by this Ladder gain th' impending Skies;
Follow the Planets thro' their rolling Spheres,
Shine with the Sun, or glow among the Stars:
From World to World, as Bees from Flow'r to Flow'r,
Thro' Nature's ample Garden take our Tour,
Oh, could I with a Seraph's Vigor move!
Guided thro' Nature's trackless Paths to rove,
I'd gaze, and ask the Laws of every Ball,
Which rolls unseen within this mighty *All*.
'Till, reaching to the Verge of Nature's Height
In God would loose th' unwearied length of Flight.

[Pp. 33–34]

In this exaltation before nature, the friends anticipated the postapocalyptic condition of the redeemed in heaven, for in the finale of "On Society" we learn,

When fix'd on Zion's ever-wid'ning Plains,
The Force of Friendship but increas'd remains:
When Friend to Friend, in Robes immortal drest,
With heighten'd Graces shall be seen confest;
And with a Triumph, all divine, relate
The finish'd Labours of this gloomy state.

Adams did not envision social formations intermediate between earthly love or friendship and the sublime friendly society of heaven. Membership in an earthly polity of love was not conceived, not even as participation in a church order. Reformed Christianity's emphasis on personal religion and the individual experience of conversion, when refracted through the doctrine of the sublime with its psychic transport of the individual witness, had a peculiar tendency to dissolve any medium between the subject and a universalized generality.

Whether Adams's poem was rhetorically successful is open to question. It is perhaps best to understand it as an attempt to work a rapprochement between the Christian interest in a sense of the transcendent and a general cultural interest in the pleasures of society. Harvard's cosmopolitans wished to retain the sublime office of oracle of the revelation yet did not wish to deny the force of friendship, the power of love, or the pleasure of society.

Whereas a Puritan saint might say God's altar needs not our polishing, the cosmopolitans thought polish and politeness were graces. Both the sublime and the literature of polite wit were aesthetic modes; sensation and pleasure stood at the heart of both modes. The cosmopolitan aesthetic program was to promulgate a literature that served the Christian imperative to assert the reality of supernatural power while endorsing the graces and sociable virtues of politeness. Christian belletrism could not resolve the contradiction inherent in yoking the sublime, a profoundly individual experience of elevation and terror, with the polite, a profoundly social experience of the sensus communis. Indeed, the dual intents of Christian belletrism were so antithetical that they could be kept in tension only in writing (and particularly in print). Polite conversation face-to-face could not well endure the intrusion of the supernal. Print's ability to bind belles lettres to a discourse of Christian instruction is a matter of historical significance.

The Polite Christian

The quintessential expression of the cosmopolitan project was the "Proteus Echo" series of essays, sketches, and poems printed in the *New-England Weekly Journal* in Boston during 1727–1728. The writings purported to be the contributions of a club of correspondents. In actuality, everything was contributed by the triumvirate of Mather Byles, John Adams, and Matthew Adams. In the fifty-two installments, sublime transports mingled cheek by jowl with polite pleasantries. The sublime prospect of the world's formation in no. 16 could have been a prose distillation of Blackmore's *Creation*. The evocation of the terrors of death in no. 17 supplied an old topos of Christian meditation with a sensual luster that would have gladdened John Dennis. Thunder and lightning took on apocalyptic intensity in no. 19. Yet these stood disconcertingly proximate to visions of the sociable world. By digesting a series of observations out of these essays, we can make 1720s Boston seem something altogether more artsy than history has allowed. To see how far polite Christianity could assimilate to genteel moralism, let us read through them, touching upon some of the issues that have occupied our attention in this study.[35]

35. The titles for this collection and the extracts are mine. The numbers of the essays as originally printed, given here with the essays, do not match the numbers of the issues of the *New-England Weekly Journal* in which they appeared: no. 2: Apr. 17, 1727; no. 5: May 8; no. 7: May 22; no. 10: June 12; no. 11: June 19; no. 14: July 10; no. 21:

THE COMMONPLACE BOOK OF MR. PROTEUS ECHO

The Age

This Age is too polite, to bear the same ill-Manners and Roughness as the former. Then a Man was thought the more Religious for being a Clown, and very honest because he used no Ceremony but downright plain dealing. But now the taste of Mankind is very much rectifyed; and the World cannot endure the Absurdity to see a Man behave himself as if he were under the Reign of Queen *Elizabeth*. [No. 21; John Adams]

Beaux

I don't know how it is, but some who maintain a bold and gallant Freedom with the Ladies, would think an injury was done them, if only for that single Accomplishment you should refuse to rank them in the number of polite Gentlemen. But till they possess the good Sense of the one sex as well as Softness of the other, the World will always be so just as to esteem them Nothing besides well bred and genteel Beaux. [No. 29; John Adams]

Club Talk

If the end of Associating is to Converse, then to start some Subject which may profit and please, is most subservient to this Design, and the Neglect so to do is a kind of Quakerism in Society. How unseemly does it look for a Club of Rational Creatures to pass away whole Hours in a solemn Silence, and all this while for a Gentleman who has a noble Talent of expressing his Sentiments, to let it lie buried in a Napkin. [No. 43; Matthew Adams]

Coffee-House Conversation

If you frequent a Coffee-House, you'l be entertained with Politicks and News, and, when the Company are a little flushed with Drink, Religion. [No. 35; John Adams]

Coffee-House Fellowship

I have observed in all the Companies I have been in, from the *Caravan-Lodge* in *China*, to the *Crown-Coffee-House* upon the *Long-Wharffe*, that all Conversation is built upon Equality; Title and Distinction must be laid aside in order to talk and act sociably, and the ungrateful Names of Superiour and Inferior must loose themselves in that more acceptable and familiar one, the Companion. [No. 30; Mather Byles]

Aug. 28; no. 26: Oct. 2; no. 29: Oct. 23; no. 30: Oct. 30; no. 35: Dec. 4; no. 36: Dec. 11; no. 43: Jan 29, 1728; no. 51: Mar. 25.

Conversation

Conversation is attended with many Advantages both of getting Good our Selves, and benefitting our Fellow-Creatures. It tends to polish our Minds, and refine our Manners; to wear away the disagreeable Roughness which we acquire by too much Solitude; and to infuse an affable and easy Deportment which will powerfully recommend us in all Companies. In a Word, it adds a Gracefulness to the Air; a Softness to the Eye; an Assurance to the Heart; and touches the Tongue with a more artful and winning Fluency of Address. [No. 30; Mather Byles]

A Critick

A Polite Critick is one who has improved the natural Sagacity and Soundness of his Judgment, by a close perusal of several the best Ancient and Modern Authors; is as quick-sighted to discern Beauties as to spy Faults, and having distinguish'd himself by some eminent Performance, is under no Temptation from Envy to pull down the Reputation of others. [No. 29; John Adams]

Disputatiousness

An agreeable Conversation may tend very much to the Improvement and Preservation of Friendship, but when our Discourse shall run on in Contradiction, till it warms into wrangling Disputation, there is Danger of being hurried on in the Transport of our Passion, to such a Bitterness, as is more the Temper of an Adversary than a Friend.

There is hardly any thing more destructive of Friendship than Disputes; especially when they are urged and prosecuted with Vehemence, and intermixt with Raillery and Satyrical Wit. [No. 26; Mather Byles]

Friendship

In order to preserve a strict and inviolable Friendship, it is necessary to mix our Intimacy with a kind of Distance and Reserve: or in other words, that we avoid that Familiarity which is always an Inlet to Indifference and Contempt. Our own Experience may instruct us, that the nearest Neighbours and Relations, are not always the most sociable and friendly; nor are those, who are at first very often together, observed to be the most kind and durable Comparions. [No. 26; Mather Byles]

A Gentleman

This Gentleman has to uncommon Natural Endowments, added Artificial ones, and made Conversation part of his Study. By this means he has

replenished his Soul with an inexhausted Fund of Ideas, big with Entertainment and Instruction. As his Mind is thus pregnant with innumber-
able Pleasantries, and other Topicks for Society, so he has a peculiar
Happiness and Dexterity to express, and set them off, in the most lively
and advantageous Manner. He can cloath his Thoughts, modulate his
Voice, and adapt his Gesture as the Circumstances require: And as he
pleases is able to awe us by his Gravity; surprize us by his Uncommoness
and quick Turn; or tickle us into an irresistable Laughter, by the Slyness
and Subtilty of his inimitable Humour. To say no more, his Company is
desired and sought by all, and none ever left it without Regret, without
Diversion, and without Improvement. [No. 30; Mather Byles]

The Grubstreet Hack

Dick Grubstreet . . . is a Fellow of a very low Descent, and compounded of
the Dregs of Mortality. His Ancestors; from all Generations, were Enemies to every thing that is great and noble; and always sordid and mean
in their Apparel, Discourse, and the whole tenour of their Actions. He is
Heir of all these their good Qualities, and has many more of his own,
which render him a perfect Original. As for his Aspect, there was never
any thing more plain, uncouth, and emblematical of his Soul. He has a
down-cast look, which proceeds not from Meditation, but Stupidity:
And his Dress, and Manners, are both alike rough and unpolished. He is
a mortal and professed Foe to good Sense, and the true Sublime in
Writing, and whensoever he reads either, (which is only by chance,) he
rejects them with an ignorant Disdain. [No. 10; John Adams]

Love

There is nothing in which Men more impose upon themselves, than in
matters of Love. No sooner has this Passion kindled in any great Degree
in the Heart, but the Eyes of Reason are put out, a Cloud hangs upon the
Intelect, and Darkness invades the whole Soul. [No. 11; Mather Byles]

Manners

Good Manners . . . is a discriminating Character of reasonable Beings,
and that which must remain as long as the Continuance of Vertue, upon
which it is founded. Our Necessities, which are various and numberless,
oblige us to a frequent Recourse to our Fellow-creatures, and their
voluntary Offices of Love and Benevolence, lay us under the the Bonds
of a perpetual Acknowedgment. . . . The decent Ceremony of a mutual

Complaisance, is therefore so near of Kin to Vertue, that I can hardly believe the want of it is reconcileable with that Religion, which is void of Offence, towards our Maker and Fellow-creatures. [No. 51; Matthew Adams]

A Merchant
Charles Gravely . . . has traded for many Thousand of Pounds in *Wit* and *Eloquence*, and all sorts of the richest *Styles* and *Figures*, that are of such Use in the Common-Wealth of Letters: And could never be perswaded to venture his Merchandise abroad, upon any other Bottom than that of *Good Sense;* for which Reason, he has in all his Adventures, succeeded to Admiration. He is of all our Society, the best acquainted with the various Humours and Passions of Mankind, and can only by the Sight of the Face, very often discover the secret Motions and Propensity of the Heart; so that it is sometimes very dangerous being in his Company. [No. 2; Matthew Adams]

Poesy
As Poesy is the highest Exercise of the noblest Powers of our Souls, it cannot but afford a superiour Pleasure to those happy Minds who are distinguished with a Taste for such raised and exquisite Entertainments. [No. 36; Matthew Adams]

Poets
Those whose Fancies teem with Images, into whose Breasts Nature has infused a Caelestial flush of Spirits, and who feel the inspiring Divinity inform their inmost Soul: They disdain to walk in the dull common pace of Prose; but bound and fly aloft upon the Pinions of Sublime Thoughts, and harmonious Numbers, till reaching their native Skies, they at the same time become the Admiration and Envy of all Mankind. [No. 7; John Adams]

The Polite Author
A Polite Author is one who weighs his Subject wisely and exactly before he ventures to chuse or write upon it; then draws a clear and regular Scheme of it in his own Mind, which being the most natural is also the most easy: Endeavours to find out what Sentiments are the most proper for his Subject, and what Words will paint them in the most clear, strong and genuine Colours: Who uses a plain, sublime, nervous or soft Stile, according to the various Themes upon which he Treats, and so grace-fully turns his Sentences, as to make them flow in the most musical

Periods to the Ear; and understands when he has said enough. [No. 29; John Adams]

A Polite Gentleman

A Polite Gentleman is one who maintains such a deference to the World as to imitate all its innocent Customs and Manners without affecting Singularity in any thing besides the Greatness of his Soul, and Beauty of his Example. [No. 29; John Adams]

Politeness

Politeness is one of those things which are more easily conceived than described. But as it begins to dawn upon the Country, and every Person has it in his Mouth, I shall throw together some Thoughts upon the subject. . . .

He that is Polite, must be born with a Genius for Politeness. He should enjoy a penetrating and solid Judgment, to give him a correct Taste of things, and a vigorous and lively imagination, else he will not be able to relish those fine Strokes of Wit, and Sublimity, which so please and astonish us in the best of Authors. [No. 29; John Adams]

The Punster

[The Punster] has a musical Ear, a quick Fancy, and a good Memory, but is undoubtedly Crack-brain'd. With these Accomplishments he sets up for a Wit, and as *Dryden* expresses it, entertains himself with *waging Harmless War with Words*. His Memory furnishes him with a Stock of Syllables; his Ear judges if they chime to one another; and his Fancy raises some uncouth and ridiculous image from them, which he is perpetually laughing at himself, and perswading others to join with him. [No. 14; Mather Byles — reflecting on his own heart-sin]

Sociability

Desire after Society is a Passion strongly rooted in human Nature; and even *Adam* breathing the Sweets of *Eden*, could not be compleatly happy without a Partner in his Enjoyments. To indulge and gratify this universal Taste of Mankind they have from the Beginning learned to form themselves into Cities, Kingdoms, and other Communities, by which they have in some Sort created an Union of Sorrows, and Hopes, and Satisfactions, and lived in a Manner agreeable to the Species. [No. 30; Mather Byles]

Society

Society is to unloose and unbend the Mind, and ought to have something of Gaiety and Sprightliness in it. If it should be serious, it ought also to be Chearful, and should never be affected; but above all, it must be Useful. [No. 43; Matthew Adams]

Vulgar Taste

THE Multitude are more eager after what glitters, and dazzles upon their Imaginations, than what instructs their Reason: But Truth is removed far from sense and fancy, while she soars upon the Wings of the most abstracted Thought. She shines high above the Ken of the Vulgar, who being us'd to nothing but their Senses, cannot behold her through those Clouds. And this her Sublimity is the Reason that they either Reproach her for being too lofty and raised, or else admire her for this only Reason, that they do not understand her. [No. 5; John Adams]

Proteus Echo's immersion in the metropolitan ethic of sociability, the ideal of genteel conversation, and the aesthetics of politeness was total. The triumvirs adapted the picture of the sociable world limned in the *Tatler*, *Spectator*, and *Guardian* to the features of Boston. The London prints had transmitted notions of the genteel world to the New World. Proteus Echo suited them to the local temper, and the *New-England Weekly Journal* broadcast them. The personal example and conversation of someone like Henry Brooke in Pennsylvania might give rise to genteel circles with an elite membership; the newspaper publication of a vade mecum of politeness could prompt a broad desire to participate in the sensus communis of polite conversation. While drawing the obvious conclusion that print led to the popularization of belles lettres and the "ingenious conversation" it subserved, we must not overlook the less conspicuous point: the rise of belles lettres was in many ways a reaction to the proliferation of print. Belles lettres was a mode of writing that disavowed its handwritten character by aspiring to transparency before the beauties of sociable communication. Yet in order to make that communication sufficiently interesting, it had to import from literature certain "flowers and ornaments" — maxims, witticisms, and the formulas that Swift mocked in his *Polite Conversation*. Consider the Proteus Echo entry "The Polite Author" (no. 29). Before venturing to communicate, the author "Endeavours to find out what Sentiments are the most proper for his Subject." This did not mean an assay of the prevailing opinion of an audience with an eye toward its philosophical refinement and correction. The proper "Sentiments" to which the Reverend John Adams alluded were sententiae, the memorable sentences from tradition. From the time of Erasmus the learning of this tradition took place in the academy by the practice of commonplacing, registering the finest passages from authors under subject headings. In the humanist scheme of education in rhetoric the commonplaces were written and reviewed until fixed in memory; ultimately they would be drawn on in a forensic performance. What could be used in one arena of oral performance could be used in another. By means of commonplaces conversation became learned.

With the publication of compendia of sententiae, such as Erasmus's *Adagia*, print instituted a canon of "proper sentiments" that academies enforced and polite companies endorsed. "Agreeableness," that desideratum of sociability, was given to conversation by the concert of sentiment achieved through the distillation of literature into a canon of commonplaces. Decomposing the Proteus Echo essays into the sentiments from which they were constructed and displaying their harmony with the original premises of belles lettres as it emerged as an expression of metropolitan sociability dramatizes the conversational consensus underwritten by print.

A peculiarity of the Proteus Echo series was its index. When the year's run of essays ended, the series shut down; and an index of its contents appeared. It revealed that the essays and poems, despite appearing over a host of initials, came from only three writers.[36] The matter of writings was not truly a sensus communis: the protean community of letters that encompassed both Christian sublimity and polite chat was shown to be the creation of two recent Harvard graduates and a middle-aged merchant. The key to the index suggested that the identities were revealed to satisfy public curiosity about the composers of such engaging material. In truth the index was published to promote the reputations of the Proteus Echo authors.

Famous Characters and the Defamer

Fame was the prerogative of talent at Harvard College. Competition in the classroom, in the undergraduate societies, and at the commencement exercises determined one's standing in class and one's prospects in society. When Benjamin Colman introduced the metropolitan standard of manners and aesthetics into New England in 1699, he established a new basis for renown. The old roles of statesman, physician, merchant, and minister were supplemented with the office of virtuoso. Colman's ability to combine ministerial vocation with the role as exemplar of the social graces vested

36. Bruce Granger, ed., *Proteus Echo (1727–28)* (Delmar, N.Y., 1986). See introduction for a discussion of authorship.

him with a double luster. His connection with important figures in the metropolis, his romance with "Philomela," and his ability to combine sublimity with the "beauties of religion" made him the model of the rising generation that hungered for renown.

For the pietists Colman was the first of the civic Christians — the believers who made an accommodation with the world. His was the moderated spiritual flame that would in the course of time be termed the Old Light. Merchant Matthew Adams captured the disposition of civic Christianity when he remarked, in his discussion of good manners, above, "The decent Ceremony of a mutual Complaisance, is . . . so near of Kin to Vertue, that I can hardly believe the want of it is reconcileable with that Religion, which is void of Offence, towards our Maker and Fellow-creatures." Matthew Adams was a capable and successful public man, perhaps most valuable for giving the young Benjamin Franklin the run of his library.

John Adams, Matthew's nephew, was the greater virtuoso. He was called to be assistant pastor to the Reverend Nathaniel Clap in Newport. But Clap was a champion of the old style and found his young associate too worldly; he denied him the pulpit. The church split. Adams presided over the Second Congregational Church until Clap's agitations forced his dismissal. Adams returned to Harvard as a tutor for four years. He had two short, unsuccessful tenures at churches in Philadelphia. The second trial was cut short by a mental breakdown. He returned to Boston and was supported by private charity until his death from fever in 1740. Rumor held too much brooding on books had ruined his sanity; he could read nine languages. His funeral was a celebration by Harvard of a cultural hero: "The Corps was carried and plac'd in the Centre of the College-Hall; from whence, after a portion of Holy Scripture, and a Prayer very suitable to the Occasion, by the learned Head of that Society, it was taken and deposited within Sight of the Place of his own Education. The Pall was supported by the Fellows of the College, the Professor of the Mathematicks, and another Master of Arts." Bookseller Daniel Gookin or uncle Matthew Adams in a preface to the posthumous collection of the poet's works observed that "sufficient to perpetuate his Memory to the latest Posterity, are the Immortal writings and Composures of the departed Gentleman; who, for his Genius, his Learning, and his Piety, ought to be enroll'd in the highest Class, the catalogue of FAME."[37] Adams's fame was fleeting, meriting a

37. *Boston Weekly News-Letter,* no. 1871, Jan. 31, 1740; Clifford K. Shipton, *Biographical Sketches of Those Who Attended Harvard College in the Classes 1713–1721,*

condescending notice in Samuel Miller's intellectual history, *A Retrospect of the Eighteenth Century* (1800). No school child in the nineteenth century was obliged to sweeten her lips with memorized lines from "On Society."

There was only one belletrist who earned lasting fame from the ranks of the Harvard cosmpolitans—Mather Byles. And no one desired literary renown or pursued it more assiduously than he. His campaign for aesthetic immortality earned him the signal distinction of being the only British American belletrist to have his personal parodist—New England's greatest master of defamation, the Harvard-educated rum distiller, Joseph Green.

In literary histories for two centuries Mathew Byles has held the rather solitary office of New England's Augustan poet. He won the post by calculating self-promotion, a fair measure of literary skill, and his legendary wit. The incidents of his life have long been matters of record, from his boyhood tutelage at the hands of uncle Cotton Mather to his expulsion from the pulpit of Old South during the Revolution for his tory sympathies. Less well known are the stratagems by which he installed himself as the great cham of New England poetry. Byles's quest for literary eminence began while an undergraduate. Adhering to the time-honored pattern, he first laid claim to public notice by floating an elegy. When in April 1724 Captain Josiah Winslow (Harvard, 1721) died in an Indian fight in Maine, Byles and John Adams (Winslow's classmate) vied to honor Winslow's memory. Adams's lamentation was conservative, employing the time-honored typological strategy of identifying the deceased with biblical Jonathan and refurbishing David's lamentation with modern diction and couplet rhyme. Byles opted for a more fashionable neoclassicism in "To the Memory of a Young Commander Slain in a Battle with the Indians, 1724." The two poems were handed about together in Cambridge as examples of the dual directions of collegiate artistry. In 1726 Ebenezer Parkman attended the Harvard commencement, had the opportunity to read both works, and declared that he "was very well pleas'd" with the performances. Parkman, that afternoon, also read another poem by Byles, one that would contribute to his elevation as chief poet of Massachusetts. "He show'd me (at my Request) his Poem to Mr. Dowding on his Verses of Eternity, Sent in a Letter to Sir Byles."[38] It appeared in one of the final

Sibley's Harvard Graduates, VI (Boston, 1942), 424–427, and citing Matthew Adams to Josiah Cotton, Curwen MSS, II, 11, American Antiquarian Society; preface to Adams, *Poems on Several Occasions*, [vii].

38. John Adams, "David's Elegy Paraphras'd, and Apply'd to the Premature Death

issues of the *New-England Courant*, recommended as "an early Production of a *Harvard* Muse." An element of incongruity attached to the character-ization of the piece as a provisional example of a Harvard poet's art; the poem presumed the poet's total mastery of the craft. Byles, it would seem, had served as (Joseph?) Dowding's poetic tutor. With specious modesty Byles disavowed any influence on Dowding's genius:

> In vain you say I form'd your Infant strains
> Taught you on stubborn thoughts to fix your chains.

Byles was merely serving as the New World lens for the true source of poetic light:

> Not I, but mighty POPE inspir'd thy Muse.
> He, wondrous Bard! whose Numbers reach our Shore,
> Though Oceans roll between, and tempests roar:
> Hush'd are the storms, and smooth the waters lie,
> As his sweet musick glides harmonious by;
> Ravish'd, my ear receives the heav'nly guest,
> My heart high-leaping, beats my panting breast:
> Through all my mind incessant rapture reigns,
> And joys immortal revel in my veins.[39]

That Byles should use the commendation of another's art as an occasion to advance the notion that he was the receptacle of Pope's fire in the New World shows an instinct for publicity. The impression is confirmed when one notices that in his elegy on the death of "Old Janus" (the *Courant*), Byles interrupts his mockery to commend the poetry (his own) that ap-peared there shortly before it expired.

> But, O my muse, some consolation bring,
> And in this doleful ditty cease to sing.
> Few thought his rev'rend vitals were so strong,
> Or that th' old fellow could have liv'd so long.

---

of Capt. Josiah Winslow, Who Was Slain in Battle with the Indians, May 1, 1724," in Adams, *Poems on Several Occasions*, 72–77; Byles, *Poems on Several Occasions*, 34–44; Francis G. Walett, ed., *The Diary of Ebenezer Parkman, 1703–1782* (Worcester, Mass, 1974), 14.

39. [Mather Byles], "To My Friend, Occasioned by His Poem on Eternity, Dedi-cated to Me," *New-England Courant*, no. 237, Feb. 12, 1726; from corrected version, *New-England Weekly Journal*, no. 11, June 5, 1727.

For, many a month did to the world display,
How all his parts were hast'ning to decay;
And (as 'tis usual, e'er one's parting breath)
He lighten'd once or twice before his death,*
For fire besure's in those who verses write;
And where, *my friends*, is fire, unless there's light?⁴⁰

 *Alluding to the two late poetical Courants.

Yet the poet's guile exceeded self-puffery. In the eighth issue of the *New-England Weekly Journal*, a year after the *Courant* published Byles's commendatory poem, "Eternity" appeared anonymously in the Proteus Echo column. It proclaimed the author's debt to his tutor (Mather Byles) in stanza 2:

While this great Thought employs my infant Muse,
And she with fluttering Wings the Task pursues,
On you, Dear SIR, she casts her anxious Sight,
Indulge, Propitious, and assist her Flight;
Taught by your Rules, by your Example fir'd;
She heard, she learnt, and instant was inspir'd.⁴¹

Exercising his prerogative as editor of the Proteus Echo series, Byles decided that one viewing of his appreciation of "Eternity" was insufficient, so he published a corrected version of "To My Friend: Occasioned by His Poem on Eternity, Dedicated to the Author" as "Proteus Echo no. 9."⁴² After persons began endorsing Byles's high opinion of "Eternity," he let it be known through the poetic grapevine that *he* wrote the poem, not Dowding! When Byles collected his poetry in 1744, "Eternity" appeared as his final work. The passage praising his tutor (that is, himself) was deleted. Byles's poem commending "Eternity" also appeared in the collection, renamed and placed so that it did not seem to refer to Byles's work. Because "Eternity" cemented his reputation, Byles made sure its celebrity would be recalled, appending a puff, "Added by a Friend, upon reading the foregoing." This friend (one hopes it was a friend and not Byles in masquerade) announced:

40. "An Elegy on the Long Expected Death of Old Janus [*The New-England Courant*]," in *A Collection of Poems: By Several Hands* (Boston, 1744), 10.

41. Proteus Echo no. 6, "Eternity: A Poem," *New-England Weekly Journal*, no. 8, May 15, 1727.

42. *New-England Weekly Journal*, no. 12, June 5, 1727.

In those bless'd Realms thy heav'n-born Soul shall stand;
And sing superiour in the radiant Band;
And while thy Hands the Palm caelestial claim,
ETERNITY shall consecrate thy Fame.[43]

Having manipulated both the sociable world of the Harvard literati and the Boston public prints to clear for himself a favored place in the realm of New England letters, Byles used his advantage to recreate the image of Harvard projected by the weeklies. He did so by lending the college the aura of wit and cosmopolitanism that the English universities had cultivated in miscellanies since the 1690s. His first effort was "Commencement" (1727), a celebration of the most important event on the academic calendar. It depicted the public disputation, the most exquisite drama in a student's life, when a candidate showed his parts and learning and perhaps won a reputation:

The work begun with pray'r, with modest pace,
A youth advancing mounts the desk with grace,
To all the audience sweeps a circling bow,
Then from his lips ten thousand graces flow.
The next that comes, a learned thesis reads,
The question states, and then a war succeeds.
Loud major, minor, and the consequence,
Amuse the crowd, wide-gaping at their sence.
Who speaks the loudest is with them the best,
And impudence for learning is confest.[44]

("Grace" here meant ease, rather than divine favor: Byles celebrated the ideal of the polite academy.)

Having consolidated authority in both institutions, college and newspaper, that circumscribed literary fame in Boston, Byles turned to London. In a letter of October 7, 1727, Byles expressed to Alexander Pope his ravishment upon reading the master's works. Byles was especially impressed by the new scope of celebrity encompassed by Pope's fame: "What corner of the earth [is] so secret as not to have heard the name of Mr. Pope? or who so retired as not to be acquainted with his admirable compositions, or so stupid as not to be ravished with them"? On May 3, 1728, Byles wrote to

43. Byles, *Poems on Several Occasions*, 111–112.
44. [Mather Byles], "Commencement," in *A Collection of Poems: By Several Hands*, 51–52.

Isaac Watts, the dean of Christian letters. Watts and Pope both responded to Byles by sending him copies of their books. Books were the medium by which fame was solidified. The new print market built around celebrity authors gave books an influence as broad as Britain's empire of the seas. Byles grasped the lesson: to serve ambition, one must bind one's muse to the press. During the 1720s in New England there existed markets for very few kinds of native poetry: for ballads on remarkable events and executions, verses promulgating practical Christianity, elegies, and public pieces commemorating important occasions. By assuming the role of volunteer laureate for the Bay Colony, Byles dominated the latter two markets. In 1727 he mourned the death of George I, in 1728 he congratulated William Burnet on his installation as governor of Massachusetts, and in 1729 he reflected on Boston's great fire. By the time of Governor Jonathan Belcher's appointment in 1730, Byles was so firmly associated in the public mind with public proclamation that he was forced to write a poem explaining why he hadn't welcomed Belcher with an ode.[45] After marrying Belcher's niece, Byles found himself the court poet of the administration.

A chorus of approbation greeted Byles's elevation to the status of state oracle. Tributes from Peleg Wiswall, John Perkins, John Adams, Joshua Gee, and Jane Turell sounded his praise, but not every devotee of the arts in Boston wished to join the choir. Joseph Green, a merchant wit, sounded the strongest discord, and in 1728 he appointed himself the antilaureate. As Byles elevated collegiate ceremony and the grace of the Harvard graduate, the antilaureate supplied *A Satyrical Description of Commencement, Calculated to the Meridian of Cambridge in New-England,* describing public diversions in 1728 in the descriptive style of a "town eclogue." The description's jest lay in its systematic redirection of attention from the action at the college to the public revelry attending commencement week:

> To Taverns some repair;
> And who can tell what Pranks are acted there.
> Some spend the Time at Pins (that toilsome Play)
> Others at Cards (more silent) pass the Day.
> In Rings some Wrestle till they're mad out-right
> And then with their Antagonists they fight.

45. Arthur Wentworth Hamilton Eaton, *The Famous Mather Byles, the Noted Boston Tory, Preacher, Poet, and Wit, 1707–1788* (Boston, 1914), 102–104. A copy of the original letter to Pope is contained in "A Collection of the Original Copies of Several Letters," MS SA BYL 2, New England Historic Genealogical Society, Boston.

For Fighting is the Effect of Wrestling, as
Men draw Conclusion from the Premises.
All kind of horrid Noises fill the Street,
While distant Woods their Eccho's back repeat.

. . . .

Vast Numbers on the Pagan Party gaze,
To see th' incarnate Devils dance the Haze.
While some intoxicated are with Wine,
Others (as brutish) propagate their Kind.[46]

The meaning of commencement did not lie in the introduction of the scholars to public life; rather, it resided in the liberty that permitted the populace to enjoy "forbidden Pleasures." The meaning of commencement was manifest everywhere in the Cambridge vicinity except college hall.

Green next harried Byles when the paintings of John Smibert inspired Byles to publish an appreciation, "To Pictorio, on the Sight of His Pictures." Immodestly Byles nominated Smibert and himself as the heralds of the coming of civilization to the "barbarous Desart" of Boston:

"Alike our Labour, and alike our Flame:
'Tis thine to raise the Shape; 'tis mine to fix the Name."[47]

Green published a demurral:

Unhappy Bard! sprung in such Gothic Times
As yield no friendly muse, t'extol your Rhymes.
Hard is the Task you singly undergo
To praise the Painter and the Poet too.
But much I fear you raise a short liv'd FAME,
Which lives but on the Pen from whence it came.
Boast on, and take what fleeting Life can give,
For when you cease to write, you cease to live.
If you to future Ages would be known
Make this Advice I freely give — your own.

46. [Joseph Green], *A Satyrical Description of Commencement, Calculated to the Meridian of Cambridge in New-England* (Boston, [1728?]) (my attribution; J. A. Leo Lemay concurs).

47. Originally published in the *Boston Gazette*, Jan. ?, 1730 (now missing), the text derives from a reprinting, *American Weekly Mercury*, no. 528, Feb. 19, 1729/30, reprinted also in Kenneth Silverman, ed., *Colonial American Poetry* (New York, 1968), 235–237.

PLATE 6 Joseph Green. *Oil by John Singleton Copley, 1767. The turban was fashionable among Boston merchants; the brocade jacket connotes prosperity. Julia Knight Fox Fund. Courtesy, Museum of Fine Arts, Boston*

Go to the Painter — for your Picture sit;
His art will long survive the Poet's Wit.[48]

The master stroke of the epigram lay in the fact that Smibert had recently completed a portrait of Byles. Consequently, its display would make it seem as though Byles had followed Green's advice!

Joseph Green realized that the sort of authorial self-creation that Byles was attempting depended upon, indeed was preconditioned by, print. In the pages of a newspaper one could recreate oneself as a character or refashion others as characters and have the results accepted as truth. Green had noticed the proliferation of posthumous "characters" of citizens published in the press. Tongue in cheek, he wrote his Portsmouth friend Samuel Pollard concerning the social utility of the practice:

> Now I am upon this Head of Characters I can't dismiss it, without congratulating my Country upon the pious and useful Custom of publishing Characters in the weekly Papers, which look upon as a great Support to Religion and Virtue. Who would be at the Pains of many Actions which they now do, were it not in hopes of havg them recorded, what more proper way of doing it then this. It is what we all expect and desire; The hopes of a long Character (for the Substance and Truth of it are less regarded then the Length) thrusts us on; there is a certain stimulating Virtue in it, which pricks us on in Religion; in short [it is] like wringing a Calf by the Tail to make him go fast.[49]

The truth of a person's character is a problem because of the perpetual resort by character writers to the formulary of virtue. Does one get to the human distinctiveness of Mrs. Anna Rust, for instance, by noting, as a character writer in the *New-England Weekly Journal* did, "She was a well accomplished Gentlewoman, and a sincere Christian, and always remarkable for her Prudence and Discretion, which with her chast Conversation, had gain'd her an uncommon Reputation with all sorts of People, and realy what Solomon said of a virtuous Woman may with Truth be said of her,

---

48. [Joseph Green], "To Mr B——, Occasioned by His Verses to Mr. Smibert on Seeing His Pictures," *Boston Gazette*, Apr. 13, 1730. This verse was transcribed from the newspaper into several commonplace books, including John Smibert's notebook and Jeremy Belknap's "Collection of Poetry," Belknap Papers (013.9b), both at the Massachusetts Historical Society. A printed version of the text is contained in Henry Wilder Foote, *John Smibert, Painter . . .* (Cambridge, Mass., 1950), 56.

49. Joseph Green to Captain Benjamin Pollard of Portsmouth, N.H., June 7, 1733, Smith-Carter MSS, Massachusetts Historical Society.

That she opened her Mouth with Wisdom. and in her Tongue was the Law of Kindness"?[50] Representing Mrs. Rust as an ideal, a simulacrum of Solomon's virtuous woman, abstracts life to an impersonal generality. Green (in a personal letter to one of the wits of the merchants' club of Portsmouth, New Hampshire) parodied the formulary of virtue by offering a character of Boston's principal whore, Mary Godfrey:

> Sometime before last Lords Day Mrs. Mary Godfrey (the Relict of Mr. Thomas Godfrey, Mariner of this Town, first Daughter to Mr. James Pitts, late of Boston, deceased, and Sister to the present Mrs. Lydia Mackcune of the said Boston) yielded up her Spirit (which was meek and quiet) to God who gave it; leaving behind her an Infant Train, being several in Number, which were not begotten without her Maternal Co-operation. — Touching her Character, which deserves a Place in a gilded *Volumn* (having in her life time been very instrumental to the large Consumption of Gilding) she was a voluptuous Woman, whose Price was not above half a Crown, the Heart of her Husband did safely trust in her; her Children rose up and call'd her, pray forsooth Mother, her husband also and he ——ed her. Again she was a strict observer of the first Comand. Vizt. To increase and multiply: And as her Pity and Vigour recommended her to the Gay and Wanton, so did her Civilities to the Vulgar for her deportment was ever humble etc., and when she open'd her ——— it was with *Wideness,* by which she acquired so universal an Acquaintance and Esteem, as perhaps has hardly been exceed by any person of her Age, Art and Opportunity. It might have been added that she was a woman of comely proportions, good Features (before the Small Pox) a genteel Mien and handsome Behaviour, but these are things of small Note; for, as Favour is deceitful, so Beauty is vain, but a Woman that pleaseth the Men, she shall be praised.[51]

The perverse application of biblical texts, moral *sententiae,* and polite commendation to a person whose calling denoted vice made the devices of praise conspicuous and the act of praise mechanical. Her public character is signally indicated in the metaphor of an elite consumer book—a gilt volume.

As a satirist, Green specialized in parody, demonstrating how the language of praise cloaked vanity. Often he pastiched notices in the public

50. *New-England Weekly Journal,* no. 321, May 14, 1733.
51. Green to Pollard, June 7, 1733.

prints because what was published carried an imputation of wide importance, or official sanction. These send-ups were distributed in manuscript. In part, Green frequently published in manuscript because his wit spoke to the private sensus communis of the mercantile clubs in Boston, Salem, and Portsmouth and not to the anonymous public of print. Green's was not a corrective satire but was designed to make its objects ridiculous in the eyes of a select audience. His parodies of the exchanges between Governor Belcher and the Assembly of New Hampshire, for instance, expressed a political perspective freed of both the parochialism of the popular party in the Assembly and the power-serving self-interest of Belcher and the prerogative party. And "The Disappointed Cooper" satirized the enthusiasm of New Light evangelists in the person of the Reverend William Cooper.[52]

The unusual feature of Green's satires of Mather Byles was that they were invariably printed. Green determined that the most effective solvent for Byles's print-constructed character had to be administered in that medium where Byles presided as chief poet. In 1733 Green performed his most astonishing deed as antilaureate: he managed to get two of his parodies printed in the "Poetical Essays" section of the *London Magazine*. One can imagine Byles's astonishment, given his hunger for fame, when he encountered Green's revisions of his character in one of the two great London periodicals. In place of Byles's self-image as master elegist and public mourner, he found "The Poet's Lamentation for the Loss of his Cat, Which He Used to Call His Muse." In place of Byles's character as sacred singer and psalmist of New England, Green supplied Byles the doggerel David. Both satires and Byles's "Hymn at Sea" have long enjoyed places in anthologies of American literature. Yet the poems have never been read insightfully. "The Poet's Lamentation" appropriated the first person in order to make Byles's expression of grief a confession of his poetic mortality. Without the aid of the cat/muse the poet's art will die, for she was the source of his music:

> When'er I felt my tow'ring fancy fail,
> I strok'd her head, her ears, her back, and tail;

52. J. A. Leo Lemay, "Joseph Green's Satirical Poem on the Great Awakening," *Resources for American Literary Study*, IV, (1974), 173–183. See my discussion of Green's satires of Governor Joseph Belcher and the New Hampshire Assembly, in *Oracles of Empire: Poetry, Politics, and Commerce in British America, 1690–1750* (Chicago, 1990), 131–137.

And, as I strok'd, improv'd my dying song
From the sweet notes of her melodious tongue;
Her purrs and mews so evenly kept time,
She purr'd in metre, and she mew'd in rhime.[53]

Moreover, she was the sole defender of the poet's art from the ravages of time, for the "quires of words array'd in pompous rhime" stand imperiled, since "Now undefended, and unwatch'd by cats, / Are doom'd a victim to the teeth of rats." In effect, the cat's death portended his own, for his poetic immortality was doubly forfeited by her loss. Green's pretense that Byles's muse was a mortal beast rather than an immortal goddess linked Byles's art to the low and perishing while permitting an exploration of the bathos of the poet's language.

Byles's elegies suffered from an excess of sentimentalism, in which the meaning of loss inhered in the intensity of subjective turmoil. For Green, sentimental effusion submerged the moral significance of elegiac memorialization. In a sentimental elegy, recollecting the virtues of the deceased did not console a reader; rather, it intensified anxiety at loss. Green satirically brought the problem to the fore. Displacing the language of virtue from its normal human sphere to the animal realm allowed Green to parody the contemporary fashion for sentimentalizing pets. Simultaneously, it afforded him an opportunity to suggest that sentimentalism subverted the act of moral commendation, transforming it from an act of judgment to a renaming of desire:

In acts obscene she never took delight;
No caterwawls disturb'd our sleep by night;
Chaste as a virgin, free from every stain,
And neighb'ring cats mew'd for her love in vain.

The poet's unnatural monopolization of the affections of his pet redefines what was meant by one's "devotion to the muse." The allegory of erotic sublimation inscribed in the myth of the muses has been recast as a humorous tale of Platonic bestiality. The egotism of the poet's dominion of his cat's affections partook of the egotism of sentimentalism in general, in which the speaker's feelings constitute the all of poetic meaning. Green linked this egotism with the private madness of the furor poeticus and

53. [Joseph Green], "The Poet's Lamentation for the Loss of His Cat, Which He Used to Call His Muse," *London Magazine*, I (1733), 579.

suggested that the loss of the one creature with whom the poet holds social commerce would relegate him to solipsistic rapture:

> Oftimes, when lost amidst poetic heat,
> She leaping on my knee has took her seat;
> There saw the throes that rack'd my lab'ring brain,
> and lick'd and claw'd me to myself again.

> Then, friends, indulge my grief, and let me mourn;
> My cat is gone, ah! never to return,
> Now in my study all the tedious night,
> Alone I sit, and unassisted write:
> Look often round (O greatest cause of pain)
> And view the num'rous labours of my brain.

By Green's design the culminating vanity of "The Poet's Lamentation" was that, deprived of his muse and armed with the knowledge that his work will be rat fodder, the poet persisted in writing. His absurd lament would testify to the futility of his labors.

Green's second satire, "On Mr. B[yles]'s Singing an Hymn of His Own Composing, at Sea, on a Voyage from Boston to an Interview with the Indians in New England," contained two parts: a ten-quatrain explanation of the motive and circumstance of Byles's composing his famous "Hymn at Sea" and a five-quatrain parody of the hymn. According to Byles's own report, the hymn was composed shipboard on an expedition upon which he served as chaplain under duress, since Governor Belcher had weighed anchor when his reverend nephew was visiting shipboard in Boston harbor. Deprived of his psalmbook, Byles had transformed his experience of the majesty of the ocean into a hymn in the style of Isaac Watts:

> Thy Pow'r produc'd this mighty Frame,
> Aloud to thee the Tempests roar,
> Or softer breezes tune thy name
> Gently along the shelly shore.[54]

In Green's travesty, the contrasting moments of softness and might are recast to highlight the impertinent decorativeness of the former and the hyperbole of the latter:

54. Matthew Byles, "Hymn at Sea," in *American Museum, or Universal Magazine*, VIII (1790), pt. 2, appendix, 1.

From raging winds and tempests free,
So smoothly as we pass,
The shining surface seems to be
A piece of Bristol glass.

But when the winds and tempests rise,
And foaming billows swell,
The vessel mounts above the skies,
And lower sinks than hell.[55]

Green, as usual, fashioned the mock-sublime climax of the parody as a moment of subjective derangement:

Our heads the tott'ring motion feel,
And quickly we become
Giddy as new dropp'd calves, and reel
Like Indians drunk with rum.

While Green metaphorically vests Byles's sublime intoxication with the semblance of seasickness in the hymn, the introduction shows his drunkenness to be of a different order. There he seems fuddled with his own ambition:

In David's psalms an oversight,
Byles found one morning at his tea:
Alas! why did not David write
A proper psalm to sing at sea?

Thus ruminating on his seat,
Ambitious thoughts prevail'd;
The bard determin'd to compleat
The part wherein the prophet fail'd.

The humor here is more subtle than a cursory reading suggests. Every good reader of Scripture would have known that the book of Psalms did not lack sea pieces. Psalm 93, for instance, was regularly sung in the seaport towns of Christendom. The point was that David, the poet cherished by God, did not provide an ocean hymn. Green showed that Byles's obsession

55. [Joseph Green], "On Mr. B[yles]'s Singing an Hymn of His Own Composing, at Sea, on a Voyage from Boston, to an Interview with the Indians in New England," *London Magazine*, I (1733), as reprinted in *American Museum, or Universal Magazine*, VIII (1790), pt. 2, appendix, 2.

was to play the role of God's poet oracle. To remedy the failure of the first, the self-appointed second supplied "The part wherein the prophet fail'd." On shipboard Byles had his vatic office confirmed.

> Our modern parson having pray'd,
> Unless loud fame our faith beguiles
> Sat down, took out his book and said,
> Let's sing a song of Mather Byles.

So Green humorously asserted that the yearning for public fame fed at Harvard had reached the extravagance of imagining oneself the penman for a modern revelation. That the message of the revelation came from an all too human ego hardly needed emphasizing.

Mather Byles did not let Green's satiric sallies strike without a counterblast. Byles dispatched a manuscript into Boston's taverns, a parody of Green's parody. The reply attempted to rob Green of his metropolitan luster by recasting him as Grub Street bard imbued with the profanity of the tavern world:

> Long paus'd the lout, and scratch'd his skull,
> Then took his chalk (he own'd no pen,)
> And scrawl'd some doggrel, for the whole
> Of his flip-drinking brethern.

> The task perform'd — not to content —
> Ill chosen was each Grub-street word;
> Strait to the tavern club he went,
> To hear it bellow'd round the board.

> With vast amazement we survey
> The can, so broad, so deep,
> Where punch succeeds to strong sangree,
> Both to delightful flip.

> Drink of all smacks, inhabit here,
> And throng the dark abode;
> Here's rum, and sugar, and small beer,
> In a continual flood.

> From cruel thoughts and conscience free,
> From dram to dram we pass:
> Our cheeks, like apples, ruddy be:
> Our eye balls look like glass.

Our brains a tott'ring motion feel,
And quickly we become
Sick, as with negro steaks, and reel
Like Indians drunk with rum.[56]

The hymn that "'stiller Josy" sang praised the unholy spirits that animated tavern vivacity and whose manufacture provided Green's livelihood. The most notorious stanza of the hymn alluded to a crude jest rumored to have taken place in Green's club in which "steaks cut from the rump of a dead negro were imposed on the company for beef." Since Byles's parody defamed the tavern world through which it was circulating, there had to be some point or image that verified the picture of cruelty and crudity sketched therein — an image that would give even the denizens of the Three Horse Shoes or the Red Lion pause. Alluding to the infamous episode of the "negro steaks" confronted the readership with an irrefutable evidence of the depravity of the world in which Green's humor held sway.

The contest between Byles and Green occasioned a final exchange in the spring of 1734. On March 25, Byles anonymously published a paean to his wife of one year in the pages of the *New-England Weekly Journal*. Despite the novelty of a new poetic role, that of lover, the tenor of the performance alerted the antilaureate to the identity of the author. Green chided Byles for provoking the bachelor segment of the population into a uproar with his descriptions of hymeneal bliss:

In am'rous [verse you] have told the Town;
How happy 'tis to have a Wife,
Rather than live a single Life:
And what fine Things you've been a doing,
Since you for *Marriage* chang'd your *Wooing*:
And made young-Fellows Mouths to water;
Impatient to be coming after.[57]

This backhanded compliment on the power of Byles's evocation of desire had the effect of suggesting that literary talent of the minister of the Hollis Street church resided in erotic poetry.

As piquant as the argument of Green's reply was his headnote in which he alluded to the techniques of self-puffery by which Byles had risen to

56. *American Museum, or Universal Magazine*, VIII (1790), pt. 2, appendix, 2–3.
57. [Joseph Green], "To the Author of the Poetry in the Last Weekly Journal," *Boston Gazette*, no. 743, Apr. 1, 1734.

preeminence in the literary columns of New England's press. Green explains, "I had wrote the following Lines; agreable to the common Custom, I desired a Friend to bestow an Encomium on them; which he declined; telling me I might as well do it my self; and that not without a late Example." (The allusion was to the Dowding episode.) The implication was that fame in the print world, because it could be manufactured occultly behind the impersonal screen of print, was a dubious quality. In a few short years events would prove Green right with a forcefulness astonishing to the antilaureate as well as the laureate. George Whitefield's meteoric transit through the colonies, the eruption of the evangelical movement, and the popular turmoil occasioned by the revivals of the Great Awakening made oral performance the means to fame with a suddenness that was shocking. Whitefield's Pauline contempt for the ceremonies of sociability put the culture of politeness and its Christian apologists on the defensive. The assiduous cultivation of the press by the sons of Harvard no longer ensured the notice of New England, much less the world. Byles and Green found themselves allied in opposition to the enthusiasts. Green ceased his attacks on Mather Byles and turned to the New Lights:

> "Hail! Davenport of wondrous fame,"
> Let *Whitefield* come and drain our Purses
> And *Crosswell* load us with his Curses,
> Let *Tennent* sentence Foes to Hell
> And *Bushnell* strip him self to yell.[58]

If stripping and yelling were the requisites of fame, then Green would rather do without. Mather Byles, for all his vanity and ambition, at least had the commendation of learning. From the New Light perspective learning was a carnal accomplishment; one's spiritual condition was the main concern. Green mockingly incited the Christian public to "stir up your talent Gifts / For want of Learning use your Fists."

Mather Byles proved more circumspect in his treatment of New Lights. Unlike Green, Byles did not commit his contempt for the evangelicals to paper. Rather, his Old Light sympathies found vent in his conversation. Consider his jest turning upon the persecution mania of the New Lights:

> In 1773, the *Massachusetts Gazette* informs us, the town authorities purchased for Boston from England two or three hundred street lamps. The

---

58. [Joseph Green], "Hail! D——p——t of Wondrous Fame," *Boston Weekly Post-Boy*, no. 396, July 19, 1742 (my attribution).

afternoon of the day they arrived a gossipy woman who had adopted so-called "New Light" opinions, and was gifted with a disagreeable whining voice, called on Doctor Byles. Her conversation irritated and bored the doctor and at last in desperation he said: "Have you heard the news?" "No, what news, Doctor Byles?" she asked eagerly. "Why, Madam," said the parson, "three hundred new lights have this morning arrived from London, and the selectmen have wisely ordered them put in irons." "You don't say so!" said the woman, whereupon she hurried away to see who else had heard the distressing news.[59]

Byles possessed a genius for spontaneous retorts, for puns, for wordplay of any sort. They erupted uncensored from his lips in conversation. He became to his contemporaries "punning Byles." His jests were the humor of the town — repeated in assemblies, transcribed in commonplace books, recorded in the newspapers, and published in the memoirs of people of the era.[60] Even his tory sympathies could not dim the popular appreciation of his pert humor. By a strange irony, Byles, like the New Light preachers he deplored, would live on in public memory for his oral performances.

Fame for Joseph Green was never the motive for writing. He was one of the few Harvard graduates of the colonial era (Robert Treat Paine and Samuel Quincy were others) who wholly imbibed the ethic of sociability wherein the pleasure of literature lay in its vivid illumination of the moment, the company, and the mood, and not in its address to some posterity. Yet Green, too, won a measure of fame. His satire of the Boston Freemasons, *Entertainment for a Winter's Evening* (1750), became the most popular satirical work published in British America before John Trumbull's *M'Fingal*.[61] During his lifetime he was known as "The Poet" and enjoyed the peculiar honor of having rural persons accost him to write elegies and epitaphs. On one occasion he obliged:

A country farmer, who was bewailing the death of a faithful servant, had resolved such distinguished merit should not pass unnoticed; he therefore ordered a gravestone to be raised to his memory, and was recommended to Mr. Green for a poetical inscription . . . who asked him the

59. Eaton, *The Famous Mather Byles,* 123–124.
60. The largest collection of Byles's jests is contained in Ephraim Eliot, Commonplace Book, III, Boston Athenaeum.
61. See my "Clio Mocks the Masons: Joseph Green's Anti-Masonic Satire," in J. A. Leo Lemay, ed., *Deism, Masonry, and the Enlightenment: Essays Honoring Alfred Owen Aldridge* (Newark, Del., 1987), 112–117.

name and qualifications of this person, and for what he esteemed him most remarkable. After drying his tears, and suppressing his sobs and sighs, he replied, that this fellow was an excellent servant, he loved him like his own soul, he was a *choice* hay raker, none could *rake* better nor *faster*, except himself. . . . Mr Green having thus received every information necessary for the ground work, took his pen and wrote the following EPITAPH   Here lies the body of *John Cole!* His Master lov'd him like his soul: He could *rake* hay, none could *rake* faster, Except that *raking dog*, his Master.[62]

With such performances Green cemented himself alongside his old nemesis, Mather Byles, in memory as the most important contributor to Yankee humor in that half-century between Silence Dogood and the Hartford Wits. It is a curious happenstance that the champion of Christian belletrism and the genius of tavern wit should unwittingly collaborate in transforming Harvard in public recollection from the Temple of Fame to the Nursery of Mirth.

The Duplicities of Print

When Byles made himself New England's literary celebrity and Green parodied the enterprise, both men had to negotiate a world of print no longer under the watch and ward of Harvard College, for by the 1720s the prints in Boston had become public. The conventions by which authors spoke and audiences responded had been imported. Mastery of the methods of publicity was a requisite of fame. Mather Byles had studied the methods and knew that one must put one's name before the public. He was distinctive for the obtrusiveness with which he advertised his, and none of his sermons issued from the press anonymously. All of his public poetry in pamphlet form bore his name; not even uncle Cotton Mather proclaimed his identity so assiduously on the title page.

One must recall the conditions that generally governed the fixing of one's proper name to a printed work in the English-speaking world. If one sought notice in the world of learning, one proclaimed one's name (or a Latinized version of it, if one sought an international audience of scholars), knowing full well that one would be subject to critical scrutiny. If one's subject were controversial, one might publish a volume anonymously in the

---

62. [Joseph Green], elegy for the servant of Mr. Cole, *Massachusetts Magazine*, I (1789), 585.

hope of avoiding censure by church or state. If one spoke in the character of one's office — as minister, professor, judge, or laureate — one employed one's name or one's title: "Rector of St. John's, Nevis." Byles published as a minister of the gospel and also as the volunteer laureate of Massachusetts.

Yet Mather Byles did not restrict himself to the usual occasions for presenting his signature. In college he began appropriating other persons' names to praise himself. He also published satires and polite verse in the newspapers anonymously, abiding by the rule of authorial obscurity in polite expressions, yet bruited about the fact of his authorship in conversation, so none of his pieces appeared without its provenance being known. Joseph Green, on the other hand, abided by the rules that governed the literature of sociability; his printed writings were all anonymous or used the cognomen, an alter ego known to the tavern literati, Clio. He also fell foul of the difficulty attending authorial identity in the realm of print — names and cognomens are simply words on paper and can be appropriated by anyone with any audacity. Green's nemesis in the tavern world, John Hammock, a vintner who usually published as V. D. or Vini Doctor, signed Clio to a doggerel screed against the Freemasons so foul in its scatology that Green was forced to advertise his lack of responsibility to avoid civil action.[63] It was the sole occasion in Green's career when he came before the public under his proper name. Among almanac publishers the appropriation of one another's name and persona was common after Swift's famous Bickerstaff hoax, with Benjamin Franklin's hoax concerning Titan Leeds the most famous example.

Something should be said about the distinction between cognomen and pseudonym in the literary world. In England and America, the literary exchanges of the court and the club took place most often through manuscripts, which served as scripts for oral performance. In these writings authors adopted cognomens to serve as fixed personae during the life of the company. The assumed names were truly cognomens — that is, other names by which persons were known, because within the conversation a person was always addressed by that name and spoke through it to others. Aphra Behn was always Amynta to members of her cabal. Proper names were restored to a writer only as an act of valediction — when a writer died or took leave of the muses, when a company disbanded or placed the con-

---

63. *Boston Post-Boy*, Jan. 14, 1751. For John Hammock, see my "Clio Mocks the Masons," in Lemay, ed., *Deism, Masonry, and the Enlightenment*, 118–120.

versation of the club before the public in print as an act of summation. Upon the death in 1744 of Archibald Home, the leading poet of New Jersey, his circle in Trenton collected his works and those of the company and supplied proper names to pieces that had been written under cognomens.[64]

Using cognomens subserved the goal of belletristic discourse in general; it aestheticized conversation by distancing it from the mundane talk of familiars. Throughout the eighteenth century, the favorite cognomens in the sociable world were neoclassical, because they lent an aura of nobility to belles lettres. Next in popularity were names that served as descriptors: Veramour (William Byrd), a Gentleman of Virginia (William Dawson), or Philo-Muses (Nathaniel Gardner, Jr.). Initials were seldom used in the literary conversation of the sociable world but were self-designations used in addressing print audiences.

Persons whose principal literary activity took place in company retained their cognomens when and if they contributed to the public prints. Indeed, the recurrent use of a cognomen by a writer of belles lettres, before 1750, suggested his or her participation in the club and salon culture.[65] Problems arose when persons adopted the same name (Constantia, for instance) in separate local literary scenes and then both bore the cognomen into the broad world of print. In contrast, those who wrote to supply the press — the Grub Streeter or the colonial sponsor of a periodical — used pseudonyms, a variety of names suggesting salable identities, personae through which to speak. If one name caught on, one kept it as a durable resource. Ned Ward spoke his maledictions in a myriad of first-person voices until his serial publication of *The London Spy* succeeded (hence the legendary difficulty of establishing his oeuvre). Thereafter, he recalled to his reader that he was the London Spy. The print writer, unlike the belletrist in the sociable world, faced the task of creating a readership. The creation of this readership was approached pragmatically, with an author assuming masks experi-

64. The editor was probably Abigail Streete Coxe, a member of the circle. The collection was prepared by a scrivener in a manuscript edition. The surviving copy is "Poems on Several Occasions By Archibald Home. Esqr. Late Secretary, and One of His Majestie's Council for the Province of New Jersey: North America," Laing Manuscripts, III, 452, University of Edinburgh Library.

65. When two or more persons ventured from the sociable world into print sharing the same cognomen, difficulties ensued. Consider Sarah Wentworth Morton's problems when she found another woman was also presenting works under the name "Constantia." Because she was already known in her society by "Constantia," Morton did not wish to surrender the name.

mentally. Taking on a range of social roles permitted one's representations to approximate more closely the vox populi. The prose disquisition spoken by a distinct persona became the favorite vehicle for periodical writers. These writers commenced an elaboration of subjectivities, projecting themselves through a range of roles whose breadth and dynamism had theretofore been achieved only in drama. Franklin, before he was Poor Richard, spoke as Silence Dogood, Hugo Grim, Timothy Wagstaff, Abigail Twitterfield, B. B., J. T., Philoclerus, Betty Diligent, Mercator, the Printer of the *Pennsylvania Gazette*, Anthony Afterwit, Celia Single, Alice Addertongue, Y. Z., and Blackamore. After he was Poor Richard, Franklin assumed personae when circumstance encouraged it.

Print's liberation of a writer into multiple identities eventuated in the author's assumption of the character of a society. John Dunton's *Post-boy Rob'd of His Mail; or, The Pacquet Broke Open, Consisting of Five Hundred Letters, to Persons of Several Qualities and Conditions, with Observations upon Each Letter. Publish'd by a Gentleman Concern'd in the Frolick* (London, 1692) marked an ambitious expansion of the projective capacity of authorship. Dunton, a Grub Street bookseller, aided by Charles Gildon, personated a multitude of distinct subjectivities; furthermore, he framed these personifications in the readings of a society of wits, a club that robbed the post as a libertine frolic. The historical interest of Dunton's book consists in its brilliant demonstration of the power of print to appropriate the uses and figures of sociable belles lettres to its own ends. Here, after all, was a book that captured the manuscript communications of friends and intimates, employed the chief institution of polite society — the club — as a persona, and posited the control of the postal service as the image of literary power. This last is a matter of signal importance. We have already seen that the newswriter came to power in the republic of letters by positioning himself in the coffeehouse, the physical situation most convenient to public business in the city. Control of the posts afforded a similar access. The authority of a newspaper depended upon access to both the conversation and writing of public persons. When John Campbell, the postmaster of Boston, began the *Boston News-Letter* in 1704, his monopoly over the public prints would not be challenged until 1719, when William Brooker wrested the office of postmaster from him and commenced publication of the *Boston Gazette*, with James Franklin as his printer.[66] When Philip Musgrave

66. It is worth remembering that Campbell began by distributing handwritten newsletters to subscribers, using his franking privilege; when he established that there

supplanted Brooker as postmaster, he discharged Franklin and hired Samuel Kneeland as his pressman. Persons establishing a paper without a monopoly of the post confronted logistical difficulties that only talent, the subsidy of a political party, and entrée with the major ship captains (the carriers of international news) could overcome.

Old Janus

James Franklin's publication of the *New-England Courant* in 1721, after his dismissal as printer of the *Boston Gazette*, must be understood as something of an adventure. Originally designed to be the organ of a party resisting the practice of inoculation, the *Courant* had overcome its exclusion from the mails by being controversial and by adopting the methods of the masters of periodical writing, Richard Steele and Joseph Addison. From Steele's *Tatler* the *Courant* had taken the idea of serving as a forum for public correspondence. Instead of merely extracting news from private letters or the London newspapers, Franklin invited literate persons to communicate with one another in the columns of the *Courant*. In 1722, when the controversy over inoculation had been exhausted and when James Franklin had been proscribed from publishing the paper, the paper had transmuted further, presenting its pieces as the proceedings of a club; the idea had been cribbed, of course, from Addison's Spectator Club. The method of the paper had been revised to conform with the sociable intentions of a club. "The present Undertaking . . . is designed purely for the Diversion and Merriment of the Reader. Pieces of Pleasancy and Mirth have a secret Charm in them to allay the Heats and Humors of our Spirits, and to make a Man forget his restless Resentments." This program explicitly disavowed the ways of Grub Street — of marshaling print to the service of profanation and malice: "Long has the Press groaned in bringing forth an hateful, but numerous Brood of Party Pamphlets, malicious Scribbles, and Billingsgate Ribaldry."[67] In place of profanation, "the main Design of this Weekly Paper would [   ] entertain the Town with the most comical and diverting Incidents of Humane Life, which in so large a Place as *Boston;* will not fail of a universal Exemplification." the *New-*

---

existed a hunger for news in outlying regions of New England, he resorted in 1704 to print.

67. Norman S. Grabo, "The Journalist as Man of Letters," in J. A. Leo Lemay, ed., *Reappraising Benjamin Franklin: A Bicentennial Perspective* (Newark, Del., 1993), 32–34; *New-England Courant*, no. 80, Feb. 11, 1723.

England Courant had announced (somewhat disingenuously) that it would perform in Boston that pacification of the prints that Steele and Addison had performed in London using the same means: infusing the politeness of belles lettres into the print world. Author and reader would be connected in printed communications that took the form of the conversation of a club. The strategy became a favorite of colonists who established newspapers in the 1730s. The *South-Carolina Gazette* had its "Meddler's Club," the *Virginia Gazette* had its Monitor Club, the *Weekly Rehearsal* in Boston had its Society of Gentlemen.

What were the consequences of periodicals' widespread adoption of the persona of the club? By metaphorizing the reading public as club, the newswriters collapsed the distance between the private society and society at large. The power of metaphor and pervasiveness of print connected a readership in a new social contract. By refiguring the intercourse of society at large as the exchanges of a friendly circle, the party animosities that troubled the public spirit were elided, and, in their place, a politics of sympathy was established. This politics of sympathy relied upon (as belles lettres did) a sense of community grounded in a shared experience of pleasure. The editor of the *New-England Courant* indicated precisely whence the stimulation would derive — from representing in print "the most comical and diverting Incidents of Humane Life." Incident became comic when apprehended from that distance that rendered it sufficiently general to seem exemplary of "Humane Life." This distance could be achieved only at the cost of surrendering one's proper name upon entry into print. Bearing one's proper name into the conversation posed the question whether one's vantage was to one's advantage. "In this Matter we desire the Favour of you to suffer us to hold our Tongues." The new social contract required a universal displacement of participants into alter egos; each speaker must generalize himself before generalizing about others. In the *New-England Courant* this compact was kept scrupulously.

In the imaginary club that conversed in the pages of the renovated *Courant* one character was granted special prominence. He was "a Doctor in the chair," or "a perpetual Dictator." This superintending personality was "old Janus . . . a Man of such remarkable *Opticks*, as to look two ways at once." The importance for Augustan aesthetics of the idea of spectatorship has long been acknowledged by historians. Even in our brief excursion in the region of belles lettres we have detected one of the major turns in the literary treatment of spectation during the period when we noticed the supplanting of the *London Spy* by the *Spectator* — the alien onlooker by the bystander who belongs — as the persona through which print bore witness to the life of the metropolis. What further development is signified in this character who looks two ways at once? The *Courant* explained the special character of Janus by analogy to the act of interpretation:

> There is nothing in which Mankind reproach themselves more than in their Diversity of Opinions. Every Man sets himself above another in his own Opinion, and there are not two Men in the World whose Sentiments are alike in every thing. Hence it comes to pass, that the same Passages in the Holy Scriptures or the Works of the Learned, are wrested to the meaning of two opposite Parties, of contrary Opinions, as if the Passages they recite were like our Master *Janus*, looking *two ways at once*, or like Lawyers, who with equal Force of Argument, can plead either for the *Plaintiff* or *Defendant*.[68]

The perpetual dictator of the *Courant* club was print itself. In the person of Janus the equivocal meaning of printed texts was metaphorized. In oral performance, clarification and specification of meaning occur by listeners' questioning a speaker. Tone of voice, too, conveys much lost to the page. The printed passage, in contrast, gives up its meanings in light of the reader's foreunderstanding ("opinion"), constrained in the hermeneutic circle. Since readers' opinions do not coincide on all points, the encounters with printed texts occasion different findings.

Of persons engaged in the act of publication, printers had special reason to stress the equivocal meaning of printed writings. Since authorship was disguised, the one known actor in publication was usually the printer. If the civil authorities were offended by a writing, they held the printer responsible for what appeared. James Franklin's stint in the Boston jail attested to this state of affairs. By insisting that texts could be construed differently, the printer called into question the interpretation that threatened his liberty. As the figure most interested in propounding the view that the meaning of printed texts was equivocal, the printer had been emblematically associated with the figure of Janus in the graphic arts. He appears as the two-headed god in "The Art and Mystery of Printing," presiding over a press manned by beasts and devils. The shop displays the drying sheets of half a dozen partisan papers, an edition of Rochester's poems *Onania*, and the most recent sheet, *Cases of Impotency*. In the rafters above the shop the

68. *New-England Courant*, no. 81, Feb. 18, 1723.

owl of wisdom looks down quizzically. The historical point of the engraving's critique is well conveyed: the printer who traditionally presided over the engine of learning now supervises the spread of Grub Street's profanations. In effect the role of print in ameliorating culture became equivocal.

The effect of that equivocality was to pluralize meaning in a culture. Take the case of learning in New England. Harvard College's proprietary dominion over the realm of learning was directly challenged by the notions of polite learning promulgated by the *New-England Courant*. The *Courant* writers attacked the pretenses of the Cambridge scholars at their most vulnerable point — their literary accomplishment. Since literary skill had traditionally been judged in New England on the basis of a writer's mastery of the elegy, the *Courant* writers made Harvard's elegiac practice appear to be provincial and archaic. The collegians' homespun mourning doggerel they dubbed "Kitelic" poetry after a particularly threadbare elegy penned by Dr. John Herwick in honor of Mehitebell Kittel of Salem. If a Harvard poet assumed a more metropolitan style of grieving, the *Courant* characterized the elegy as a rote exercise in disposing images cribbed from Joshua Poole's *English Parnassus* according to the rules for elegy laid down by Edward Bysshe's *Art of English Poetry*. Benjamin Franklin's contribution to the paper war, Silence Dogood's "Receipt to Make a New-England Funeral Elegy," was the most famous in a series of attacks on the witless effusions of Harvard's sons. Hypercriticus in issue 67 supplied a historical overview of the New England elegy, showing how the dullness of old John Danforth had been absorbed by the younger generation of Harvard elegists, personified by Amos Throop. Tibullus in 105 satirized three elegies by J. Calf. In 156 and 158 T. S. showed how a recent Harvard elegy, "Pitchero-Threnodia," warmed over phrases from Dryden and Cowley, adding awkward ejaculations as its only original contribution to the message. In the *Courant*'s campaign the critical strategy was invariably the same — show that beneath the facade of a learned man of parts lay the visage of a dull provincial. That is, Janus showed every rival to be Janus-faced.

The *Courant* employed the technique of imputing duplicity to the character of a rival as early as its third issue. The newswriters might have adopted the strategy from the first of the paper's Harvard-trained opponents, the Reverend Thomas Walter. In the guise of Zechariah Touchstone, this nephew of Cotton Mather lashed out at the paper with his *Little-Compton Scourge*. He ridiculed "Couranto's" learning ("Selfconceit supplies the want of Sense") by dissection of his persona:

But to be sure get your self *Dissected* (according to your Promise) that the World may have a full View of your *Outward Man*, for you are a Misterious Piece of Skin, that cannot disclose your *Exteriors*, without the Help of Anatomy. And, Sir, as for the Dissection for the Discovery of the *inward Man*, the World thinks it needless, for that your Works declare, your *Guts are in your Brains*.[69]

By exploiting the picture of man as a being with an exterior and an interior life, Touchstone indicated that Couranto's pretense to learning hid a nature in which thought had been reduced to appetite. Couranto did Walter one better; he wielded the scourge to flay Touchstone, revealing beneath the surface Tom Walter and then revealing Tom Walter to be a libertine. In the pseudonymous world of print, the revelation of a rival's name constituted the extreme of aggression, since it forced the writer prematurely before the tribunal of public judgment. Couranto printed a ribald letter signed T. W. and recalled an episode from Walter's youth before his reformation by uncle Mather:

The very same Night (or about the same Time) that he wrote this Letter, he was with another Debauchee at a Lodging with two Sisters, of not the best Reputation in the World, upon the Bed with them several Hours, and this Spark sent for *Punch* to treat them with, and would have had *the Candle put out*, but they not having a Conveniency to light it again, it was *lock'd in a Closet*, and . . .

In order that the reader not mistake that it was a rake that was being portrayed, "Couranto" added an epigram to flesh out the portrait:

No Wonder Tom thou wert so wroth
   Since *Bacchus* did inspire
'Twas *Rum, raw Rum* and *Cyder* both
   That rous'd thy *Grubstreet* Ire.[70]

To call the minister of Roxbury a raking libertine, to represent Cotton Mather's learned nephew, the single figure most responsible for rendering psalm singing more beautiful in New England, a Grub Street hack on a jag was to make imputations about character exceeding impudence. In-

---

69. Zechariah Touchstone [Thomas Walter], *The Little-Compton Scourge; or, The Anti-Courant* (Boston, 1721). Franklin's printing of the screed against his own paper suggests that he wished to promote the newspaper by fostering controversy about it.

70. *New-England Courant*, no. 3, Aug. 21, 1721.

deed, the furor Couranto provoked forced James Franklin to advertise that he had muzzled Couranto—the Church of England provocateur John Checkley:

> Several Gentlemen in Town believing that this Paper (by what was inserted in No. 3) was published with a Design to bring the Persons of the Clergy into Contempt, the Publisher thinks himself oblig'd to give Notice, that he has chang'd his Author; and promises, that nothing for the future shall be inserted, any ways reflecting on the Clergy or Government, and nothing but what is inocently diverting."[71]

In November 1721, someone lobbed a bomb through Cotton Mather's window, presumably to silence his advocacy of inoculation. Franklin felt compelled to vindicate himself at length from the charge of vilifying the clergy and inspiring mob action. Shortly thereafter Cotton Mather bestowed upon the *Courant* its second face. Instead of being a polite company of cosmopolitans, it was "a *Hell-Fire Club* with a *Nonjuror* at the Head."[72] The paper war of traded imputation continued until the authorities arrested James Franklin in June 1722 for the *Courant's* sardonic comments on Judge Paul Dudley's election as councillor for northern Maine, where he did not reside, and repeated fusillades against the clergy. The arrest was celebrated in a verse satire "Thrust into the Grate by an Unknown Hand." The hand might have been unknown, but the text makes clear that a Harvard muse (Joshua Gee?) was doing the crowing:

> *O Rare Couranto!* We justly triumph in your righteous Fate,
> You impious Wretch, that lash'd both Church and State.
> Father of Discord, maker of Division,
> Broacher of Strife, and sower of Sedition;
> Fomenter of Contention and Debate,
> And Feuds, in Family, in Church and State.
> What! Such a scoundrel Rascal take in Hand,
> To banish Vice, and to reform our Land,
> Boldly to reprimand our Reverend Seers,
> And Lug our Ghostly Fathers by the Ears;
> To tax our learned Youth with want of Knowledge
> and impudently satyrize *our Colledge,*
> To load our pious Judges with Disgrace,

71. *New-England Courant*, no. 9, Sept. 4, 1721.
72. *Boston Gazette*, no. 155, Nov. 12, 1722.

And fault our Rulers to their very Face?
Ah scoundrel Wretch! Your vile Courant has spread
Its Poison far and wide! No matter you were dead,
And your Courants all burnt, that have such Discord bred.
Your scandalous *Defamatory Libel*,
Is prais'd and priz'd by some above the Bible,
And more devoutly read: But yet we dare aver,
It does more hurt than Famine, Plague and War.[73]

The charges of libel did not stick, for the General Court voted against Franklin's indictment. Posterity has read the legislature's nonconcurrence as an endorsement of liberty of the press. In all likelihood it arose from the Old Charter faction's desire to irritate Judge Dudley and the party for prerogative. Franklin did not prove so lucky in January 1722/3 when the governor's Council prohibited Franklin from publishing the *New England-Courant* without the direct supervision over contents by the secretary of the province. What provoked the prohibition was an essay in issue 76 lambasting the hypocrisy of the New England clergy. Even Elisha Cooke and the Old Charter faction could not wholly countenance calling the reverend clergy two-faced.

The tale has often been retold of James Franklin's circumvention of the injunction — how he freed brother Benjamin from his indentures (rebinding him with a secret document) and published the *Courant* in Benjamin's name. The first issue published under the new imprimatur introduced the character of Janus as the genius of the *Courant* club. We can appreciate the jest in selecting the double-headed god to personate a paper forced, because of an essay on hypocrisy, to publish with the public face of Benjamin and the face of James kept private. From 1723 until mid-1725, the *Courant* maintained its two roles in Boston. Old Janus was champion of polite learning, inviting critiques of dull poetry (issues 97, 99, 100, 105, 108, 140) and the manners of the sexes (87, 101, 107, 112, 121, 136, 138, 144, 146, 161, 186). Old Janus was also the scandalmonger and fomenter of contention, advancing attacks upon New England filiopietism (93, 129), the polity of Congregationalism (130, 132, 135), magistrates (103, 149, 151, 154), the militia (163, 164), and Harvard scholars (50, 67, 83). In mid-1725, perhaps because of Benjamin's departure, the *Courant* began to lose vitality. Old Janus disappeared from the pages. From October 9 through Decem-

73. *New-England Courant*, no. 50, July 16, 1722; and see also [Joshua Gee], "On the Foregoing," in *A Collection of Poems: By Several Hands*, 11–13.

ber 25 every issue of the paper was devoted to republishing a Grub Street criminal biography, *The Life of Jonathan Wild*, London's underworld mastermind. Since the book was available from local booksellers, James was committing suicide with his subscription list. In June 1726 the paper expired. In an exquisite piece of irony the Harvard poet Mather Byles had the last word on the paper, offering "An Elegy on the Long Expected Death of Old Janus."

I Mourn, alas! for in the grave is laid
Old rev'rend JANUS with his double head.
Assist, ye nine, my mournful song inspire,
And thou, O *Bacchus*, and thy gen'rous fire;
Let high *Parnassus* weep in ev'ry place,
And let each summit celebrate a face:
Tears from all *Argus'* eyes this death demands,
While griev'd *Briareus* wrings his hundred hands.

Mourn, all ye scribblers who attempted fame,
Screen'd by the umbrage of his pow'rful name:
Whose works now cease each rolling weed to rise,
A grateful cov'ring over smoking pies;
Or when a squib a holliday declares,
To mount in air, and blaze among the stars.
You, woeful *Wights!* his lost protection mourn,
And let your griefs flow plenteous o'er his urn;
Alas! no more shall your bright souls be shown,
In foreign shapes, and features not your own:
No more you'll write beneath his shade conceal'd,
But in full dulness be abroad reveal'd.[74]

Byles memorialized precisely those aspects of Old Janus new to the world of provincial letters: his mystification of authorial identity and his sponsorship of polite literature.

If Janus symbolized the mystery of identity with which printing cloaked the author, Proteus Echo symbolized the surmimetic potentiality opened up by printing. In the introduction to the series, Proteus Echo declared, "To such a Perfection am I arrived in the Art of Mimickry, that I am able

---

74. [Mather Byles], "An Elegy on the Long Expected Death of Old Janus," in *A Collection of Poems: By Several Hands*, 9 (the poem had circulated in manuscript for several years).

not only to take any sound I hear, but have a Faculty of looking like any Body I think fit." The introduction's epigraph taken from Ovid's *Metamorphoses* — "Sunt quibus in plures ius est transire figuras" ("Some have the power to change into many shapes") — suggested the extravagance that Proteus Echo's transformations could assume.[75] Proteus Echo experimented with impossible narrators, for instance, presenting the memoirs of a piece of wood in issue 6. Yet the protean powers of Proteus Echo were not exercised on experiments in alien subjectivity so much as presiding over metamorphosing of Boston into the sociable world. And to do this Proteus Echo favored one guise over all others — that of the polite Christian gentleman who brokered the conversation of Boston's beau monde.

75. Proteus Echo no. 1, *New-England Weekly Journal*, no. 3, Apr. 10, 1727.

8

Gaining Admission

In late July 1739 a young gentleman stepped off a New York trading vessel at the wharf in Speightstown, Barbados. His fine dress, despite the summer heat, advertised his status. His ruddy, even-featured face and candid expression invited approach. One was struck in particular by the stranger's remarkably straight teeth, a rare possession in the Sugar Islands. He showed them off when he spoke, and he spoke volubly and well: "His Discourse is polite, and he is of a spritely Look and Gesture." The gentleman gave his name to the port authorities, "Gilbert Burnet," and displayed a letter of introduction bearing an image of the great seal of Massachusetts. He was immediately accorded those courtesies due a son of ex-governor William Burnet of Massachusetts. He was feted at the plantations of the local gentry. When one of the principal Jewish merchants on the island secured Burnet as guest of honor for the wedding of his heir, he deemed it a social coup. Imagine Mr. Lopez's surprise when a substantial sum of money disappeared during the ceremony while Mr. Burnet was alone in the house nursing a headache. Lopez and several guests attacked Mr. Burnet and had him arrested, but no cash was found upon his person. Public indignation at Burnet's treatment grew violent; a mob burned the local synagogue and drove the Jews out of town. Mr. Burnet was released on bond and enjoyed the hospitality of his bondsmen until news of the incident reached Boston. Word was sent back that no member of the Burnet family had gone to the West Indies. Furthermore, Bostonians speculated that the sham gentleman was none other than Tom Bell, the Harvard-educated rogue and confidence man. Burnet / Bell was captured attempting to escape the island. As a disconsolate bondsman wrote, "He owes about Two hundred and fifty

Pounds to several People; if he had got off, his Intentions were to *Jamaica*, there he would have got larger Sums than here, being well equipped with several costly Suits of Cloaths, one of black Velvet."[1]

Tom Bell's modus operandi suggests a great deal about the ways a male stranger gained admission to the company of the genteel in the colonies. His habit of adopting the role of an itinerating son of a famous family (Bell was at various times a Livingston, Winthrop, De Lancey, Wendell, Hutchinson, and Middleton), his cultivation of a fashionable appearance (clothes were favorite items of theft), and his displays of wit and learning (Harvard's contribution to his livelihood) suggest certain features of self-presentation that contributed to being accepted by a colonial elite. Since Bell was concerned only with gaining that degree of acceptability that enabled him to borrow or steal, and run, his adventures afford only a tantalizing first glimpse of assimilating into colonial society.[2] In order to understand how an immigrant transmuted himself into a local fixture, one must examine other case histories — histories that reveal the procedures and pitfalls of assimilation and detail the crucial contributions made by literary skill, wit, and manners in earning the embrace of ruling elites.

In societies as volatile as the British American port cities, the rites of admission were administered decisively and speedily. If one had relatives who belonged to the gentility, if one carried proper letters of introduction or professional certificates, if one belonged to the Freemasons, the Royal Navy, the Society for the Propagation of the Gospel in Foreign Parts, or any other transatlantic institution, if one was not notorious, and if one performed well in public arenas, then the embrace by local society could be swift. Town elites flourished by incorporating the most talented or best-connected newcomers. To understand how a man installed himself into a provincial elite, Dr. Thomas Dale's supremely successful penetration of the upper stratum of Charleston society in 1732 is our handbook.[3] Dale's

1. *Boston Evening-Post*, no. 227, Dec. 10, 1739, no. 437, Dec. 19, 1743; Clifford K. Shipton, *Biographical Sketches of Those Who Attended Harvard College in the Classes 1731–1735*, Sibley's Harvard Graduates, IX (Boston, 1956), 377.

2. A list of his aliases was provided in a warning notice published in the *Boston Weekly News-Letter*, Mar. 10, 1743.

3. The most telling portrait of the volatility of elite population in colonial South Carolina is Richard Waterhouse, "South Carolina's Colonial Elite: A Study in the Social Structure and Political Culture of a Southern Colony, 1670–1760" (Ph.D. diss., Johns Hopkins University, 1973), revised as *A New World Gentry: The Making of a Merchant and Planter Class in South Carolina, 1670–1770* (New York, 1989).

history will lay bare the dos and don'ts of introducing oneself to a provincial city. It will dramatize the roles of conversation, good manners, and polite letters in making one's way and provide a chart of the complex social organization of colonial centers—the taverns, churches, clubs, parlors, parties, and official arenas in which one had to shine in order to be invited into the quality. Dale's triumph was registered in his letters to the Reverend Thomas Birch of Middlesex and London, a correspondence extraordinary for its candor about the mechanics of social climbing.

The Rapid Rise of Dr. Dale

In March 1732 Dr. Thomas Dale abandoned London, a medical practice troubled by debt, and parents agitated by his recent marriage to a woman whose intellectual attainments greatly exceeded her fortune. He and wife Maria sailed for Charleston, South Carolina, the port city nearest the richest botanical area known in British America. Having defended a dissertation in medical botany for his doctor of medicine degree at the University of Leyden, Dale hoped to supplement the returns from medical practice by manufacturing drugs from Carolina plants for the homeland. His father, Frances Dale, was a pharmacist in Hoxton, England. Uncle Samuel Dale, one of England's premier pharmaceutical botanists, provided a model for success.[4] Dale and his wife arrived in Charleston in late spring, and summer brought a virulent outbreak of yellow fever, which created an immediate demand for Dale's services. On August 1 Maria died of the disease.

Ironically, the death of Dale's wife removed the greatest obstacle to his local success. Reports of problems attending the marriage had followed the couple into Carolina. Dale believed these rumors sped Maria to the grave: "She could not bear thoughts of having been the Cause of my lossing my Share of my Patrimony, nor of the false and malicious Character that had

4. Thomas Dale, *Dissertatio medico-botanica inauguralis de Pareira Brava et Serapia officinarum* (M.D., Leyden University, Sept. 23, 1723); Robert E. Seibels, "Thomas Dale, M.D. of Charleston, S.C.," *Annals of Medical History*, III (1931), 50 (Seibels misdates Thomas Dale's arrival in South Carolina as 1725, instead of 1732); Miller Christy, "Samuel Dale (1659?–1739), of Braintree, Botanist, and the Dale Families: Some Genealogy and Some Portraits," *Essex Naturalist*, XIX (1918–1920), 49–69.

The identity of Dale's first wife, Maria, has never been determined. His Latin epitaph indicates that she was thirty-five years old at the time of her death, Aug. 1, 1735. A love letter dated Mar. 2, 1725, also survives, among the Birch correspondence, with the recipient unnamed.

been sent from Home of Her to these parts of the world, under these thoughts I say She could not support herself but now lies down with those, who rest from Care and anxious Life."[5]

Rumor could be a sharp affliction for a new immigrant to the colonies. If countervailing evidences were not ready to hand, the Atlantic's expanse kept a bad report alive. Rumor possessed an entertainment value. Notoriety of any sort risked a report in the local newspaper. The arrival of Tom Bell in any city, for instance, was sure to occasion a public greeting: "Notice hereby is given to the Publick to be upon their Guard, for in all probability, the famous, or rather infamous Tom Bell is upon the Line" (*Boston Weekly Post-Boy*). For persons less notorious, a suggestive notice (initials or descriptors, no names) appeared in the public prints, such as "A Hue and Cry, after an Irish Dear Joy" (*South-Carolina Gazette*), or "An Epigram, Occasion'd by the News of the Transportation of Two Lawyers from England, the One for Stealing Books out of Publick Library in Oxford, the Other for Robbing on the Highway" (*Barbados Gazette*). The slow pace of transatlantic communication could work in someone's favor if one's malfeasance were not generally known. A man could outrace rumor, leaving Britain and establishing himself in the colonies before the truth came out. Samuel Cardy, Charleston's principal public builder at midcentury, fled Dublin after misappropriating public money. By the time report of his misdeeds came to Carolina, he had already established himself as the most competent manager of large-scale building projects in the colony.[6]

Intelligence did not simply flow from Britain outwards; it often traveled from the colonies to Britain. James Ralph, Benjamin Franklin's friend, abandoned a family in Philadelphia in 1724 to seek fame and fortune in England. With the aid of Thomas Dale's friends, the Reverend Thomas Birch and bookseller William Meadows, Ralph eventually established a name as a writer. In 1732 Dale confirmed the substance of a rumor that was circulating about Ralph: "I have been assured here that a certain friend

5. Thomas Dale to the Reverend Thomas Birch, "Charles-Town Nov 17 1732," Correspondence of Thomas Dale, M.D., from Charleston, S.C., 1731–36, MS 4304, fol. 53, British Library, London. All subsequent citations of this correspondence will be by letter date and folio.

6. *Boston Weekly Post-Boy*, Aug. 22, 1743; *South-Carolina Gazette* (Charleston), no. 26, July 27, 1734; *Barbados Gazette*, reprinted in *American Weekly Mercury*, no. 914, July 7, 1737; Kenneth Severens, "The Irish Career of Samuel Cardy, Charleston's Master Builder," lecture, Gibbes Art Museum symposium, Charleston, S.C., March 1992.

whose marriage we doubted at London really left a wife at Philadelphia who now teaches School at that place, do not let this piece of news be made publick because it will be easily ghessed from what quarter the intelligence came." Dale's remark about the ability of persons on the other side of the Atlantic to guess the source of information highlights the curious way in which transatlantic institutions (the Church of England, the printsellers' network, the navy) were webs of personal acquaintance operating over five thousand miles' distance. Dale would see this truth dramatized three years later when a second wave of rumor about his English marriage broke in Charleston. "There are two or three little Stories about yr humble Servt. which have made him and some of his friends laugh at and curse the little malice of some folks, for the heaviest accusation that has been brought five or six thousand miles against me is, that I did not pay the parson who married me to my first wife, which had it been true as it is false, would not have carried any thing hugely criminal in it." Dale identified the origin of the slander: "I know it must come from Mr Meadows's Shop."[7]

Maria's death lifted from Dale the pall of rumor. It allowed him to turn what was, in life, a social embarrassment into what, in death, was a romantic tale of elopement in the face of disapprobation. Dale formed Maria's story into an elegant and affecting Latin epitaph. She was the virtuous heroine ("Fides, Prudentia, probitas, mores, pudor") who defied with solitary fortitude common gossip until she could bear the world's calumny no longer. Death released her to enjoy the sublime hospitality of heaven. Displayed in the burial yard of St. Philip's Church, the inscription (no longer surviving) stood as an attractive monument to conjugal loyalty. A copy of the text was dispatched to England for circulation. It would elicit sympathy for Dale among friends and repair the breach with his parents; in Charleston its eloquent Latin publicly advertised Dale's learning and literary ability.[8]

7. Robert W. Kenny, "James Ralph: An Eighteenth-Century Philadelphian in Grub Street," *Pennsylvania Magazine of History and Biography*, LXIV (1940), 219–221; Elizabeth R. McKinsey, *James Ralph: The Professional Writer Comes of Age* (American Philosophical Socety, *Proceedings*, CXVII [1973]), 59–78; Dale "To Rev. Mr. Gough at Mr. Meadows Bookseller in Cornhill London," July 8, 1732, fol. 194; Dale "To Revd Mr. Thomas Birch St. Johns Lane near Smithfield London," Oct. 2, 1735, fol. 61. Dale's work for the London bookseller Thomas Coxe in the late 1720s connected him with the publishing world and with Meadows and Ralph.

8. Dale to Birch, Nov. 17, 1732. Birch corresponded with Samuel Dale. Thirty-nine of Samuel's letters to Birch survive in the British Library, over the course of which he discusses the breach and the reconciliation after Maria's death.

The funeral monument was a traditional medium for fixing the social eminence of one's family in public view. The act of interment, too, enabled families to assert the worth of deceased members by the lavishness of the trappings. The number of gloves and rings dispensed, the elegance of the painted hatchments, and the sumptuousness of victuals at the wake all communicated the degree of a family's eminence. Historians of material culture have increasingly turned to graveyards and churches as indexes of social organization. The church building was one public space where persons of every social class had visual access to one another. In colonial Virginia's Anglican churches the church interior inscribed the scheme of social precedence in a community, with the reserved pews informing the congregation of a family's standing. Dale arrived in Charleston at a fluid moment in the city's church life. The Church of England's principal house of worship, St. Philip's, was under construction after relocating to Church Street from the corner of Meeting and Broad. By being a regular attendee during the period of construction, Dale got a reputation for devotion: "I am . . . very remarkable for going constantly to Church tho' they are half done, and for carrying a Greek Testamt with me."[9] The Greek Testament reinforced the public perception that he was a learned man. This perception was crucial in his professional competition with other physicians resident in the city. While his Leyden degree elevated him above uncredentialed practitioners of medicine in South Carolina, it put him only on a par with other medical doctors. His problem was to assert precedence among these professionals.

Dale carried into Charleston one credential that Charleston's other practicing doctors lacked, books bearing his name on the title page. In London he had translated several Latin medical texts into English for booksellers Thomas Cox and John Wilcox: Henry Francis Le Dran, *A Parallel of the Different Methods of Extracting the Stone out of the Bladder*; Jodocus Lommius, *A Treatise of Continual Fevers*; John Freind, *Nine Commentaries upon Fevers: And Two Epistles concerning the Small-Pox*; and Freind's landmark treatise on menstrual disorder, *Emmenologia*.[10] Dale's name on the title page proclaimed his medical authority while his introductory remarks

9. Dell Upton, *Holy Things and Profane: Anglican Parish Churches in Colonial Virginia* (Cambridge, Mass., 1986), 56–59; Dale "To Revd Mr Birch Preacher to the New Chapel in Hampstead Middlesex Charles-Town febry 8. 1732," fol. 55.

10. Henri Francois Le Dran, *A Parallel of the Different Methods of Extracting the Stone out of the Bladder* (London, 1731); Jodocus Lommius, *A Treatise of Continual Fevers . . .* (London, 1732), John Freind, *Nine Commentaries upon Fevers: And Two Epistles concerning the Small-Pox* (London, 1730); Freind, *Emmenologia* (London, 1729; 2d ed., 1752).

advertised his adherence to the "mechanical" school of medicine (which treated the body as an integral machine).

There were limits, however, to the authority of these imprints. The modest level of general education in the city hindered the formation of informed judgment. Public opinion might favor one physician's manner more than another's expertise. In 1734 Dale observed, "We have much less Learning or Encouragement for Letters, there being two or 3 blockheads, who can hardly write or read their own names who are reckoned as great Drs tho' not altogether so learned as Yr humble Servt." During the 1730s the professionalization of medicine had not advanced sufficiently to suppress the odor of quackery surrounding the art of physick. To earn respect as a gentleman physician, a practitioner had to distinguish himself as much as possible from the surgical barbers and Whacums that figured prominently in popular imagination. Brandishing one's credentials and demonstrating one's learning in public places elevated one from the cadre of medical "blockheads, who can hardly write or read." By such displays Dale, John Lining, and John Moultrie began ameliorating the status of physicians in South Carolina. Over the course of the eighteenth century, the status of physicians rose greatly in Charleston. In part their social exaltation was due to the constellation of talented doctors drawn by the city's wealth; in part, to the repeated dependence of the citizenry upon its physicians as waves of smallpox, cholera, yellow fever, and malaria broke upon the port and spread through the countryside. In a place as unhealthy as Charleston the physician was a welcome figure.[11]

Dale might have been singularly lucky in the timing of his arrival. The outbreak of yellow fever afforded him an immediate occasion to display his skill before the widest possible audience. Then, too, after presenting his credentials to Governor Nathaniel Johnson, the governor's wife suffered a terrible accident. Her injuries eventually proved fatal, but newspaper reports indicated that she experienced some relief from pain in the days before she expired. Though the attending physician was not named, it might have been Dale who provided the anodyne. Such a service might

11. Dale "To Rev Mr. Thomas Birch at the sign of the Coffee-mill in St. John's Lane near West Smithfield London," Nov. 25, 1734, fol. 57; Diane Meredith Sydenham, "Practitioner and Patient: The Practice of Medicine in Eighteenth-Century South Carolina" (Ph.D. diss., Johns Hopkins University, 1979).

For public resentment of the growing wealth and status of doctors at midcentury, see the two satirical verses printed in *South-Carolina Gazette*, no. 1097, July 3, 1755.

explain how Dale, a mere half a year after arriving in the country, could claim, "I have the honour to stand very Fair with our Governor."[12]

Charleston doctors, like the majority of British doctors, earned their incomes from treating patients or from salaried positions with institutions. In the American colonies, however, the shortage of cash caused great problems for service professions. "As to great monied Fortunes they do not grow here, we have no Currency but a little paper, and that not enough, whatever our Great Merchants and Userers may say to the contrary."[13] With more than thirty practitioners competing for what moneyed trade there was, the rivalry was intense. Having so conspicuous a client as the governor put one in the first rank of practitioners. Yet the governor operated as a client, not a patron, of Dale. Dale had to establish himself in the local market without the securities of a salary or a sinecure; he had to attract a client base.

Patronage mattered in the provinces, yet the absence of a hereditary aristocracy, the transiency of imperial officials, and the vicissitudes of mercantile life made the patron system unstable. To compensate, established gentlemen in the American port cities formed private associations named after the patron saints of the British nationalities — St. Patrick's Society, St. David's Society, St. Andrew's Society, and St. George's Society — to sponsor likely newcomers. On the Masonic model, these societies were affiliated with a mother society in Dublin, Cardiff, Edinburgh, or London. Unlike the Masonic lodges, the mother society exercised no oversight over affairs in the local clubs. In Charleston these societies held formal quarterly meetings, they adopted local taverns or coffeehouses as informal gathering places, and they sponsored festivities on the saints' days — feasts, balls, and skimmingtons (mock parades). Non-British residents, like the Huguenot French and the Germans, developed similar institutions, the French Coffeehouse and the German Friendly Society. The organization of these patronage associations by ethnicity indicates the extent to which the empire was perceived as an aggregate by its constituent peoples and colonies; yet these distinct peoples recognized the same means, patronage and sociability, for furthering the interest of their members.[14]

12. *South-Carolina Gazette*, no. 17, July 8, 1732; Dale to Birch, Nov. 17, 1732, fol. 53, verso.

13. Dale to Birch, Nov. 25, 1734, fol. 57, recto.

14. The issue of social organization by ethnicity within the empire prompted a debate in the pages of the *Georgia Gazette* (Savannah) during late 1764. Scoto-Britannico-

Thomas Dale, as an Englishman, was taken up by the St. George's Society, which met at Poinsett's Tavern in the city, a handsome two-story brick inn two blocks inland from the most active section of Charleston's waterfront.[15] The membership had a reputation for frivolity. Shortly before Dale's arrival in Charleston the society's laureate, "Dismal Doggrel," published a verse announcing a mock attack on "Fort Jolly" (a rival local tavern) to honor St. George's Day, April 23, 1732.

> *Twenty-third*, did I say! no-that will be *Sunday*,
> Excuse the Mistake — on the following *Monday*
> The Gates of *Fort Jolly* we resolve to attack,
> And, without Fire or Sword, that strong Garison sack.

> The Commander, we know, 's a tough militant Blade,
> And may not perhaps be so easily taken;
> Yet, as stout as he is, no Defence can be made
> 'Gainst th' Havock design'd on his *Fowls* and his *Bacon*.[16]

This is a sample of the low humor of masculine sociability. The announcement's single noteworthy element is its mock military dress, for it reveals how competition among the English, Scots, Irish, Welsh, and native Carolinians was humorously sublimated through the imagery of war. Ethnic

---

Americanus, a member of the St. Andrew's Club, wrote: "A love for one's country is a virtue, but I think it does not at all follow, that a love to one part of a nation of which we are a member, in preference to another part of it, is a vice, because the very same reason that induces me to love Britain better than Denmark, namely because the former is my native country, will induce me to love Glasgow better than Aberdeen, or to speak plainly, Scotland better than England, from its being more particularly the place of my nativity. These, Sir, are honestly my sentiments, and I think I have no more prejudice for my country than every man ought to have" (no. 87, Nov. 29, 1764). A. B. C. objected: "The intent and spirit of the union . . . doubtless was meant to bury in oblivion the distinction of Englishmen and Scotsmen; and the name of Briton, as it was to be general to bother nations, so it was thought would inculcate in every breast an undistinguishing and impartial love for ever part of Britain: If these generous views have been defeated Scoto-Britannico-Americanus plainly and honestly accounts for it, as he confesses that he loves Scotland better than England, and of course a Scotchman better than an Englishman" (no. 89, Dec. 13, 1764).

15. The building still stands, a private residence.

16. "Lines, by Way of Advertisement, to All Concern'd in That Honourable Engagement," *South-Carolina Gazette*, no. 9, Mar. 4, 1731/2. J. A. Leo Lemay suggests that Dale might have been the author of this verse, but it predates his arrival in Charleston (*A Calendar of American Poetry in the Colonial Newspapers and Magazines and in the Major English Magazines through 1765* [Worcester, Mass., 1972], 37).

solidarity served as an armament in the struggle for social precedence. Patronage systems presupposed a public life in which networks of persons with common interests competed for mastery in the public sphere. Dale availed himself of the advantages of the St. George's Society, eventually becoming an officer of the organization and a patron of a younger generation of English immigrants. Membership in St. Philip's Church and the St. George's Society advertised Dale's affiliation with the Anglican English element in Charleston. Yet for a professional man to prosper, he had to attract a clientele beyond his denomination, club, and circle of home countrymen. He had to engage with those elements that made up the broader public of Charleston. Fortunately for Dale, by the 1730s Charleston had a number of arenas in which expressions of a corporate public spirit were emerging — places where the particularities of religion, ethnicity, and vocation were attenuated in the social conversation. The most important of these arenas was the long room in Gignilliat's Tavern on the corner of Broad and Church Streets. Called "the Court Room" because the Court of Common Pleas regularly met there before the erection of the State House in the 1750s, the space housed most of the city's principal public diversions until the Revolution.[17] In the Court Room the city's music concerts and balls were held until the establishment of Pike's Dancing Academy in the 1760s. Itinerant painters and lecturers on electricity addressed the public. Important town associations held meetings there — the Charleston Library Society, the St. Cecilia Society, the Scottish Rite Masons. There the acting companies performed before the erection of the city theater, presenting Thomas Otway's *Orphan*, farces, and comedies. The Court Room's regulations and permissions differed from those of other city taverns. Adopting the mores of the inns at the English spas, the Court Room allowed women to attend public functions without any blot upon their reputations. For sixty years it was Charleston's single most important arena for competitive social display, the center of the beau monde.

Dale was struck by the love of social diversion found among Charleston's gentility: "We live very gaily and pleasantly here and find much more good Company and Conversation than I could possibly have expected." To cut a figure in the brilliant company at the Court Room was expensive. "I have been at very great charges in fitting up my House and pharmacy, burying my Wife, and dressing myself out the people here being extremely

17. Leola Willis, Research File, "Taverns," MS Collection, South Carolina Historical Society, Charleston. Her notes are largely concerned with "the Court Room."

shewy in their Dress, so that I am grown a greater Beau than Ever I expected to have made."[18] Henrietta Johnston's pastel portraits of Charlestonians of the 1710s and 1720s give a concrete sense of the concern for a fashionable appearance. In a likeness such as that of Mrs. Prioleau one sees a woman confident before the public gaze. Her beauty refracts the metropolitan canons of taste; her hair is coiffured in the court style of Queen Anne, and her clothing is imported, not homespun. That citizens from the Huguenot community made up their appearance in the English court style suggests the extent to which London fashion served as the unifying force for the aspirants to gentility.

The gentility's vanity about appearance and its indulgence in the diversions of the Court Room eventually earned rebukes from Christian critics. Josiah Smith was the Court Room's local nemesis. When evangelist George Whitefield came to town in 1740, he took up the complaint, thundering at the carnality of the public balls. Whitefield's denunciation of the Charleston beau monde probably contributed to the willingness of Bishop Alexander Garden to arraign him before an ecclesiastical court in Charleston during the Bryan affair of 1740. Dale and other wits of the Court Room harried the evangelist with epigrams in the local papers.[19]

Dale's characterization of himself as a beau specified the image he wished to project in the Court Room: that of a young, marriageable man of fashion equipped with fine manners and an easy wit. Maria's death had rendered him marriageable, money had purchased fashionable clothing, and professional life in London had polished his manners. His primary task in 1732 to become a complete beau was to establish himself as a wit. No

18. Dale to Birch, Nov. 17, 1732, fol. 54, recto.

19. Josiah Smith, the Harvard-educated minister of the Independent Congregational Church, was an influential apologist for George Whitefield among Reformed Christians in British America. *On the Character, Preaching, etc. of the Reverend Mr. George Whitefield . . . Preach'd in Charlestown . . .* (Boston, 1740) was the most important southern vindication of the evangelist published during the revivals.

My suspicion, based on stylistic evidence, is that Dale wrote, under the pseudonym Misanaides, "The Congratulation, Humbly Address'd to the Rev. Mr. Whitefield on His 68 Preachments in Forty Days, with the Great and Visible Effect of Meat and Money That Ensued Therefrom," *South-Carolina Gazette,* no. 330, June 26, 1740, republished in Philadelphia and Boston. His friend George Seamon probably wrote C——, "A Poetical Epistle from a Gentleman of this Town to a Friend, Which May Serve as an Epilogue to the Late Polemical Writings on Religion," *South-Carolina Gazette,* no. 326, May 24, 1740. Clues to Seamon's authorship are provided in Z——'s verse rejoinder, printed in *South-Carolina Gazette,* no. 328, June 7, 1740.

sample of his verbal repartee has come down to us, but conversational skill might not have contributed importantly to Dale's winning a reputation. In November Dale wrote Birch, "You must know we have a newspaper here, wherein I now and then insert a Letter, which has got me the reputation of a great wit and a great Scholard." The *South-Carolina Gazette* was still a novelty when Dale arrived in Carolina, begun by Thomas Whitmarsh at the beginning of 1732. Whitmarsh, who had been a journeyman under Franklin during his brilliant reformation of the *Pennsylvania Gazette* in 1729, followed Franklin's recipe for success: timely digests of foreign news, accurate transcriptions of provincial political addresses and communications, a column for local news, a broad range of advertisements, and belletristic essays of an entertaining and useful sort. From the first, Whitmarsh disavowed any parochial identification with sect, class, or ethnic group. He reprinted Henry Baker's signature poem for the *Universal Spectator*, claiming its sentiment as his own: "I'm not High-Church, nor Low Church, nor Tory, nor Whig."[20] Whitmarsh invited that cosmopolitan range of discussion instituted by the British periodical press with the *Tatler* and the *Spectator* and recently reconstituted in the *Gentleman's Magazine* (1731) and the *London Magazine* (1732). Dale accepted Whitmarsh's invitation. Since every submission to the newspaper bore a pseudonym during 1732, we cannot identify with certainty what came from Dale's pen. Two letters on manners signed Meznikoff are the most likely candidates. Whatever the case, to have won his reputation as a wit in the Court Room, he must have revealed his authorship in conversation.

Dale's skill as a wit would have its most celebrated exercise in January 1734/5, when his "Prologue" was read before a performance of Otway's *Orphan* at the Court Room. In the poem Dale assumed the office of civic oracle:

Prologue, Spoken to the ORPHAN, *upon it's being played at* Charlestown, *on Tuesday the 24th* of Jan. 1734–5

When first Columbus touch'd this distant Shore,
And vainly hop'd his Fears and Dangers o'er,
One boundless Wilderness in View appear'd!
No Champain Plains or rising Cities chear'd
His wearied Eye.——
Monsters unknown travers'd the hideous Waste,

20. *South-Carolina Gazette*, no. 1, Jan. 8, 1731/2 (J. A. Leo Lemay's attribution).

And men more Savage than the Beasts they chac'd.
But mark! how soon these gloomy Prospects clear,
And the new World's late horrors disappear.
The soil obedient to the industrious Swains,
With happy Harvests crowns their honest Pains,
And Peace and Pleanty triumph o'er the Plains.
What various Products float on every Tide?
What numerous Navys in our Harbours ride?
Tillage and Trade conjoin their Friendly Aid,
T'enrich the thriving Boy and Lovely Maid.
Hispania, it's true, her precious Mines engross'd,
And bore her shining Entrails to its Coast.
Britannia more humane supplys her wants,
The Brittish sense and Brittish Beauty plants.
The Aged Sire beholds with sweet Surprize,
In foreign Climes a numerous Offspring rize,
Sense, Virtue, Worth and Honor stand confest,
In each brave Male, his prosp'rous hands have blest,
While the Admiring Eye improv'd may trace
The Mother's charms in each chast Virgins Face.
Hence we presume to usher in those Arts
Which oft have warm'd the best and bravest Hearts.
Faints our endeavours, rude are our Essays:
We strive to please, but can't pretend at praise:
Forgiving Smiles o'erpay the grateful Task,
They're all we hope and all we humbly ask.[21]

This is a public poem; indeed, it attempts to define the public sphere for the province. To appreciate its civic mythology we must look beyond the conventional images of civilization's westward transit and the stage-by-stage improvement of the colony to discern the peculiarities of the "Prologue." It was significant, for instance, that the public spirit must compass both tillage and trade, overcoming the traditional division between the countryside (backcountry) and city (Charleston). The benefits of this harmony would then be projected upon the rising generation, the youth and maid. Success would be measured for Carolinians in the future prosperity

21. *South-Carolina Gazette*, no. 54, Feb. 8, 1734/5. He enclosed also a copy of his "Epilogue," in Dale "To Revd. Thomas Birch St. John's Lane West Smithfield London," Feb. 29, 1735/6, fol. 60, recto.

of one's posterity. The image of a British family, with a loving patriarch admiring numerous colonial offspring, presented a benign figure of empire posed against recollections of Spanish rapacity. (Dale invoked the provincial anxiety over Spanish depredations on British trade, an anxiety that would shortly erupt in the War of Jenkins's Ear.) The British sense and beauty of those offspring asserted Carolina's achieved civility. No distinction pertained between metropolis and province except that between age and youth. The nascence of the colony lent its situation the quality of romance embodied in the sexual potentiality of the youth and maid. The inclusion of both sexes in British American civic myths was unusual. Yet, given Dale's family paradigm of empire and his projection of the value of Carolina in terms of a posterity's riches, it was inevitable. More distinctive was his assimilation of conventional gender qualities (male sense and virtue, female charm and beauty) to his argument about the development of Carolina civility. The stage theory of empire envisioned the culmination of the work of empire in the coming of arts. Thus enterprise led ultimately to pleasure. Dale correlated masculinity with the sphere of trade and tillage, femininity with the arts. We can understand thereby the symbolic transition between the image of the virgin's face and the prologist's announcement that he and the players have come to usher the arts into Carolina with their performance.

Dale was a moving force in the attempt to establish a theater in Charleston in 1735. The successful performance of *The Orphan* enabled the erection of a playhouse two blocks west of Gignilliat's Tavern on Church Street. For his efforts Dale "was desired to write the Epiloge" for George Farquhar's *Recruiting Officer*." He obliged with a verse to be recited by Sylvia while dressed in a man's clothing:

> In truth Dear Ladies! 'tis a curious matter,
> To prove, *Tiresias*-like, a double nature;
> To bid farewel to petticoats and stitching,
> And, wearing breeches, try their force bewitching;
> From belle to belle with janty air to rove,
> Play idle tricks, and make unmeaning love;
> With scandal and quadrille address the dames,
> And strut the fair ones into wanton flames.
>
> But, faith! I pity *Rose*, poor willing tit,
> Of all her joys, and promis'd transport bit;

Her eager amorous soldier prov'd at last,
As *Cynthia* cold, or *Farinelli*, chast;
For how could I, alas! the nymph delight
Or how perform the Duties of the night?
A mere poetical hermaphrodite![22]

Dale's epilogue reflected upon the limits of art. Art could permit a woman to seem a man, or a man (Dale) to speak as a woman (Sylvia). It could even incite passions in people with its representations. It could not manage that consummation of passion identified with heterosexual union, "the Duties of the night." Its "mere" accomplishment was an unnatural conjunction of opposites — a hermaphroditism engendered by poetry, the emasculated masculine vocal art of the celebrated castrato Carlo Farinelli. In the theater the conjoint power and powerlessness of art became peculiarly apparent. Just as poetic hermaphroditism explained heterosexuality for Aristophanes, Sylvia's sham amours revealed what meaningful love might entail. Dale's playful exploration of the contradictions of fictive truth gestured toward the profoundest tension in his thought. For Dale the theatrical art metaphorized the unsettled circulation in the sociable world. He observed to Birch that his life was "neither Tragedy-Comedy or farce, but a medly of all three, for such has been my Life since the Death of poor Mrs Dale. I am sometimes Dr M—— or Sr H—— another Glysterpipe; one while Caesar, another Sr John Dale; one while I herd with quality and revel all night, another I converse with your grave Cits and go soberly to bed by nine."[23] The variety of society's demands and desires required that one play a multitude of public parts. Against the ever changing masquerade of social life Dale symbolically posed the family.

One wonders whether Dale suggested that the players inaugurate their Charleston season with Otway's *Orphan*. Having suffered within six months both disinheritance and the death of the wife for whom he had endured

22. Thomas Dale, "Epilogue to the Recruiting Officer, Written by Thomas Dale, M.D., and Spoken by Silvia in Man's Cloaths, at the Opening of the New Theatre, in Charles-Town in South-Carolina," *Gentleman's Magazine*, VI (1736), 288. Dale and Birch were both friends of Charles Ackers, the editor, and Dale suggested that Birch might forward a copy of the poem for inclusion in Ackers's magazine. Dale to Birch Feb. 29, 1735/6, fol. 60, recto. "The Epilogue to the Orphan" appeared in the *South-Carolina Gazette*, no. 56, Feb. 22, 1734/5.

23. Dale to Birch, Feb. 8, 1732/3, fol. 55, recto.

disinheritance, Dale would have been peculiarly sensitive to Otway's exploration of familial dislocation.[24] In composing a "Prologue" for *The Orphan* that projected the future well-being of the colony in terms of the formation of new families — the conjunction of the rising generation of youths and maids — and by envisioning the inauthenticity of art in terms of an incapacity for heterosexual union, Dale communicated the weight he attached to the urge to incorporate himself into some familial order.

Yet we may be reading these writings too personally. The association of political stability and the formation of good matches among the rising generation was an ideological commonplace among the English upper classes. Indeed, Dale's difficulties with his parents stemmed precisely from his violation of a conventional concern with making a familial alliance that would have economic, social, or political benefits. After the death of Maria, Dale did not allow himself to be governed by private affection in the choice of a spouse. As a marriageable professional man of exceptional talent and parts, he had an opportunity to ally himself directly with the families that dominated Charleston life. Dale permitted Attorney General Charles Pinckney and his wife to act as patron–marriage broker for him. They "have brought me into a very good and extensive Acquaintance, they have likewise made up a Match between me and a young Lady a very intimate friend of theirs, whose Father is [a] very considerable Man here, and was some time since Lieut. Governr." The young woman in question was the twenty-two-year-old Mary Brewton; the father, Miles Brewton, was the wealthiest merchant in Carolina. The rapidity (August to November) with which Dale passed from mourning to inclination to matrimony inspired some trepidation. On February 8, Dale wrote Birch, "I should have been married this time, but that our old Lady [Mrs. Miles Brewton] thinks it too carnally minded to think of any such thing much less to act it at this holy Season of Lent; wherefore you may think of the Stocking on Easter day next."[25]

When the wedding occurred, it occasioned a sumptuous public display. "The wedding Cloaths are ready on both sides, and do you think I shan't look wonderful for a Bridegroom in an olive-green Grogrom trimed with

24. For the cultural and political resonances of *The Orphan* in British America, see my *Oracles of Empire: Poetry, Politics, and Commerce in British America* (Chicago, 1990), 166–169.

25. Dale to Birch, Nov. 17, 1732, fol. 53, verso, Feb. 8, 1732/3, fol. 55, verso. A. S. Salley, Jr., "Col. Miles Brewton and Some of His Descendants," *South Carolina Historical and Genealogical Magazine*, II (1901), 139.

Gold and lined with a pink Italian Mantle." Dale's character as a man of fashion was confirmed. Dale did not describe the bride's clothing, either before or after the ceremony. Indeed, Mary Brewton Dale had only a tenuous presence in letters subsequent to the letter of February 1732/3 announcing his marriage, there being a single mention noting her avid attraction to him. More space was allotted to the two sons she brought into the world. Dale might have viewed his second wife as an instrument for bringing forth children; he was "expecting a good many being going into a fruitful family." At the time of marriage she was also of immediate material benefit, enabling him to improve his manner of living, for she owned her own house. Dale's cramped quarters before his marriage housed "four Negroes, 2 Dogs, a Cat and A Raccoon." (He crossed out the word "Negroes" and overwrote "Devills.")[26] Mary Brewton's building, Daughterdale, still stands on Church Street in the block between Tradd Street and Atlantic. It is an unprepossessing two-story structure built on the compact scale of the oldest Charleston town houses. The facade is devoid of architectural ornament. A single door afforded access on the street end. A carport currently occupies the space used by Dale for his pharmacy. The interior lacked the entertainment space found in contemporary merchants' houses, such as the Thomas Rose house five doors away. Nowadays the primary attraction of the house is that it harbors the ghost of Mary Brewton Dale, who haunts the premises out of a disquiet born of a hard marriage (the ghost tale dates from the early twentieth century and has no substantiation in the historical record). In fact, all evidences point to a successful marriage troubled only by the death of two small sons by disease. Indeed, the matchmaking Pinckneys increased their patronage of Dr. Dale after his marriage, sponsoring his elevation to the Carolina bar. After Mary Brewton Dale's death in childbirth in 1737, they arranged two subsequent marriages — one to Anne Smith, granddaughter of the legendary landgrave and governor Thomas Smith, the other into the powerful Simons family. Hannah Simons Dale, the doctor's fourth wife, was renowned for her hospitality and the brilliance of her conversation at the tea table she maintained for Charleston women.[27]

Marriage into the Brewton family and friendship with the Pinckneys gave Dale access to a more exclusive company than that found in the tavern

26. Dale to Birch, Feb. 8, 1732/3, fol. 55, verso.

27. H. S., "Verses upon Mrs. Dale's Death . . . ," *South-Carolina Gazette*, no. 887, May 13, 1751, is an elegy composed by a female member of Hannah Dale's coteries.

clubs or the Court Room — the parlor society overseen by the great families. One's conduct in the public parties predicated whether one would be invited into the homes of the consequential families. From the viewpoint of the established families everyone was a known quantity except the newcomer. Repeated scrutiny in public situations quickly determined whether the newcomer was sufficiently fashionable, powerful, or talented to warrant cultivation. Dale understood Charleston to operate like the British provincial cities. "Our Country is as fruitful of scandal as one of your Countrey-towns in Engld. because Here we all know one another of any fashion or Consequence, and we have so many publick or family parties." Once in the orbit of the families, one merely had to withstand the normal assaults of gossip. Gossip in a society that entertained itself with malicious talk lacked the potency of certain report; thus it was received more as an expression of envy than as truth.

> A person must take any disadvantageous Character with great allowance, for example some people shall represent yr hum Serv. as a tolerable clever fellow, and others at the same time shall allow him no more knowledge or Experience than a Cobler, the truth is we have above thirty who pass for Doctors here tho' they still want the participle, and their several Relations must support them and their Characters by all manner of means, besides in my Case there is more particular Envy and Spleen because I am raised so much above the herd as to civil Employmts.[28]

That Dale's professional rivals generated the gossip directed against him suggests that the doctor's success in business spurred envy. The novelty of Dale's practice lay in his determination to manufacture and sell medicines on a scale never attempted in Carolina. By establishing a pharmacy he augmented his income by selling medicines directly to the public. "I make shrift to sell a good deal of Physick, but when I shall be paid for it the Ld knows. I have a well-stock'd Shop, and at present a very good Shopman."[29] In 1734 he determined to get around the local credit crunch by "sending some Quant. of Drugs etc to London Market when I shall be able to keep Monies there." Dale also set up a distillery, supplying the local taverns with alcohol and perhaps manufacturing cordials. Dale's one rival as a dispenser of medicines in the city was the uncredentialed but brilliant James Kill-

28. Dale to Birch, Oct. 2, 1735, fol. 61, verso.
29. Ibid., Nov. 25, 1734, fol. 57, recto.

patrick. In 1738 their professional rivalry would break out into the most memorable controversy in the annals of early southern medicine.

Killpatrick's career in Charleston was less spectacular than Dale's. A native of Carrickfergus, Ireland, he attended the University of Edinburgh in 1708, leaving before he earned a degree. He attempted to make a living in the Irish towns as a medical practitioner before removing to South Carolina in 1717. His uncle, David Killpatrick, was already established in the city. The uncle's immediate assistance was needed because James lost his small store of portable wealth to pirates during the crossing. In 1724 David Killpatrick's death improved James Killpatrick's status in the world, permitting his marriage to Elizabeth Hepworth, daughter of the province secretary.[30] The marriage allied Killpatrick to the class of imperial place-holders rather than to the native-born gentry. One mark of this affiliation lay in his sympathy for the Georgia experiment. The imperial bureaucracy understood the strategic importance of Georgia as a military buffer against the Spanish in Florida and the French in Mobile. Most established Carolinians, Dale included, saw Georgia as a threat to Carolina's control over the Indian trade.[31] Killpatrick, like Dale, valued literary skill as a means of asserting one's presence in public affairs. In February 1732/3, Killpatrick published "An Address to James Oglethorpe, Esq; on His Settling the Colony of Georgia," in verse. His support for Oglethorpe would eventually contribute to his appointment as physician for the expedition against St. Augustine. Admiral Charles Thomson of the West Indies fleet thereupon became his patron, engineering Killpatrick's return to London. After a name change to James Kirkpatrick and the receipt of a doctor of medicine degree, he would win medical renown for his *Analysis of Inoculation* (1754).[32]

Killpatrick's ambitions in literature (as well as in medicine) were di-

30. Joseph Ioor Waring, "James Killpatrick and Smallpox Inoculation in Charlestown," *Annals of Medical History* (1938), 301–308.

31. At one juncture during the running publicity war between the colonies, Dale began collecting materials for a history of South Carolina that might have been intended as a fusillade in the the the war. William Stephens, secretary of Georgia, wrote of Dale in *A Journal of the Proceedings in Georgia . . .* (London, 1742), "I looked upon him as one of the most inveterate Opposers of any good that might befal it [Georgia]; and that he was generally so esteemed" (II, 340). Stephens details Dale's participation in anti-Georgia publicity.

32. *South-Carolina Gazette*, Feb. 10, 1732/3 (my attribution; the poem gains its title later); J. Kirkpatrick, *The Analysis of Inoculation: Comprizing the History, Theory, and Practice of It: With an Occasional Consideration of the Most Remarkable Appearances in the Small Pox* (London, 1754).

rected by a metropolitan vision of success. When in Carolina he addressed verse epistles to Alexander Pope pledging his allegiance to his dominion as chief British poet. Meanwhile, Killpatrick labored at his own poetic masterwork, *The Sea-Piece*, a five-canto celebration of the British sea empire, which he believed (incorrectly) would establish him as imperial laureate.[33] Dale's ambitions were the inverse of Killpatrick's. Having experienced the travails of metropolitan practice, Dale had abandoned London to establish himself as a colonial fixture. His labors bound him to the local scene; his writings spoke, not to London, but to Carolinians, to aid them in the creation of a public spirit.

In 1738 the outbreak of smallpox in Carolina brought the rivalry of Dale and Killpatrick to a head. A slave ship, the *London Frigate*, had discharged its human cargo in April on the barrier island; the usual quarantine procedures were not followed. Disease exploded through the countryside, spreading "so extensively that there were not a sufficient number of persons in health to attend the sick, and many persons perished from neglect and want." It was said that 1,675 persons (647 white, 1,028 African slaves) contracted the disease, of whom 295 (157 white, 138 African slaves) died. The Cherokees suffered an even more appalling mortality, losing as much as 50 percent of the tribal population. In the face of so virulent an epidemic, Carolina's few doctors resorted to the controversial practice of inoculation, instructed in the method by a surgeon attached to the Royal Navy squadron. Citizens objected on moral and other grounds in the pages of the *South-Carolina Gazette*. Yet the effectiveness of inoculation was statistically confirmed. Only 16 patients of the 683 inoculated died. One of these, however, was a patient of Killpatrick, a young girl named Mary Roche. Killpatrick had disagreed with Dale about the method of treating the girl (Charleston's doctors worked together during the epidemic). In a general essay on smallpox in the newspaper Killpatrick attempted to head off public criticism of his treatment of Mary Roche.[34]

No professional body of physicians existed to adjudicate the dispute. Thus the conflict concerning the correct manner of treating Mary Roche

33. David S. Shields, "Dr. James Kirkpatrick: American Laureate of Mercantilism," in David R. Chesnutt and Clyde N. Wilson, eds., *The Meaning of South Carolina History: Essays in Honor of George C. Rogers, Jr.* (Columbia, S.C., 1991), 39–49; *South-Carolina Gazette*, nos. 228, 229, June 8, 15, 1738; Edward McCrady, *The History of South Carolina under the Royal Government, 1719–1776* (New York, 1899), 180.

34. Joseph Ioor Waring, *History of Medicine in South Carolina, 1670–1825* (Charleston, S.C., 1964), 38.

became a matter of public determination, and one's rhetorical skill counted more than one's medical knowledge in the contest for public approbation. Killpatrick's newspaper piece did not quell criticism, so he published a pamphlet, *The Case of Miss Mary Roche Who Was Inoculated June 28, 1738*. Dale replied with *The Case of Miss Mary Roche, More Fairly Related*. The point of dispute — whether a blistering agent should be administered in the first fever of the disease — quickly became submerged in a mounting war of personal invective. Killpatrick supplied *A Full and Clear Reply to Doctor Thomas Dale . . . with Some Diverting Remarks on the Doctor's Wonderful Consistence and Exquisite Attainments in Physic and Philology* (Dale's skill as a poet was impugned). Dale answered with *The Puff; or, A Proper Reply to Skimmington's Last Crudities*, wherein Killpatrick appeared as a caricature lunatic: "Mad with revenge, he gather'd all his wind, / And bounc'd like Fifty Bladders from behind."[35] The Assembly's prohibition of inoculation on September 21 rendered the medical dimension of the dispute moot. Killpatrick attached himself to Oglethorpe's expedition shortly thereafter, leaving Dale master of the field in Charleston.

What cannot now be determined is whether Dale played any part in the political actions that forestalled the activity of inoculation's foremost champion. Would Dale have used his political influence to embarrass his rival despite practicing a form of inoculation himself? The most that can be asserted is that Dale, alone of Charleston's medical practitioners in 1738, possessed the political clout to have effected a legislative ban.

Dale's attainment of political influence marked his apotheosis in Charleston society. The circumstances of his elevation to public office in 1734 were remarkable. Dale had no training in the law and no experience in the halls of government. Nevertheless:

> The Governour and His majesty's Council looking upon me as a vir literatus and a pretty diligent reader they did me the honour to appoint me one of His Majesty's Judges for this Provinces, and a Justice of the Peace, and I was engaged to accept these Commissions, I have been obliged to make a handsome Collection of Law-books and to study them with some application in order to support my new Character with Reputation and Honour, and I have hitherto met with the applause of the publick. Who would ever have thought to have seen me a Juris Autistes,

35. There is some question whether Dale actually published *The Puff*; the quotation is taken from an advance advertisement for the piece found in the *South-Carolina Gazette*, no. 260, Jan. 25, 1739.

and buried in Cook upon Littleton. As to a Justice of the peace, I, like my Brethren of Middlesex, make my office keep my house, tho' with something more Justice than they sometimes distribute for their money.[36]

By his elevation into public employments by the Pinckney coterie, Dale became an actor in Carolina's political theater. He served initially as an associate justice but eventually was appointed assistant justice on the South Carolina Court of General Sessions. His place in the government helped his medical practice to assume semiofficial status. When the queen of the Catawbas required treatment, Dale was put in charge. Because of his participation in the government and his membership in the Pinckney circle, Dale risked forfeiting that portion of his medical business that identified with the popular party in the Assembly. During heated moments in 1735 in the battles over the prerogative, Dale experienced a drop-off in custom: "When parties ran high, I lost some of my first practise yet I have recovrd it with so much encrease that some days last week all three of us could hardly make up the physick fast enough."[37]

Dale's ability to generate income from two sources, coupled with his membership by marriage with the wealthy Brewton clan, made him a valuable ally. Members of the Charleston elite cemented their interest with other members by entering into bonds of financial obligation with them. By accepting another's loans, by signing another's loan notes as guarantor, or by subscribing to another's projects, one fixed oneself as a necessary participant in the welfare of a group. These obligations were undertaken with a double risk, loss of money and loss of friendship. "The greatest uneasiness I at present labour under is the several obligations to my friends, which I cannot easily cancel; for tho' I never got so much money in my Life, yet I cannot command so much as I want, and hardly know what fatality keeps me bare, indeed it is principally owing to L[e]nity and Good-nature, I cannot sue any Deb[to]r without being convinced of any knavish Inclinations, and my heart is so tender I must relieve if in my power."[38] The primary commercial disadvantage of being a physician lay in the reputation for greed one might get by denying treatment to suffering persons unable to pay.

36. Dale "To Revd Mr Thomas Birch St. John's Lane West Smithfield London," Dec. 19, 1736, fol. 36, recto.

37. Waring, *A History of Medicine in South Carolina*, 204–205; Dale to Birch, Nov. 25, 1734, fol. 57, recto.

38. Dale to Birch, Oct. 2, 1735, fol. 61, recto.

Dale's yearning for financial security probably accounts for his prominent part in the development of Carolina's first insurance scheme. Following the English model, Dale helped organize his circle of acquaintance into a "Friendly Society . . . mutually to ensure each other from fire." The method of minimizing the loss to houses and business premises from fire was to gather by subscription a pool of money (£170,000 sterling) and use it as capital for a bank that would lend at 10 percent interest. Theoretically, the return on the loans would recompense the original subscribers with a healthy 30–40 percent profit after a few years. Dale himself had £1,750 invested.[39] But all fantasies of gain would go up in smoke when the Great Fire of 1740 consumed Charleston from the Cooper River waterfront to Church Street. Dale's house was spared, but the entire insurance pool was paid out, bankrupting the scheme.

After collaborating in the establishment of the insurance scheme in 1735, Dale took a further step to secure his fortune. "I design to turn Grasier and Cow-penner." Using the six hundred acres of land in Williamsburg township granted him by the Carolina Assembly as headright, Dale became one of the many suppliers of the beef market near Meeting and Broad, the central brokerage for meat supplying the West Indies. On a second granted tract, a headright town lot in Williamsburg township — "The Best of all our Eleven new Towns and surprisingly settled for the time" — Dale set up a distillery.[40] Although every free male immigrant was entitled to headright land, the selection of the tract was a right of the Carolina executive. Thus, Dale's political connections had served him in good stead.

The oligarchs of Carolina, being themselves ambitious, understood the industry that drove Dale to establish a medical practice, a pharmacy, a botanical supply business, a distillery, and a cattle farm. Yet there were many industrious persons avid for fortune in Carolina who were not embraced by the ruling few. Dale's elevation to civic employments had been enabled by one talent that few in the colony possessed to a supreme degree: Dale was a master of words, an expert reader as well as writer. Mastery over texts was one of the warrants to rule in the eyes of the ruling oligarchy. Appearing as a "vir literatus" brought him to the forefront of the medical profession; demonstrations of his expertise suggested to Carolina's rulers that Dale might succeed in a second profession, law. The law was an

39. Ibid.
40. Ibid., Feb. 29, 1735/6, fol. 59, verso.

arcane text to master, yet its grasp brought to those who mastered it political power.

The master reader held an important place in the world of letters, serving as a receiver and conductor of ideas. While publishing a letter in the local newssheet might cement one's reputation as a wit and scholar, a profounder benefit accrued to one who communed with the finest minds of the age. Nearly every letter that Dale directed to England contained a request for reading matter: "Please tell Mr Cox that if he will send me any Books that you approve of I will pay Him very honestly."[41]

Before coming to Charleston, Dale, because of his medical translations, had been immersed in London's literary world, but his departure from London separated him from the center of the world of letters. Birch was Dale's liaison to the printshops and bookstalls that had once been his haunts. In letter after letter Dale pumped Birch for intelligence about literary matters in the metropolis. "I [than]k you for all Yr news, and beg you always to send me as much as you can about my old Acquaintances, and Authors and if in your walks thro' Moorfields and the Stalls you would pick me up some pamphlets and 2 or 3 penniworth of Learning good and old, you would do me a singular favour." Dale, to move his friend to compliance, would assume the mask of literature-starved provincial thirsting for news of the world of letters:

> For Fortune plac'd me in a ruder soil,
> Far from the Joys that with my Soul agree,
> From wit, from Learning — far, oh far from thee![42]

Certain of the letters, such as that for December 19, 1736, were wholly concerned with musings about "Acquaintances, and Authors." Besides calling James Thomson "the Homer of our Island," he requested titles concerning a controversy over the sacrament, letters by Shylock and Gripes, and John Jackson's metaphysical speculations, *A Dissertation on Matter and Spirit* (1735). In turn, he suggested that Birch read the report the South Carolina Assembly printed attacking the Georgia scheme, which Dale probably had a hand in composing.[43]

Birch was a force in literary circles. In 1736 he had already begun his

41. Ibid., Nov. 17, 1732, fol. 53, recto, margin.
42. Dale to Birch, Dec. 19, 1736, fol. 65, recto.
43. South Carolina, Assembly, *Report of the Committee Appointed to Examine into the Proceedings of Georgia* . . . (Charleston, S.C., 1736).

distinguished career as a biographer, having published *The Life of Atterbury*. His translation of Pierre Bayle's *Dictionary* had eclipsed all competing English versions (Dale served as an overseas subscription agent). Birch, in 1736, was turning his hand to the biography and collected works of John Milton, the first of a series of literary editions that would eventually include the works of Edmund Spenser, Sir Walter Raleigh, and the theologian John Tillotson. After becoming secretary of the Royal Society, Birch turned his hand to biographies and editions of the natural philosophers Ralph Cudworth and Robert Boyle. His four-volume *History of the Royal Society of London* (1756–1757) was the second great history of that institution. In later life he became the foremost documentary historian of the reigns of Elizabeth I, James I, and Charles I. Birch's acquaintance with operators in the literary world was large. His regard for Dale moved him to perform a range of literary services besides providing books and recommending titles. It was Birch, for instance, who had Dale's "Epilogue to the Recruiting Officer" printed in the *Gentleman's Magazine*. Dale, for his part, had writings by Birch inserted in the *South-Carolina Gazette*, spreading his fame.[44] Birch's celebrity in London served as a benchmark against which Dale could always measure his own rise in Charleston. No doubt it served as a powerful hindrance to vanity.

Though Dale became no Thomas Birch, nor even a James Killpatrick in worldly fame, he enjoyed as successful a career as any immigrant to Carolina managed during the first half of the eighteenth century. He came to Carolina in 1732 a failed physician in a problem marriage. He died in 1755 as the colony's chief pharmacist related by three Carolina marriages to the great provincial families. He had successfully projected his worth in every arena that provincial society possessed: the church, the bench, the legislature, the male tavern world, the mixed-sex public world of the Court Room, the parlors of the great families, the pages of the local gazette, the exchange, and the medical community. He was a respected jurist, a noted wit, and a paragon of learning. If the rise of colonial culture was marked by a growth in public civility and the amelioration of manners, then Thomas Dale was as important an agent in "the rise of empire and arts" as South Carolina had in the pre-Revolutionary era.

Dale's career is most interesting for the clarity with which it shows the complex of discursive institutions that must be negotiated before a man be-

44. [Thomas] Birch, "On Printing," *South-Carolina Gazette*, no. 57, Feb. 17, 1732/3.

came a social success in British America. It illustrates with peculiar precision the role of print in an individual's self-projection in society. In London he had worked for booksellers; in Carolina he had been the subscription agent for Bayle's encyclopedia. He published in both the local newspaper and English magazines. He assisted in the founding of the Charleston Library Society and built one of the great personal libraries in the colony. His professional standing depended upon his mastery of two literatures, medicine and law. He contributed to the transatlantic pamphlet campaign that his government waged against Georgia, and his appreciation of the role of print is attested in his sponsorship of publication of Birch's most famous poem in the *South-Carolina Gazette*, "The Art of Printing." Nevertheless, this standing in public depended on his projection of his virtues and talents in private society, where conversation and handwritten communications reigned. Success for Dale required that he consolidate his standing in his church, the St. George's Society, and the Court Room while making his name professionally as a physician to the public at large. Then he had to gain the parlor society of the great families and get a patron. He had to marry into the elite. Once installed in the government, through the activities of his patron, Dale had to reinforce his place in the oligarchy by binding his economic, political, and cultural connection with other elite actors in partnerships, insurance companies, party caucuses, and the library society. When Thomas Dale died, his eulogist in the *South-Carolina Gazette* understood the interpenetration of public career and private virtues of sociability and conversation:

> Yesterday afternoon died, aged 50 years, Thomas Dale, Esq: esteemed a Man of great Virtues, Abilities and Learning in general, and in his Profession of Physic in particular, in which he took his Doctors Degrees at *Leyden* in the year 1724 or 25: In his public Character, (for he has been a Judge in the Supreme Courts of the Province about 16 Years past) he always acted with great Integrity and Honour; and in his private Life exhibited a truly amiable Character, being possessed of many Virtues and Qualifications which made him valuable and agreeble to his Friends and Acquaintance, and without Envy, Malice or Resentment to his Enemies, for such, he, like many other good Men, undeservedly had; He was open, generous and free in his Sentiments; and from his great and extensive Reading had a great Fund to entertain in Conversation: He was a loving, tender and affectionate Husband, a kind Neighbour, a humane Master, and a sincere and hearty Friend, a Lover of true Reli-

gion, and a Practiser of the Rules, and Precepts of it; and has died as sincerely lamented, by all who had the Happiness of an intimate Acquaintance with him, as any Man ever did.[45]

An Anatomy of Hospitality

Not every colony built a metropolis or created an urban beau monde. Certain of the staple colonies — Virginia, North Carolina, East Florida, and several of the Sugar Islands — developed as agricultural countrysides, networks of estates served by modest arrays of trading towns. The families of the great landowners presided over the social lives of these countrysides, entertaining strangers and one another according to the customs of hospitality, the ethic of entertainment traditional to the European landed upper classes. Hospitality differed from sociability in several features. Whereas sociability promoted the free and friendly conversation of persons meeting in public space, hospitality organized social exchange under the auspices of a family in its household. Whatever hierarchy of authority governed the family was reinforced by a hierarchy among host and guests based on property. As plantation tutor Philip Vickers Fithian observed to a friend in New Jersey, the egalitarian table fellowship of farmers and laborers in New Jersey did not exist in the Old Dominion, where property was concentrated in the hands of the few. "Such amazing property . . . blows up the owners to an imagination, which is visible in all, but in various degrees according to their respective virtue, that they are exalted as much above other Men in worth and precedence, as blind stupid fortune has made a difference in their property."[46]

Hospitality tested the status of host and guest. Fithian indicated that in Virginia a visitor was judged on the basis of property, "posts of honour, and mental acquirements" — in that order. A college degree at Nassau-Hall, for instance, rated ten thousand pounds in the eyes of the gentry. A degree holder could devalue his standing as a gentleman if he proved deficient in "Dancing, Boxing, playing the Fiddle, and Small-Sword, and Cards." A male guest's first care had to be never to underrate himself in the eyes of the hosts; his greatest peril lay in inappropriate familiarity with a female mem-

---

45. *South-Carolina Gazette*, no. 853, Sept. 17, 1750.

46. John Rogers Williams, ed., *Philip Vickers Fithian: Journal and Letters, 1767–1774* (1900; rpt. Freeport, N.Y., 1969), 285–287. This letter dated Aug. 12, 1774, to John Peck contains Fithian's famous assessment of the plantocracy from the viewpoint of a middle-class New Jerseyan.

ber of the host family. Fithian warned his friend to give up all amorous ambition when in the employ of a plantation owner. Fithian's warning brings to view a second distinction between sociability and hospitality. Spa style had influenced urban heterosociability in the colonies by loosening the superintendence of chaperons and families upon the conversation between the sexes. At the public balls, and particularly in the masquerades, much could be ventured. In the hospitable world of the great estates, the scrutiny of the family could be escaped only with great industry or with the wish of the family.[47]

Hospitable conversation was not so witty as sociable chat. The presence of gentlewomen restrained masculine jest. Male Virginians cultivated the cockfight as a scene of masculine permissions, where swearing, gambling, drinking, and joking prevailed. Horse races and fish fries were lesser sites of male revelry because women could and did attend both.[48] The presence of gentlewomen proved so inhibiting to candid talk that Fithian endured six months of plantation conversation before he experienced as "sociable and unconstrained" a chat with ladies as he had since leaving "Home, and my forgiving Friends." For a temporary resident such as Fithian the restraints on conversation and the formalities of behavior could be endured as an experimental education in an alternative code of manners. For free-spirited persons whose livelihoods depended upon long-term residence in the hospitable world, its protocols were suffered with less forbearance. The Virginia of Fithian's day would spawn several satirists of plantation manners: schoolmaster James Reid, dramatist Robert Munford, and poet Robert Bolling. Munford and Bolling were scions of plantation stock who viewed their world while acutely sensitive to its absurdities. Bolling's 1760 diary of his unsuccessful wooing of Anne Miller survives as an exemplary

47. Ibid., 287. When Robert Bolling courted Anne Miller in 1760, he managed to secure some private occasions for intimacy when parents were away during weekend sleep-over parties at plantations. He indicated that among the elite class of "familiars" there was greater liberty permitted for access between the sexes. J. A. Leo Lemay, ed., *Robert Bolling Woos Anne Miller: Love and Courtship in Colonial Virginia, 1760* (Charlottesville, Va., 1990), 52–53.

48. These scenes are described and condemned by schoolmaster James Reid, in "The Religion of the Bible and the Religion of K[ing] W[illiam] County Compared," in Richard Beale Davis, ed., *The Colonial Virginia Satirist: Mid-Eighteenth-Century Commentaries on Politics, Religion, and Society* (American Philosophical Society, *Transactions*, VII, pt. 1 [1967]), 43–71. This satire circulated in manuscript; a copy is in the Southern Historical Society Collections, Wilson Library, University of North Carolina at Chapel Hill.

portrait of the problems troubling the courtship rituals of Virginia's hospitable world.[49]

When did the hospitable world come into being in British America? Although the consolidation of great agricultural estates was well under way during the final quarter of the seventeenth century in the staple colonies, the institution of a culture of hospitality along Old World lines was by no means widespread until the 1720s. Even in the Sugar Islands, where wealth and power consolidated quickly in the hands of certain families, the rites of the big house were imperfectly understood.

Consider the jaundiced assessment of hospitality in Barbados supplied by Captain Thomas Walduck to James Petiver in 1710. An urbane man of commerce, Walduck criticized the sugar planters with a candor that suggests he had no long-term stake in the island's welfare. The captain had a stranger's liberty of opinion. Writing his summary view of island manners at the request of Petiver, London's most enterprising seed dealer, Walduck pitched his observations to his correspondent's sure sense of urban civility and country hospitality. "The people to Strangers and those that do not live amgt them appear to be noble Spirited Generous and brave but indeed they are naturally covetous Pusilanimous and Cruel, they are very fond of new faces, and shall make noble treats to Entertain a forreigner, from one to the Other all over the Island, but afterwards, you shall find nothing in their houses but Irish beef that has been a 12 month in brine Salt fish dry Bonivess fair water or Cowjou worse than water."[50] Walduck's reduction of Barbadian hospitality to a hunger for novelty damned the society for a boredom caused by island insularity and social overfamiliarity. Twenty years later the publisher of Barbados's first newspaper attempted to put a good face on the gantlet of hospitality that a stranger had to endure.

> The whole Community is like a single Family. Each Individual is known to the rest; and as all are supposed to come at first with an Intention, and the Hopes of making or mending their Fortunes, so by a constant Intercourse of Business and Pleasures, there is an Opportunity of conversing almost at once, with Men of every Condition and Circumstance of Life. In that Island . . . the true Characters of Persons are soon discovered, and their Talents or Foibles seldom long concealed; which is partly owing to the Hospitality of those already settled, who it is acknowledged

49. Lemay, ed., *Robert Bolling Woos Anne Miller*.

50. Thomas Walduck to James Petiver, Nov. 13, 1710, Sloane MS 2302, British Library. All subsequent citations of Walduck will refer to this letter.

receive and entertain Strangers in the kindest and most generous Manners, provided they bring any Recommendations, or can give a tolerable Account of themselves.[51]

While Barbados might have resembled Charleston in the extent to which those in society knew one another, it lacked Charleston's public arenas of sociability. The dominion of familial hospitality over the social conversation in the islands was absolute. The stranger's character was discovered by the dominant families in business and pleasure; that is, in his behaviors in the market and in the plantation parlor.

Walduck had little favorable to say about plantation hospitality, indicting the hosts for presuming to a wealth and power that they did not possess. He wrote that the plantation houses that were supposed to give material form to the islanders' quality were ramshackle villas with

> neglected bare walls and unfurnished like an Empty Sepulchre the first room shall be pretty well furnished when they know of any Stranger Coming if there is as much furniture in the parish for they shall borrow of all their Neighbour's Chairs of one Spoones and forks of another, the bread they eat and the butter that makes the Cause is particularly provided for the day for they keep neither of these in their houses.

The splendor of a Barbadian household was borrowed, not possessed. Given the pains exerted by the planter families to appear splendid, Walduck suggested that the planters wished to seem worthy in the eyes of a stranger as much as the stranger did in the eyes of the planter. (Certainly no planter family would appear majestic in the eyes of a neighbor from whom it borrowed the silver.) At times the pretentions of the planters were not addressed to any audience at all but were exercises in self-gratulation. When planters died, for instance, hatchments and escutcheons adorned the casket. "They out do the Dutch in Heraldry for every man assumes what Coat he pleaseth or [that] the fancy of a vain Dream invent, and they are such unthinking Devills here that if two brothers dye the Year one after the other, they generally have different Coates." Heraldry in Barbados has degenerated from an archive of family emblems to a temporary display of glyphs of personal ambition.

Barbadian funerals, like funerals throughout British America, were so-

---

51. [Samuel Keimer], "Preface," in [Keimer, comp.], *Caribbeana: Containing Letters and Dissertations, Together with Poetical Essays on Various Subjects and Occasions,* 2 vols. (London, 1741), I, iv.

cial occasions, when the family of the deceased could assert its worth. Walduck, however, viewed such assertions of social precedence as futile because of the corruption of those attending and the disorder of the ceremonies:

> There is always carried to the Church 10 or 12 Gallons of burnt wine or a Pail full or 2 of Rum-punch to refresh the people (for a funeral sermon makes them squeamish) where as soon as the Corps are interr'd they sit round the Liqour in the Church porch drinke to the obsequies of the defunct, smoke and drink, untill they are as drunk as Tinkers, and never think of the dead afterwards. . . . After they are buried there is no care taken of the graves or the Church-Yards, Hogs has routed up Children, and Dogs carried away their bones the town people make fire of the rotten Coffins.

Walduck's sketch presents the paradox of a social occasion that annihilates society. The family of the deceased absorb themselves in solipsistic vanity. The guests debauch themselves to insensibility. Finally, even religion's profound community between the living and the dead dissolves into an indifference that makes grave desecration a casual activity.

Walduck, a churchman, was singularly sensitive to Barbadians' tendency to convert the solemn passages of life into secular revels. He particularly noted their tendency to remove the ceremonies marking these events from the church sanctuary. He was bothered, for instance, that persons married in their houses, "never in the Churches." Even christenings were performed in domestic settings. "I have seen fount and Common prayer bookes in some of the Churches, but never saw water put in the one, or all the Service read through out of the Other." Christenings, marriages, funerals — all became occasions of festivity rather than solemnity. For Walduck such indulgence in social pleasure seemed a vanity. For instance, love of festivity prompted families to postpone christenings until the season "when the hog is fat," risking the loss of an infant's baptismal entitlement to the Kingdom of God if it should suddenly die before the months of plentitude.

Walduck's caricature of the vanities of Barbados depicted the society's failings as provincial innovations departing from English standards in religion, morality, and politeness. Old stereotypes of London as the Babylon of luxury exporting its depravities to the provinces do not appear in Walduck's letter. On the contrary, the one commendable picture of Barbadian society provided by Walduck is the Bow Bell Club, a society of ex-Londoners (all had to have been born within the sound of the bells of St. Mary-le-

Bow Church) who celebrated by feast and reveal the civility of the metropolis on St. George's Day. Walduck judges the island's hospitality against this imported standard of metropolitan sociability. Deviation from the metropolitan standard betokened provinciality at least, creole degeneration at worst. Unlike Dale, Walduck could not speak of the achieved civility of the province.

Walduck realized that the struggles for precedence in the plantation ballrooms of Barbados depended upon a more fundamental and pernicious exercise of the prerogatives of class and race. To Petiver he wrote that Barbadian planters

> are unmercifully cruell to their poor Slaves by whome they get their living without a wet finger they never give them clothes to wear or victuals to eat all days of their lives but works them 18 hours in 24 without any intermission (it is a common saying amgt the planters that if they give 30£ St for a Negro and hee lives one year he payes for himself.) they shall be at 1000 times more charge and care of their horses for their pleasure than for those poor Souls wthout whom they would be worse than the Negroes — themselves.

Walduck unambiguously attributed the cruelty of the planters to their irreligion. Lacking religious scruples, planters felt little restraint upon their appetites for material wealth. Walduck's assessment was blunt: their "Discourse and Conversation of no moral honesty of no profest religion hardly think of God but in their Curses and Blasphemies." Against this hedonism Walduck asserted Christian cosmopolitanism and the morality of trade. His Christian cosmopolitanism can best be seen in his condemnation of ethnic boosterism. The rhetoric of the St. Patrick's and St. Andrew's Societies belied the true legacies of the European nations in the colonies:

> This nation were a Babel of all Nations and Conditions of men English, Welsh, Scotch, Irish, Dutch, Deans [Danes?] and French, The English they brought with them drunkeness and Swearing the Scotch Impudence and Falshood, The Welch covetousness and Revenge The Irish Cruelty and Perjury the Dutch and Deans Craft and Rusticity and the French Dissimulation and Infidelity and here they have Intermarri'd and blended together that of what Quality this present Generation must be of you shall Judge.

Walduck visualized colonial history as a process of ethnic mongrelization that resulted in the coalescence of the Old World's vices. His vision is recognizable as a jeremiad. Indeed, at the end of the letter, Walduck pronounced prophetic words of woe against the island. He would be the first in a succession of Christian moralists during the century who cried of coming judgments upon the staple colonies.

While Walduck's writing merits notice as a precursor of the literature of abolitionism, it commands our attention for its delineation of the differences between sociability and colonial hospitality. Sociability is associated with urbanity, egalitarian conviviality, innocence, the arts, table fellowship, and wit. Hospitality is associated with provinciality, vanity, familial competition, and hypocrisy. The starkness of the oppositions is interesting, given the fact that cross-pollination of the modes of interaction was taking place in Britain and America. In Carolina, for instance, where the larger plantation owners lived part of the year in Charleston, the country style of hospitality was strongly influenced by the fashions of the Court Room. Conversely, as the eighteenth century wore on, the sociable institutions of Charleston became increasingly dominated by the city's great families until membership in certain organizations became a matter of heredity. In 1710 in Barbados, however, the distinction between sociability and hospitality was a matter of moral consequence to an intelligent trader. A man committed to the imperial meritocracy of trade saw the importation of hospitality into the New World as a historically retrograde emulation of the customs of traditional hierarchies. Since neither estate nor custom in the New World warranted such hierarchies, the planters could assert rank only by arrogating to themselves the material symbols of landed station; to do this they had to seize wealth by will and by the violence of forced labor.

Walduck allows us to see why hospitality constituted a problem for those who did not participate in the staple colonies' elite networks. It suggests a troubling reason why the literature of hospitality is so insistent upon asserting the virtues of the host and family in treating the stranger. Only where a stranger is subjected to the host's power is the virtue of a host an issue. Hospitality admits the stranger to the benefits of society, roof, and table by forcing the guest to enter a contract of voluntary subordination to the host and his family.

9

Toward the
Polite Republic

Though the American Revolution dissolved the legal ties binding the colonies to England, it did not break their dependence upon metropolitan manners or insulate them from the international market in fashionable goods. In 1787 Noah Webster complained: "The present ambition of Americans is, to introduce as fast as possible, the fashionable amusements of the European courts. Considering the former dependence of America on England, her descent, her connexion and present intercourse, this ambition cannot surprise us."[1]

We do not doubt the point of Webster's plaint — that manners and fashions in the United States owed much to London and Paris. His fretting over the influence of European courts, however, recycled old republican myths rather than announced any newly observed truths. The influence of the Hanoverian court over British and imperial culture had waned with every passing year of the dynasty. Parisian fashions in clothing and thought emanated from the salons, more than from the entourage of Louis XVI. Throughout the colonial period the attempts to set up satellite courts around governors had only desultory success. For every courtly Lord Botetourt there were half a dozen dour Dinwiddies more intent on imperial policy or pelf than making social life richer and more civil in the

---

1. Noah Webster, "Remarks on the Manners, Government, and Debt of the United States" (1797), in Webster, *A Collection of Essays and Fugitiv Writings (1790)* (1790; rpt. Delmar, N.Y., 1977), 85; Alexandre-Marie Quesnay de Beaurepaire, *Memoire...* (Paris, 1788).

colonies. No, the engine for civilizing America upon European lines was not the court, nor was it that other metropolitan institution that supplanted the courts in fashioning manners and modes, the theater. The visits of the itinerant acting companies were too infrequent, the antitheatrical prejudice was too virulent among the Reformed Christians in the population, for the stage to direct changes in social commerce.

In England, the stage served as a mirror for all the innovations of each social scene. Every assemblage from the gaming table to the army camp had its characteristic talk and behavior mimicked for the general public. Their novelties were reviewed for the delectation of local citizens, and in the more insightful plays the words and ways that were merely modish were distinguished from those that were liberating and enlivening. In British America the stage never proved potent enough to be the mediator of the discursive styles and manners of private society. At most, it served as a reference — a style prompt — for the Henry Brookes and Thomas Dales in the colonial cities. Instead, the play of manners took place in those institutions of private society that had crossed the Atlantic and set up in the colonies. Just as the forms of private society were various, so were the manners and modes they encouraged. Even the most generalized types of conduct — politeness, sociability, familiarity — were not manifested uniformly among clubs, coffeehouses, salons, and tea tables. Even the commonest of common denominators among associations, the pursuit of pleasure in the exercise of fellow feeling, seems too abstract a category for making sense of the rich diversity of behaviors cultivated in voluntary associations.

Radical Republican charges in the 1780s and 1790s that such organizations were expressions of luxury or aristocracy seem beside the point. The Revolution, for all the talk of republicans about simplicity, equality, and virtue, did not alter the play of private society. Yet it was a private society profoundly different from that established in the European capital cities. Without a court or the stage to discipline the activity of private society, European mores were never established authoritatively. Instead, Old World fashions, discourses, and behaviors combined with local improvisations. Every form of private society predicated upon pleasure survived the Revolution to shelter experiments with manners and modes of self-expression. These customary forms were joined by new institutions, such as Alexandre-Marie Quesnay's Academy of the Polite Arts that began operating in Philadelphia in 1780 and briefly opened a New York branch in

1785. Quesnay's Academy sponsored theatricals and offered instruction in French, "all sorts of dances most in fashion in Europe, and principal graces and manners."[2]

The public prints testified to the continuing vitality of all the old arenas of sociability. In 1784, a satirist encountered in Philadelphia's Coffee House the same international batch of newshounds, commercial men, and practical sages that one would have met in the London Coffeehouse in Philadelphia half a century before or the Pennsilvania Coffeehouse in London a century before:

> What various faces here we thronging view
> From Nova-Zembla down to swart Peru,
> Met for the mutual benefit of each,
> To gather news or useless lore to teach;
> Here men of *straw* with men of fortune meet,
> And men of neither both familiar greet.[3]

Around the urn Philadelphians Bully Bragwell, Billy Button, and Adam Archly talked the same talk about commercial ruin, politics, and taxes that had made the coffeehouse the political academy of Restoration England. New York's Tontine Coffee House formalized the commercial exchanges of its clientele, becoming the New York Stock Exchange.

The tavern's persistence as a haven of masculine appetite and jest was most memorably observed in Washington Irving's *Rip Van Winkle*. The tavern sign might have substituted the face of President George for royal George, yet the inn's unchanging company — the neighborhood congress of indolent talkers — remained the only society congenial to the country's undomesticated Rips.

Tea tables remained places where women asserted prerogative, according to *The Tea-Drinking Wife*. They also continued to cultivate a distinctive mode of conversation, if we accept the instruction of Richard Johnson's *Tea-Table Dialogues*. Salons diversified their practices. Coteries that fol-

---

2. *Freeman's Journal; or, The North American Intelligencer,* Jan. 9, 1784. An advertisement for the opening of the New York branch appears in *New-York Packet,* Mar. 21, 1785. Kenneth Silverman discusses the financial difficulties that thwarted the New York venture in *A Cultural History of the American Revolution . . .* (New York, 1976), 445–446.

3. "Coffee House," in *The Philadelphiad; or, New Pictures of the City . . .* (Philadelphia, 1784), I, 61.

lowed the bluestocking model — those of Sarah Wentworth Morton or the anonymous author of *Effusions of Female Fancy, by a Young Lady*, for instance — projected a presence in print. Others, most notably Anne Willing Bingham's drawing room in Philadelphia, created a haven of conversation where politics, art, and economics were discussed by men and women of influence after the fashion of Paris.[4]

Assemblies enjoyed unparalleled popularity with the coming of the peace. Rules and regulations of the Dancing Assembly organized in Savannah were published in broadside in 1790. John Griffiths, a dancing master at Quesnay's Academy in New York, competed with Andrew Picken, a London master, instructing persons in the latest steps, the rivals teaching on alternate days in the City Assembly rooms. Picken's success would drive Griffiths out of the city and on to Boston, Providence, Litchfield, and other New England towns as an itinerant master. Griffiths also supported himself by compiling and publishing the first American dancing manuals, beginning in 1788 with *A Collection of the Figures of the Newest and Most Fashionable Country-Dances.*[5] At times, one suspects that the new political liberties led to an embrace of novelties. Francisco Miranda (later the father of Venezuelan independence) remarked on the overthrow of old austerities in Wilmington, Delaware, in January 1784 when he visited an assembly ball. It was

the first diversion of its kind in this place, for as the settlement is Quaker they do not dance. However, as good daughters of the republic, with changing customs, they adapt themselves. The Assembly was small, and

4. *The Tea-Drinking Wife* . . . (New York, 1797); [Richard Johnson], *Tea-Table Dialogues* . . . (Philadelphia, 1789); *Effusions of Female Fancy, by a Young Lady* . . . (New York, 1784); Wendy A. Nicholson, "Making the Private Public: Anne Willing Bingham's Role as a Leader of Philadelphia's Social Elite in the Eighteenth Century" (master's thesis, University of Delaware, Winterthur Program, 1988). Nicholson does not address the intellectual dimension of Bingham's coterie. Morton belonged to the Stone House Club and was the most famous New England salonniere of her day. The writings by men and women belonging to a New York City salon of the 1780s appeared in *Effusions of Female Fancy.*

5. *Rules and Regulations for the Dancing Assembly of Savannah* (Savannah, Ga., 1790); Kate Van Winkle Keller, "John Griffiths, Eighteenth-Century Itinerant Dancing Master," in Peter Benes, ed., *Itinerancy in New England and New York*, Dublin Seminar for New England Folklife, 1984 (Boston, 1985), 94–97. Keller supplies a complete bibliographical chronicle of *A Collection* (103–104).

in a very little room; but it was pleasant and appropriate. Here for the first time Quaker men and women mingled in this sort of diversion, although they did not dance themselves.

We enjoyed a very good supper, consisting of tea, coffee and chocolate, cold tongue, ham, wine, etc. The contra-dances and cotillions lasted until three in the morning, when the greater part of the company retired.[6]

Wilmington's assembly might have catered to new American tastes by featuring contradances, but it understood its social function in light of an old model of civic celebration, for the occasion of the ball was the birth night of General George Washington.

Clubs flourished. In New York City the Friendly Club, Calliopean Society, Horanian Society, Ermenian Society, Information Society, Belles Lettres Club, Anacreontic Society, Sub Rosa Dining Club, Union Club, Belvedere Club, St. Tamany Society, Philological Society, and Debating Society pursued their various projects.[7] R. B. Davis's "Ode for the 5th Anniversary of the Calliopean Society, November 20, 1793," indicated that beneath a public face of rationality the time-honored play of appetite, raillery, liberty, and pleasure seeking went on in male company:

> Quick let the smiling glass
> Bear Mirth and Pleasure round,
> And bursting from the heart,
> Gay let the song resound.
> No cares intrudes upon our feast —
> our Guardian Muse Presides
> And while in Pleasure's paths we rove,
> approving Reason guides.[8]

Projecting societies also retained the rites of private sociability. The Belvedere, an Antifederalist club formed in the wake of Citizen Genêt's transit across the American firmament, was, according to John W. Francis, "an hilarious association." In a 1793 cartoon satirizing the club, we see its

6. Quoted in John Gardner, "Contradances and Cotillions: Dancing in Eighteenth-Century Delaware," *Delaware History*, XXII (1986–1987), 43.

7. Eleanor Bryce Scott, "Early Literary Clubs in New York City," *American Literature*, V (1933–1934), 12.

8. Entry for Nov. 20, 1793, Calliopean Society Minute Books, New-York Historical Society.

PLATE 7 Green Dragon Tavern. *Pen-and-ink sketch with watercolor wash by John Johnson. Boston, 1773. Meeting place of Sons of Liberty and the Lodge of St. Andrew. Courtesy, American Antiquarian Society, Worcester, Mass.*

ideals posted on the wall: "Liberty is the Power of doing any thing we like," and "This Society Up and all else Down."[9]

Let us not mistake the lesson of the Belvedere. Democratic-Republicans depended on the same "entre nous" liberties of expression cultivated by their opponents. Their polemics denouncing private association must be taken with salt. The proliferation of Democratic-Republican clubs illustrates that association (and secret association, for that matter) was not the flash-point issue in the culture wars of the 1780s and 1790s.[10] What generated heat were the manners promoted by the various forms of private association.

Republicans attacked private societies as institutes of luxury. The jeremiad against luxury is historically significant not for its effectiveness in quashing politeness or repressing social institutions. It could not stop either. Rather, the failure of the campaign exposed a critical weakness in

9. John W. Francis, *Old New York; or, Reminiscences of the Past Sixty Years* (New York, 1858); *A Peep into the Anti-Federal Club*, Aug. 16, 1793, engraving, American Antiquarian Society copy.

10. For the explosive spread of these political societies, see Eugene Perry Link, *Democratic-Republican Societies, 1790–1800*, 2d ed. (New York, 1965).

republican ideology: the failure to conceptualize the place of leisure in civic culture other than in negative terms or atavistic notions of rural retreat — *otium*, "leisure."[11] This failure was the most visible symptom of a larger incapacity to appreciate the central role of pleasure in human action, an incapacity that would limit the effectiveness of republican attempts to counteract the growth of a consumption-driven economy and a liberal ideology.

Consumption lay at the center of the most spirited paper war over cultural values of the 1780s, the battle about the Tea Assembly in Boston. Though tea drinking retained its broad popularity in post-Revolutionary America, its association with the Boston Tea Party colored it with the taint of metropolitan privilege. The cultural innovation of the Tea Assembly lay in its amalgamation of two forms of sociability: the tea party and the dancing assembly. Membership was by subscription. Merchant families, particularly those with marriageable sons and daughters, flocked to the company. In 1785 the public prints erupted. A satirical play script bearing the rumored name of the assembly, *Sans Souci, alias Free and Easy*, quickly sold out and went into a second edition.[12] The letters columns of the newspapers filled up with complaints about the pursuit of pleasure and the degeneration of the Republic. One newspaper critic asked:

> Did ever effeminacy with her languid train, receive a greater welcome in society than at this day. New amusements are invented — new dissipations are introduced, to lull and enervate those minds already too much softened, poisoned and contaminated, by idle pleasures, and foolish gratifications. We are exchanging prudence, virtue and economy, for those glaring spectres luxury, prodigality and profligacy. We are prostituting all our glory as a people; for new modes of pleasure, ruinous in their expences, injurious to virtue, and totally detrimental to the well being of society.[13]

11. The ideological preoccupation with otium among literary Federalists is treated at length in William Dowling, "Literary Federalism in the Age of Jefferson: Joseph Dennie and the Port Folio, 1801–1811," MS.

12. Silverman, *A Cultural History of the American Revolution*, 509–510; *Sans Souci, alias Free and Easy* . . . (Boston, 1785). Mercy Otis Warren denied authorship of the piece.

13. *Massachusetts Centinel* (Boston), Jan. 15, 19, 1785, reprinted in Gordon S. Wood, ed., *The Rising Glory of America, 1760–1820*, 2d ed. (Boston, 1990), 137–143.

Novelty, luxury, effeminacy, prodigality, and profligacy offended a customary simplicity and frugality of manners. The name Sans Souci ("without worry") invoked simultaneously the aesthetic ideals of the art of sociability (ease and liberty of expression) and the extravagances of the French court (Sans Souci was the name of Marie Antoinette's palace). The amusements enjoyed there — dancing, tea drinking, card playing — were vices, according to the critic, "marked with the epithet 'polite.'"

This procrustean Cato of Massachusetts republicanism confessed that humans needed recreations to alleviate the strain of toil, yet these recreations had to be "rational," not amusements tending to levity. This vision of republican manners as a virtuous and masculine austerity marked the rhetorical limit of the attack upon the institutes of polite sociability. The attack was immediately answered. Perhaps the most telling reply was one that asked what good liberty possessed if one were limited to maintaining oneself frugally:

> Have I not then a right to spend some part of the fruits of my industry to procure amusements most agreeable to myself, whilst I do not act contrary to the laws of my country, or so as to injure my neighbour. To what end do we toil, if not to promote our ease, and to procure an exemption from labour; for my part I think it is better to die at once than for years, and without relaxing, to be a slave to what is called our interest.

The respondent raised the issue of leisure explicitly. What did the liberty procured by the Revolution mean if one could not escape the compulsion of labor and necessity? Beyond mere rest one should be free to pursue ease and amusement. Another correspondent, Candidus, observed that such private pursuit of happiness was unobjectionable, except when one's cash underwrote the activities of an institution that subverted the good of society. Here we approach the crux of the debate over the Sans Souci. The peril posed by the Sans Souci seemed new precisely because the integrity of public culture of the United States was new. Society in the form of a virtuous public stood freshly revealed to be subject to peril. Certainly dancing assemblies were not new in Boston, nor objections to them — in March 1723, a gang of scowrers had wrecked Gatchell's Dancing School in the city.[14] Soirees serving tea and featuring chat in mixed company were not new; they had been features of provincial culture from the 1710s

14. Ibid.; *New-England Courant* (Boston), no. 84, Mar. 11, 1723.

(Chapter 4). Yet there can be no doubt that the relationship between sociable institutions and society at large (that is, the public) had changed with the creation of the United States.

Here we must follow Michael Warner in seeing the new and threatened integrity of the national, not in terms of a "national imaginary," but in terms of the abstract republic cherished by the eighteenth-century republic of letters. It was this idealized entity that republicans declared to be in peril from the pursuit of pleasure. Republican literature was, in large measure, a jeremiad against sumptuary practice. In *Letters of the Republic* Warner observed, "The republican paradigm of literature had an anti-aesthetic tendency, where aesthetics was increasingly being formed around private appropriation and distinction."[15] Thus politeness posed a problem for a republicanism dependent upon the market yet ideologically committed to a politics of common virtue. This problem became critical in the world of letters when print and polite letters began supplanting conversation and gift exchange of literary manuscripts in private society. Print raised the issue of vanity for both the production and the consumption of polite literature. Vanity had been less important when politeness was a watchword of conversation, for polite talk and manners incorporated one into a community that shared these conventions; the company of the genteel mitigated the vanity of gentility, for it was not an individual practice. Politeness, because of its conventionality (that is, its potential for mass reception), its cultural associations with gentility, and its aura of worldliness, became a vehicle for literary fame. If one could supply a sufficiently easy, elegant, and diverting performance, one might become the American Chesterfield. (And the literary departments of the magazines testified how many penmen and -women aspired to this office.) On the consumption side of the literary transaction, an individual's subscription to a polite magazine or purchase of a novel served as a marker of one's imaginative commitment to gentility, cosmopolitanism, and the pursuit of pleasure. Unless one belonged to a reading club, this subscription asserted an individual identity as a genteel person.

Warner's study is noteworthy for its sensitivity to the rhetoric of republicanism, particularly when criticizing literary consumption in the United States. Yet it overestimates the power of republicanism to constrain the market ideologically. In print, politeness performed tasks the ideology of

15. Michael Warner, *The Letters of the Republic: Publication and the Public Sphere in Eighteenth-Century America* (Cambridge, Mass., 1982), 132–137.

virtue, the culture of domesticity, and the critique of luxury could not accomplish. For instance, it supplied a repertoire of mannerly expression for courting couples at a time when negotiating marriage was being freed from patriarchal oversight. The republican vision of courtship as the mutual recognition of virtue between partners was deficient, for it made nothing of the frisson of adventure for women or the pleasures and anxieties of the contest for the fair among men. Moral censors might sing, "Court me not to scenes of pleasure," to the young citizenry of the United States; such strictures only attested to the power of pleasure.[16] In courting, aesthetics came irresistibly into play in the lives of Americans, and in courtship differentiation was all. One had to distinguish oneself, like the fair Shulamite from the company of women, or the Beloved from the company of men. Polite literature indicated how to do this — how to become a virtuoso of wit or a maestro of amusement. And it gave voice to the pleasure one felt in the company of the object of one's desire.

Yet in print polite letters could only represent courtship: supply a lexicon or instruct one in technique. In fictions or narratives the displacement from actual communication, the inauthenticity of polite expression concerning the heart, became the obsessive point of discussions about courtship novels and gallant verse. The linkage in courtship novels between seduction and the rhetoric of politeness became a commonplace of the criticism of novels.[17] For this reason, old distinctions between true politeness and false politeness became attached to the differentiation between print expressions and manuscript expressions of affection. In the hierarchy of worth, a love letter in the suitor's hand had a higher standing than an ode to Chloe in the local paper.

While courtship was the central transaction demanding polite and personal communication, it did not monopolize the posts. Every social interaction in which trust, personal connection, and privacy were crucial made use of the manuscript letter as its principal medium of contact. Commercial negotiation, motherly advice, friendly admonition, and commiseration all used private letter. To the extent public prints obtruded a notion of a contentious, self-interested, ideologically fixated sense of the public, per-

16. Jay Fliegelman, *Prodigals and Pilgrims: The American Revolution against Patriarchal Authority, 1750–1800* (Cambridge, 1982), 123–135; [Sir Henry Bate Dudley], *Court Me Not to Scenes of Pleasure* (Philadelphia, [1795?]).

17. Cathy N. Davidson, *Revolution and the Word: The Rise of the Novel in America* (New York, 1986), 89–109.

sons resorted to a familiar, polite, and careful communication by letter. As the public prints burgeoned during the 1780s and 1790s, a powerful reactive expansion of epistolary writing and communication took place. With this expansion came a shift of emphasis away from the individual letter as an event of communication to the idea of correspondence in which an enduring relationship grounded in feeling might be cultivated. Elihu Hubbard Smith, the Connecticut physician-poet, communicated something of the intellectual weight attached to correspondence in a letter to Idea Strong on March 29, 1796:

> Letters are designed as substitutes for conversation; and that regular succession of them, which obtains the title of a Correspondence, may be considered as analogous to the intercourse of neighbours. Yet, tho' this account of their use be just, it should not be hence inferred, that, like conversations and neighborhood visitings, they are to be devoted to prattle and gossiping. Correspondencies, like partnerships and marriages, may produce important consequences, and ought to be engaged in with some caution, and much meditation. Neither caprice, nor vanity, nor ambition, nor any selfish feeling, should have any thing to do in this matter. . . . We are not made for ourselves alone, but for each other; for all. For the benefit of all, therefore, should our lives, our thoughts, our energies, be employed; and each act must be pronounced good or bad; only in proportion as it promotes the welfare of all.[18]

Here a Federalist man of letters declared the new discursive situation of private communication in the United States. Anything that institutionalized social relationships in the new Republic (correspondence between two persons, for instance) had to answer to the needs of society at large, had to avoid private interest or frivolity, and had to withstand moral scrutiny. Smith believed the moral health and "welfare of all" depended upon the mutual edification of citizens. He lived his conviction. Smith involved himself repeatedly with publication projects, particularly in connection with medicine, abolition, and national literature. Yet these educational endeavors could succeed only when a harmony of moral feeling pervaded the citizenry. Such harmony was best cultivated by personal correspondence, not in the public prints.

18. Elihu Hubbard Smith, *The Diary of Elihu Hubbard Smith (1771–1798)*, ed. James E. Cronin, Memoirs of the American Philosophical Society, XCV (Philadelphia, 1973), 147–148.

Publishers recognized the peculiar authority of correspondence that arose from its personality — its connection with authentic lives. The frequent resort of authors and editors to epistolary forms of address in print is a fact of eighteenth-century literary history. The letter's ability to span geographic distance with the intimate word was put to service in overcoming the impersonality of print marketed to an unknown audience. Novels, political tracts, economic treatises, and homilies increasingly assumed the form of correspondence. Over the course of the century one sees a shift from the rhetorical use of "A Letter" to representations of correspondence: *Letters from an American Farmer, Letters from a Farmer in Pennsylvania, Letters on Various Interesting and Important Subjects, Letters of Friendship.*[19] In these, a course of education in morality, politics, aesthetics, or manners was laid out within a frame of friendship or association. Invariably, the personal character of the relationship was stressed.

The gap between virtual friendship and actual friendship, between a fictive correspondence in which a single author concocts the letters of all parties and a genuine correspondence, proved to be critical for those who most valued authenticity of sentiment. The avoidance of print to communicate sentiment became a hallmark not so much of gentility as of those discursive communities that most avidly embraced moral sentimentalism. In particular, it marked the discursive practice of educated women. One of the major contributions of the new feminist historiography has been the reconstruction of the civic sorority, a women's community of continental scope constituted in letters in the decades preceding the American Revolution. Within this epistolatory sorority certain women — Hannah Griffitts, Elizabeth Graeme, Annis Boudinot Stockton — became literary celebrities without participating in the hurly-burly of print or, in the case of Susanna Wright out on the Susquehanna frontier, without participating in the society of tea tables and salons. These networks were amorphous, much as the readerships for women's novels in the early Republic were. Nevertheless, they constituted a fundamental part of the republic of letters. Most important, they supplied the filaments of affection that bound the nation together. As late as 1831 Sarah Hale(?) observed, "Those who have felt, in

19. J. Hector St. John [M. G. St. J. de Crèvecoeur], *Letters from an American Farmer* . . . (Philadelphia, 1793); [John Dickinson], *Letters from a Farmer in Pennsylvania* . . . (Philadelphia, 1768); Robert Slender [Philip Freneau], *Letters on Various Interesting and Important Subjects* . . . (Philadelphia, 1799); [Joseph Huntington], *Letters of Friendship* . . . (Hartford, Conn., 1780); [George Logan], *Letters Addressed to the Yeomanry of the United States* . . . (Philadelphia, 1791).

their own hearts, the effect of this intercourse by letters with dear and distant friends, or witnessed its influence on others, will not need be told how strong a bond of sympathy it creates between different sections of our country."[20]

With the creation of the United States and the political assertion of a civic integrity of federal scope, the question arose how manners and morals would be adjudicated. With no established church and a proliferation of denominations competing for spiritual authority, no federal project of civic piety could be enacted. With the rejection of schemes for a national university, the college could not stand as a national institute of manners and morals. While various periodicals and newspapers aspired to be the national tribune, all suffered from the problem of being intellectual commodities. The average magazine lasted fifteen months before folding from lack of cash.[21] The typical newspaper found economic survival depended upon being a vehicle of partisan politics rather than an impartial censor of morals. Then, too, morality and manners both depended on the ethos of an exemplar in order to be conveyed. Mores lived in the behavior of persons. One could write telling a youngster that General Washington had a noble bearing on a horse, but, until that child experienced the quiddity of Washington on horseback, he or she would have only an inkling of the general's style.

Into the vacuum stepped Martha Washington. Her establishment of a drawing room for the governing classes in New York, and later in Philadelphia, created an arena for a new civic style of sociability and conversation, combining the heterosociality and sensibility of the polite salon with the simplicity of manners and emphasis upon civic and domestic virtue demanded by republicanism. Her republican court also served as the primary courtship theater in the new nation — the place where an unattached legislator or official might find a genteel spouse. The many marriages made in the court (James Madison's with Dolley Payne was only the most

20. Susan Stabile, " 'I Saw Great Fabius Come in State': Philadelphia Women's Court Poetry in the Age of Washington," paper, Sixteenth Annual Meeting of the Society for Historians of the Early American Republic, Boston College, July 15, 1994; [Sarah Hale?], "Letter Writing: In Its Effects on National Character," *Ladies' Magazine, and Literary Gazette*, IV (1831), 241–243. Fredrika Teute discovered this important essay.

21. Michael T. Gilmore, "Magazines, Criticism, Essays," in Sacvan Bercovitch, ed., *The Cambridge History of American Literature*, I, *1590–1820* (New York, 1994), 558–572.

conspicuous) contributed greatly to the consolidation of a governing class interrelated on a continental scale.[22] It also provided a public space for elite women where their conversation could instruct public men in manners, morality, and policy.

The republican court and its network of affiliated salons provided a venue in which women could constitute a civil interest and conduct projects. Although historians might not have recognized this function until recently, Radical Republicans of the 1790s certainly did and found reason to fear. A newspaper campaign against Martha Washington's levee portrayed it as the seedbed of aristocracy and the laboratory of luxury. Republican ideology insisted that feminine activity must be entirely contained within domesticity to be virtuous. Virtue, as Linda K. Kerber has so forcefully shown, was conceived in terms of gendered spheres of activity.[23] Yet this ideological insistence that one perform within the ambit of a gender role was contravened by a host of practices and, in the activities of the republican court and its successors, subverted well into the nineteenth century.

Nineteenth-century cultural commentators extensively discussed the cultural and political influences of the salon world.[24] Their concerns, however, did not extend to the sorts of questions that stimulate current inquiry. They did not remark the extent to which permissions granted to women's conversation in the salon could be projected elsewhere. Could matters treated by women in the salon be broached in a lecture by a woman at an athenaeum?

The republican court's continental network of salons and the simultaneous growth of lyceum circuits for speakers raises the issue of scale. The creation of the Republic and the spread of public prints seemingly required

22. Daphne O'Brien, "The First Congress, Polite Society, and Courtship in New York City: The Case of Margaret Lowther Page," paper, Sixteenth Annual Meeting of the Society of Historians of the Early American Republic, Boston, July 15, 1994.

23. David S. Shields and Fredrika J. Teute, "The Republican Court and the Historiography of the Women's Domain in the Public Sphere," paper, ibid.; Linda K. Kerber, *Women of the Republic: Intellect and Ideology in Revolutionary America* (Chapel Hill, N.C., 1980).

24. Rufus Wilmot Griswold, *The Republican Court; or, American Society in the Days of Washington* (New York, 1855); E[lizabeth] F. Ellet, *The Court Circles of the Republic; or, The Beauties and Celebrities of the Nation* (Hartford, Conn., 1869); Anne Hollingsworth Wharton, *Salons Colonial and Republican* (Philadelphia, 1900), and *Martha Washington* (New York, 1897).

that those venues of oral communication that aspired to public influence organize into something more than local institutions. While Freemasonry supplied a model of a network of private associations that connected the city with the countryside, it was a model with problematic political overtones, particularly for republicans. The idea of a vast, international network engaged in projects whose character was hidden behind a cloak of secrecy did not accord with republicanism's vision of a virtuous and wholly public civic life (whereas privacy was connected with the domestic sphere). The network of Democratic-Republican clubs shows that such theoretical objections were no hindrance to the practical embrace of the idea of networks of associations as vehicles for politics. (Indeed, the continental network of committees of correspondence during the Revolution had demonstrated the effectiveness of such organizations to the patriots.) So we witness in the early Republic the expansion and rationalization of certain institutions of private society, with the result that the influence of the spoken word and manuscript writing broadened. While the gross features of this cultural development are now apparent, a detailed and careful assessment of what actually happened in the networks of salons and clubs and in the speakers' circuits should be undertaken.[25]

The proliferation of newspapers and spread of ideas and knowledge by means of a paper's reprinting information from books and other newspapers were developments recognized by even the dullest of cultural commentators in the 1790s. Recognition of the cultural potency of print might have prompted projectors of various sorts to expand the scope of private discursive institutions in response. The complexity of the relationships between print, manuscript, and oral communication during the early Republic is fascinating. Consider how both the production and reception of print are tied to institutions of private society. Many newspapers and most magazines were edited and composed by "a society of gentlemen." On the reception end, private corporations, styled "social libraries," selected, collected, and maintained collections of books and periodicals. In Albany, Boston, New York City, Philadelphia, Newport, and Charleston, library societies had formed before the Revolution. In the post-Revolutionary era these private corporations were supplemented by an array of "public" li-

25. William J. Gilmore, *Reading Becomes a Necessity of Life: Material and Cultural Life in Rural New England, 1780–1835* (Knoxville, Tenn., 1989); Philip F. Gura, *The Crossroads of American History and Literature* (University Park, Pa., 1996).

braries in the 1790s maintained by municipalities. Around these institutions subsidiary constellations of reading circles and debating societies formed in ever increasing numbers from the 1790s through the 1830s. As Mary Kelley has shown, reading was often a profoundly social activity. The post-Revolutionary era also saw the coalescence of writers and readers in the society of the bookstore. In Philadelphia, for instance, Bell's bookstore became the favorite haunt of printers, writers, and book purchasers. It became the personification of the republic of letters:

> Here authors meet who ne'er a sprig have got
> The poet, player, doctor, wit and sot;
> Smart politicians wrangling here are seen,
> Condemning *Jeffries* or indulging spleen,
> Reproving Congress or amending laws,
> Still fond to find out blemishes and flaws;
> Here harmless *sentimental-mongers* join
> To praise some author or his wit refine,
> Or treat the mental appetite with lore
> From *Plato's*, *Pope's* and *Shakespear's* endless store;
> Young blushing writers, eager for the bays,
> Try here the merit of their new-born lays,
> Seek for a patron, follow fleeting fame,
> And begs the slut may raise their hidden name.[26]

Bell's bookstore here has become the temple of fame where aspirants to notice congregate, absorbing the example of past celebrities and performing the rituals of praise and dispraise that were theretofore the preserve of the coffeehouse. Sometime during the 1790s, Asbury Dickens's bookshop on Second Street eclipsed Bell's as the center of Philadelphia's literary firmament.[27] Dickens's shop became the haunt of poets John Blair Linn and Samuel Ewing, playwright Charles Jared Ingersoll, novelist Charles Brockden Brown, and the editor of the *Port Folio*, Joseph Dennie.

One peculiarity of the bookstore community was that it never fully served the imperatives to sociability that the literati felt. Perhaps the competitive ethos of the marketplace could not be escaped in a commercial set-

---

26. *The Philadelphiad*, I, 39–40.

27. John Davis, *Travels of Four Years and a Half in the United States of America during 1798, 1799, 1800, 1801, and 1802* (New York, 1909), 204.

ting. Whatever the case, these companies tended to formalize their intercourse into clubs that met elsewhere. The Dickens bookshop group formed the nucleus of Philadelphia's Tuesday Club.[28] Brown and Linn, when they were in New York, participated in the Friendly Club. These aggregations of authors and booktrade people became fixtures of nineteenth-century cultural life, with Washington Irving's Cheshire Cheese and Oliver Wendell Holmes's Saturday Clubs being the most conspicuous of a dozen or so such assemblies. What service did they perform in the world of letters? They provided a nonconfrontational place to work out problems of aesthetics, politics, and commerce affecting those interested in the production of literature. In print, the rhetoric of crisis or boosterism suffused criticism. Among members of a literary fraternity, one could dispense with adversarial or partisan posturing and collaborate on common problems and concerns. The diary of Elihu Hubburd Smith, a member of the Friendly Club, records the activity of his literary fraternity. Manuscripts of plays, novels, poems, and essays circulated among the membership for evaluation. New books were read in common and subjected to analysis. Debates about issues of the day took place. Smith and Charles Brockden Brown, on Monday, December 19, 1796, got into a "long and disputatious argument, 'On the difference between poetry and prose' — or rather on 'the wherein are poetry and prose distinct'; which ended, as such discussions usually do, with the conviction of either party; and with no clearer ideas on the subject, than before."[29] Clubical conversation did not ensure that debate would not decay into adversarial posturing. Nevertheless, within the company of such persons arguing such issues, the identity of the man of letters was formed. Here literary men developed a sense of common cause that was something beyond the shared interest in letters possessed by amateurs.

Somewhere between amateurism and professionalism was the peculiar self-consciousness projected in print by the circle of writers who formed the New York Calliopean Society during the 1780s. The group provided the impetus for the *New York Magazine; or, Literary Repository*, which published from 1792 to 1796. In each issue they supplied contents for a column titled "The Drone." The offerings were the cream of belles lettres prepared to be read during the weekly dinner meetings of the club. The club and its literary endeavors survived the short life of the magazine, its

28. Lewis Leary, "John Blair Linn, 1777–1805," *William and Mary Quarterly*, 3d ser., IV (1947), 162.

29. Smith, *The Diary of Elihu Hubbard Smith*, ed. Cronin, 273.

minute book and manuscript repository suspending in 1831.[30] When the group appeared in print, it did so under a name that mocked republican rebukes of belles lettres as the fruit of indolence. By embracing the status of "drone" and by brandishing its marginal, unvirtuous, and elite status as its identity, the club burlesqued the rhetoric of industry, virtue, and egalitarianism inspiring the public prints. What was gained by confessing that the club was something other than a miniature republic of virtue? A liberty of perspective that permitted members to conceive, for instance, of "The Science of Lying." Thus in "Drone XIX" the club offered an anatomy of lying, elaborating the distinguishing marks of "the stretch," the "twang," the "bounce," and the "humbug." Of all the discussions of rhetoric and oral performance to appear in print in the United States during the 1790s, this brief essay supplied the most prescient glimpse of the Barnumesque America of hoaxes, tall-tales, and humbuggery.

Something about the convergence of humor, liberty of conversation, and society remained attractive to readers well into the nineteenth century. It was no fluke that the most popular author in the English-speaking world during the century, Charles Dickens, won success by his representation of *The Posthumous Papers of the Pickwick Club* (1837). Yet Dickens's success had curious effects in terms of the public image of clubbing. Despite the documentable popularity of clubs in the United States throughout the century, clubbing became associated in the literate imagination (the mind of the republic of letters measured in clichés and customary associations found in myriads of texts) with English gentlemen's clubs. Clubical liberty of wit would be domesticated in popular imagination under the idea of English eccentricity. Now when one mentions "The Drones" to a literate American, the immediate image is of Bertie Wooster, Gussie Finknottle, and an oddly named assortment of upper-class twits holed up in their London clubhouse conducting the annual dart tourney or practicing the newt mating dance. The dark counterpart to this image — colored by the notoriety of the Cambridge Apostles — is that of a secret homosexual brotherhood practicing dangerous politics and cultivating forbidden pleasures.

The fate of the club in print was to serve as an institution forever marked by peculiarity. It was homosocial in a society increasingly adamant in its insistence on heterosociality, indolent in a culture that paid lip service to industry, upper-class in an egalitarian public sphere, humorous to the point

---

30. One MS of seven hundred pages, from 1788 to 1795, survives in the New York Historical Society, NYHS 1222.

of eccentricity, and, at times, secret. For these reasons the club was invested with an exoticism that lent it interest in the print market.

The fate of the club in American society is not so simply characterized. Clubbing became immensely popular during the course of the nineteenth century, practiced by all classes and ethnic groups except native Americans. It ceased to be practiced exclusively by men; indeed, by 1910, women's clubs might have eclipsed men's clubs in numbers — this despite the exponential growth of clubbing among men.[31] Should we interpret the increasing popularity of clubbing among men as a reaction to the feminization of American culture — a social analogue to the popularity of male fantasy genres in print? Or should we see it as an expansion of its traditional custom of supplying an emotional resort for commercial men at a time when business grew increasingly insistent on a serious and professional demeanor? Should we view the embrace of the club by women as a sign of their determination to master the institutions customarily denied to them? Despite the ample literature on voluntary associations in the United States, fundamental questions concerning the cultural work of the club — and the other forms of private society — in the nineteenth century remain unanswered.

For the eighteenth century, however, certain conclusions can be advanced. The sociable world of the early Republic — the arenas of conversations, display, courtship, and amusement — withstood the attacks of Radical Republicans who feared urbanity and evangelical champions of simplicity, piety, and domesticity. The visions of civility promulgated by the clubs, coffeehouses, salons, fraternities, and the republican court were culturally powerful because they confessed the sharing of pleasure as an ideal of society at a time when increasing numbers of persons understood the pursuit of pleasure to be an end of action. They remained powerful because they instituted practices that enabled persons to interact easily and pleasurably. The forms of private society clearly articulated styles and manners that secured persons in attractive identities; and, because a larger world recognized mannerliness, stylishness, and wit, these identities proved useful for anyone who traveled within the United States and beyond its bounds. Attempts to tie the aesthetics of private society to a notion of aristocratic

31. Starting points for an examination of the explosive growth of women's clubs during the nineteenth century are Karen J. Blair, *The History of American Women's Voluntary Organizations, 1810–1960: A Guide to Sources* (Boston, 1989); and Anne Firor Scott, *Natural Allies: Women's Associations in American History* (Urbana, Ill., 1991).

luxury in large measure failed. As Richard L. Bushman has shown, gentility was appropriated as the public mode of the middle classes, becoming in the course of time "respectability." The early-twentieth-century attack by George Santayana and Bernard De Voto on the genteel tradition challenged bourgeois, not aristocratic, civic conduct.[32]

By concentrating upon the internal dialectic of civility and examining the discursive institutions and manners developed within Anglo-American culture, I have brought to the fore the tensions and opposition between discourses and manners. Yet perspective is everything. When one considers the external dialectic of civility — that which operated between Anglo-Americans and the various American native cultures — certain distinctions between republican and genteel styles collapse. Diplomatic missions from the United States government to negotiate treaties with the various tribes were emphatically theatrical. As Andrew R. L. Cayton has argued, feasts, oratory, display of manners, dress, and exchange of gifts dramatized civility.[33] Whether Federalist or Democratic-Republican, the diplomat made the demonstration of politeness a central matter of the negotiation. The old dream of European commercial imperialists that the "savage" peoples of the world would exchange their goods for the "arts of peace" — that is, the material tokens of civility — did not dissolve with the founding of the Republic. Nor did the natives seem less "savage" or in need of civilizing in the eyes of government policy makers.

Although successive administrations brandished civility in diplomatic parleys and agents of the United States made much to Europeans of the virtuous manners and simplicity of a population that enjoyed liberty, governmental promulgation of civility as an explicit policy diminished with the accession of Jefferson in 1800. So we close with a mystery. Why did Jefferson, who had experienced firsthand the intellectual vitality of the French salons, who possessed an exquisite sense of the role of manners in the good order of a nation, allow the social-institutional zone between the state and the citizenry to become less public? Why did he dismantle the republican court, calling a halt to the levees? Why did he reframe the sociability of the

32. George Santayana, *The Genteel Tradition: Nine Essays*, ed. Douglas L. Wilson (Cambridge, Mass., 1967); Bernard De Voto, *The Literary Fallacy* (Boston, 1944).

33. Andrew R. L. Cayton, " 'Noble Actors' upon 'The Theatre of Honour': Power and Civility in the Treaty of Greenville," paper, Institute of Early American History and Culture, Conference, "The Frontier," September 1994.

governing classes, rendering it more domestic, by making small supper parties its primary scene? And why did he allow the refinement of persons, houses, and things to fall under the management of the institutions of a private society dominated by rich merchant, planter, and rising professional families — persons about whose virtuousness he had strong doubts?

These closing questions invite us to take up the question of civility anew, posing it for the social world that evolved during the nineteenth century, the century of sectional strife, civil war, and class division in the United States. I will not write that history. But I can envision an account, building upon Bushman's *Refinement of America*, that would chronicle the competing projects of various private social institutions (voluntary associations, if you will) in the name of civility. My book will serve that unwritten history by glossing the imagery and language pervading the nostalgia for things colonial in the wake of the Civil War. It will suggest that something more than old furnishings and Georgian architecture was being reanimated by the Colonial Revival. Civility once again came to be conceived as a means of building personal bonds across social divides. This time it would be dominated by a picture of an aestheticized, derealized colonial past. In this Williamsburg of civility, the white populations of both North and South could meet and become sociable again, discovering atavistic affinities in shared pleasures and old-time gentility. The problem was that the United States during the last half of the nineteenth century included increasing numbers of people — African-Americans, recent Southern European immigrants, Jews, Asians — who did not have a readily recognizable place in the colonial period room of the national imagination. Would the symbolic language of American civility be sufficiently flexible to incorporate them?

INDEX

Recitation, 28, 30, 36, 74

Refinement, xxvi, 141–142, 176, 222–223, 242

Reform: associations for, xv–xvi, 188; of elite, 69–70; and Reformation of Manners movement, 211–213; of conversation, 211–214

Republican court, xxviii, 320–322, 326–327

Republican ideology, xxi, 189; and private society, xxviii, 308–309, 313–317; and leisure, xxix, 314–315; abstraction of, 8; and civic virtue, 10, 176; and republican court, 321–322

Republic of letters, xv, xxii, 12, 162, 164, 219, 240, 265, 298, 319

Reputation, 50, 73–74, 76–77, 106–109, 144–158, 219; and skill, 161–174, 243, 281–282; and self-publicity, 243–266; and professional competition, 280–281, 295–296

Restoration, 20, 32, 55, 57, 59, 113, 310

Revolution, 308, 315, 322

Rhetoric, xvii, 74, 80, 98, 124–125, 194, 197, 228, 295

Rhode Island, 176, 187, 244, 322

Riddles, 161–164

Ridiculous clubs, 17, 177, 197–198, 207, 312

Ritual: and society, xvii, xix, 141–145, 171–173, 196; as semiotic frame, 143–144; at college, 214

Roberts, Phineas, 197–198

Robie, Thomas, 216

Roche, Mary, 294–295

Romps, 99, 101, 120

Rose, Aquila, 94

Rosee, Pasqua, 20, 59

Rota, 182, 184, 199, 202

Roth, Rodris, 116

Rowe, Rev. Louis, 61

Rowzee, Dr. Lodowick, 40

Royal Society, 210

"Rule for Conversation" (Brooke), 34–35

Rumors, 277–279

Rush, Benjamin: "Account of the French fete," 1–5

Russell, Lucy, countess of Bedford, 15, 17

Rust, Anna, 252–253

Rye House plot, 184

S., T., 269

St. Cecilia Society, 284

St. Serfe, Thomas, 26

Salonnieres, xxix, xxx, 14–16, 45, 104, 138–140, 144

Salons: as private society, xiii–xxxiii, 14–17, 144; and sensible conversation, xviii, xxvi, 100–101, 120, 139, 311; in France, xxxi, 12–13, 119, 308; in Italy, 14; women's sponsorship of, 12–15, 119–121; and Platonism, 45–46, 138–140, 209; and authorship, 263–264, 311; in the early Republic, 310–311; and republican court, 320–322, 327–328

Sans Souci, alias Free and Easy, 314–315

Santayana, George, 327

Satire: of social aspirants, 47–48, 90; theory of, 88, 91; of women, 99–101, 253; of male rivals, 170–173; of government, 194–195; and disputatiousness, 238; and parody, 253–254; of clergy, 270–271; of plantation manners, 302–303; of club ideals, 325

Satyrical Description of Commencement (Green), 249–250

Savagery, xix, 3, 106, 180, 287; and commerce, 11, 327

Saturday Club (Boston), 324

Scarborough. *See* Spas

Schuykill Fishing Company, 190–198

Schuykill Swains, 128, 139

"Science of Lying," 325

Scottish common sense philosophy, xvii, 181

Seccomb, John, 61, 214–216

Sedgewick, Eve Kosofsky, 204–205

Sedition, 175, 182, 184–187, 189, 271